# CASTES OF MIND

# CASTES OF MIND

## COLONIALISM AND THE MAKING
## OF MODERN INDIA

*Nicholas B. Dirks*

PRINCETON UNIVERSITY PRESS    PRINCETON AND OXFORD

*Library of Congress Cataloging-in-Publication Data*

Dirks, Nicholas B., 1950–
Castes of mind : colonialism and the making of
modern India / Nicholas B. Dirks.
    p. cm.
Includes bibliographical references and index.
ISBN 0-691-08894-2 (alk. paper) — ISBN 0-691-08895-0 (pbk. : alk. paper)
1. Caste—India. 2. Social classes—India. 3. India—
History—British occupation, 1765–1947. I. Title.
DS422.C3 D58   2001
305.5′122′0954—dc21      2001021236

British Library Cataloging-in-Publication Data is available
This book has been composed in Times Roman

Printed on acid-free paper. ∞

www.pup.princeton.edu

Printed in the United States of America.

10  9  8  7  6  5  4  3  2  1

10  9  8  7  6  5  4  3  2  1
(Pbk.)

**For Naki**

# Contents

## Acknowledgments _____

ALTHOUGH this book has in some ways grown quite naturally out of its predecessor, *The Hollow Crown*, it was not the book I had at first intended to write. I had spent a year at the India Office Library and Record Room in 1986 engaging in research on a Scottish antiquarian and collector, Colin Mackenzie, a man whose life and work is discussed in the fifth chapter but who plays a far less significant role in the story to follow than was my original plan. I had intended then to write a book on the early colonial archive: the collection, formation, and then transformation of early canons of British colonial knowledge concerning India, for which the Mackenzie collection was to be the centerpiece. Mackenzie, whose massive collection of vernacular texts and miscellaneous records from peninsular India—assembled by an extraordinary group of assistants and translators during the late eighteenth and early nineteenth centuries—produced many of the texts used in my earlier study of local kingship and society in early modern southern India, still warrants a book of his own. Instead, I became preoccupied with one of the major absences in the early colonial archive: namely, caste. My study of the early colonial archive made it clear how peculiar the colonial fascination with caste from the middle of the nineteenth century on really was. I had already argued that caste—at least in the areas of southern India that I had studied intensively—was profoundly embedded within political society, not at all as it has been portrayed in contemporary anthropological literature. But, now that I could document this claim in much more extensive ways given the provenance of the Mackenzie collection, I soon became preoccupied with two central questions concerning the modern career of caste. First, I sought to understand how caste had come to exercise such pride of place in the colonial imagination. Second, I wanted to document the effects of this transformation on modern Indian society. If knowledge was both an effect and an instrument of power, as Foucault has suggested, it seemed necessary to write an account of caste that was both about ideas and their materialization in, and through, history.

As the idea for this book began to take shape—amid a series of other research trips to India as well as back to London—the explosion of caste anxiety and violence around then Prime Minister V. P. Singh's decision to implement the recommendations of the Mandal Commission in the summer of 1990, dramatically increasing quotas for Backward Caste representation in government and education, raised a third question. Would my effort to write a critical account of the colonial history of caste become affiliated with critiques of Mandal? By extension, what was the relation between colonial critique and postcolonial politics in India? Although attention shifted from caste to the growing communalism of the 1990s, most dramatically around the Hindu nationalist assault on Babur's mosque in Ayodhya, I kept my focus trained on the politics and history of caste in contemporary India. And I discovered that the question of caste brought together a wide range of historical, anthropological, and political concerns, even as it connected the two most distant points of my own scholarly relationship to India. As an undergraduate, I had begun to study Indian history through the figure of E. V. Ramaswamy Naicker and his relation to Gandhi and Indian nationalism, on the one hand, and the extraordinary history of caste politics in southern India, on the other. At the point that I began to draft the manuscript that makes up this book, I found myself convening the seminar at Columbia University where B. R. Ambedkar had presented his first critique of caste. The critical visions of E.V.R. and Ambedkar made it possible for me to connect the first two questions of this book with the third.

I have been extremely fortunate during the fifteen years of this book's gestation to have the support of a variety of institutions and individuals. The California Institute of Technology, the University of Michigan, and Columbia University have all supported the research and writing of parts of this book, as have the Social Science Research Council (1986), the Guggenheim Foundation (1989–1991), the American Institute for Indian Studies (1989; 1991), and the Institute for Advanced Study in Princeton (1989–1990). I am grateful to the staff of the following institutions where the research for this book was carried out: the India Office Library and Records, London; the library and archives of the School of Oriental and African Studies, London; the National Archives of India, New Delhi; the Nehru Memorial Museum and Library, New Delhi; the Tamil Nadu Archives, Madras; and the Government Oriental Manuscripts Library, University of Madras.

Above all, this book owes its origin to the work and influence of my Ph.D. advisor, Bernard Cohn. Cohn's work over many years has made clear how constitutive the history of colonial knowledge in general and the census in particular has been for modern understandings of caste. In his scholarship, his teaching, and his sustained and profound encouragement of this project, he has played a key role in making this book possible.

Val Daniel and Gyan Prakash have been the most generous and loyal of intellectual comrades during the many years I have worked on this project. In addition to reading and commenting on just about everything else I have written over the years, they read and gave detailed comments and suggestions on an earlier version of the manuscript. Partha Chatterjee, whom I came to know when he invited me to a conference in Calcutta in 1989, where I gave an early version of Chapter 8, has also been an invaluable intellectual partner since then, even as his provocative suggestions about colonial modernity and postcolonial politics in India have made this effort to understand caste seem worthwhile long after I started it. Peter van der Veer provided several opportunities to present and discuss parts of this work over the last decade and has been a

terrific interlocutor and critic. David Ludden has also been supportive throughout the project, and a continuous source of material, insight, advice, and
friendship.

During my years at the University of Michigan, Tom Trautmann was not
only the finest colleague any academic could hope to have but also a regular
source of detailed help on specific aspects of the history of Orientalism in
India. My early efforts on the history of caste were encouraged by many wonderful colleagues at Michigan, including Bill Sewell, Geoff Eley, Ray Grew,
Fred Cooper, Fernando Coronil, and Sally Humphreys. Sherry Ortner was one
of the first to welcome me to Michigan and has supported this project and
argued about it with me ever since. I worked closely with Ann Stoler, whose
shared interests in colonial archives helped me formulate some of the concerns
that animate this book. I was fortunate that Gyan Pandey spent two semesters
at the University of Michigan, making him a captive (and yet always generous)
audience for my developing ideas, especially when I could entice him to a
local pub.

Gananath Obeyesekere, a resolutely unanonymous reader for Princeton University Press, gave me wonderful feedback, and important advice, about the
manuscript; I am in his debt, even if I have not always heeded his remarks as
much as I should have. Arjun Appadurai has been generative in working
through many of the questions that we both began to ask when studying with
Bernard Cohn at the University of Chicago. Mahmood Mamdani lugged my
manuscript to Kampala and gave me the benefit of his extraordinary reading of
the argument and material in the context of his own important work on the
legacies of colonial history in Africa. Aamir Mufti was especially encouraging
and suggestive in his responses to my efforts to relate the question of caste to
the subject of minorities.

Joan Scott and Clifford Geertz invited me to deliver versions of what have
become the first and last chapters at the Thursday Seminar in the Institute for
Advanced Study (in 1990 and 1999, respectively), and on each occasion made
helpful and encouraging comments. Tom Laqueur and Stephen Greenblatt first
asked me to publish an early version of this project in *Representations* (in
1992). The late Burton Stein, who would have preferred that I wrote the book
on Mackenzie, was always supportive of my work even (perhaps especially)
when he disagreed with me; he always provided me with a home away from
home when I was in London. Jean-Claude Galey hosted me for a semester at
the Ecole des Hautes Études in Paris in 1992 and engaged me in constant and
scintillating debate on questions around history, caste, and Louis Dumont, all
the while plying me with wonderful food, wine, and gossip.

Other colleagues and friends have played important roles at various points
in this project. Ranajit Guha read large parts of the manuscript and made enthusiastic comments. Stanley Tambiah read and commented on papers based
on several chapters with his characteristic insight and encouragement. Judy

Walkowitz helped to deepen my sense of British history while making many suggestions about the history of British social and anthropological theory. Chris Fuller and Jonathan Parry have been worthy critics and warm hosts, both when I was an academic visitor at the London School of Economics and Political Science in 1986 and during my visits to London since then. Shahid Amin has discussed William Crooke and colonial sociology more generally over the years, at the same time that his own work has been a model for the historical anthropology of South Asia. Dharma Kumar provided me with a home in New Delhi and with robust and witty argument whenever we met. Anjan Ghosh did me the honor of being my student, while giving me the benefit of his extraordinary erudition and interest over the course of much of this project.

There are many others who have helped me in various ways with this book, engaging with my arguments, sponsoring me to give or publish papers, making arguments of their own that have forced me to rethink and expand my views, helping me with archives, and offering their encouragement. I would like especially to thank Lila Abu-Lughod, Amrita Basu, Laura Bear, Akeel Bilgrami, Carol Breckenridge, Natalie Davis, Nancy Farriss, Michael Fisher, Saloni Mathur, Tim Mitchell, M.S.S. Pandian, Peter Pels, Gloria Raheja, Arvind Rajagopal, Sumathi Ramaswamy, Anupama Rao, H. L. Seneviratne, Jonathan Spencer, and Tom Wolfe.

I am grateful to my graduate students at the University of Michigan and Columbia University for their critical role in making this work seem worthwhile (though always subject to withering critique) from start to finish. I am especially indebted to the students who took my graduate seminar in the spring of 2000 for reading an earlier version of the manuscript; Arjun Mahey, Nauman Naqvi, and Nathaniel Roberts in particular made extraordinarily detailed and helpful comments on issues ranging from argument to style and organization. I have been lucky to have superb research assistants over the course of this project, including Pamila Gupta, Lisa Mitchell, Nauman Naqvi, Parna Sengupta, Vazira Zamindar, and Karin Zitzewitz.

It has been a pleasure to work with Princeton University Press. I thank Walter Lippincott for his interest in this project since I first discussed it with him in 1988. Mary Murrell has facilitated the process at every stage and been a supportive and perceptive editor. Fred Appel has collaborated to keep the project moving along. And Margaret Case has been the most patient, and painstaking, of copyeditors.

During the years that I finished this book, my daughter, Sandhya, left home to start a life of her own (wondering why her father never wrote that book he kept talking about), and my son, Ishan, was born, survived two long hospital stays in his first year, and learned the function of the delete key before his first word. Even when I have been most consumed by the writing of this book, both have done their best to remind me of the important things in life.

Most of this book was written in the quiet and gentle sanctuary of the southern Berkshires over the last three summers. During that time, Janaki Bakhle not only insisted that I finally write this book (putting aside my more frivolous undertakings to concentrate on the great task of history) but has made it possible for me to do so. She has also read through repeated drafts of my work, giving me both my severest criticism and my most devoted approbation. In hopes of more of the same for many future books, I dedicate this book to her.

*Southfield, Massachusetts*
*January, 2001*

## *Abbreviations*

BC     Board's Collections, India Office Library, London
G.O.    Government Order
IOL    India Office Library, London
NAI    National Archives of India, New Delhi
SIR    Survey of India Records, New Delhi
TNA    Tamil Nadu Archives, Madras

# Part One

## THE "INVENTION" OF CASTE

# One

## Introduction: The Modernity of Caste

> In that Country the laws of religion, the laws of the
> land, and the laws of honour, are all united and
> consolidated in one, and bind a man eternally to the
> rules of what is called his *caste*.
> —Edmund Burke[1]

### Caste as India

When thinking of India it is hard not to think of caste. In comparative sociology and in common parlance alike, caste has become a central symbol for
India, indexing it as fundamentally different from other places as well as expressing its essence. A long history of writing—from the grand treatise of the
Abbé Dubois to the general anthropology of Louis Dumont; from the piles of
statistical and descriptive volumes of British colonial censuses starting in 1872
to the eye-catching headlines of the *New York Times*—has identified caste as
the basic form of Indian society. Caste has been seen as omnipresent in Indian
history and as one of the major reasons why India has no history, or at least no
sense of history. Caste defines the core of Indian tradition, and it is seen today
as the major threat to Indian modernity. If we are to understand India properly,
and by implication if we are to understand India's other core symbol—Hinduism—we must understand caste, whether we admire or revile it.

In *The Discovery of India*, Jawaharlal Nehru wrote that "Almost everyone
who knows anything at all about India has heard of the caste system; almost
every outsider and many people in India condemn it or criticize it as a whole."
Nehru did not like the caste system any more than he admired the widely
heralded "spiritual" foundations of Indian civilization, but even he felt ambivalence about it. Although he noted that caste had resisted "not only the powerful impact of Buddhism and many centuries of Afghan and Mughal rule and
the spread of Islam," as also "the strenuous efforts of innumerable Hindu reformers who raised their voices against it," he felt that caste was finally beginning to come undone through the force of basic economic changes. And yet
Nehru was not sure what all this change would unleash. "The conflict is between two approaches to the problem of social organisation, which are diametrically opposed to each other: the old Hindu conception of the group being
the basic unit of organisation, and the excessive individualism of the west,

emphasizing the individual above the group."[2] In making this observation, Nehru neatly captured the conceptual contours of most recent debates over caste: he evaluated it in relation to its place as fundamental to Hinduism, as well as in terms of a basic opposition between the individual and the community, an opposition that has provided the bounds of most modern social theory and political imagining. This opposition constitutes the basic limit to most understandings of caste, both in the West and within India itself.

Louis Dumont, the author of the most influential scholarly treatise on caste in the last half of the twentieth century, believed that the West's excessive individualism was the single greatest impediment to the understanding of caste. Dumont began his book, *Homo Hierarchicus*, with a critique of individualism, claiming Marx and Durkheim as his sociological ancestors. For Dumont, "the true function of sociology is . . . to make good the lacuna introduced by the individualistic mentality when it confuses the ideal with the actual. . . . To the self-sufficient individual it [sociology] opposes man as a social being; it considers each man no longer as a particular incarnation of abstract humanity, but as a more or less autonomous point of emergence of a particular collective humanity, of a *society*."[3] Dumont based his suspicion of modern individualism on Tocqueville's analysis of American democracy, in which he noted that "individualism . . . disposes each member of the community to sever himself from the mass of his fellow-creatures; and to draw apart with his family and his friends; so that, after he has thus formed a little circle of his own, he willingly leaves society at large to itself . . . not only does democracy make every man forget his ancestors, but it hides his descendents, and separates his contemporaries from him; it throws him back for ever upon himself alone, and threatens in the end to confine him entirely within the solitude of his own heart." Dumont thus began his study of caste in India by placing it at the center of the sociological endeavor, and aligning himself with Tocqueville's critical lament about the rise of the "novel idea" of individualism.[4]

For Dumont it is this same commitment to individualism, even within the sociological space of theorizing the social, that rejects the possibility that hierarchy, the core value behind the caste system, has not only been foundational for most societies but is naturally so. Dumont wrote that "To adopt a value is to introduce hierarchy, and a certain consensus of values, a certain hierarchy of ideas, things and people, is indispensable to social life. . . . No doubt, in the majority of cases, hierarchy will be identified in some way with power, but there is no necessity for this, as the case of India will show. . . . In relation to these more or less necessary requirements of social life, the ideal of equality, even if it is thought superior, is artificial."[5] Dumont made this point here in the service of a straightforward epistemological assertion, namely, that a Western audience (and as his prose makes clear, he could imagine no other) will misunderstand caste, and hierarchy, because of the modern denial of principles that seem opposed to individualism and equality. But his claims about the ideological foundations of hierarchical values in India—that India has always been mired in spiritual and otherworldly concerns—are not only deeply problematic, they are as old as Orientalism itself. For Dumont, caste is seen to express a commitment to social values that the modern world has lost, and it is hard not to read Dumont's scholarship as a peculiar form of modern Western nostalgia, if with a long colonial pedigree. Dumont's faith in a communitarian ideal may have little in common with Nehru's anxiety about the demise of caste, but it asserts the view, largely shared in India as well as in the West, that caste is the sign of India's fundamental religiosity, a marker of India's essential difference from the West and from modernity at large.

This book will ask why it is that caste has become for so many the core symbol of community in India, whereas for others, even in serious critique, caste is still the defining feature of Indian social organization. As we shall see, views of caste differ markedly: from those who see it as a religious system to those who view it as merely social or economic; from those who admire the spiritual foundations of a sacerdotal hierarchy to those who look from below and see the tyranny of Brahmans (all the more insidious because of the ritual mystifications that attend domination); from those who view it as the Indian equivalent of community to those who see it as the primary impediment to community. But an extraordinary range of commentators, from James Mill to Herbert Risley, from Hegel to Weber, from G. S. Ghurye to M. N. Srinivas, from Louis Dumont to McKim Marriott, from E. V. Ramaswamy Naicker to B. R. Ambedkar, from Gandhi to Nehru, among many others who will populate the text that follows, accept that caste—and specifically caste forms of hierarchy, whether valorized or despised—is somehow fundamental to Indian civilization, Indian culture, and Indian tradition.

This book will address this question by suggesting that caste, as we know it today, is not in fact some unchanged survival of ancient India, not some single system that reflects a core civilizational value, not a basic expression of Indian tradition. Rather, I will argue that caste (again, as we know it today) is a modern phenomenon, that it is, specifically, the product of an historical encounter between India and Western colonial rule. By this I do not mean to imply that it was simply invented by the too clever British, now credited with so many imperial patents that what began as colonial critique has turned into another form of imperial adulation. But I *am* suggesting that it was under the British that "caste" became a single term capable of expressing, organizing, and above all "systematizing" India's diverse forms of social identity, community, and organization. This was achieved through an identifiable (if contested) ideological canon as the result of a concrete encounter with colonial modernity during two hundred years of British domination. In short, colonialism made caste what it is today. It produced the conditions that made possible the opening lines of this book, by making caste the central symbol of Indian society. And it did its work well; as Nehru was powerfully aware, there is now no simple way of wishing it away, no easy way to imagine social forms that would transcend the languages of caste that have become so inscribed in ritual, familial, communal, socioeconomic, political, and public theaters of quotidian life.

In the pages that follow I will trace the career of caste from the medieval kingdoms of southern India to the textual traces of early colonial archives; from the commentaries of an eighteenth-century Jesuit missionary to the enumerative obsessions of the late nineteenth-century census; from the ethnographic writings of colonial administrators and missionaries to those of twentieth-century Indian scholars. I will focus on early colonial efforts to know India well enough to rule it and profit by it, as they brought together the many strands of scientific curiosity, missionary frustration, Orientalist fascination, and administrative concerns with property and taxation in the service of, among other things, colonial governmentality.[6] I will follow these conjunctural imperatives as they increasingly substituted statistical and ethnographical techniques for historical and textual knowledge, as they drew from an ample inheritance of Orientalist generalization to articulate the justifications for permanent colonial rule, and as they took on the racialized languages and conceits of late nineteenth-century imperial world systems. And I will illustrate some of the ways in which this history provided the frame for an alternative history of social reform and nationalist resistance which worked to throw out colonialism while absorbing from colonial encounters many of the terms and arguments of self-determination and self-government. I will also survey the rise of caste politics in the twentieth century, focusing in particular on the emergence of movements that threatened to fracture nationalist consensus even as they revealed the problematic charters, and entailments, of anticolonial nationalism. For the purposes of this book, this history will attain its apotheosis in the debates over the use of caste for social welfare in the postindependence contexts of "reservations," quotas, and affirmative action.

## Specters of Caste

It is impossible to write about India today, particularly when addressing issues concerning community, without referring to the current crisis over secularism and religious nationalism. The rise of Hindu fundamentalism has made it necessary to engage explicitly with the ways that Hinduism, as a set of ritual practices, a "world religion," and an ethnic identity, has increasingly claimed India as its own. The uses of *Hindutva* as a political call to arms, and the demise of secularism as a legitimate national ideology, have led to a crisis that might make a book on caste seem beside the point. But it is in part because of the crisis around communalism that it is well worth directing some attention to the ways in which caste haunts discourses of community and nation in India today. This study will perforce address a range of concerns relevant to the current crisis. First, there is now general acceptance of the fact that the bitter debates over caste reservations were triggered by the implementation of the Mandal Commission Report by V. P. Singh in 1990. Once caste started to be used as the basis for denying rather than conferring social privilege, Hindu nationalists captured ground by calling for a notion of religious community to replace one of caste. Second, one of my arguments in this book will be that caste was configured as an encompassing Indian social system in direct relationship to the constitution of "Hinduism" as a systematic, confessional, all-embracing religious identity. Indeed, caste has generally been seen as fundamental to Hinduism—a curious irony in a context in which the problems of caste are today being used to justify the necessity of Hinduism as a noncontestatory form of community to cushion the turmoil of political modernity in India. My examination into the colonial history of caste will complement any investigation of the affiliation of religious identities with political communities in the current geopolitics of South Asia, even as it builds on the important suggestions of Gyanendra Pandey that religious *communalism* was also in large part a colonial construction.[7]

It is not as if the Hindu nationalists, any more than either fundamentalist or secularist reformers in days past, have managed to wish caste away. Caste continues to dominate Indian social worlds, even if in some larger political contexts it has been effaced by the conflict between Hindus and Muslims. In regions of India that witnessed particularly significant anti-Brahman (and by implication anticaste) political movements, as for example in what are today Tamil Nadu and Maharashtra, as well as in regions where caste provided the basis for "lower-caste" political mobilization, as for example in parts of Bihar and Uttar Pradesh, caste seems to be as prominent a fact of social life as ever. Increasingly, all-India forms of Dalit ("untouchable") politics carry on B. R. Ambedkar's insistent identification of caste as the most powerful vehicle of dominance—ritual as well as political and economic—in India. At the same time, the process of what has been called the ethnicization, or substantialization, of caste, heralded by many social scientists as the necessary death of the old caste system (based as they thought it was on interdependency rather than conflict) has provided new mechanisms for the strengthening of caste identity. Caste may no longer convey a sense of community that confers civilizational identity to the Indian subcontinent, but it is still the primary form of local identity and, in certain contexts, from Dalits to Brahmans, translates the local into recognizably subcontinental idioms of association far more powerful than any other single category of community.

Caste thus continues, even as it continues to trouble. But despite the tone here—and I will be critical of the British role in the reification of caste even as I am critical of those, Indian or Western, who advocate the values of the *caste system*—I do not seek to join the chorus of those who view caste as either emblematic of Indian civilization or as opposed to modernity. Although my principal concern will be to unravel the historical process that has worked to naturalize the idea of a (uniform, all-encompassing, ideologically consistent, Indologically conceived) caste system, I am particularly concerned to register my conviction that caste has at times been the necessary vehicle of social and political mobilization, even as it carries as many traces of the modern as the institutions it is said to inhibit or oppose. When figures such as Ambedkar in western India or Periyar in the south organized political movements around caste, they worked to transform both the cultural meanings and the political uses of caste in ways that went well beyond the colonial mandate. On occasion, caste has indeed been a worthy synonym of community in the best of senses, even if political movements have all too often failed to transcend in any way the problematic relationship of caste to exclusion. Nehru observed that "In the constructive schemes that we may make, we have to pay attention to the human material we have to deal with, to the background of its thought and urges, and to the environment in which we have to function. To ignore all this and to fashion some idealistic scheme in the air, or merely to think in terms of imitating what others have done elsewhere, would be folly. It becomes desirable therefore to examine and understand the old Indian social structure which has so powerfully influenced our people."[8] More to my point, since I can share neither Nehru's precise pronouns nor his own political project, leave alone his understanding of caste, I would argue that caste endures and is so significant today because it has been the precipitate of a powerful history, in which it has been constituted as the very condition of the Indian social. This book is principally about the historicity of caste, the ways caste has come into being, and as such been conditioned by history to condition (and make conditional) any possibility of a future beyond, or without, caste.

What follows is principally about the colonial role in the historical construction of caste. I argue that the history in which caste has been constituted as the principal modality of Indian society draws as much from the role of British Orientalists, administrators, and missionaries as it does from Indian reformers, social thinkers, and political actors. Indeed, my argument is about the power of the colonial leviathan to produce caste as the measure of all social things, a feat that could not have been accomplished had caste not become one of the most important emblems of tradition (the not-so-obscure object of desire for many Westerners and Indians alike, across the full course of India's modern history) at the same time as it was a core feature of colonial power/knowledge. And yet this is not a simple story of either epistemic domination or of elite collaboration. This book not only culminates in the heroic attempts by Ambedkar and Periyar to change the terms of caste; it builds on the work of critics of colonial modernity such as Ranajit Guha and Partha Chatterjee, who have been as concerned to chart new historical patterns of influence as they have been to find new ways to chart alternative futures. Guha, whose work has ranged from his brilliant intellectual history of the Bengal Permanent Settlement to his more recent studies of anticolonial insurgency and the manifold historical entailments of colonial domination, has both demonstrated the power of colonial rule and the need to write not just against but beyond colonialism.[9] And Chatterjee has always insisted on the need to chart the history of colonized negotiations with both the brutality of foreign domination and the spectral hail of the modern. Drawing inspiration from these and many other scholars, I hope to weave an argument far more complicated than that the British invented caste, though in one sense this is precisely what happened. But when I assert the power of colonial history I do so in the wake of the now canonic demonstrations by Bernard Cohn and Edward Said of the hegemonic character of colonial rule on the history of the colonized.[10]

We now know that colonial conquest was not just the result of the power of superior arms, military organization, political power, or economic wealth—as important as these things were. Colonialism was made possible, and then sustained and strengthened, as much by cultural technologies of rule as it was by the more obvious and brutal modes of conquest that first established power on foreign shores. The cultural effects of colonialism have until recently been too often ignored or displaced into the inevitable logics of modernization and world capitalism; and this only because it has not been sufficiently recognized that colonialism was itself a cultural project of control. Colonial knowledge both enabled conquest and was produced by it; in certain important ways, knowledge was what colonialism was all about. Cultural forms in societies newly classified as "traditional" were reconstructed and transformed by this knowledge, which created new categories and oppositions between colonizers and colonized, European and Asian, modern and traditional, West and East. Through the delineation and reconstitution of systematic grammars for vernacular languages, the control of Indian territory through cartographic technologies and picturesque techniques of rule, the representation of India through the mastery and display of archaeological mementos and ritual texts, the taxing of India through the reclassification and assessment of land use, property form, and agrarian structure, and the enumeration of India through the statistical technology of the census, Britain set in motion transformations every bit as powerful as the better-known consequences of military and economic imperialism.[11]

Most saliently for the argument here, British colonialism played a critical role in both the identification and the production of Indian "tradition." Current debates about modernity and tradition fail to appreciate the extent to which the congeries of beliefs, customs, practices, and convictions that have been designated as traditional are in fact the complicated byproduct of colonial history. Bernard Cohn has argued that the British simultaneously misrecognized and simplified things Indian, imprisoning the Indian subject into the typecast role it assigned under the name of tradition: "In the conceptual scheme which the British created to understand and to act in India, they constantly followed the same logic; they reduced vastly complex codes and their associated meanings to a few metonyms. . . . India was redefined by the British to be a place of rules and orders; once the British had defined to their own satisfaction what they construed as Indian rules and customs, then the Indians had to conform to these constructions."[12] Edward Said has illuminated the process through which the Orient was "Orientalized" precisely because of the byzantine reinforcements of colonial power and knowledge.[13] Partha Chatterjee has called this general process the "colonial rule of difference": referring thereby to the historical fact that colonialism could only justify itself if under the regime of universal history it encountered the limit of alterity, the social fact that India must always be ruled because it could never be folded into a universal narrative of progress, modernity, and, ultimately, Europe. "To the extent this complex of power and knowledge was colonial," he tells us, "the forms of objectification and normalization of the colonized had to reproduce, within the framework of a universal knowledge, the truth of colonial difference."[14]

It is here that we come up against the special perversity of colonial modernity, for the traditional was produced precisely within the historical relationship between the colonizer and the colonized. The colonizer held out modernity as a promise but at the same time made it the limiting condition of coloniality: the promise that would never be kept. The colonized could be seduced by the siren of the modern but never quite get there, mired necessarily (if colonialism was to continue to legitimate itself) in a "traditional" world.[15] On the other side of the colonial divide, the colonized, sometimes in direct reaction to the colonial lie of universality, would appropriate tradition as resistance and as refuge, but under conditions of colonial modernity tradition was simultaneously devalued and transformed. As a result, tradition too suffered from loss, even as it was tainted by its evident historicity. In the case of caste, many Indian social reformers and critics mistook this history as linear decline, the degradation of a noble system into a corrupt structure of power and dominant interests. Only a few, most notably the extraordinary sociologist G. S. Ghurye, blamed colonialism.[16] But whatever the argument, attempts at historical recuperation typically took the form of finding an Orientalist golden age, a time when caste was an ideal system of mutual responsibility, reasoned interdependence, and genuine spiritual authority. Only a few non-Brahman and Dalit voices rejected this kind of Orientalist nostalgia, all the while feeling increasingly trapped by the demands of anticolonial nationalism to downplay, and defer, all critiques of Indian culture and civilization.

## The Indian Political

Perhaps the most troubling legacy of the colonial idea of a golden age is the disavowal (shared in large part by nationalist thought) of the political forms and affiliations that were an important part of India's precolonial history. It is this last concern that was the subject of my previous study, *The Hollow Crown*, which took as its focus the social and political fortunes of a small kingdom in southern India from the seventeenth to the early twentieth century. I argued that "until the emergence of British colonial rule in southern India [and by implication India at large] the crown was not so hollow as it has generally been made out to be. Kings were not inferior to Brahmans; the political domain was not encompassed by a religious domain. State forms, while not fully assimilated to western categories of the state, were powerful components in Indian Civilization. Indian society, indeed caste itself, was shaped by political struggles and processes."[17] The vital world of political action and community was, in fact, overtaken by colonial rule, and public life became increasingly defined as Western at the same time that the promise of universal modernity became more and more marked in national and racial terms. Meanwhile, public life was emptied of all "traditional" components—as old forms of politics were condemned as feudal and old forms of association rendered atavistic. The permanent Zamindari settlements of Bengal and Madras, and the intractable histories leading to indirect rule of one form or another in one-third of India (leaving princely states "intact"), produced a hollow simulacrum of India's ancient politics. The British maintained in style these kingdoms, which had facilitated colonial conquest, as lavish museums of old India. At the same time, these states were constant reminders of the justifications of British rule: India had been unable to rule itself because its political system was commanded by grand but quarrelling kings who would shamelessly exploit their subjects in order to accumulate unlimited wealth and prestige, and had neither attended to basic principles of justice nor concerned themselves with the formation of organized administration and stable, centralized power. Thus Britain sustained the fiction that it had walked into a vacuum and had conquered India, as the Cambridge imperial historian John Seeley said, "in a fit of absence of mind," after which the British ruled India for the sake of its own subjects, rather than for any gain of their own.[18] This astonishing failure of historical consciousness was, of course, justified through the attribution of a lack of history, and caste was taken as a sign thereof.

These colonial narratives seemed justified by case after case in which landlords and princes would fail to exploit the economic opportunities afforded by permanent settlement and indirect rule; "theater states" grew up all over India in which issues of ceremonial and prestige, hierarchy and protocol, accumulation and expenditure seemed of far greater moment than either sound management or popular representation. A kind of embarrassment set in, I would suggest, in which it became difficult to point to recent history, and the vast estates and quasi-autonomous tracts under royal control, as arguments for national self-confidence—let alone self-rule. In cities like Calcutta, the elite was in large part supported by the profits that came from landlord rights to these same

rural estates; in this environment, recognition of the power of the West became the basis both for what has been called colonial mimicry in areas
ranging from political theory to cultural production and for the development
of forms of resistance that were justified by the glorious past record of India's
civilizational achievement. A new vision, following what by now was an authoritative Orientalist script coauthored in many cases by those who accorded
no particular prestige to political authority, celebrated the civilizational and
spiritual achievements of old India. This vision did not address the political
history of recent times; a conspicuous silence was maintained around the material basis of the vision's own conditions of possibility. In thinking about the
efflorescence of current debate around the subject of tradition, it is accordingly necessary to call again for the recuperation of that part of Indian tradition, or history, that had been compromised by the vain pomp, circumstance,
and exploitation of colonial feudalism—not to argue return but rather to
counter the otherworldliness of colonial fictions about history. It is time again
to "tell sad stories of the death of kings: how some have been deposed, some
slain in war, some haunted by the ghosts they have deposed. . . . All
murdered."[19]

In subsequent chapters I shall say more about kings, and about the Indian
political. The point here is to suggest that the death of kings cleared the way
for the transformation of caste under colonial rule. Caste was refigured as a
distinctly religious system, and the transformation had immense implications
for everyday social life. The confinement of caste to the realm of religion
enabled colonial procedures of rule through the characterization of India as
essentially a place of spiritual harmony and liberation; when the state existed
in India, so the argument went, it was despotic and epiphenomenal, extractive
but fundamentally irrelevant. British rule could thus be characterized as enlightened when it denied Indian subjects even the minimal rights that constituted the basis for the development of civil society in Europe. Caste itself was
seen as a form of colonial civil society in India, which provided an ironic, and
inferior, anthropological analogue for the colonized world. In Europe, the rise
of new nation-states in the eighteenth century went hand in hand with the
construction of a new form of civil society. Civil society was to free individuals in new and progressive societies from "traditional" modes of social organization and from the myriad constraints of premodern and/or feudal polities.
Civil society had been constituted by and institutionalized in a range of
bodies—the church, educational institutions, civic organizations—that represented the interests of a private domain, interests construed to be autonomous
from the state even as they were simultaneously protected by it. The modern
state, more powerful than ever before, had legitimated itself in part through its
claim to free the social realm from the politics of the past. In India, however,
caste was understood always to have resisted political intrusion; it was already
a kind of civil society in that it regulated and mediated the private domain,

such as it was. But a society based on caste could not be more different from modern Western society, for caste was opposed to the basic premises of individualism, and it neither permitted the development of voluntarist or politically malleable social institutions nor worked to reinforce the modern state. Further, caste conferred citizenship only in social and ritual rather than in political contexts, and opposed the ideas of both individual action and social mobilization. According to some, caste actively resisted the modern state even more than it did the old, for the modern state opposed rather than supported the dharmic order of things. At the same time, many British officials were convinced that caste would stand in the way of nationalist mobilization, claiming as it did primordial loyalty from its members.

Under colonialism, caste was thus made out to be far more—far more pervasive, far more totalizing, and far more uniform—than it had ever been before, at the same time that it was defined as a fundamentally religious social order. In fact, however, caste had always been political—it had been shaped in fundamental ways by political struggles and processes; even so, it was not a designation that exhausted the totality of Indian social forms, let alone described their essence. What we take now as caste is, in fact, the precipitate of a history that selected caste as the single and systematic category to name, and thereby contain, the Indian social order. In precolonial India, the units of social identity had been multiple, and their respective relations and trajectories were part of a complex, conjunctural, constantly changing, political world. The referents of social identity were not only heterogeneous; they were also determined by context. Temple communities, territorial groups, lineage segments, family units, royal retinues, warrior subcastes, "little" kingdoms, occupational reference groups, agricultural or trading associations, devotionally conceived networks and sectarian communities, even priestly cabals, were just some of the significant units of identification, all of them at various times far more significant than any uniform metonymy of endogamous "caste" groupings. Caste, or rather some of the things that seem most easily to come under the name of caste, was just one category among many others, one way of organizing and representing identity. Moreover, caste was not a single category or even a single logic of categorization, even for Brahmans, who were the primary beneficiaries of the caste idea. Regional, village, or residential communities, kinship groups, factional parties, chiefly contingents, political affiliations, and so on could both supersede caste as a rubric for identity and reconstitute the ways caste was organized. Within localities, or kingdoms, groups could rise or fall (and in the process become more or less castelike), depending on the fortunes of particular kings, chiefs, warriors, or headmen, even as kings could routinely readjust the social order by royal decree.[20]

Social identity was importantly political, as too were the contexts in which different units became formed, represented, and mobilized. And politics took on its shape and meaning in relation to local and regional systems of power in which headmen (of lineages, temples, villages), religious leaders (gurus, leaders of sects and monasteries, saints, priests, muftis, and imams), warriors, chiefs, and kings were figures of central importance, with authority over constituencies that from certain perspectives could look and act like caste groups. To read and organize social difference and deference—pervasive features of Indian society—solely in terms of caste thus required a striking act of history and studied disregard for ethnographic specificity, as well as a systematic denial of the political mechanisms that selected different kinds of social units as most significant, and as most highly valorized, at different times. Brahmanic texts, both Vedic origin stories for caste and the much later dharma texts of "Manu," provided transregional and metahistorical modes of understanding Indian society that clearly appealed to British colonial interests and attitudes; they also secured for Indians pride of place in a civilizational lexicon of cultural reconstitution, reaffirmation, and resistance. The idea that *varna*—the classification of all castes into four hierarchical orders with the Brahman on top—could conceivably organize the social identities and relations of all Indians across the civilizational expanse of the subcontinent was only developed under the peculiar circumstances of British colonial rule. Hierarchy, in the sense of rank or ordered difference, might have been a pervasive feature of Indian history, but hierarchy in the sense used by Dumont and others became a systematic value only under the sign of the colonial modern.

## Caste and the Colonial Modern

The transformations associated with modernity in India were overdetermined by the colonial situation. On the one hand, what was useful for British rule also became available for the uses of many Indians who were recruited to participate in one way or another in the construction of colonial knowledge. On the other hand, new forms of and claims about knowledge, products as they were in large part of early colonial Orientalism and late colonial state practices, could take root only because colonial interventions actively obliterated the political dynamic of colonial society. Ironically, it was the very permeability and dynamism of Indian society that allowed caste to become modern India's apparition of its traditional being. Under colonial rule caste—now systematic, and systematically disembodied—lived on. In this new form it was appropriated and reconstructed by colonial power. What Orientalist knowledge did most successfully in the Indian context was to assert the precolonial authority of a specifically colonial form of power and representation.

When caste became political again (if, necessarily, in a different sense), whether in response to census classifications at the beginning of the twentieth century or in reaction to the implementation of the Mandal Report at the end, no one should have been surprised. Caste had been political all along, but under colonialism was anchored to the service of a colonial interest in maintaining social order, justifying colonial power, and sustaining a very particular form of indirect rule. By indirect rule in this context I mean the mechanisms that were used both to buttress and to displace colonial authority. In the early years of colonial rule, these mechanisms were organized principally through "land systems" that were linked to modes of property, agrarian relations, and revenue collection. Zamindars, individual cultivators, and village communities were variably constituted—after long debates over Indian history and colonial policy—as the authentic heirs of precolonial local authority and as primary agents of revenue collection and local order. This was the period when Charles Cornwallis and Philip Francis took their cues from the physiocrats and argued in favor of the resurrection of local lords as a loyal and newly gentrified elite, indebted to British rule and dedicated to improvement; when Thomas Munro made his career by arguing against landlords both because he saw these survivals of older political systems as dangerous and because he was convinced they, unlike the ryots or cultivators whose role he championed, had no actual involvement in agricultural cultivation; and when Charles Metcalfe and Mountstuart Elphinstone established their reputations by identifying and advocating the resilience of the ancient village republic or community, writing histories to justify their position and drafting land policies to demonstrate the wisdom of their views.

As agrarian revenue issues were provisionally resolved, they were at the same time increasingly taken over by other kinds of revenue concerns tied into the diversification of the colonial economy, ranging from changes in international trade, the success and transformation of industrial development in Britain, and the rise of major investments in railways and other infrastructures, to new kinds of world strategic concerns. Thus the crises of early conquest and rule began to give way to other issues of control. This was so particularly in the wake of the Great Rebellion of 1857, after which the Company's ambitions of complete conquest were necessarily curtailed, and the British state assumed "direct" rule. At the very time that Awadhi talukdars were being bought off and other princes and zamindars feted as the ceremonial center of old India, British interest in the institution of caste intensified in very new ways. District-level manuals and gazetteers began to devote whole chapters to the ethnography of caste and custom; imperial surveys made caste into a central object of investigation; and by the time of the first decennial census of 1872, caste had become the primary subject of social classification and knowledge. Although the village continued to be seen as the dominant site of Indian social life, it became understood as more a setting for caste relations than the primary building block of Indian society. By 1901, when the census commissioner H. H. Risley announced his ambition for an ethnographic survey of India, it was clear that caste had attained its colonial apotheosis.

And yet caste was never easily contained, either by spiritual otherworldliness or by Risley's racial empiricism. If caste, like the women's question, became an increasing embarrassment to the nationalist project in the twentieth

century, it never disappeared from the politics of the day. An avalanche of
petitions to census commissioners over caste status led to the dropping of caste
as a census category after 1931, even as caste politics vied significantly with
certain forms of nationalism in places such as Bombay and Madras presidencies. Even as temple entry, under Gandhi and many regional leaders, continued
to occupy pride of place in certain political agendas, Ambedkar threatened the
unity of nationalist purpose by pressing his case for separate electorates for
scheduled castes in a heroic struggle with Gandhi in 1932. Caste politics did
not interfere with the triumph of the nationalist movement, as did communal
strife between Hindus and Muslims in the tragic preemption of Partition, but
it returned soon after independence to contest the easy assurances of modernity
in the new Nehruvian secular vision of society, both at the national level and
once again in regions such as Madras. The sociological assurance that caste
would disappear except as a form of domestic ritual or familial identity when
it entered the city and new domains of industrial capital turned out to be a
bourgeois dream disrupted both by steady reports of escalating caste violence
in the countryside and then the turmoil over reservations in the principal cities
of the nation. Caste did not die, it did not fade away, and it could no longer be
diagnosed as benign. At the same time, caste remains the single most powerful
category for reminding the nation of the resilience of poverty, oppression,
domination, exclusion, and the social life of privilege. And some of the most
eloquent expressions of political community now come in the form of movements that take caste as a primary focus of social mobilization. One could even
argue, following recent formulations by Partha Chatterjee, that caste has
moved from its place as a colonial substitute for civil society (or, in Chatterjee's terms, the colonial argument for why civil society could not grow
in India) to a new position as a specifically postcolonial version of political
society.[21]

And so, for better and for worse, caste did replace the crown that came
before. If the crown was literally emptied of the political dynamic and authority that characterized precolonial regimes in India's history, caste entered,
Athena-like, into the places left behind. Recounting the history of caste, in
other words, is one way of narrating the social history of colonialism in India.[22]
This is a history in which the past itself was colonized, in which the domain of
civil society was abandoned to theories about the weight of tradition, in this
case the totality represented by the caste system. Caste became the colonial
form of civil society; it justified the denial of political rights to Indian subjects
(not citizens) and explained the necessity of colonial rule. As India was anthropologized in the colonial interest, a narrative about its social formation, its
political capacity, and its civilizational inheritance began increasingly to tell
the story of colonial inevitability and of the permanence of British imperial
rule. If caste occupied the place of the social and constrained the possibility of
the political, colonial rule could consist largely of the enumerative technology

of the census and the ethnographic survey, producing by the late nineteenth century what I call the "ethnographic state." This is not the whole story, of course, for at the very time that caste was consolidated as the primary object of social classification and knowledge, it was appropriated in other ways, as well. And it was also steadily subordinated to the political mobilization around the nationalist movement, which disproved one colonial myth after another. But caste remained, and was in fact recast, in ways that have caused embarrassment and critique and have provided the basis for new forms of social mobilization and progressive politics. Caste has become uniquely Indian, and not always in ways that satisfy either liberal or conservative agendas of national identity.

Caste is a specter that continues to haunt the body politic of postcolonial India. Whether in constitutional claims about the abolition of caste discrimination or in political claims about the formation of the national community, it has become the subject of national shame. In part this is an extension of the "women's question" that emerged so powerfully in relation to social reform debates and movements of the nineteenth century. Most of the issues that attracted the attention of social reformers, from widow burning to prohibitions around widow remarriage and controversies over the age of consent, were embedded within caste protocols and related to caste status. The fundamentally gendered character of caste as an emergent cultural system will only occasionally be remarked in the argument that follows, even as I must note at the outset that many of the most egregious effects of caste have been expressed through gender.[23] Colonial sociology was almost as silent as nationalist sociology about the ways in which caste encoded the treatment and management of women in Indian society; it either assumed the pervasiveness of India's abuse of women or anthropologized the whole set of questions around marriage, reproduction, and the family. In the nationalism of the twentieth century, Gandhi was one of the few major figures to attempt to keep the women's issue alive, if in registers that have attracted considerable dissent. Gandhi's principal amendment to the social reform agenda was, in fact, his plank concerning "harijan uplift," although this too became severely contested as his efforts at compromise and incorporation fell afoul of increasing Dalit mobilization.

Nevertheless, whether in relation to the history of gender, the victimization of Dalits, or the rise of anti-Brahman and backward-caste politics, caste has worked to compromise the easy affiliations of national unity and civilizational history. Caste has become the focus of progressive movements and of debates—both local and national—about the character of postcolonial politics. It has also become the uncomfortable reminder that community is always segmented by class, gender, and region, that the nation might be threatened less by religious difference than by other pervasive grounds of difference; it is a reminder that all claims about community are claims about privilege, participation, and exclusion. Caste has been the site of collisions between patriarchy and tradition; in its valorization of Brahmanic ideals around the status of women and the general subservience of women to marriage rules and domestic conditions, caste has simultaneously preserved the patriarchy of premodern society and worked to sanction the continued oppression and exclusion of women in nationalist reimaginings of the past. But it has also made it clear that neither Brahmanism nor Hinduism can be the genuine basis for a national community, even as religion itself cannot be sequestered (indeed never has been so sequestered) into a private sphere, whether in traditional or modern terms. And caste haunts all assertions of return to a premodern past, all claims about the glories and values of tradition. Caste may be the precipitate of the modern, but it is still the specter of the past.

# *Two*

## Homo Hierarchicus: The Origins of an Idea

### In the Beginning

The Portuguese have been credited with the initial use of the term *casta* to refer to the social order of India, although according to at least one source the first use of the word was applied only to the lowest Indian classes in contradistinction to their overlords.[1] In the early sixteenth century, the traveller Duarte Barbosa reported some features of a caste order after extended stays in India, in particular on the basis of his stay in the great kingdom of Vijayanagara. He wrote that there were "three classes of Heathen, each one of which has a very distinct rule of its own, and also their customs differ much one from the other."[2] The first, and principal, class included the king, "the great Lords, the knights and fighting men." The second class were "Bramenes, who are priests and rulers of their houses of worship."[3] Brahmans were accorded a position of respect, and endogamy within caste units was said to be a general custom, as too the application of sanctions within castes to maintain caste discipline. Barbosa expressed no surprise or shock about Indian society, and although he reported the position of Brahmans as exalted and that of untouchables as inferior, he did not mention the varna system of the four ideal caste groups, nor did he moralize about caste one way or the other.[4] Subsequent European writings about India add little to his account, and frequently comment even less on things like caste. Jean Baptiste Tavernier, a French merchant who traveled to India frequently in the middle of the seventeenth-century, reported on the reign of Aurangzeb as well as on commercial relations between India and Europe, and made some mention of Hindu beliefs, rituals, and customs. But caste was barely mentioned, except as the report of the priests who say there are seventy-two castes, though "these may be reduced to four principal [castes], from which all others derive their origin."[5]

The Mughal rulers of India were aware of a formal varna scheme that could be used to encompass in textual terms the entirety of the Indian social order. Abu'l Fazl, the author of the late sixteenth-century gazetteer and administrative codebook of Akbar's court, the *A'in-i-Akbari*, noted that the four varnas—the brahmans or priests, the ksatriyas or warriors, the vaisyas or merchants and agriculturalists, and the sudras or laborers and servants—had been born from the primordial body of Brahma, and that all subsequent subdivisions of caste groupings were due to intermarriage among these four original categories. But

the A'in-i-Akbari spent far more time delineating the kin-based social categories that actually made up the local social order than it did commenting on
caste—predictably, no doubt, given the concern of the book to systematize
forms of revenue collection and local government under Mughal rule. And
under direct Mughal rule, the most salient titles conferring status were those
that signified a relationship to or an honor derived from the Mughal court, such
as Mansabdar, Zamindar, or Bahadur.[6]

It was not that caste was not there—the earliest writings report Brahmans
and untouchables, and touch on caste concerns in marriage practices and religious matters, among other things—but rather that it did not seem particularly
striking, important, or fixed. This was not only because the European world
was itself mired in hierarchical forms but also because caste did not present
itself as either dominant or especially clear. When it did appear as a phenomenon that was even remotely coherent, it did so as the explanation of Brahman
"informants" about the Hindu order of things, and was presented at a level of
abstraction that made its formal structure appear exotic and not especially relevant. One of the first British reports of this nature came in a treatise by Alexander Dow, an officer in the East India Company's army who had studied Persian
and published a translation of a standard history of India by Firishtah (*The
History of Hindostan*) in 1768. In his introduction to the translation, he wrote
about matters he thought would complement the history, ranging from the
nature of Mughal government to the character of Hindu customs, manners, and
beliefs. Dow relied on the tutelage of a Brahman pandit in Banaras and
adopted a textualist and Brahmanic view of Indian society. Dow was critical of
Mughal ignorance of Hinduism and disregard for Brahmans, though he tells
the story of how Abu'l Faz'l's brother studied Sanskrit and the Vedas under
false pretenses—an illustration of Akbar's famed tolerance of and interest in
these matters. Dow was clearly impressed by the erudition of the Brahmans
with whom he conversed, and was aware of the shortcomings in his own scholarly capacity to write about them, since he had studied Persian rather than
Sanskrit.

Dow reported the existence and elegance of the Vedas, and dismissed some
rampant reports about Hindu society, such as that sati was widely observed,
noting that it had, "for the most part, fallen into desuetude in India; nor was it
ever reckoned a religious duty, as has been very erroneously supposed in the
West." But he wrote only perfunctorily about social life, which consumed a
mere seven pages of text.[7] His section on "caste" is only a page long. He wrote:
"The Hindoos have, from all antiquity, been divided into four great tribes, each
of which comprehends a variety of inferior casts. These tribes do not intermarry, eat, drink, or in any manner associate with one another, except when
they worship at the temple of Jagganat in Orissa. . . . The first, and most noble
tribe, are the Brahmans, who alone can officiate in the priesthood like the
Levites among the Jews." Dow then described the other three varnas, which he

called tribes, by noting their formal associations: "Sittri-s" or Ksatriyas, "ought to be military men; but they frequently follow other professions," "Bise-s" or Vaisyas "are for the most part, merchants, bankers, and bunias or shop-keepers," and "Sudders . . . ought to be menial servants, and they are incapable to raise themselves to any superior rank." According to Dow, all those who are excommunicated from the four tribes are, with their posterity, "for ever shut out from the society of every body in the nation," becoming members of the Harri cast, presumably the "untouchables." The threat of excommunication was so severe that any intermixture of blood was prevented. This, however, was all there was to it—an account clearly based on his Brahman pundit's exposition of the basic outlines of the Dharma Sastras.

## Missionary Views

The first extensive, and in the early years of the nineteenth century the most influential, European account of caste united textual formulations with empirical observation. It appeared in the text published under the name of the Abbé Dubois in 1816, *Description of the Character, Manners, and Customs of the People of India, and of Their Institutions, Religious and Civil.*[8] I say "under the name" because the scholar Sylvia Murr has recently discovered that Dubois's original manuscript was in large part based on an obscure manuscript written by Père Coeurdoux in the 1760s. Dubois himself went to India to escape the "ravages" of the French revolution.[9] He presented "his" text to Mark Wilks—the British resident in Mysore and author of an extensive history of Mysore—in 1806. Wilks forwarded the text to the Madras government the following year, with an enthusiastic endorsement, after studying it for some time and using it for his own study of Mysore history.[10] He wrote:

> The Manuscript of the Abbé Dubois on Indian Casts . . . contains the most correct, comprehensive, and minute account extant in any European language of the Customs and Manners of the Hindus. Of the general utility of a work of this nature, I conclude that no doubt can be entertained. Every Englishman residing in India is interested in the knowledge of those peculiarities in the Indian casts which may enable him to conduct with the natives the ordinary intercourse of civility or business without offending their prejudices. These prejudices are chiefly known to Europeans as insulated facts, and a work which should enable us to generalize our knowledge, by unfolding the sources from which those prejudices are derived, would, as a manual for the younger servants of the Company, in particular, be productive of public advantages, on which it seems to be quite superfluous to enlarge.[11]

Madras bought the copyright for 2,000 star pagodas, which Dubois asked to be put in government paper, the interest from which served him for some years as a kind of regular pension. The purchase of this manuscript was reported by the

Madras government to the Board of Directors of the East India Company in 1807 as "an arrangement . . . of great public importance."[12] Lord William Bentinck, the governor of Madras, explained the importance of Dubois's work thus:

> The result of my own observation during my residence in India is that the Europeans generally know little or nothing of the customs and manners of the Hindus. . . . We do not, we cannot, associate with the natives. We cannot see them in their houses and with their families. We are necessarily very much confined to our houses by the heat; all our wants and business which would create a greater intercourse with the natives is done for us, and we are in fact strangers in the land. . . . I am of opinion that, in a political point of view, the information which the work of the Abbé Dubois has to impart might be of the greatest benefit in aiding the servants of the Government in conducting themselves more in unison with the customs of the natives.[13]

Dubois performed an anthropological service to the British rulers of India, doing so in part because as a French Jesuit missionary he was thought to be able to cross social worlds far more readily than the imperial British themselves. But, as was true with all missionary perspectives, social worlds were crossed in order to convert souls, a social fact that led to very strong views on the subject of caste.

The manuscript was sent to London, where it was eventually translated into English and published in 1816, without benefit of the fact that at the same time Dubois was engaged in making extensive changes to the text. Copies had remained in Madras, where they were examined by a group of scholars at the College of Fort St. George, in particular A. D. Campbell, secretary of the Madras Board and a noted scholar of Dravidian languages, who had recommended revisions. The college had also attained a dictionary and a work on Hindu ethics from Dubois, but returned these as of little interest, noting "that the most useful part of the former [materials] had been compressed in the Abbé's work on castes."[14] Dubois apparently did make major changes. He "expunged the whole of the 8th and 9th chapters of his work as too incorrect for publication, and in lieu thereof has substituted a new chapter containing about 400 pages of close writing. He has also forwarded about 300 pages of the same kind, being additions and new matter which he wishes to insert in different parts of his work."[15] Campbell further noted that "The Board in submitting this letter have directed me to explain to the Government that the alterations, additions and corrections of the Author, though considerable, appear to them the least which the work requires. There is nothing perhaps of more importance to the Hindoo community than that their distinctions of cast should be well understood by the civil officers of the government in the interior of the country, yet there is no subject at present on which it is so difficult to procure correct information."[16] The exact nature of Campbell's concerns is unclear; what does

come through from the correspondence is the fact that although Dubois's treatise was clearly considered inadequate in some respects and deeply flawed in
others, it nevertheless continued to receive the support and approbation of
Company servants in Madras well after it was submitted and, judging from
Murr's account, more than fifty years after some of the material was written.
The British were aware that despite their growing expertise in matters concerning land revenue issues on the one hand and linguistic and grammatical issues
on the other, they still knew painfully little about local social life and customs.
And given Bentinck's description of British interactions with the colonized
populations of India, it was unlikely they could do better than Dubois's book,
flawed, and apparently dated, though it was.

Many years later, in a prefatory note to the revised edition, the noted Orientalist Max Müller gave testimony to the importance of Dubois's text by noting
that it contained

> the views of an eye-witness, of a man singularly free from prejudice and of a scholar
> with sufficient knowledge, if not of Sanskrit, yet of Tamil, both literary and spoken,
> to be able to enter into the views of the natives, to understand their manners and
> customs, and to make allowance for many of their superstitious opinions and prac-
> tices, as mere corruptions of an originally far more rational and intelligent form of
> religion and philosophy. Few men who were real scholars have hitherto undertaken
> to tell us what they saw of India and its inhabitants during a lifelong residence in the
> country, and in spite of the great opportunities that India offers to intelligent and
> observant travellers, we know far less of the actual life of India than of that of Greece
> and Rome.[17]

While confessing the extraordinary limits of Orientalist knowledge in India,
Müller made clear both the prestige of Dubois's text and his supposition that
he was a man free of prejudice, if firmly located in the eighteenth rather than
the nineteenth centuries. But although Dubois was neither English nor a colonial servant, he was a Christian missionary, and his other writing on India,
which was at the time far more controversial, concerned his observations on
the potential position of Christianity in India. In 1823 he published a pamphlet
entitled "Letters on the State of Christianity in India; in which the conversion
of the Hindoos is considered as impracticable, to which is added a vindication
of the Hindoos, male and female, in answer to a severe attack made upon both
by the Reverend *****."[18] He wrote that "The Indians are a people so peculiarly circumstanced that I consider it next to impossible to make among them
real and sincere Christians; the force of the prejudices and customs among
them is known by all."[19]

Dubois was not unimpressed by the intellectual merits of Hinduism, but was
extremely critical of Brahmans, both because he saw them as the chief impediment to Christianization and because he viewed them as given over to sensual

pleasures and preoccupations, the "empire of the senses." According to the Rev. James Hough, who took issue with Dubois, "his arguments are founded upon the bad character of the Hindoos, but especially of the Brahmins—upon the extensive influence of the latter over all other castes of Hindoos—upon the nature of their superstitions and the inveteracy of their prejudices."[20] And Dubois was particularly critical of the efforts of early missionaries to use pageantry and festival to attract Hindus, as the net effect had been to interest only the "outcasts, or persons left without resources and without connexions in society; or among stupid and quite helpless fellows."[21] As we shall see, much early "colonial" ethnography was in fact written by missionaries, who observed Indian society more closely than did British officials, but experienced it in relation to their primary concern with Christian conversion. Dubois was one of the first such missionary ethnographers and, as Bentinck duly noted, a great authority at a time when the colonial administration knew so little.

Dubois began his book by describing the "caste system" in India, referring to the varna system as outlined in the *Dharma Sastras*. He then noted that there were many prejudices against caste, and persons who believe that "caste is not only useless to the body politic, it is also ridiculous, and even calculated to bring trouble and disorder on the people." But he went on to say: "For my part, having lived many years on friendly terms with the Hindus, I have been able to study their national life and character closely, and I have arrived at a quite opposite decision on this subject of caste. I believe caste division to be in many respects the chef-d'oeuvre, the happiest effort, of Hindu legislation. I am persuaded that it is simply and solely due to the distribution of the people into castes that India did not lapse into a state of barbarism, and that she preserved and perfected the arts and sciences of civilization whilst most other nations of the earth remained in a state of barbarism." His high opinion of caste was linked to his very low opinion of Hindu morality: "We can picture what would become of the Hindus if they were not kept within the bounds of duty by the rules and penalties of caste, by looking at the position of the Pariahs, or outcastes of India, who, checked by no moral restraint, abandon themselves to their natural propensities. . . . For my own part, being perfectly familiar with this class, and acquainted with its natural predilections and sentiments, I am persuaded that a nation of Pariahs left to themselves would speedily become worse than the hordes of cannibals who wander in the vast waste of Africa, and would soon take to devouring each other." If Dubois had negative views of Brahmans, they were nothing to what he took the "outcaste Pariahs" to be. Without a Brahmanically ordered caste system, Dubois felt that India would "necessarily fall into a state of hopeless anarchy, and, before the present generation disappeared, this nation, so polished under present conditions, would have to be reckoned amongst the most uncivilized of the world."[22]

Dubois's chapter on "Pariahs" demonstrated his "upper-caste" contempt for them, as well as for those—including Europeans—who lived in any proximity

to them. Thus it was that Dubois believed that a Christian mission was destined to fail if it could convert only "untouchables" and have no success at all
with Brahmans. He had nothing but admiration for the great early seventeenth-
century Jesuit missionary Roberto de Nobili, who took on Brahman customs
and modes of life, and managed to convert a number of upper-caste Hindus to
Christianity, in part because he did not insist, as many other missionaries did,
that they break caste mores. But once the Catholic Church challenged this form
of conversion, leading to the famous controversy about the so-called "Malabar
Rites," the Jesuits had to fall in line with stated Church policy that religious
conversion should lead to social conversion, as well.[23] And through his own
experience, Dubois despaired even of the possibility of religious conversion,
taking a far dimmer view than did de Nobili.

Dubois made a separation between caste as a kind of civil institution and
Hinduism as the religious basis of it. Although he wrote of caste in approving,
sometimes even glowing, terms, he made no secret of his revulsion to Hinduism as a religion. He argued that "caste regulations counteract to a great extent
the evil effects which would otherwise be produced on the national character
by a religion that encourages the most unlicensed depravity of morals, as well
in the decorations of its temples as in its dogmas and ritual."[24] And yet caste
was not unconnected to religion, since he suggested that it was the genius of
caste to protect India—and by implication Hinduism—from foreign influence.
"The Hindus have often passed beneath the yoke of foreign invaders, whose
religions, laws, and customs have been very different from their own; yet all
efforts to impose foreign institutions on the people of India have been futile,
and foreign occupation has never dealt more than a feeble blow against Indian
custom. Above all, and before all, it was the caste system that protected
them."[25] Thus caste protected Hindus from a fall into barbarism but was also
the reason why Christian missions were so woefully unlikely to succeed.

For Dubois, highest praise was reserved for the ancient Hindu lawgivers or
"legislators," who conceived the caste system and organized it in terms of
sufficient sanction and conviction to prevent the possibility of systematic
breakdown for millennia to come. So impressed was he that he not only explained the failure of Christianity through caste, he also recommended against
substantial interference in Indian affairs on the part of the colonial rulers.

> It is in the nature of the Hindus to cling to their civil and religious institutions, to
> their old customs and habits. . . . Let us leave them their cherished laws and preju-
> dices, since no human effort will persuade them to give them up, even in their own
> interests, and let us not risk making the gentlest and most submissive people in the
> world furious and indomitable by thwarting them. Let us take care lest we bring
> about, by some hasty or imprudent course of action, catastrophes which would re-
> duce the country to a state of anarchy, desolation, and ultimate ruin, for, in my
> humble opinion, the day when the Government attempts to interfere with any of the

more important religious and civil usages of the Hindus will be the last of its existence as a political power.[26]

Dubois's writings attained extraordinary authority for the British rulers for
a number of reasons, not least because he justified British opinion that interference in social and religious customs should be kept to an absolute minimum.
Even though he was a Christian missionary, he thus advocated Company policy designed precisely to keep missionaries out of India. For years, in fact, the
Company prohibited as much missionary activity as it could and tried to interfere in social and religious matters as little as possible. When William Carey
and John Thomas arrived in Bengal in 1793, they were not only the first Bap-
tist missionaries in India, they were the first English clergymen who went to
India as missionaries with official Company sanction. Even so, they were not
encouraged to proselytize, but expected rather to restrict missionary activities
to educational and linguistic pursuits, to set up schools and translate the Bible.
Indeed, in the eighteenth and early nineteenth centuries, the Company actively
involved itself in local religious activities, it regulated endowments for temples and other religious institutions and compelled "untouchables" and Christian converts from the lower castes to assist in Hindu festivals. In addition,
European soldiers were posted in attendance at various religious rituals to bolster the appearance of Company pomp and circumstance.[27] It was only because
of the efflorescence of evangelical Christianity in early nineteenth-century
Britain and the rise to political power of evangelical Christians such as Charles
Grant and William Wilberforce that the East India Company was forced to
change its policy and allow missionary work in India. After 1813, licenses
were regularly granted for missionary work, and after 1833, the requirement
for licensing was lifted altogether.[28] But even with the growing rapprochement
between missionaries and Company officials, there were still tensions between
the two and major differences in attitudes toward India and opinions about
how much the British government should intervene. After the Great Rebellion
of 1857, official British opinion once again veered away sharply from the
encouragement of any active intervention, expressly assuring Indian subjects
that they would not be coerced to change their beliefs or customs. Accordingly, missionaries became even more concerned about the missed opportunities of empire and the general failure of British crown rule to take Christianization as its primary mission.

If Dubois was peculiar among missionaries in his high regard for caste and
his discouragement of official intervention, he nevertheless held an opinion
that became a convention among missionaries—that caste was the chief impediment to conversion. Carey and his colleagues operated the Serampore
schools for some years before realizing that caste was a potential problem.
Soon, however, Carey's colleagues wrote that they saw caste as "a prison, far

stronger than any which the civil tyrannies of the world have erected; a prison which immures many innocent beings." In some despair, Carey wrote that "All are bound to their present state by caste, in breaking whose chains a man must endure to be renounced and abhorred by his wife, children and friends. Every tie that twines around the heart of a husband, father and neighbor must be torn and broken, ere a man can give himself to Christ."[29] Missionaries concluded that caste was "the most cursed invention of the devil that ever existed," and began to insist on the renunciation of caste as a clear sign that converts had renounced idolatry, as well. That the missionaries had little success except among the lower castes fueled their resentment. And thus it was that missionaries came to accept Dubois's characterization of caste as a system that brooked neither individual dissent nor freedom of movement. Given the preoccupation with, and history of, conversion, missionaries came to hold a special contempt for caste; their ascription to it of a totalizing power was not seen in other contemporaneous British writings.

Missionaries who felt the need to move gradually, as well as those who maintained some interest in converting Indians of upper-caste backgrounds, tended to argue that caste was principally a civil rather than a religious institution, not unlike other systems of social rank and privilege. The principal missionary society in Madras wrote to its constituents in 1809 that it "does not countenance the adherence of the Christian converts to any former religious restrictions which are not consistent with their Christian liberty, yet it cannot be in the power or wish of the Society to abolish all distinctions of ranks and degrees in India."[30] Bishop Heber, who set important mission policies in the 1820s, subscribed to this view as well, as did the "Tanjore missionaries" who argued that "caste had existed as a purely civil institution before the coming of the Brahmans, who had made of it something sacred and immutable."[31] But a report commissioned by the bishop of Madras in 1845 suggested instead that caste "distinctions are unquestionably religious distinctions, originating in, and maintained by, the operation of Hindu idolatry." As Duncan Forrester has observed, "They defended their negative approach as being based on a new and far more profound knowledge of Hinduism and Indian society than had been available to Bishop Heber and the early missionaries."[32] By the middle of the century, missionaries came overwhelmingly to agree that caste was an unmitigated evil. In a resolution made by the Madras Missionary Conference of 1850, it was stated that caste "is one of the greatest obstacles to the progress of the Gospel in India . . . whatever it may have been in its origin, it is now adopted as an essential part of the Hindu religion."[33] Such opinion had ramifications for missionary policy, as missionaries had different views on whether caste should be tolerated in the Church and in its educational institutions, or whether the breaking of caste scruple around issues such as interdining be considered requirements for inclusion within the Christian fold (or for

acceptance into Christian institutions). It was also significant in that missionaries wrote far more about caste and other social matters than did any others
during the first half of the nineteenth century. Missionaries were obsessed with
caste.

## Caste and Early Colonial Historiography

It is not that other British commentators were entirely unimpressed by the
salience of caste or its significance for a whole series of civilizational diagno-
ses. Late-eighteenth- and early-nineteenth-century British writings on India,
however, tended to say relatively little about caste and to be formulaic at best,
long after Alexander Dow. Most British writing on India in the eighteenth
century concerned military matters, and reflected a painstaking and painful
history of conquest, negotiation, alliance, deception, and warfare. The great
hero of the century was Clive, whose military successes in Bengal and Madras
had established the basis for Company control over vast sections of India's
most fertile lands. But even after the successes of Plassey and Arcot, the history of colonial conquest was highly fraught. The Mysore rulers Haidar Ali
and Tipu Sultan had to be engaged four times before their final defeat in 1799,
before which many commentators noted the possibility of a very different
political future for the subcontinent. And the Marathas were a potent force
until the military and diplomatic successes of the British in 1818. In writings
about warfare and military and political intrigue, and in basic concerns about
conquest and control, caste figured as of little significance. The belief that the
British, like the Mughals and the Sultanates before them, had merely walked
into India, facing only minimal resistance because of caste divisions, could
hardly have been generated, let alone sustained, at times of open and regular
military engagement.

Even when they were no longer explicitly engaged with matters of conquest,
the British were concerned about land revenue and the growing need to provide regular income from agriculture to supplement the mercantile profits of
international trade; this also mitigated a preoccupation with caste in favor of
the village. Thomas Munro, Mark Wilks, and Charles Metcalfe all wrote eloquently about the importance of the village community. Metcalfe's words are
perhaps the most quoted: "The village communities are little republics, having
nearly every thing they can want within themselves, and almost independent
of any foreign relations. . . . Dynasty after dynasty tumbles down; revolution
succeeds to revolution; . . . but the village community remains the same."[34]
Thomas Munro, the architect of the Madras ryotwari settlement (which, unlike
Cornwallis's zamindari settlement in Bengal, was made with individual cultivators), wrote in a report from Anantapur of May 15, 1806, that "Every village,
with its twelve Ayangadees as they are called, is a kind of little republic, with
the Potail at the head of it; and India is a mass of such republics. The inhabi-

tants, during war, look chiefly to their own Potail. They give themselves no trouble about the breaking up and division of kingdoms; while the village remains entire, they care not to what power it is transferred: wherever it goes the internal management remains unaltered; the Potail is still the collector and magistrate, and head farmer. From the age of Menu until this day the settlements have been made with or through the Potails."[35] The Fifth Report of 1812 quoted Munro liberally in an endorsement of the view that village government had been in place "from time immemorial," though it also reflects the debate over land tenure in Madras as to whether individual cultivators or the headman of the village should be the agent of revenue settlements, about which much more in a later chapter.[36] Charles Metcalfe and Mountstuart Elphinstone elaborated the idea in relation to the abiding belief in the evanescent but extractive presence of Oriental despotisms. Elphinstone wrote that "These communities contain in miniature all the materials of a State within themselves, and are almost sufficient to protect their members, if all governments are withdrawn";[37] and Metcalfe elaborated his comment quoted above by noting that the village communities have "nearly everything that they want within themselves, and [are] almost independent of any foreign relations."

The focus on the village was part of the early colonial preoccupation with questions of property, landholding, and revenue collection. In late eighteenth-century Bengal, the views of John Shore, Philip Francis, and Charles Cornwallis had all led, after extensive debate, to a permanent settlement with zamindars, or landlords. This led to a massive reorganization of local power meant simultaneously to coopt the chiefs and magnates of late Mughal rule and install a loyal and landed aristocracy to serve a physiocratic vision for a new India.[38] But as the immediate concerns of conquest gave way to the need for more revenue, Thomas Munro and others made their political careers by arguing for a completely different organization of revenue collection in the countryside. The colonial concern to know India began with the desire to understand local forms of landholding and agrarian management, and voluminous statistics and narratives both reflected this concern and fueled continuous arguments about the best ways to rule India and collect revenue. Suspicion of local magnates turned into a paternalist romanticism around the figure of the rural yeoman, and thus the colonial interest in local history and social organization crystallized first around images of gentry landlords, village republics, and sturdy yeomen. There were many different views, but virtually all colonial commentators were impressed by the integrity, and relative autonomy, of the village.[39]

Although by far the greatest number of early colonial records concerned questions of revenue and property, the Company, and numerous Company servants, were interested in discovering a more broadly based context in which to situate polemical debates over property, rent, and agrarian structure. Colin Mackenzie, who played a particularly important role in the rescuing of south India's precolonial history (and he will play an important role in the story ahead), tried to distance himself from revenue debates, and committed himself to the collection of local texts while he engaged in his cartographic and surveying activities in the subcontinent between 1784 and his death in 1821. Significantly for our story here, he encountered very little concerning "caste" in his vast collection of local texts, traditions, and histories, nor did he comment frequently about it. In Mackenzie's initial project of collecting representative texts, histories of places (particularly temples) and political families (and lineages) predominated. The south Indian landscape that he traversed was dotted with temples that served as convenient reference points for trigonometrical surveying and general route maps, due to the tall gopuram towers built over the gateways into temple structures that often served as centers for marketing and defense in addition to worship. Every temple had a history that inscribed the significance of its deity and the ground of the deities' worship with a special past of miracle and power. The south Indian landscape had also been controlled by myriad little kingdoms, ranging widely in size, each with a family history for the chief or king. Thus the set of local tracts collected by Mackenzie contain literally hundreds of accounts of one lineage headman after another who managed to become a little king through a combination of strategies and successes. Frequently, of course, these stories were told as bids to become recognized as zamindars, if not as arguments per se for a zamindari-like settlement in the south.

Mackenzie's preoccupation with local chiefs and kings was in part the result of his clear recognition of the political landscape of late precolonial peninsular India; it was also in part a reflection of the more general recognition—both military and economic—of the need to understand the native aristocracy, its immediate past, and its claims to local authority. When Mackenzie began his survey of Mysore after the defeat of Tipu Sultan in 1799, the general assumption among most East India Company officials was that a revenue settlement with the local lords or zamindars, along the lines of the 1793 Permanent Settlement in Bengal, would be the most suitable form of local governance and revenue collection for Madras presidency. Thus Mackenzie's archival concern with the political history of the Deccan made a great deal of sense for early colonial administration because of its emphasis on the pasts and pedigrees of the potential landlords of a zamindari revenue settlement. As the consensus around the need for a ryotwari settlement grew, interest among many of Mackenzie's old friends in the results of his labors diminished.

From my earlier work, I was aware of the prevalence of texts that concerned kings and temples. However, when I first turned to the Mackenzie collection as a repository for early ethnographic knowledge about southern India relatively uncontaminated by the official interest in land tenure, I was surprised to find very few caste histories.[40] There were some general texts about castes, as also some curious lists of caste groups that resembled Borges's Chinese encyclopedia more than later ethnographic surveys. But there were only a few specific caste histories. Those that did exist seemed of uncertain textual genre, hastily put together from the chance concerns and remarks of local subcaste headmen. Although Mackenzie occasionally mentioned the need to collect texts with information about caste, I found systematic material about caste only in his statistical and cartographic collections, as also in some of his drawings. In the statistical tables called *caneeshamari*s, "the population of the districts by castes, families, and villages" was carefully counted and presented by local public officials.[41] Some of these tables were transcribed on his actual maps of Mysore and the Ceded Districts. Here, the compilations of population data under caste headings seemed to have the same indexical function for the map as the delineations of field types and irrigation sources. These lists were highly particularistic and idiosyncratic. Though Brahmans were usually at the head, the lists were neither highly formalized nor easy to compare across districts or regions. I was surprised by the discovery that my interest in finding early (and little mediated) texts on caste turned up so little.

Only when I turned to Mackenzie's drawings did it seem that I had finally found caste. One of Mackenzie's largest portfolios has eighty-two drawings depicting different groups in the northern Deccan drawn during the early years of the nineteenth century, labeled as drawings of "costume."[42] Costume was the key sign and objective focus of ethnographic difference. This emphasis on costume was in part a reflection of the fact that clothes in India (as in England) were important markers of hierarchy and difference. It was surely also because of the lack of any clear sense of what a pictorial survey of the castes and tribes would be like, as well as, perhaps, because of the influence of the cult of the picturesque, which was preoccupied with the colorful and exotic aspects of the Indian social order. The castes and groups that found their way into Mackenzie's portfolio reveal a very particular ethnographic sensibility. There were portraits of the ancient kings of Vijayanagara, royal Darbar scenes, court servants and soldiers, and of court officials. Both in the absence of any kind of systematic and autonomous sense of a "caste system" and in the concentration of attention on characters who reflected the political landscape of the eighteenth-century Deccan—the same characters who figured in most of Mackenzie's local texts—we can see major differences between Mackenzie's vision of India's ethnography and the ethnography that became canonized in the late nineteenth century.

Despite Mackenzie's years of collecting historical materials, he never prepared a historical synthesis of his own, let alone a catalogue of his collection. And the great Orientalists—Sir William Jones, Nathaniel Halhed, Henry Thomas Colebrooke, and so on—never actually wrote histories or systematic accounts of India, either. The first such history was written instead by James Mill, a Benthamite journalist who secured lifetime employment with the East India Company soon after publishing his magisterial, and voluminous, history of British India in 1817.[43] In the House of Commons, Thomas Macaulay declared it to be the greatest work to appear in English since Gibbon's *Decline and Fall of the Roman Empire*. Mill's text, unsurpassed as a general British history—and as a canonic text for the training of East India Company servants—for the rest of the century, was in part an argument for Utilitarian principles, in part a challenge to Orientalists such as Sir William Jones.[44] As suggested by Javed Majeed, it "shaped a theoretical basis for the liberal programme to emancipate India from its own culture."[45] An attack on Orientalist knowledge in several senses, it held praise of India's civilizational greatness, even if lodged firmly in the past, accountable for blocking serious attention to the need for progress and modernization. Mill had written earlier about the problems of "Oriental rhetoric on the riches of India," criticizing Sir William Jones's susceptibility to the "idea of Eastern wonders," by which he meant wonders both cultural and economic.[46] Throughout his history, Mill systematically debunked the claims of Orientalist scholars that there was anything of merit in India's past: "Rude nations seem to derive a peculiar gratification from pretensions to a remote antiquity. As a boastful and turgid vanity distinguishes remarkably the oriental nations they have in most instances carried their claims extravagantly high." Mill cautioned his reader that "the legendary tales of the Hindus have hitherto, among European inquirers, been regarded with particular respect"; but "because, without a knowledge of them, much of what has been written in Europe concerning the people of India cannot be understood," he proceeds reluctantly to relate the mythological origins of Indian civilization.[47] He made clear, however, his contempt for India's early cultural heritage, and for its government and law in particular. As a further claim for his own authority against that of the Orientalists, he argued in his preface that his lack of knowledge of any Indian language was no disadvantage in his quest, and that his lack of firsthand experience of India—he never journeyed there—rendered his capacity to evaluate the myriad writings on and testimonies of India with the dispassionate objectivity necessary for an adequate historical account.

Mill argued his case polemically, for he was concerned that if the British nation, and government, "conceived the Hindus to be a people of high civilization, while they have in reality made but a few of the earliest steps in the progress to civilization, it is impossible that in many of the measures pursued for the government of that people, the mark aimed at should not have been wrong." And he was clear who the culprit for this misconception had been: "It was unfortunate that a mind so pure, so warm in the pursuit of truth, and so devoted to oriental learning, as that of Sir William Jones, should have adopted the hypothesis of a high state of civilization in the principal countries of Asia." The claim of civilization had weighty consequence, then as now. Had this been mere scholasticism, Mill's alarm would have been less severe, but as "Sir William was actuated by the virtuous design of exalting the Hindus in the eyes of their European masters; and thence ameliorating the temper of the government," Mill was clear that he was attacking both a general cast of mind and a set of governmental policies.[48] In particular, as a good Utilitarian, Mill was concerned about Jones's influence on legal policy, for the Company had sought to disrupt legal precedent as little as possible in the matter of personal law. But Mill was also concerned about the Company's general commitment to the maintenance of the status quo wherever possible, whether in matters of local government, or social policy: "We have already seen, in reviewing the Hindu form of government, that despotism, in one of the simplest and least artificial shapes, was established in Hindustan, and confirmed by laws of Divine authority. We have seen likewise, that by the division of the people into castes, and the prejudices which the detestable views of the Brahmans raised to separate them, a degrading and pernicious system of subordination was established among the hindus, and that the vices of such a system were there carried to a more destructive height than among any other people."[49] In keeping with this general position, the "Anglicists"—of whom Thomas B. Macaulay, who had authored condemnations of Indian literature and learning in defense of his advocacy of the expansion of English education, was the other prime example—would have the Company overturn as much as possible of the weight of the past in order to prepare the way for new modernizing policies and institutions.

Mill's (and Macaulay's) critiques of Indian society were very like, in tone and content, those of the missionary Charles Grant, despite the marked political differences between the two camps of Utilitarians and Evangelicals. As early as 1796, Grant had written his "Observations on the Asiatic Subjects of Great Britain," to make his case against prevailing Orientalist policies of respect for Indian custom, religion, and law that had been promulgated by Warren Hastings.[50] He began his diatribe by asking, "Are we bound for ever to preserve all the enormities in the Hindoo system? Have we become the guardians of every monstrous principle and practice which it contains?" Like Mill, Grant believed that "the true cure of darkness is the introduction of light. The Hindoos err because they are ignorant; and their errors have never fairly been laid before them. The communication of our light and knowledge to them, would prove the best remedy for their disorders."[51] Although Grant's conviction was that Anglicization and Christianization would bring in this light, Mill was concerned with a more general notion of modernization, one that critiqued even some aspects of English institutions. Both held, however, that the religion of the Hindus was an abomination, and believed Brahmans and Brahmanism to be responsible for social depravity. Mill wrote that "by a system of priestcraft, built upon the most enormous and tormenting superstition that ever harassed and degraded any portion of mankind, their minds were enchained more intolerably than their bodies; in short that, despotism and priestcraft taken together, the Hindus, in mind and body, were the most enslaved portion of the human race."[52] Mill's view of caste followed, accordingly, as a prime example of an Indian institution predicated on priestcraft and adapted to despotism.

Mill's idea of caste, however, was entirely textualist. Despite his virulent critique of the Orientalists, on the subject of caste he completely conceded their authority, though he maintained a missionary-like disdain for the institution. Like most colonial commentators in the early nineteenth century, Mill's view of caste derived from Jones's 1794 published translation of *The Laws of Manu (Manu Dharma Sastras)*.[53] Jones achieved his early reputation from his prodigious accomplishments in Oriental literatures and languages, and eventually proposed, on the basis of his linguistic studies, the historical kinship of Sanskrit and European languages. Jones went to India as a jurist, and among his many other achievements played a critical role in the translation, explication, and advocacy of classical canons of Indian law. His translation of *Manu* was the last of his legal contributions, as he died shortly after its publication, but the text became important for reasons well beyond its place in the delineation of personal law. *Manu* concerned such topics as the social obligations and duties of the various castes (*varna*) as well as of individuals at different stages of life (*asrama*), the proper forms of kingship, the nature of social and sexual relations between men and women of different castes, ritual practices of many kinds but mostly those connected with life-cycle transitions and domestic affairs, as well as procedures for the adjudication of different kinds of everyday quarrels and disputes. The text is about dharma, which means duty as well as law, religion as well as practice. According to Wendy Doniger and Bardwell Smith, "By the early centuries of the Common Era, Manu had become, and remained, the standard source of authority in the orthodox tradition for that centrepiece of Hinduism, *varnasrama-dharma* (social and religious duties tied to class and stage of life)."[54] The text was the subject of nine separate commentaries, which suggests its importance over the years. Sanskritists have debated the significance of the text for actual legal practice, and it reads more like a synthetic compilation than a code of law. Whatever its historical status, however, most scholars today agree that it took on unprecedented status as an "applied" legal document only under early British rule.[55] I would argue further that the canonic importance of this text for understanding the foundational nature of Indian society was an even more significant break with the past; it encapsulated British attempts to codify not just law but also social relations in a single, orthodox "Hindu"—and therefore necessarily "Brahmanic"—register. From Jones and Mill to Dumont and Marriott, *Manu* has taken on a general anthropological significance it could never have had before, with enormous consequences for the refashioning of basic assumptions about both religion and society.

The *Manu* text was self-evidently the compilation of Brahman scholars; it could hardly have been otherwise. But the canonization of the text in colonial thought has both rendered caste by definition Brahmanic and opened the

"Hindu" social world to charges of the kind made by both Grant and Mill, namely, that caste society was under the exclusive domination of Brahmans who reserved for themselves not only pride of place in the caste hierarchy but such perquisites as the right to receive rather than give gifts and general exemptions from corporal punishment even if found guilty of serious crimes. Along with a text from the *Rg Veda* that gives a canonical origin story for the caste system (the Brahman being born from the head of Purusa, the Ksatriya from the arm, the Vaisya from the thigh, and the Sudra from the feet), the *Manu* text has been trotted out for the last two hundred years as the classical statement of the caste system. It provides both an originary account of the four varnas, and an explanation, through the process of intermarriage and miscegenation, for the generation of the myriad actual caste groups, or *jatis*, reported by every ethnographer of Indian society. Thus the text has been seen as both prescriptive and descriptive, and the two functions have frequently collapsed into one. Given the history of colonial and anthropological textualization, the text has had a life far outside its own textual confines, and certainly beyond a narrow group of scholastic Brahman jurists. For Mill, who eschewed as much as possible reference to the very texts canonized by Orientalist scholarship, the *Manu* text seemed unavoidably central in his account of caste. Ironically, he relied on the work of Sir William Jones to mount his own devastating critique of Jones.

Mill wrote that "On the division of the people, and the privileges or disadvantages annexed to the several castes, the whole frame of Hindu society so much depends, that it is an object of primary importance."[56] Interspersed with disparaging functionalist asides about the requirements and susceptibilities of "rude" societies, the chapter on caste reiterated a fairly standard account of the four varnas, with the law of Manu as the primary authority. Although Mill conceded that the division of society into four classes or castes represented the first step in civilization—a step taken by the Egyptians but not by the Arabs— he was contemptuous of the relative primitiveness of the system, as also its reliance on the superstitious power of the priestly caste. He wrote:

> As the greater part of life among the Hindus is engrossed by the performance of an infinite and burdensome ritual, which extends to almost every hour of the day, and every function of nature and society, the Brahmans, who are the sole judges and directors in these complicated and endless duties, are rendered the uncontrollable masters of human life. Thus elevated in power and privileges, the ceremonial of society is no less remarkably in their favour. They are so much superior to the king, that the meanest Brahman would account himself polluted by eating with him, and death itself would appear to him less dreadful than the degradation of permitting his daughter to unite herself in marriage with his sovereign.[57]

And yet, with no trace of contradiction, Mill's next chapter is on government, which he opened by noting that "After the division of the people into ranks and occupations, the great circumstance by which their condition, character, and operations are determined, is the political establishment, the system of actions by which the social order is preserved. Among the Hindus, according to the Asiatic model, the government was monarchical, and, with the usual exception of religion and its ministers, absolute."[58] Here Mill proposed the well-worn theory of Oriental despotism, quoting *Manu* to suggest the divinity of the king. By his acceptance of this account, and his use of it to describe Indian society in its entirety, Mill provided his readers with a view of caste that confused commensal and conjugal regulation with the total social order, and denigrated the role of the king, and the status of political life, in a way perfectly consonant with British interest in justifying their rule. Mill's Utilitarian critique of colonial misrule shared far more with those he attacked than with any who would assert either the ideological or institutional importance of political rule in the period before British conquest.[59] In the end, the chapter merely rehearsed his view of the rudeness of Hindu society and polity rather than the limits of the textual version of the position of Brahmans in society.

When Mountstuart Elphinstone published his two-volume history of India in 1842, he felt the need to explain why he would write a history so soon after Mill's had seemed to set the standard for any such work and make all subsequent efforts seem redundant. Elphinstone justified his work principally on the grounds of his Indian experience, which might, he believed, "sometimes lead to different conclusions."[60] Elphinstone had been appointed to the Bengal Civil Service as early as 1796, had later been a resident in Poona before playing a prominent part in the final Maratha war, and was appointed the first governor of Bombay, a position he held from 1819 to 1827. But despite all his time in India, his anthropology was also based predominantly on the *Manu Dharma Sastra*. In his opening sections, entitled "State of the Hindus at the Time of Menu's Code" and "Changes since Menu, and State of the Hindus in Later Times," he reproduced a textual view of caste and early Indian society, writing for pages about the four varnas, the complex rules and formulations about the separation and mixing of castes, and the consequent proliferation of the myriad jatis that would later become the recognizeable caste units of contemporary ethnography. Nevertheless, Elphinstone also wrote about changes in caste, suggesting that many Brahmans had taken a worldly turn—a view not surprising for one who was the resident to the Peshwas in the last days of Maratha rule. Elphinstone also noted, more charitably than either Grant or Mill, that the institution of caste, "though it exercises a most pernicious influence on the progress of the nation, has by no means so great an effect in obstructing the enterprise of individuals as European writers are apt to suppose. There is, indeed, scarcely any part of the world where changes of condition are so sudden and so striking as in India."[61] And Elphinstone granted India the status of a major world civilization, although some of the qualifications in his admiration had to do with caste, or rather with a system in which, as he noted, the "priests, as they rose into consequence, began to combine and act in concert: that they invented the genealogy of casts, and other fables, to support the existing institutions."[62] Elphinstone's history differed markedly from Mill's, and he wrote with the detail and passion of one directly involved in Indian affairs. And yet it is striking how little changed was the ethnographic account, if only because, as he wrote like Bentinck before him, of the limits imposed on Englishmen, who "have less opportunity than might be expected of forming opinions of native character."[63] Once again, the sacred text was held to be reliable and important because of both the extreme variability of the Indian situation and the limited knowledge of the English about the social lives of Indians.

Elphinstone's account was far more nuanced than Mill's, at least in part because he sought to use his understanding of Indian history and society as the justification for the fashioning of new systems of rule and revenue collection, whereas Mill was content with nothing less than a complete break with the past.[64] Although as a practical matter Elphinstone did not always disagree with the reformist recommendations of the Utilitarians, he was opposed to the Utilitarian spirit, and argued repeatedly, in broad agreement with Thomas Munro, Charles Metcalfe, and John Malcolm, for the importance of establishing governmental policy in harmony with Indian social, if not political, institutions. Thus for Elphinstone the break with Orientalist knowledge was never complete, though the preoccupations often differed markedly. But Elphinstone's history never took on the importance of Mill's text, and it is significant that H. H. Wilson, an accomplished Orientalist and the first Boden Professor of Sanskrit at Oxford, decided to edit Mill's *History*, using this as the pretext to make myriad editorial emendations for the publication of Mill's fifth edition, as late as 1858. Even after the Great Rebellion, Mill's history was canonic.

Wilson, who made his initial reputation preparing a catalogue of the Mackenzie collection, soon took on the task of translating and editing classical Sanskritic texts, but he never lost his interest in history or in adapting Orientalist scholarship to questions of concern to colonial rule. His reedition (and "continuation") of Mill's text was a grudging acknowledgement of the extraordinary influence of Mill and his views. Nevertheless, Wilson was scathing about Mill's ignorance of India, and his preface made it clear that the reedition was less an endorsement of Mill than an attempt to use Mill's own status to disturb official opinion. He wrote:

Considered merely in a literary capacity, the description of the Hindus in the History of British India, is open to censure for its obvious unfairness and injustice; but in the effects which it is likely to exercise upon the connexion between the people of England and the people of India, it is chargeable with more than literary demerit: its tendency is evil; it is calculated to destroy all sympathy between the rulers and the ruled; to preoccupy the minds of those who issue annually from Great Britain, to monopolize the posts of honour and power in Hindustan, with an unfounded aversion toward those over whom they exercise that power. . . . There is reason to fear that these consequences are not imaginary, and that a harsh and illiberal spirit has of late years prevailed in the conduct and councils of the rising service in India, which owes its origin to impressions imbibed in early life from the History of Mr. Mill.[65]

And yet, despite these obvious differences between Wilson the Orientalist and Mill the Anglicist, it is extraordinary how similar their views were about caste. Wilson corrected Mill's notion that Brahmans were primarily priests, or that their high status depended upon a relationship to the priesthood, and made numerous other corrections and revisions to Mill's early chapters on the Hindus. And yet he relied on the very same textual source, the *Manu Dharma Sastra*, to provide the corrected evidence for an understanding of caste and Hindu society.

## Caste and the Orientalists

The Orientalists lost the force of their influence soon after the opening decades of the nineteenth century, battered by the combined attacks of the Evangelicals and the Anglicists, not to mention the development of new administrative knowledge that began to develop an empirical density of its own from as early as the 1790s. They nevertheless left an important mark, not least in the canonization of certain texts as the basis on which empirical observations and Anglicist judgments about Indian society would be made.

The last major Orientalist contribution to fundamental debates concerning the character of Indian civilization and the nature of Indian society can be seen in the writings of Max Müller, whose general popularity is in retrospect perhaps less important than the fact that he strongly influenced certain Indian social reformers and nationalists, most significantly Gandhi. Müller wrote an essay on caste in 1858, just after the Great Rebellion, or in colonial reference, the "Sepoy Mutiny."[66] Müller's essay on caste sought specifically to clarify the terms of the discussion around caste that had been vastly exacerbated by the rebellion; as he put it, "Among the causes assigned for the Sepoy mutiny, caste has been made the most prominent." The rebellion led to passionate debate about caste, a debate that licensed missionary denunciation of the Company's toleration of it, on the one hand, and prompted severe criticisms of missionaries for their role in alarming Indian subjects about British intentions to make them lose caste altogether, on the other.[67] The debate over caste was joined by Müller with his characteristic belief that textual authority should have pride of place in official knowledge about India. He carefully distinguished himself from those missionaries who advocated an attack on caste as retribution for the revolt, while he also asserted in different ways his Christian convictions and credentials. He was clear that neither India nor regard for Indian civilization should suffer from the effects of the revolt: "Whatever the truth may be about the diabolical atrocities which are said to have been committed against women and children, a grievous wrong has been done to the people of India by making them responsible for crimes committed or said to have been committed by a few escaped convicts and raving fanatics; and . . . it will be long before the impression once created can be effaced, and before the inhabitants of India are treated again as men, and not as monsters."[68] Müller asked the fundamental question about the religious or social status of caste, and noted that there was no easy answer: "Now, if we ask the Hindus whether their laws of caste are part of their religion, some will answer that they are, others that they are not." In characteristic Orientalist fashion, he advised resort to the texts themselves: "We are able to consult the very authorities to which the Hindus appeal, and we can form an opinion with greater impartiality than the Brahmans themselves."[69] Müller made clear his concern that religious beliefs—determined by textual standards—be respected in all events. But he also made clear that his study of the texts suggested that the caste of the Vedas and of later— degraded—periods were altogether different.

Despite his manifest approval of Vedic civilization and his increasing contempt for later developments, Müller recommended against major governmental intervention, arguing instead for a gradualist approach. His recommendation seems somewhat contradictory, though it was motivated in large part by a general sense of political caution: "It is now perceived that it will never answer to keep India mainly by military force, and that the eloquent but irritating speeches of Indian reformers must prove very expensive to the tax-paying public of England. India can never be held or governed profitably without the good-will of the natives, and in any new measures that are to be adopted it will be necessary to listen to what they have to say, and to reason with them as we should reason with men quite capable of appreciating the force of an argument. There ought to be no idea of converting the Hindus by force, or of doing violence to their religious feelings."[70] Müller revealed a combination of admiration and sensitivity, while at the same time he held the view that Indian problems were the result of degradation and corruption from the Vedic ideal, rather than related to colonial rule. Although few British administrators were compelled by such understandings, even when they accepted Müller's advice to respect, or at least attempt not to outrage, Indian opinion, Müller's views became influential among many Indian subjects. Most notably, his general views about Indian civilization had great significance for the development of Gandhi's thought. Gandhi followed Müller in identifying the soul of Indian civilization as that of the Vedic age, and the distortions of later history as beginning in the time of Manu. But Gandhi could never agree with Müller, as did most other social reformers, that the social and the religious could be separated.

Despite the bitter reaction in Britain to the rebellion, and the outcry against caste among missionaries and the general public, the British government, which assumed direct rule in 1858, was obviously concerned to do nothing further to threaten the continuation of its rule over the subcontinent. In the queen-empress's proclamation of the establishment of direct British authority over India, it was said that "We disclaim alike the right and the desire to impose our convictions on our subjects. We declare it to be our royal will and pleasure that none be in anywise favoured, none molested or disquieted, by reason of their religious faith or observances, but that all shall alike enjoy the equal and impartial protection of the law; and we do strictly charge and enjoin that all those who may be in authority under us that they abstain from all interference with the religious belief or worship of all of our subjects, on pain of our highest displeasure."[71] Although Orientalist opinion ceased from this point on to have major influence on British policy makers, a pragmatic desire to avoid further complications from such intervention, or perceptions thereof, overrode missionary wishes to use the moment to strike a fatal blow against both caste and Hinduism. And since there was general agreement among missionaries and officials alike that caste was simultaneously religious and social—given among other things the shared assumption about the perverse character of Hinduism as a religion—this also meant that the government would seek to disturb caste sensitivities, whatever they were and however they were sanctioned, as little as possible. Ironically, the most difficult challenges to the policy of nonintervention came from Indian social reformers, who throughout the nineteenth century sought to mobilize support from government and private citizens alike for major assaults on caste, in relation to issues that emerged from the treatment of women in upper castes to treatment of lower castes and in particular "untouchable" groups. In this endeavor, missionaries clearly played an important role, though what began as a concern with the impediments to conversion soon became used by others to resist both conversion and the embarrassment that accrued from missionary criticism.

If caste never succumbed to an analytical dualism that allowed the easy separation of the social and the religious, it was in part because the ideological underpinnings of separate religious and social (or political) domains had only developed—however uncertainly—in Europe from the middle of the eighteenth century, and were still imposed in ways that made little sense in Indian society, let alone in the colonial contexts that such deliberations inherently took place. England's own secularist self-representations were irrevocably tied to Christian assumptions and ideology.[72] In India, colonial rulers saw caste as the quintessential form of civil society, simultaneously responsible for India's political weakness and a symptom of the overdevelopment of its religious preoccupations. Missionaries and officials both viewed caste, and Hinduism, from a position in which Christianity was heralded not just as the true religion but as one that allowed for genuine separations between the political and social on the one side and the religious on the other. It is true that there was both disagreement about and confusion over what caste really was—whether it was a convenient or at the very least necessary institution for empire or an impediment not just to conversion but to the moral justifications of empire, whether it should be attacked or ignored until the nationalist cause would allow it to be taken care of outside of the imperial glare, and whether it referred primarily to the textual varna scale of four orders or the empirical muddle of myriad jati groups. By 1858 there was nevertheless general recognition that caste was the foundational fact of Indian society, fundamental both to Hinduism (as Hinduism was to it) and to the Indian subcontinent as a civilizational region. Caste emerged, stronger than ever, from the legacy of Orientalist forms of knowledge.

As the Orientalists faded away, and as missionaries lost out to the imperatives of empire, British officials increasingly felt the need to find other means to answer the disturbing questions raised by their rule and the revolt against it. If questions of conquest and then revenue collection dominated the formation of official knowledge in the years between Plassey and the rebellion, questions of order and the maintenance of rule took pride of place for the next century. The last half of the nineteenth century witnessed the development of a new kind of curiosity about and knowledge of the Indian social world, exhibited first in the manuals and gazetteers that began to encode official local knowledge, then in the materials that developed around the census, which led to Risley's great ambition for an ethnographic survey of all of India. During this same period, missionaries continued to play a role, contesting official policies of nonintervention and continuing their critique of caste and religion. But the critique of caste that was heard loudest now came from a very different place, mobilized by Indian critics and activists as varied as Rammohun Roy and Dayananda Saraswati, M. G. Ranade and G. K. Gokhale, J. G. Phule and Rabindranath Tagore, and, into the next century, M. K. Gandhi, B. R. Ambedkar, and E. V. Ramaswami Naicker. The importance of caste in the census led to increasing focus on the recognition of caste categories by the official apparatuses of government, but the critique of caste began, like the not unrelated questions around the position of women, either to disappear or be seen as a domestic issue that should be addressed only after self-rule had been instituted. Caste itself did not disappear. Instead, it seemed stronger than ever, and the massive proliferation of vernacular texts concerning caste (especially for "backward" castes) in the first two decades of the twentieth century confirmed the transformation even as they provided a principal mechanism for the mobilization of new political identities and strategies. As a result, caste continued to embarrass and to enliven debates over tradition and modernity, the relationship of civil society to religion, and the place of politics in Indian culture and the development of nationalist ideology. In moments of civilizational assertion, caste could be seen as something that had united India as a nation many years before the arrival of the British, and in moments of civilizational embarrassment caste could be held accountable for the ease of the British conquest of India itself. It was in this context that both the rise of official fascination with the centrality of caste, on the one hand, and reformist critiques of caste, on the other, would unfold.

# *Three*

## The Ethnographic State

### Toward an Imperial Sociology of India

By the second half of the nineteenth century, the colonial state in India was about to undergo several major transformations. Whereas the revenue and authority that accrued from the relationship between land and the state were fundamental to the formation of the early colonial state, the general agrarian revolts that followed hard on the heels of the 1857 "Mutiny" and the steadily increasing economic investment in imperial power (propelled in particular by the joint stock arrangement of the railways and other infrastructural projects) made it clear that things had to change. Land tax was still an important source of revenue through the century, as was much of the trade that had been fundamental to the mercantile origins of empire. It became clear, nevertheless, that the extractive colonial state was facing other challenges that required a new kind of imperium; accordingly, imperial ambition, and anxiety, moved to different levels and concerns. The steady absorption of new lands through the aggressive policies of Lord Dalhousie—that in the taking of Awadh in 1856 had led directly to the Great Rebellion—was brought abruptly to a halt, and policies of indirect rule were mobilized to accommodate, and ultimately appropriate, the incomplete project of colonial conquest. At the same time, the rebellion made it clear that some communities in India could be counted as loyal, whereas others became doomed to perpetual suspicion. These latter groups were to be replaced in the armed forces by the "martial" races; Macaulay's hyperbole was translated into state policy. In the new rhetorical economy of colonial rule, political loyalty replaced landed status, and the form of knowledge and argument that seemed most appropriate to assess matters of loyalty rather than revenue was, of course, knowledge of peoples and cultures. To put the matter in bold relief, after 1857, anthropology supplanted history as the principal colonial modality of knowledge and rule. By the late nineteenth century, as I will go on to show, the colonial state in India can be characterized as the ethnographic state.

In the wake of the Great Rebellion, and as British rule became increasingly secure, caste began to spin a career of its own. Whereas in the early part of the century India's feudal past and then its village communities seemed far more important than the caste system, the colonial ethnographic curiosity that flowered, especially from 1870 on, took caste as the primary object of social classification and understanding. The relative silence about caste matters in early official writings as well as in collections of local texts such as Mackenzie's gave way to new kinds of compendia—from miscellaneous collections and volumes, official manuals and gazetteers, to the census—in which caste figured as the most important subject and classificatory schema for the organization of India's social world. With the memory of the "Mutiny" still lively, concerns about revenue gave way to a preoccupation with social order and the maintenance of rule. To keep India, the British felt the need to know India far better than they had, and now the knowledge had to be about the society of India, not just its political economy. Thus colonial ethnology took the place that had once been held by colonial history. The recognition on the part of Bentinck and Elphinstone that certain forms of knowledge were inaccessible to the British was replaced by the obsessional conceits of high imperial ambition (and anxiety). The ethnographic state was driven by the belief that India could be ruled using anthropological knowledge to understand and control its subjects, and to represent and legitimate its own mission. By the late nineteenth century, ethnological knowledge became privileged more than any other form of imperial understanding, much as Kipling suggests when he made Colonel Creighton both head of the Ethnological Survey and a master spy in the Great Game in his classic colonial novel, *Kim*.

The more the British believed they could know India—with that peculiar colonial intransitivity that made it possible for them to think the more they knew the less the native could know them in turn—the more, of course, they doubted their knowledge. The confidence of imperial empiricism was always accompanied by a sense that facts spin out of control. As Colonel Creighton, Kipling's head of the Ethnological Survey, says, "The more one knows about natives the less can one say what they will or won't do."[1] Indeed, the more H. H. Risley, census commissioner and superintendent of the Ethnographic Survey, went on to refine caste categories to allow the enumeration of the entire population of India by caste, the more it seemed that caste categories were overlapping, unstable, and contested. But such difficulties never made Risley, or the British more generally, doubt their fundamental methods, let alone their ultimate capacity to know. The problem was that knowledge of India was always put in terms of alterity, with unknowability a natural implication of the language of difference. Between difference and the perpetual possibility of deception, knowledge was invariably uncertain. The empiricist response was always to know more, even as the British could never acknowledge the deep uncertainty about the possibility of real knowledge about subjects increasingly cast in terms of incommensurability. The flip side to imperial empiricism was the sense of ultimate inscrutability. And the story that follows charts the murky waters created as a result.[2]

Throughout the nineteenth century, the collection of material about castes and tribes and their customs, and the specification of what kinds of customs, kinship behaviors, ritual forms, and so on, were appropriate and necessary for ethnographic description, became increasingly formalized and canonic. Gradually the institutional provenance of caste expanded, affecting the recruitment of soldiers into the army (particularly after the Great Rebellion), the implementation of legal codes that made the provisions of the law applicable on caste lines, the criminalization of entire caste groups for local policing purposes, the curtailment of the freedom of the land market when excessive amounts of land were thought to be sold by "agricultural" to "merchant" groups, and the assessment of the political implications of different colonial policies in the area of local administration in caste terms—to mention only a few examples.[3] In the years after the rebellion, the detailed compilation of empirical material on British India escalated dramatically, first in occasional manuals of local districts, such as J. H. Nelson's *The Madura Country*,[4] then in the gazetteers and statistical surveys that proliferated as the ethnographic state gained momentum. Early manuals were faulted for being prolix and insufficiently statistical. This concern was expressed throughout the century, for example in response to Buchanan's account of his journeys through Mysore and Kerala in the years just after the 1799 defeat of Tipu Sultan. When some years later Buchanan was commissioned to engage in a similar survey of the Bengal districts, he was instructed to reduce the narrative sections of the account, and to collect more statistics, to make his findings both more readily digestible and comparable. Similarly, when Nelson submitted his manual of the Madura country to the Madras government, he received a lukewarm response: "The board [of Revenue] are of opinion that much greater brevity is desirable, a larger proportion of facts as compared with arguments and theories, and more copious references to the sources whence further details on the various points treated of may be obtained."[5] The board noted in general terms that although the preparation of district-level manuals would be necessary to provide the background for the preparation of a gazetteer for Madras presidency, they were concerned about the "deficiency in statistics, and the prolixity of details" in a work such as Nelson's. Nelson's volume was declared "useless to the general public."[6] This raised special questions for the Madras government because Nelson's work had been commissioned to serve as an example for other district manuals.

The government was concerned to find some method that could produce useful and uniform knowledge for all of India. "His Excellency in Council declared his conviction that immediate steps should be taken to ensure uniformity, and, to that end, appointed Mr. W. W. Hunter, LL.D., of the Civil Service, to visit the Local Governments, and ascertain what had been done in each, with a view to his drawing up a comprehensive scheme, prescribing the principles for the compilation of the Provincial Gazetteers and for their ultimate consolidation into one work."[7] In 1869, Hunter was accordingly appointed director general of statistics to the government of India, and over the years he produced and supervised a series of gazetteers that sought to systematize official colonial knowledge about India. Each manual and gazet-teer had an ethnological chapter, in which the local castes and tribes were listed and described, with more detail reserved for certain caste and tribe groups specific to the area, under the heading of "manners and customs." Marriage systems and kinship patterns, funeral rituals, adherence to Brahmanical priest-hood and principle, clothing, and the geographical distribution of different groups made up the bulk of the descriptive material. By the time of Maclean's general manual of Madras presidency, published in 1892, the subject matter of ethnology had become standardized: "An ethnological account of an Indian people must consist of not less than five separate subjects; their race or de-scent, their language, their caste, their religion or sect, and their traditional habits and customs." Maclean went on to be more specific: "Of these subjects the first [the issue of race] is the most difficult to examine because it is the most involved, and the second [language] is the easiest because it is the most capa-ble of definition and the most accessible. The other three, caste, religion and customs, are little more than matters of observation; but on the other hand they are very imperfect elements in anthropological inquiry, *caste probably taking precedence in India among the three*."[8] By this time, the ethnological section had become more important than the historical prologue, both preceeding it and exceeding it greatly in length.

One of the first general compilations of material on caste after the rebellion was assembled by the Reverend M. A. Sherring, who, starting in 1872, pub-lished an influential three-volume work entitled *Hindu Tribes and Castes*. The work aims to be the first text to "give in English a consecutive and detailed account of the castes of India," and finds it strange that no one had hitherto attempted to do so.[9] It is encyclopedic in coverage, starting with Brahmans then moving to Ksatriyas and on "down" the varna scale. But unlike earlier colonial works that relied on textually derived varna categories as a general guide about Indian society, Sherring used these categories as the frame for his attempt to marry textual and empirical knowledge. The footnotes refer to dis-trict manuals, James Tod's three-volume work on Rajasthan, early settlement reports, and Wilson's glossary, among many other sources. Manu's text is hardly abandoned; it helps to orient the chapters on Brahmans and the genera-tion of myriad actual castes, and provides a dharmic explanation for multi-plicity because of intermarriage. But this becomes in part a pretext for a strictly biological theory of origins for caste groups that are seen now to hold to en-dogamous principles without breach: "it would be . . . correct to regard the numerous Indian tribes and castes as so many distinct integers, complete in themselves, independent and unassociated . . . the honourable condition of marriage between separate castes, and to a large extent between branches of the same caste, is absolutely prohibited."[10] The tone of Sherring's work is more empirical than textual, and provides a bridge between early Orientalist forms of knowledge and a new kind of empirical quest. The text seems a perfect prelude for the census, the first all-India version of which was conducted the year of its publication.

Sherring's text betrayed not only a new empiricist tone but also the author's Christian affiliation.[11] It is striking that a certain kind of Christian position could now accommodate official views of caste, rather than simply being at war with them. By this time Sherring had already accepted the impossibility of mass conversion across India, and even he wrote with approval of Hindu social reformers who had clearly refused to abandon their own religious convictions. But his condemnation of caste, and of Brahmans in particular, carries on a long tradition of missionary and evangelical writing. Sherring followed Max Müller in asserting that "caste as now existing was totally unknown to the Hindu race on first entering into India." He then explained the rise of caste distinction in terms reminiscent of the most frustrated of Christian missionaries. First, caste explains the total religiosity of the Hindu ("the Hindu, from the outset . . . has been engrossed by his religion, which has been at once a magnet to draw him and a pole star to direct him)." Second, caste has made the Hindu servile, and it is "this credulous and servile condition of the Hindu mind [that] has afforded a golden opportunity to the wily Brahman, thirsting for rule and for the exercise of his superior gifts. And third, it is the "wily Brahman" who is especially at fault. The Brahman is not only wily, he is "arrogant and proud," "selfish," "tyrannical," "intractable," and "ambitious." Sherring maintained that the rise of caste after the Vedic period was most certainly the result of a Brahman conspiracy. "Caste, therefore, owes its origin to the Brahman. It is his invention."[12]

In inventing caste, the Brahman secured his claim to his very being: "The Brahman could not now exist, and could not have existed at all, . . . without having caste as the objective form in which his ideas were realized." Sherring used a theory of divide and rule, one that, like his theory of invention, would in fact seem far more appropriate for his own tribe than that of the colonized Brahman. He noted that the Brahman was "pleased that all the castes were animated by the spirit of themselves—pleased at the prospect of their own authority and majesty with every increment added to the castes—and pleased above all at the thought that their own order was at the head of the entire system, and exercised command over all its ramifications." And although caste did not exist at the beginnings of Aryan life in India, the Brahman was able to engineer it in the "childhood of the Hindus."[13] In his concluding essay on the "Prospects of Hindu Caste," he began his opening series of paragraphs with the following assertions: "Caste is sworn enemy to human happiness"; "Caste is opposed to intellectual freedom"; "Caste sets its face sternly against progress"; "Caste makes no compromises"; "The ties of caste are stronger than those of religion"; and "Caste is intensely selfish."[14] Sherring held, however, that the greatest force of change in India was not missionizing but the actions of certain "caste-emancipated Bengalees." Although he was ambivalent about the social reform movement in Bengal (unsure as he was about the adoption of Western customs across the board—he observed that in "our judgment, it is far better for natives of India to adhere to their own customs than to adopt those of foreigners"), he believed that a great change for the better has commenced with the the first steps of "some of the foremost thinkers and actors in Bengalee society." And although he was uncharacteristically optimistic about indigenous transformations in India, he encouraged the formation of serious anti-Brahman sentiment: "let them suddenly awake to the thought that they are as well educated, as able, as intelligent as the Brahmans . . . and exert a much deeper and a far better influence over Hindu Society at large; and they can, if they be so inclined, destroy Brahmanism, root and branch—can utterly annihilate it."[15] Although Sherring's text reiterated earlier missionary condemnation of Brahmans, it accepted the salient reality of racial and cultural difference, which for the missionary always meant the general impossibility of conversion.

Such explicit editorializing did not feature in the census, which from 1872 took over the authoritative function of producing empirical information on caste from the writings of missionaries and officials alike. By the time of the census, caste had become especially important both because of strongly held official views and because of the ways caste was confronted by a variety of Indian reformers, activists, and intellectuals as emblematic of Indian society. The spirit of caste attained its apotheosis with the census. A vehicle for the consolidation of imperial ideology, the census became the means for the collection of empirical knowledge the likes of which could not have been imagined by previous commentators. And yet even the extraordinary compilations of the census were ultimately seen as inadequate to the task of colonial ethnology. The inauguration of the ethnographic survey of India, announced in the first issue of *Man* in 1901, made clear that the census was necessary for colonial knowledge, but hardly sufficient for colonial rule:

> It is unnecessary to dwell at length upon the obvious advantages to many branches of the administration in this country of an accurate and well-arranged record of the customs and the domestic and social relations of the various castes and tribes. The entire framework of native life in India is made up of groups of this kind, and the status and conduct of individuals are largely determined by the rules of the group to which they belong. For the purposes of legislation, of judicial procedure, of famine relief, of sanitation and dealings with epidemic disease, and of almost every form of executive action, an ethnographic survey of India, and a record of the customs of the people is as necessary an incident of good administration as a cadastral survey of the land and a record of the rights of its tenants. The census provides the necessary statistics; it remains to bring out and interpret the facts which lie behind the statistics.

Thus at the start of the twentieth century the political centrality of caste was formally announced. Caste was the site for detailing a record of the customs of the people, the locus of all important information about Indian society. This information, which the colonial state felt increasingly compelled to collect, organize, and disseminate, would thus become available for a wide variety of governmental initiatives and activities, and would relate to "almost every form of executive action."

If the ethnographic survey announced the preeminence of caste for colonial sociology, it was the decennial census that played the most important institutional role not only in providing the "facts" but also in installing caste as the fundamental unit of India's social structure. There was general agreement among most of the administrators of the census, which began on an all-India basis in 1871/2, that caste should be the basic category used to organize the population counts. But there was far less agreement about what caste really was. Various commissioners, for instance, debated whether a caste with fewer than 100,000 persons should be included, or how to organize the "vague and indefinite" entries that in 1891 exceeded 2,300,000 names. There were also debates about whether, and if so how, to list the castes on the basis of "social precedence." When Risley adopted a procedure to establish precedence in the 1901 census, caste became politicized all over again. Caste associations sprung up to contest their assigned position in the official hierarchy, holding meetings, writing petitions, and organizing protests. By 1931 some caste groups were distributing handbills to their fellow caste members to tell them how to answer questions about their religious and sectarian affiliations, as also their race, language, and caste status. After 1931, the British could no longer ignore the political fallout of the census, and abandoned the use of caste for census counting altogether.

The rise of caste as the single most important trope for Indian society, and the complicity of Indian anthropology in the project of colonial state formation, are documented in a great many texts, perhaps nowhere more fully than in H. H. Risley's classic work, *The People of India*.[16] Risley, who was the census commissioner of India for the 1901 census (the regulations of which greatly influenced the 1911 census, as well), had earlier produced the multivolume work *The Tribes and Castes of Bengal*, published in 1891.[17] *The People of India* resulted directly from Risley's work as census commissioner, and is an expanded version of the commissioner's report on the 1901 census (written with the assistance of E. A. Gait) that, among other things, summarized his views on the origin and classification of the Indian races based on his historical speculations and his anthropometric research. Risley was criticized by contemporary as well as subsequent writers for overemphasizing the racial basis of caste and stressing anthropometry. William Crooke, author of many ethnographic works and perhaps his most important critic, argued against Risley with particular vehemence, suggesting that occupational criteria provided much more comprehensive and accurate indices for understanding caste as a system than did race.[18] The anthropometric researches of subsequent scholars steadily eroded the confidence of the anthropological establishment that racial types in India were anywhere near as pure or clear as Risley had assumed. But Risley's general views of caste as a social system and force in India were little challenged. Risley seemed to speak for many in both colonial and academic establishments when he wrote that caste "forms the cement that holds together the myriad units of Indian society. . . . Were its cohesive power withdrawn or its essential ties relaxed, it is difficult to form any idea of the probable consequences. Such a change would be more than a revolution; it would resemble the withdrawal of some elemental force like gravitation or molecular attraction. Order would vanish and chaos would supervene."[19] At the dawn of the twentieth century, it would be difficult to put the case much more strongly than that.

In the proposal for the ethnographic survey of India, it was observed that anthropometry was a science that would yield particularly good results in India precisely because of a caste system that organized social relations through the principle of absolute endogamy: "Marriage takes place only within a limited circle; the disturbing element of crossing is to a great extent excluded; and the differences of physical type, which measurement is intended to establish, are more marked and more persistent than anywhere else in the world."[20] Thus the government justified its project, and its choice of Risley, for a survey that was specifically directed "to collect the physical measurements of selected castes and tribes." Risley's advocacy of anthropometry and his theories about the relation of race and caste were clearly fundamental to the definition of the ethnographic project in turn-of-the-century colonial India. The scientific claim about caste reflects Risley's assumption that he could actually test in India the various theories about race and the human species that had been merely proposed on speculative grounds in Europe. At the same time, these claims concealed the continuity between the assumption that castes were biologically discrete and his belief that in cultural as well as biological terms castes in India were like individuals in the West.

The ethnographic survey resulted in a series of volumes organized around the encyclopedic delineation of the customs, manners, and measurements of the castes and tribes of the different regions of India, and although not all the surveyors shared Risley's anthropological views entirely, the volumes nevertheless reflect Risley's general sense of what the survey should entail. Each entry includes such salient ethnographic facts as caste origin stories, occupational profiles, descriptions of kinship structure, marriage and funerary rituals, manner of dress and decoration, as well as assorted stories, observations, and accounts about each group. The texts were obviously designed as easy reference works for colonial administrators, for the police as well as revenue agents, district magistrates, and army recruiters. It was clear you could know a man by his caste.

Although colonial ethnographers rarely addressed directly the political implications of their scientific projects, Risley did precisely that in his *The People of India*, where he confronted the question of nationalism. In one of the two new chapters written for the 1909 publication of the book, Risley assessed the role caste might play in the future of India's political development. And he quoted with approval the words of Sir Henry Cotton, who surmised that "The problem of the future is not to destroy caste, but to modify it, to preserve its distinctive conceptions, and to gradually place them upon a social instead of a supernatural basis."[21] Here Cotton, and Risley, advocated precisely what I have suggested colonialism in India set out to do: to reconstitute caste as a necessary complement to social order and governmental authority, and to formulate it as a new kind of civil society for the colonial state.

In Risley's view, caste has an ambivalent status. It is both a religious institution and a social or civil one. It is anarchic, yet encourages the development of monarchy. It is particularistic, though the necessary and inevitable basis for any unity in the Indian context. On the one hand Risley noted, basing his conclusions largely on the lectures of Sir John Seeley, that "The facts are beyond dispute, and they point to the inevitable conclusion that national sentiment in India can derive no encouragement from the study of Indian history." On the other hand, Risley wrote that "the caste system itself, with its singularly perfect communal organization, is a machinery admirably fitted for the diffusion of new ideas; that castes may in course of time group themselves into classes representing the different strata of society; and that India may thus attain, by the agency of these indigenous corporations, the results which have been arrived at elsewhere through the fusion of individual types." These contradictions are interestingly resolved in (and by) the colonial situation. And here we confront the colonial mind in its most liberal guise. For Risley wrote that "The factors of nationality in India are two—the common use of the English language for certain purposes and the common employment of Indians in English administration."[22]

Risley thus held out a kind of limited but realistic hope for national development in India, measured by his sense that caste ideas and institutions would stand in the way, though optimistic that a steady (and English) pragmatism on the part of Indian leaders could sow the seeds of a new mentality. But of course his liberalism was entirely complicit in the general project of British colonialism, since it supported the idea that caste was simultaneously a barrier to national development and an inevitable reality for Indian society in the foreseeable future. Furthermore, he suggested that caste, as he had interpreted it, could be made into a virtue out of its necessity. It could accommodate and shape a gradually developing class society, perhaps even softening its potential conflicts and antagonisms, and provide a model (in its idealized varna version) for the articulation of an all-embracing ideology that might work at a general level to confound and even counteract the fissiparous tendencies of caste as a specific social institution. Caste in this sense was the key to the great transition from feudalism to capitalism/democracy—except that in the colonial situation that transition could never fully be made; the teleology of self-rule was here, as always, couched in a future that had no temporal reality.

And so once again caste expressed the fundamental nature of India, and opposed itself to the possibility of history, past or future. At the same time that Risley's work united official and academic knowledge, it also revealed the extent to which basic understandings of caste, and of India more generally, were tied to colonial assumptions about the absence of politics and the over-powering and yet divisive force of caste as a social principle. And it will be-come clear that this view of both caste and India has continued to the present day to be pervasive in Western academic views of India, long after the end of empire.

## The State of Ethnography

G.F.W. Hegel was not the first to suggest that the absence of history in India was a consequence of the natural force of the caste system, but he was among the most influential. Curiously, Hegel viewed India as advanced beyond China, on his civilizational scale, in part because of the break between state and society produced by caste. "The different castes are indeed, fixed; but in view of the religious doctrine that established them, they wear the aspect of natural distinctions."[23] For Hegel this meant that in India the whole of society was not absorbed into the despotism of the ruler, as was the case in China. However, the admirable inauguration of a separation between the religious and the secular is distorted by the fact that caste is ultimately a religious principle. Caste resists not just despotism but also any meaningful exchange between social and political developments. For Hegel, as a result, caste fails to establish a relationship with history, and India remains plunged in a dreamlike state that necessitates its subjection to Europe.[24]

If Hegel thus confirmed the British colonial sense that India had no history, and that the entire force of the caste system was to hinder political develop-ment, he also naturalized the establishment of a sociological view of India that went well beyond the specific claims of colonial representation. Marx's writ-ings on India, both in his journalistic coverage of the Great Rebellion and in his development of a theory of the mode of Asiatic production, also drew on colonial sociology (though more with respect to the village community and an associated view of despotism than with respect to caste); this was true even when Marx was critical of British imperial rule. Max Weber also ratified colo-nial views in his comparative sociology, which led him to write long treatises on India and China to accompany his extraordinary work on economy, society, and values in the West. Weber not only saw caste as the fundamental institution of Hinduism, organized in relation to and by the Brahman, he accepted the categories (and even the lists of social precedence) of the 1901 census as the empirical basis for his own attempt to correlate caste to religious orders, status groups, kinship categories, and economic units (such as guilds).

Classical social theory both reiterated the conventional wisdom of colonial ethnography and influenced later colonial ethnographers, one of the last of whom was J. H. Hutton, who returned to Britain after his stint as census commissioner in 1931 to assume a professorship in anthropology at Cambridge.[25] Although he strayed well away from both the racial and textual views of Risley, having quarreled with Risley's legacy concerning the use of caste in the census when he directed it in 1931, he still drew his principal material not just from colonial sources and preoccupations but from the census itself. Perhaps most importantly, however, he served as a direct bridge between colonial officialdom and academic certification, directly calling upon his colonial experience as the basis for his anthropological expertise. In fact, academic anthropology, at least in Britain, had been preoccupied not with the peasant societies represented by caste but rather with the idea of primitive society and with the islands and hill regions that were often on the borders of imperial rule. Hutton, who also had the acuity to draw upon a growing interest in French anthropology concerning the nature of the caste system (viz. Émile Senart and Célestin Bouglé), worked to change all that, and to train a new generation of anthropologists in Britain who sought to unite the study of primitive and peasant.

The effects of World War II and the decolonization it brought in its wake had an even greater impact on the world of academic knowledge. Perhaps most important, the United States academy took charge in the years after the war, fortified by massive investment from government and private foundations in an interest to understand, and control, the processes of modernization that colonialism and decolonization had unleashed in the third world. A new empiricist social science felt itself freed from the shackles of a colonial past, and combined positivist method with a vaguely developmentalist agenda. Modernization was viewed as a natural process rather than one linked to political projects and interests in ways that might still bear the traces of imperial ideologies. And yet it is now clear how postwar America assumed a new imperial role, displacing earlier imperial regimes both by its own political position and by its genealogical relationship to these regimes through theories that used cultural theory to excuse colonial history as much as to disguise American hegemony.

*Village India*, a volume of essays edited by the young American anthropologist McKim Marriott, was the herald of a new anthropology of South Asia.[26] A product of the new American interest in "underdeveloped" societies (driven, and funded, in part by the imperatives of the cold war), the turn of anthropological interest to peasant societies was dramatically linked to modernization theories that operated as the ideological charter of a new American claim for postimperial domination.[27] Spawned in large part under the influence of Robert Redfield, whose concern was to locate anthropology around the study of little communities in complex societies and in relation to civilizational processes, *Village India* made a strong case for the fundamental relationship between caste as a civilizational idea and the village. Beyond the particular theoretical imperatives of the project, the volume exemplified a more general trend of the 1950s, when American anthropologists joined British and Indian social scientists in villages across the subcontinent to chart the social organization of the primary unit of India, namely, the village itself. Some American social scientists sought to see caste as one particular instance of social stratification in a comparative context that linked racial discrimination in the United States with caste prejudice in India. Others sought to document in rich detail the way actual relations of intermarriage and interdining determined each local manifestation of caste. But as language study in the United States developed to a new level, and area studies initiatives linked the social sciences with the humanities, caste came increasingly to be seen as a marker of something unique in Indian civilization, a sign at once of general tradition and specific alterity. During the 1960s, caste became central once again to the academic study of India. And the impetus for this came not only from internal developments within British, American, and Indian anthropology but also from the monumental intervention of the French anthropologist Louis Dumont, whose major work on caste, *Homo Hierarchicus*, was published in 1966.[28]

When I first went to graduate school in the early 1970s I was told that I was joining a group of scholars who were on the verge of a major breakthrough in the understanding of caste.[29] Those were heady days in the history of American area studies, when the accumulation of language learning and field experience made it possible for some American academics to believe they could discover authentic Indian categories of social and cultural knowledge.[30] Using theoretical prescriptions from Talcott Parsons and David Schneider, two centuries of Indological knowledge, and the accumulation of research experience based on intensive studies by anthropologists during the twenty-five years since Indian independence, social scientists such as McKim Marriott and Ronald Inden at Chicago developed a comprehensive theory of caste society that claimed to reveal the conceptual underpinnings of caste relations, based on the monistic indissolubility of natural substance and moral code. Like James Mill one hundred and fifty years before, they announced their views in the new edition of the *Encyclopedia Britannica*.[31] The appeal of the theory was in part its apparent sensitivity to Indian conceptual categories and in part the accompanying claim to be working against both British colonial understandings and Western social science. In retrospect, the theory and the claim were both seriously flawed; not only was the approach to theory ahistorical, it was based on an idealist notion of knowledge that refused any contamination by the politics of knowledge. It was not so opposed to Western social science, or colonial understandings, after all.[32] In recent years, the theoretical impact of postcolonial studies has made all such knowledge claims deeply problematic. And leaving aside the epistemological disrepute into which this neo-Orientalist project of idealist representation would necessarily fall in the wake of Edward Said's devastating critique, the implication of this kind of area studies in the constitution of a timeless Hindu India available for use by the forces of right-wing Hindu fundamentalism has subsequently sent shudders down many a scholarly spine. When Inden and Marriott wrote in 1976 that they had "found that the presumptions evident in Vedic thought do provide a good basis for formulating Indian unity and for understanding much of South Asian history and ethnography consistently,"[33] they wrote in an idiom that has since been taken over by the Hindu right.

The Chicago school of ethnosociology had a certain impact through the many graduate students who imbibed it throughout the 1970s, but it suffered from the abstruse objective of converting social science to a methodological monism, with the ultimate objective (at times mystical, and not a little colonial) of making "the knowers—somewhat like those South Asian objects that they would make known."[34] In any case, it never produced a systematic work of social theory, and as a result failed to overturn the work of its chief interlocutor and critic, Louis Dumont. Dumont, along with his collaborator David Pocock, had announced his initial proposals not in the *Encyclopedia Britannica* but in a journal he founded that soon became the leading journal of South Asian anthropology, *Contributions to Indian Sociology*. Like Inden and Marriott later on, Dumont was interested in generating a holistic theory of the caste system that took into account belief as well as action, though it soon became clear how different were the perspectives of French and American social science. But well before most American anthropologists began searching for the clues to Indian society in ancient texts, Dumont proposed, in the inaugural volume of *Contributions*, that "the first condition for a sound development of a Sociology of India is found in the establishment of a proper relation between it and classical Indology." Dumont went on to clarify the sociological implications of this methodological assertion: "By putting ourselves in the school of Indology, we learn in the first place never to forget that India is *one*. The very existence, and influence, of the traditional higher, Sanskritic, civilisation demonstrates without question the unity of India."[35] In the first major theoretical and synthetic work on caste since those of J. H. Hutton and G. S. Ghurye, Dumont provided a theoretically rigorous and all-encompassing theory of the caste system that based its argument on the idea that India was one, across both time and space. The proposals of *Contributions* anticipated the publication of *Homo Hierarchicus* in 1966, an ambitious book that was hailed as a major work of theory and insight by anthropologists and Indologists alike, and was immediately installed as the benchmark for debates on Indian society and culture for years to come.[36]

Edmund Leach, a prominent British social anthropologist who was critical of Dumont's work, nevertheless wrote that "it is probably the most important work ever published," on the subject of caste.[37] Other important anthropologists also took the book very seriously, for the most part praising its originality and elegance. Stanley Tambiah wrote that *Homo Hierarchicus* was "a profound contribution to Indian studies . . . perhaps the time was ripe for a man of vision to attempt a telescopic view of the society as a whole."[38] Ravindra Khare wrote that *Homo Hierarchicus* was "a brilliant piece of intellectual accomplishment . . . that by all odds secures a pioneering place in Indian caste studies with deserved amour propre," in the context of a long and at times critical review essay.[39] Khare noted, as did others, that Dumont was writing primarily for a French audience. Gerald Berreman dismissed Dumont's work by characterizing it as based on the Brahman's point of view, but this important critique was curiously taken by most on both sides of the Atlantic at the time as reductive.

One of the most engaged, if critical, early reviews of Dumont's work came from McKim Marriott, who nonetheless saw the book as replacing the "older standard works by Ghurye and Hutton."[40] Marriott faulted Dumont for his use of data and his choice of texts, but was most disturbed by the intellectualism of the work, the ways in which "ideology" seemed abstracted from the countless interactions that produce the effective ranks and orders that make up hierarchy in Indian society. Although he had not yet fully formulated a monistic theory of Indian society by this time, Marriott was already distressed by the dualism of the account, which made ideology seem arbitrary and removed from the possibility of either empirical test or effective action in the world (other than the world of French theory). As Marriott developed his new view of caste in collaboration with the cultural historian Ronald Inden, he took as his primary target the work of Dumont, even though to some outside observers the two views (one deriving from French structuralism, the other from American culturalism, but both seeking certification from Sanskritic texts and key Hindu ideals), shared in a great deal more than they differed. From within, however, the debate was bitter. And Dumont, whose position was indeed unabashedly intellectualist, if committed in its own way both to ideological and empirical analyses, was perhaps correct in his critique of Marriott's later position. In a new preface to *Homo Hierarchicus*, he wrote that Marriott combined his early empirical "transactionalism" with his later "analysis of culture, or of symbols and meanings, in the manner of David Schneider, thanks to a monist metaphysic that permits them to coincide like matter and idea. . . . He does this unstintingly, and in Marriott and certain of his followers one finds a syncretism of disparate notions, taken out of context, which goes far beyond the known feats of Hinduist popularization."[41] He did not realize, of course, how a similar characterization, differing only in emphasis, could be applied to his own effort to devise a sociology for all of India (ancient, medieval, and modern).

Dumont's work thus indexed not only a particular trajectory within postwar French social theory but also a far more general anthropological fascination with "caste society" that worked to reinstall caste once again as the major symbol for Indian society. This symbol was a powerful reminder of how that society is organized by religious (read Hindu) rather than secular values. Despite the abstractness of Dumont's account, what is astounding in retrospect is how very seriously it was taken—in France, Britain, North America, and India—and how, as a European work of social theory, it overshadowed many other issues relating to India in disciplines as diverse as anthropology, sociology, history, political science, and Indology for many years, at a time when there were arguably more important issues to contemplate. Perhaps most astounding of all is the fact that at the very time that postindependent India was struggling with the resilient legacies of colonial history in the context of the question of secularism, a proposal that religion encompassed politics in India would take such pride of place in international scholarship. Although Dumont's intent was not specifically colonial, and although he attended to modern changes in India in a variety of important essays, he resurrected colonial categories and arguments at a time when the West mistook their overdetermined reality for an explanation of the East's failure, and colonialism was either forgotten or consigned to Raj nostalgia. India's postcolonial struggle to reinvent the nation and the state, and to find a basis for civil society that would neither be overtaken by conflict between religious and ethnic loyalties nor defined by religious principles, was hardly helped by the rebirth of colonial Orientalism in contemporary Western social science.

Dumont argued that the political and economic domains of social life in India had always been encompassed by the religious domain, articulated in terms of an opposition between purity and pollution. For Dumont, as for Weber and others before him, the Brahman represents the religious principle, inasmuch as the Brahman represents the highest form of purity attainable by Hindus. The king, although important, only represents the profane political world, and is accordingly inferior to and encompassed by the Brahman. The overarching value accorded to the religious domain is the central feature of the ideology of caste—which Dumont characterized with the single word "hierarchy." Dumont argues that the sociological significance of hierarchy has been systematically missed by modern writers obsessed with the ideology of equality. Caste is fundamentally religious; and hierarchy is about the valorization of society over the individual. Dumont reasoned, in ways not entirely dissimilar from later formulations by Marriott and Inden, that varna and jati were not opposed but rather that the principles of varna underlay the actual organization and articulation of hierarchical relations between and among jatis. But what was distinctive for Dumont was his sense that even if the classical Brahman and Ksatriya were not present in a distinct social system, the values associated with them—status and power, respectively—would always be there, and were always held as foundationally separate and resolutely hierarchalized. And, as he put it, "this was not enough: for pure hierarchy to develop without hindrance it was also necessary that power should be absolutely inferior to status. These are the two conditions that we find fulfilled early on, in the relationship between Brahman and Kshatriya."[42] Whereas Marriott and Inden encoded the significance of the Brahman in a monistic theory of "biopower" that sought to avoid what they took to be an exogenous dual categorization of status (the domain of the ideal) and power (the domain of the real), Dumont insisted on the separation and hierarchical encompassment of the two categories as generative of the caste system itself.

Dumont thus identified the political and economic aspects of caste as relatively secondary and isolated. In assessing recent changes in the caste system, he noted that the British colonial government's policy of "not meddling in the domain of religion and the traditional social order, while introducing the minimum of reforms and novelties on the politico-economic plane," significantly reduced the extent of change and conflict under colonial rule.[43] Not only did this accept the self-representations of colonial policy, it also suggested that the British were right to make the distinctions they did between religion and society (distinctions that were always vexed, and that even according to colonial policy makers never worked quite right). In fact, the British introduced these distinctions for the convenience of colonial rule and, given the force of colonial presence and power, they took root in serious ways during two hundred years of rule. Dumont thus not only relied, perforce, on colonial sources, he also reproduced colonial ideology even when he assumed he was being most critical of Western social and political theory. The peculiar complicity of Dumont's sociology in colonial sociology was clear in his original call for a "sociology of India." His insistence on the unity of India—an insistence he claimed had nothing to do with the somewhat spurious political uses of the idea in the independence movement—not only worked to seal India's borders from the rest of the world but to mark India as unique in particular because of the "existence of castes from one end of the country to the other, and nowhere else."[44] Dumont used an argument about history to deny India history, much as Hegel did before: "If history is the movement by which a society reveals itself as what it is, there are, in a sense, as many qualitatively different histories as there are societies, and India, precisely because she is indifferent to history, has carefully laid it down in the form of her society, her culture, her religion."[45] Thus Dumont not only exempted the colonial state from any role in the constitution of modern India, he exempted India from history altogether. With this view, it is hardly surprising that in his theories the state—traditional or modern—would be of so little importance.

In Dumont's view, caste not only subordinated the political, it also reduced the individual to a position of relative unimportance. The individual only has ideological significance when placed outside society, or to put it in Dumont's terms, as "the individual-outside-the-world."[46] This is the individual as the renouncer, the *sannyasi* who must leave both society and the mundane world to attain transcendental truth. Dumont's position was stated more forcefully by Jan Heesterman, a Dutch Indologist who with Dumont played an important role in defining the discourse of Indian sociology: "Here we touch the inner springs of Indian civilization. Its heart is not with society and its integrative pressures. It devalorizes society and disregards power. The ideal is not hierarchical interdependence but the individual break with society. The ultimate value is release from the world. And this cannot be realized in a hierarchical way, but only by the abrupt break of renunciation. . . . Above the Indian world, rejecting and at the same time informing it, the renouncer stands out as the exemplar of ultimate value and authority."[47] The individual as renouncer thus occupies a critical position in what Heesterman called the "The Inner Conflict of Tradition," in a transcendental critique of the possibility of politics, economics, or history in the Indian world.

The prominence of Indologists and Indology in anthropological discourses on India has not only elided the monumental role of Islam in the history of the subcontinent, it has also worked to secure a specialized scholasticism for India. For much of the academic anthropology of India, Indology replaced history, and has been used to dehistoricize both India and anthropological practice in India. Not only has Islam been erased and the state been ignored as a potent force in the constitution and transformation of Indian society but the colonial history of India has been rendered entirely insignificant, as we have just seen in Dumont's peculiar sense of caste's compatibility with empire.[48] I find this compatibility unsettling, and as must be clear by now, see other, not unrelated, similarities between the view that the precolonial state was weak, the assertion that traditional society was organized by social and religious rather than political principles, and the conferral on caste of the exemplary status of a traditional form that has resisted the development of modern state and social structures. I become even more unsettled when I read words such as those written by Jan Heesterman, in the introduction to his book: "The modern state . . . wants to bring the ideal of universal order from its ultramundane haven down to earth. The inner conflict then becomes explosively schismatic, as eventually became clear in the drama of the Partition."[49]

And so the endless rehearsals of the essential difference between East and West, between the recent histories of India and Europe. In India caste, so colonial sociology had it, always resisted political intrusion, and was already a kind of civil society in that it regulated and represented the private domain, such as it was. But caste could not be more different from modern Western society, for it neither permitted the development of voluntarist or politically responsible social institutions nor did it work to collaborate with the modern state. Indeed, caste actively resisted the modern state even more than it did the old, for the modern state opposed rather than supported dharma. The catch here was that under colonialism the modern state was not a viable option, since its development depended in large part on the conquest and exploitation of lands where premodern states fell to the technological, military, and economic power of the ascendant West. But colonialism was predicated on more than simple economic exploitation, and its effects were as various as they are difficult to untangle, even now, from the presumed weight of tradition on colonized societies.

Colonialism in India produced new forms of society that have been taken to be traditional; caste itself as we now know it is not a residual survival of ancient India but a specifically colonial form of (that is, substitute for) civil society that both justified and maintained an Orientalist vision. This was a vision of an India in which religion transcended politics, society resisted change, and the state awaited its virgin birth in the late colonial era. Thus caste has become the modernist apparition of India's traditional self. Under colonial rule, caste—now defined by the dharmic idea of varna, disembodied from its former political contexts, and available as the principal object of colonial knowledge—could take on a new and different form. In this dissociated form it was appropriated, and reconstructed, by British rule. And even after decolonization, academic preoccupations have continued to be fascinated with the same chimeric forms that so preoccupied the British, even as they have mistaken the effects of British rule for the traditional predicates of it.[50] What anthropology and Indology together have done most successfully in the postcolonial context has been to assert the precolonial authority of a specifically colonial form of power and representation, not only disguising the history of colonialism and the essentially contingent and political character of caste but also reproducing what might be the most extraordinary legacy of colonial rule in the contemporary social life of caste and Hinduism in India today. The state of ethnography—British, French, and American—turns out to be a direct descendent of the ethnographic state.

# Part Two

COLONIZATION OF THE ARCHIVE

# *Four*

## The Original Caste: Social Identity in the Old Regime

### Colonial Conquest

The British conquest of India was anything but absent-minded. Despite the self-serving rhetoric about political chaos and social involution, the British conquest was one of the most comprehensive, long-lasting, and successful campaigns in world history. The British mobilized military, diplomatic, and economic means to transform makeshift beachheads into the major imperial jewel of modern times. The East India Company arrived in India to engage in trade for goods craved by Europe, only to find local political struggles irresistible, and opportunities for wealth—both private and public—incomparable. While beseeching the Mughal emperor to treat them as a privileged vassal, they engaged in dubious negotiations that led to celebrated victories in Arcot and Plassey, and established significant power in the local affairs and fortunes of the Mughal nawabs in the Carnatic and in Bengal. They gained ground through sleight of hand rather than absence of mind, initiating skirmishes against the French on Indian soil with local allies, and conducting campaigns against Mysore, the Marathas, and the Afghans, as well as against countless local chiefs and warriors across the subcontinent. Many battles met with little success; it took four wars to break Mysore, the Marathas were undefeated until 1818, and the Afghans humiliated the British time after time. But by securing rights to trade and then to collect revenue from Mughal grants of jagir lands, even military defeats were turned into justifications for further encroachment and expansion.

British ambivalence about the private scandal and public greed represented by eighteenth-century imperial activity in India was expressed in Burke's famous tirades during the impeachment of Warren Hastings, but it paved the way for colonial consolidation rather than retreat. By the time Hastings was acquitted by the House of Lords in 1795, the Company had secured significant control over major territories in Bengal and Madras presidencies—Bengal was already two years into the Permanent Settlement, and the nawab of Arcot had been a Company pensioner for three—and was only four years away from defeating Tipu Sultan in the last battle at Srirangapattinam in Mysore. In subsequent years, Company directors were undecided about how expansionist a policy to pursue even as they debated questions such as missionary activity, but when Dalhousie annexed Awadh—after a century or more of bad faith—

and the Company stumbled into armed confrontation first with its own sepoys and then with rebels fighting to restore the Mughal Empire, only a third of the subcontinent was left under the nominal control of Indian rulers, most of whom had already been converted into treaty kings for the imperial fiction of indirect rule.

The political histories of late precolonial India, and of early colonial conquest, were erased in the institutionalization of indirect rule. In 1858, when the Great Rebellion was quelled and the British Crown assumed direct rule as it disbanded the mercantile reign of the East India Company, India was a patchwork quilt of principalities and powers, colonized remnants of vital political histories. Princely states were thenceforth to be ruled indirectly, sanctioned by a colonial archive that invariably found textual precedent to justify its own domination. The "traditional" agencies of maharajas and chiefs were to be incorporated into empire through a political economy of honor (displayed in gun salutes and darbars) and isolation (the "foreign" policies of these states were to be managed by the British). Through the strict control of succession—an early colonial anthropology of restrictive kinship—internal policy was also carefully monitored. Despite perpetual uncertainty about the exact nature of the political relationship between the Raj and these states, some things were clear: princely India preserved the old, provided playgrounds for the British civil service, presented bold contrasts between the rapacity and ceremonial narcissism of feudal India and the progressivism of colonial rule, and protected the cause of imperial expansion both by symbolizing (however perversely) British liberality and by creating a powerful colonized elite. Princely India also covered over the history of British conquest. Mysore, one of the largest of the southern states, was handed by the British to a defunct family of rulers after the defeat of Tipu Sultan to avoid insurrection and ensure dependence. Satara—once the jewel of Maratha power—was similarly propped up by colonial convenience. The treaties and *sanad*s of British rule, when they hadn't been the pretexts for earlier annexation, became the predicates for a subordinated politics rather than the obvious outcome of two centuries of infiltration, negotiation, and battle.

History had been erased in other senses, too. I will review how early British interest in the histories of kings and dynasties yielded progressively, as the nineteenth century wore on, to the ethnological fascinations that oriented late colonial knowledge about India. But in the early years of British occupation, these histories were inescapable. By the time of Mill and other formal British accounts of the rise of their rule, these histories were punctuated by stories of treachery and atrocity, political inconstancy and military deficiency, sufficient to explain both why a trading company intervened in local affairs the way it did and how trivial such intervention was (despite the legendary bravery of heroes such as Clive). And yet these histories reflected the vitality of kings and their regimes long before they became the museological fixtures of later colonial display. What was never translated into the later colonial ethnological imagination was the extent to which a history of social relations and forms was frozen within this political history. As soon as one looks within the political structures of the old regime one sees the historical forces that produced a whole host of ranks, titles, emblems, honors, alliances, ruptures, and dynamics that constituted the fundamental features of social identity for all but those positioned at the extreme ends of the caste order. And even those icons of the ethnologically defined caste system—Brahmans and Dalits ("untouchables")—were hardly exempted from their political histories and locations, however much idioms of purity and pollution were used to explain, and reproduce, certain components of social prestige and ritual hierarchy.

## The Social History of the Old Regime

Some caste groups were formed directly out of the social classes that made up the feudal armature of the kingdoms of the old regime, as occurred throughout the southern part of the Tamil country. Other caste groups literally came into being around the forces of centralization and affiliation that were spawned by political movements and outcomes, as in the case of the Marathas, a caste that was formed in large part through a process of community formation that was activated by the success of Shivaji and his band of warriors. The Marathas later claimed Ksatriya status for themselves as an attempt to displace the residual authority of the Chitpavan Brahmans under Peshwa rule; this struggle played itself out in the early years of East India Company control over the Maratha country.[1] In northwestern India, kingdoms emerged out of the success of clan brotherhoods in establishing political power that extended well beyond the villages and forts of original settlement and control, as happened cyclically in many Rajput territories.[2] And new groups of Rajputs emerged in central India as a consequence of the political emergence of new kingdoms during the seventeenth and eighteenth centuries, and there is similar evidence of social mobility around the royal traditions and claims of Rajputs elsewhere.[3] Whatever the particular political history, dominant landed groups could not sustain their power within either villages or localities without establishing and maintaining strong relationships with chiefdoms and kingdoms well beyond their local domains. This is where ethnological views of caste and the village community have collaborated, for despite Dumont's claim that the "myth" of the isolated village has eclipsed the civilizational significance of caste as an Indian system, both notions have neglected the foundational importance of larger political systems for the construction of social relations vis-à-vis caste and the village alike.

   To view one example of this process in some detail, I turn to the southern Tamil kingdom of Pudukkottai.[4] The Tondaiman dynasty of Kallar kings wrested control over a significant swath of land in the central Tamil country between Tanjavur and Madurai in the last quarter of the seventeenth century. Whereas "Kallars" had been branded as thieves in much early Tamil literature and as criminals by the British far later under the Criminal Tribes Act, in Pudukkottai—a little kingdom that became the only princely state in the Tamil-speaking region of southern India—they became the royal caste. Kallars controlled much of the land, occupied the greatest number of authoritative positions, particularly as village and locality headmen and as the dominant village elders, and ran the most important temples as trustees. These were often their lineage, village, or subcaste territorial temples, in which they received honors only after the king (or his local representative) and Brahmans. If one can make such distinctions, Kallars were dominant for economic and political as well as ritual reasons.

Kallars, like Maravars, Akampatiyars, and some similar groups from the Andhra country who migrated southward during the period of Vijayanagara rule, settled in mixed economy zones such as Pudukkottai on the borders of the central political and economic regions of the south. In these areas they quickly attained dominance in late medieval times by exercising rights of protection over local communities and institutions. The Kallars were successful in part because of their strong kin- and territory-based social structure. In addition, their cultural valorization of heroism and martial honor was highly conducive to the corporate control of the means of violence, coercion, and local authority. It was no accident that Kallars—like these other affiliated groups—were often the very groups from which others sought protection when they themselves were not granted rights to protect. And it was groups like the Kallars, Maravars, Vatukas, and others who, through the establishment of formal protection arrangements, rose to the status of major chiefs in the Tamil (and Telugu) countryside, called *palaiyakarar*s (or, in British parlance, poligars). The palaiyakarars, singly and sometimes collectively, made the expansion of British rule in southern India halting and difficult. Their resistance to British occupation in what became known as the Poligar Wars lasted from the 1740s, when the British joined the efforts of the nawab of Arcot to subdue them, to 1801, two years after the defeat and execution of the great rebel chief Kattabomman of Tirunelveli. The Tondaiman kings of Pudukkottai cast their lot with the Company, and played an instrumental role in the final defeat of the other palaiyakarars which explains why they attained the sole princely status they did under British rule. But more important for my story here, the fact that Kallars became kings of Pudukkottai, whereas in other areas of the south they were consigned to low-status positions seen by some as completely outside the ambit of formal Brahmanical civilizational culture, suggests the extent to which the political fortunes of particular groups were crucial in shaping both the nature of their own social formation and the ways in which they were situated within a larger set of social relations.

Pudukkottai rose, as did many other "little kingdoms" in the south, within the context of a late-medieval political order. This was defined by such forces as the Vijayanagara kingdom and the various lower-level Nayaka rulers who ruled from the important cities of Tanjore and Madurai, as well as the powerful agents of Mughal rule, in particular the nizam of Hyderabad and the Carnatic governor, the nawab of Arcot (soon to become a principal debtor and supporter of the East India Company). The cultural mix of the time was reflected in political ideology as well as cultural form, and purveyed in languages as various as Tamil, Telugu, Kannada, Persian, Marathi, English, French, and Sanskrit. This was a time of massive social mobility and cultural transformation, and although there was competition for Brahman scholars and priests to lend cultural legitimacy to fledgling kingdoms and active temple building, there was also a serious Islamic presence in symbolism, protocol, and beliefs, as well as in royal architecture including many of the buildings of the Vijayanagara rulers. Some of the traditional centers of power yielded to some degree in significance to previously more marginal areas and groups, but the decentralization of political forms and processes was neither a sign of the inadequacy of the capabilities of Indian states nor a natural prelude to British colonial rule, as suggested in many of the old colonial accounts that depicted the eighteenth century as a period of decadence and degradation. The economy was thriving, in part because of the new role of smaller chiefdoms and political actors—and the regional economies that supported them. The small and local-level states that proved increasingly powerful were also actively learning the political, military, and administrative lessons that the French and the English were learning at the same time. Until the fall of Srirangapattinam in 1799, the most aggressive new state system was ruled from Mysore, first by Haidar Ali and then his son Tipu Sultan, who succeeded in large part because of their capacity to capitalize on the cultural transitions of the time even as they put in place new forms of bureaucratic systematization and regulation.

Much of Haidar Ali's and then Tipu Sultan's attention was taken up by an attempt to establish a central bureaucracy. They funded and provided the political basis for these innovations by attempting to absorb local palaiyakarars and resume the myriad local privileges and benefices that had been fundamental to the political organization of the old regime. Like the British, the Mysoreans became heavily involved in the assessment not just of revenue but of the multiple claims to local office, title, honor, privilege, and tax-free status, the latter having already been grouped by earlier regimes under the heading of the Persian term *inam*. In my own research on Pudukkottai, it took little study of local land records to uncover the most extraordinary historical characteristic of the political system: how little of the land was taxed. According to early-nineteenth-century records, 70 percent of cultivable land was classified as inam, or tax-free benefice. Of the rest, less than 30 percent of the cultivated land was either taxed (around 9 percent) or given out from year to year on a share basis

(18 percent) in which the king's revenue establishment received the putative share of four-ninths of the produce. This statistic was, if anything, more dramatic in the mid-eighteenth century, when there were at the very least another 5,000 military retainers supported by inam, before the gradual dismantling of the military system of the state under the influence of British "indirect" rule. By the early period of British control, only 30 percent of the inams (by number rather than extent) were for military retainers, their chiefs, and for palace guards and servants (the number before must have been closer to 50 percent); 25 percent were allocated to village officers, artisans, and servants; and the remaining 45 percent were for the support of temples, monasteries, rest and feeding houses for Brahman priests and pilgrims, shrines for Muslim saints, and land grants to Brahman communities.

This structure of privileged landholding reflects the structure of political power and sociocultural participation within state and village institutions under the old regime.[5] The chief landholders were the great Kallar *jagirdars* and *cervaikarars*. The former were the collateral relations of the raja. Jagir estates were created for the two brothers of the raja after a succession dispute in 1730 severely threatened the stability of the state. These collateral families kept these estates intact until their "settlement" in the late nineteenth and early twentieth century. The jagirs were, in effect, mini-kingdoms in their own right, each containing a small court and a full set of inam grants, including military ones. Just below the jagirdars came the cervaikarars, all but one of whom were of the same "subcaste" as the raja, and most had one or more direct affinal ties with the royal family. These collateral chiefs were given larger grants of land, titles, honors, and emblems, as well as ample (though specified) lands for military retainers to serve under them. Lesser chiefs, called *kurikarars*, came from Kallar "subcastes" other than the royal one. Additionally, lands and privileges throughout the state were given to other Kallar families, even more distant in kinship and status terms, with the stipulation that these families protect villages and localities not dominated by loyal Kallars. The royal family and court were protected by a group of *uriyakarars* made up of an allied though "separate" caste group, the Akampatiyars. These royal protectors, in fact, became a separate "subcaste" group of their own, marked off terminologically and affinally from other Akampatiyars in the region by virtue of their connection with and service to the raja. A number of these guards had prominent roles in the kingdom but, like most of the lesser chiefs, were given no formal group of military retainers under them, even when they were awarded extensive lands.

Within each village in the state, headmen were given lands in recognition of their rights of local authority as well as to render their position representative of the state's power at large. These headmen came from the locally dominant castes, Kallars in the northern and eastern parts of the state, Maravars in the south. They were called *ampalams*, a title that in certain places became used as the caste title for dominant groups rather than separately as an occupational or administrative term. Various village officials, artisans, and servants were also given inam (more properly, *maniyam*) lands by the state. *Maniyam*, a term meaning honor or privilege, was used at times for all inams, though in a more marked sense it was used to label land grants given to village servants whose task was to maintain and operate irrigational facilities, to village officers or headman, to priests of small village temples or shrines, or to other local personages whose obligations ranged from service in village festivals to service to the local officials or state servants. Inam titles often became used as social (that is, caste) titles, designating as they did a local privilege/occupation that established a direct link with the king and with the local political/social system.

In addition to many inams granted to village and local temples in the form of maniyam lands given to local priests and village servants, many inam grants were also made to Brahmans, temples, and charities of various sorts, including mosques and shrines to Islamic saints. One of the fundamental requirements of Indian kingship (Hindu as well as Islamic) was that the king be a munificent provider of fertile lands for Brahmans who would study and chant the Vedas, perform sacrifices, and provide ritual services for the king so as to ensure and protect his prosperity and that of his kingdom; for temples that were centers of worship as well as for the articulation of various social and locality structures; and for *chatram*s, feeding and lodging houses for itinerant Brahmans and pilgrims. The merit of the king who made the grant could be shared by all those who protected the gift, a duty enjoined in the inscriptional rhetoric upon all subsequent kings. In spite of Pudukkottai's marginal social and political position, it was well endowed with temples and Brahmanic institutions precisely because of the prevailing force of royal ideology. The respect accorded to Brahmans was not seen to anchor a spiritual worldview in which—*pace* Dumont—the temporal world of the king was resolutely overshadowed by the world of the Brahman, but rather to signify that powerful kings could not do without Brahmans—who became signs of a certain form of kingship—even as Brahmans, in a series of compromises that were of consequence only to them, required the resources made available by royal patrons. Although Brahmans were indexed at the top of the ritual order of things, when honors were given in temple festivals throughout the state, they were given first to the king, and only afterward to the Brahman.

The history of *inam* grants—itself a Persian bureaucratic term used from late medieval times to impose a new kind of state order on older political forms—reveals the extent to which the terms that came to be used as "caste" titles were themselves political in origin and meaning. Caste appears in part as the sedimentation of older political systems, the residue of a social formation that had lost its political dynamic as a direct result of British colonial conquest. Thus it is imperative to reconsider caste in relation to the histories in which the now standardized titles of caste and social position were once markers of complex political relations centered on the court and the politics of kingship (across so-called "religious" boundaries) in the old regime.

## Caste and the Old Regime

There is little doubt that in many medieval Hindu contexts kings derived much of their power from worship, and bestowed their emblems and privileges in a cultural atmosphere permeated by the language and attitudes of worship. At the same time, however, royal practices mixed "religion" and "politics" so thoroughly that it would seem ludicrous to try to separate them. Further, royal protocol and ideology became progressively permeated by Islamic forms that increasingly appeared in the language and customs of political authority, from the eleventh century in the north, and from the fourteenth century in the southern peninsula. Indeed, the more one engages in a study of political and cultural history of medieval and early modern India, the more peculiar would seem a textualist view that privileged a small body of dharma texts from a very specific period and provenance. This peculiarity is magnified when one realizes the extent to which these texts themselves have a particular history, in which (as we saw in Chapter 2) they became authoritative in large part because of a specific collaboration in the late eighteenth and early nineteenth centuries between British Orientalists, Brahman pandits, and the spaces that were open to ethnological textualism because of the contemporaneous historical emphasis on issues relating to land, sovereignty, and revenue.

Within the context of kingdoms such as Pudukkottai, Brahmans were certainly respected, and the *brahmadeyam* lands granted to them were among the best lands available. Competition for the most learned, and respected, Brahmans was sometimes fierce, and suitable provision had to be made to be able to boast of their residence within a particular kingdom. Kings and commoners both were aware of the separatist practices of Brahmans, their refusal to eat cooked food given by other castes, their steadfast avoidance of pollution and taint. Brahmans were also vital for royal rituals, both in annual festivals such as Dassara and in domestic rituals on a more frequent basis. But Brahmans were ironically more adamant than most in insisting on the divinity of the royal office, and on the respect they maintained for the person of the king. Although Brahmans lived apart—both literally in special hamlets and ritually in the myriad ways in which they kept to themselves—they lived very much within a world in which the power and authority of the king seemed paramount, even for their own self-respect and position. When Dumont and other ethnological commentators insist that the high position of the Brahman is the ideological proof of the hierarchical nature of the "caste system"—arguing that despite the great muddle in the middle, the strict hierarchy placing Brahmans on the very top and "untouchables" on the very bottom indicates the absolute priority of the categories of purity and pollution—they mistake a part for the whole. Brahmans may have been necessary, both for a great many aspects of Hindu thought and practice and for the ideological maintenance of Hindu kingship, but they neither defined nor provided the principles that organized hierarchy for the entire Indian social order throughout all time.

The Kallars of Pudukkottai, for example, were very clear about the reasons for their own hegemonic position, and they depended neither on Brahmans nor on Brahmanic principles. To some extent, all Kallars participated in the kingship of the royal Tondaiman family, though to varying extents. The forms of clan and subcaste structure within the group of Kallars were vitally affected by proximity to the king; the political hierarchy turned out to determine the social hierarchy as well, with alliance structures working out the political gradations and relations of proximity in fine detail. The royal subcaste occupied a preeminent position, dominating all other segments or subcastes. And the "hierarchy" of chiefs revealed a layering of relationships, all focused on the person of the king. All members of the royal subcaste were loosely called *rajapantu*, meaning that they had some kind of connection with the raja. Although this term was used to designate all members of the subcaste in an unmarked sense (and was used among Kallars from other subcastes, as well, even more generally), within the subcaste itself there were multiple distinctions of rank, again all having to do with a logic of proximity to the king. Proximity was reflected both in kinship terms and in relation to a brand of royal ideology that stressed the principle of "control and order" (*kattupatu*). The Kallars saw themselves as having the most "order" and "discipline," which included both disciplinary procedures to maintain order, deference, and command within the social group, and adherence to a variety of social rules that could variably be affiliated to Brahmanic or Islamic aristocratic practice—such as proscribing widow remarriage and insisting on purdah for royal women. The term *kattupatu* was used among all Kallars (and in different ways among all groups in Pudukkottai), though only within the royal subcaste did it carry the particular meanings described above. For all these groups, though again most importantly for the royal subcaste, kattupatu did not mean simply a code for conduct but also a set of authoritative (and inherently political) procedures that rendered this code enforceable within the community.

The significance of the term *kattupatu* no doubt reflects in part the particular history of Kallars as bandits, agents of disorder. The term is used, however, by many other castes to signify appropriate codes of conduct and modes of social enforcement, and some groups placed lower down in the order of things asserted, or accepted, that their kattupatu was too loose. Indeed, there was a steady decrease of a certain kind of definitional order as one went "down" the caste hierarchy, in the sense implied by many Kallars but also by others. Maravars, for example, in all respects like the Kallars except in that they were ruled by Kallar rather than Maravar kings (who lived just to the south of the border of the state), had found it impossible to organize their social relations consistently within their local territorial units (*natus*) in the same way as had been done by Kallars—a social fact much lamented by the Maravars themselves (and attributed by some to the lack of a Maravar king). For other groups, there was not only a noticeable decline in caste order, and a laxness in defining and maintaining the kattupatu, but also a decline in the autonomy to define what that order was. Discursive hegemony, organized by Kallar rule and deployed throughout the social order, worked in large part through this notion of order. Among some groups typically labeled as "untouchable," namely Pallar and Paraiyar, there was the sense that kattupatu could not exist properly without more control over the order of things, both within and without the caste. Thus, the sense of disorder implied by a position of subordination was reflected in the way caste ideology was articulated. Dominant groups asserted that they controlled the castes that worked for them, usually as landless laborers and village servants in locales over which they asserted total domination. Although differences were expressed as to whether this was legitimate authority or the raw exercise of power, the idiom within which notions of order (internal and external) were expressed was strikingly consistent across castes. Untouchable groups used the locality, and sometimes the lineage names, of their dominant-caste patrons as their own self-designations. The fundamental structures of their social relations were inscribed by the hegemony of the dominant classes. Notions of honor, order, royalty, and command were deployed, in other words, in the practices that produced and reproduced hierarchy through the workings of power. The autonomy accorded to pollution issues for Brahmans was the luxury of a particular kind of dominance, and thus, contra Dumont, could only be mistaken as the ideological principle of the whole if one was blinded by power itself.

Power functioned in the service not only of Brahmans but of men more generally. As caste had been constructed as a social system, first in the political milieu of the old regime and then in increasingly Brahmanical forms under colonial rule, the most pervasive forms of oppression were directed at women. Hidden from view even as they were the most important objects of social regulation, women lost out from the top to the bottom of the caste scale. In Maharashtra, for example, the elevation of the Peshwas to a position of greater power in the eighteenth century already conferred great authority to Brahmanic values. Fukuzawa has shown that the caste system in Maharashtra was the outcome of state-regulated social reform rather than a "spontaneous" social order of the people. Fukuzawa has further suggested that the Peshwai and its central bureaucracy used the legal apparatus of the state to preserve the caste hierarchy in the areas under its control.[6] Uma Chakravarty has argued that the consequences of this were as devastating for women as they were, in Fukuzawa's argument, for groups such as the "untouchables." As she has written,

"The Peshwai, with its notions of Brahmanya and the rigid hierarchies of the caste system, could not but have a direct bearing on gender relations in eighteenth-century Maharashtra. Apart from other things, the Brahmanya implied a certain strictly regulated code of conduct for women, differing to some extent according to caste, but always the index in fixing ranking within the caste hierarchy."[7]

In Pudukkottai and other "poligar" areas of the south, Brahmans had by no means the same position in political arenas, and had to await British colonial rule for the conditions of their own attainment of secular power. Before the British arrived, however, the Kallar royal family emulated some Brahmanic conventions involving women, such as female seclusion, strictures on widow remarriage, and sati. During the same period, the relative independence of women within many caste groups (including some Kallar groups, Maravars, and most other landed groups) in making decisions concerning marriage, divorce, and remarriage was increasingly brought under the control of patriarchal structures and values. This also affected the allocation of certain forms of property, such as maintaining control over the movable property involved in inheritance and marriage transactions of different kinds. The Brahman administration in Pudukkottai state, for example, legislated that no temple in the land could be used for marriage ceremonies involving widows or divorcees, in direct contravention of some of the practices of castes who had previously had full control over their constituent temples. In these cases, Brahmans were simply following procedures that had been introduced through the Ministry of Hindu Religious and Charitable Endowments in Madras presidency under British rules. The British, to maintain their neutrality, had resorted to priestly and textual mediation for all matters deemed religious, thus in effect legislating a steady "sanskritization" of custom and convention.[8] At the same time, the use of Brahman interpreters of legal traditions for matters involving "personal law" worked to confer fewer and fewer rights on women in cases concerning property and inheritance. The identification of women's issues as fundamental to the mobilization of social reform projects and movements in the nineteenth century soon fell prey to the increasing sense that social reform in matters such as caste and women's questions should be reserved until after the nationalist movement could be successful. Caste worked to suppress the autonomy of women, in both its success and its failure.

Structures of power were enacted in the social organization of caste and kinship, in terms of both underlying principles and explicit ideology. Politics, in the terms outlined above, was fundamental to the processes of hierarchy and the formation of units of identity. These units of identity were multiple and hardly exhausted by the general idea of caste. Localities, known in Tamil as *natu*, defined many social forms and served as the focus for temple festivals, agricultural management, law and order among social groups, irrigation, and sectarian affiliations. Most caste groups were organized in units that were markedly territorial, though the idea of territory—as much as it preexisted specific political regimes—was also a vehicle for the expression of forms of political power. Villages were also significant for everything from political economy to cultural activities and identities, as were hamlets, even units identified as "streets" within villages. The kingdom itself was an important unit of identity. It shaped the conditions of regional dominance, and, focused the political system upon a single court and kingly family with enormous implications for the character of social and cultural life. The kingdom also organized the structures of local hierarchy through the distinctions made across and within castes relating to proximity to the king and participation within the kingdom. The political logic of social things was expressed both territorially and institutionally, through kings as well as temples, economic resources as well as social processes.

These observations apply as well to the other "poligar" kingdoms of the Tamil country, including, for example, the Maravars of the southern districts. Indeed, one of the few early "caste" documents that surfaced in the early years of the nineteenth century concerned the Maravars, but began with an account of the way Maravar organization was structured according to the same logic of proximity to the king as outlined above in the case of Kallars.[9] After listing the seven major groups of Maravars, the text noted that four families were related to the king of Ramnad, said to be heads of palaiyakarar families whose status was based on their affinal relations to the royal family. The account of "customs and manners" was like a roll call of the privileges that were accorded to members of the royal family, as well as a list of the particular customs that were attached to this status (including, for example, the practice of sati). This "ethnographic" text asserted:

> Among those Maravars who are in power, some are palaiyakarars, some hold land rights in villages and some are village headmen, some hold protection rights over villages; also that they have held these important positions and rights over a long period of time is known from references to them and their names in villages and in various literary works. Aside from these above-mentioned important persons, other important Maravars are: village watchmen, village headmen, others who are cultivators who give a share of the produce to the government as well as other taxes, and others who pay their taxes to the headman of the district and obey faithfully that which is said and the punishments which are meted out by the munsifs.[10]

Later in the text we are told that "the eighteen palaiyakarars of the Tanjore country all worship the raja with reverence," for which reason the sovereign of Madurai bestowed upon him the right to use his name as well as the requisite royal insignia, presented him with a lion-headed palanquin, made him one of the family of princes, and fed him with his own rice. The text concludes by listing different systems of military tenure, or the benefices that are provided for military service, among different groups of Maravars. One group of these, for instance, were military retainers for local kings: "Those who carry a spear and a sword are granted land measuring five kalams . . . ; those bearing muskets seven kalams; those bearing sarbogi nine kalams; those bearing a large gun fourteen kalams—the double allowance being due to the fact that the gun is carried by two men. A sardar [chief] of one hundred men is granted land of fifty kalams and half as much for a sardar of fifty men. These grants are made in various villages of the Marava country." In short, the text told the kind of story I narrated concerning Pudukkottai, in which social rank, privilege, and position were both correlated with and determined by participation in the political hierarchy. Although the text does provide some details of marriage customs and other domestic rituals, the largest part of the text concerns the political hierarchies within the caste group, freely mixing "ritual" and "political" idioms to express the authority of the king and his kingdom. Caste, in this example from one of the few extant texts from the early nineteenth century that might be deemed a "caste history," was little more than the precipitate of local political structures and social relations.

If these texts suggest a rather specific political context and genealogy for understanding the social order of dominant groups such as Maravars and Kallars in the Tamil country, they also suggest by extension similar kinds of political histories for groups that range from the Telugu country to Maharashtra, and from the older Rajputs of northwestern India to the new Rajputs of central India. The very dominance of these groups suggests the extent to which their own political ideologies and structures exerted influence over the organization of social relations generally, as well as the principles underlying them. But this is not to generalize on this basis without modification, and indeed my argument is that there were multiple logics organizing social relations—all, however, socially and politically contingent in various ways. We have already noted a far more complex position for Brahmans than would be guessed from the texts, even as we have seen the forced implication of "untouchable" groups within the political and discursive structures of their "patrons" and overlords. Additionally, there were many other kinds of groups that would hardly fit within the terms of a single caste system. The term "caste" appears to have united a vast variety of different kinds of groups and social types, from Brahmans to Dalits, from Kallars to Muslims. It also united territorially dominant and/or populous groups with a whole set of occupationally defined groups that, by definition, lived in small groups across extensive territories, with different kinds of social relations and forms.

If royal castes have been exemplary for my argument (in contrast to the exemplary position of Brahmans and untouchables for ethnologists such as Dumont), the occupational groups specific to village life such as washers, blacksmiths, barbers, and carpenters have been seen by others to express the quintessential character of caste as being defined by the division of labor and the provision of a complete array of social services for an agricultural economy. Principal players in the traditional drama known often by the name of jajmani, these were the "village servants" who provided local services to dominant, landed families for a yearly share of the village harvest; they also received other traditional perquisites for roles that linked the political and economic with the ritual (as, for example, the role played by washermen and barbers in funerals and other domestic rituals). These so-called castes, however, had very different kinds of kinship systems and locality relations. No village contained more than a few of these families, which made them very different from locally dominant agricultural castes or, for that matter, the even larger groups of agricultural laborers. They were marked by occupation rather than by such principles as purity and pollution, and their role in relations marked by exchanges of bodily substances and the like have been used to characterize them in terms of the wider logic of caste. Many early theories of caste stressed these occupational groups because they seemed to provide a key to the pervasive forms of social differentiation indexed by caste as a system, understood in functional terms as a means to allocate different necessary jobs to different groups. My point here is not to dispute the role of occupation as such, but rather to note the enormous difference between these kinds of caste designations and the others discussed above—one reason why a general occupational theory of caste has never prevailed in the anthropological literature.

One classificatory distinction that was extremely important in southern India during the seventeenth, eighteenth, and nineteenth centuries disappeared almost entirely from writings about caste after the late nineteenth century, and never did appear in northern India. This was the distinction between right- and left-hand groups, used to differentiate social groups between those who were tied to the land and those who were tied more to economic and social functions not directly involved in local agricultural regimes. This distinction at times rivaled the capacity of caste as a general rubric to order social groups; it suggested serious differences not only between castes (in a factional sense) but also between kinds of caste groups. Although the exact specification of left- or right-hand status varied across region (and according to different accounts), the left-hand group was typically made up of traders and merchants, artisans, and some lower "Sudra" caste groups, as well the leather workers. The right-hand group was typically made up of higher Sudras—usually the dominant landed groups such as Vellalars, Mudaliyars, Kavuntars, Maravars, and so on—along with the untouchable Paraiyas. According to the Abbé Dubois, who recognized this general division of castes as disruptive for his idealized sense of unified caste relations, "The Brahmins, Rajahs, and several classes of Sudras are content to remain neutral, and take no part in these quarrels," although some other accounts have placed Brahmans on the left. Dubois further wrote that "This division into Right-hand and Left-hand factions, whoever invented it, has turned out to be the most direful disturber of the public peace.

It has proved a perpetual source of riots, and the cause of endless animosity amongst the natives. . . . The opposition between the two factions arises from certain exclusive privileges to which both lay claim. But as these alleged privileges are nowhere clearly defined and recognized, they result in confusion and uncertainty, and are with difficulty capable of settlement."[11] Whereas kings were no doubt used to settling these disputes, the British were extremely perplexed when in the native quarters of Madras just outside the gates of Fort St. George, disputes arose, some very bitter, which they found themselves unable to arbitrate and at a loss to control.

Disputes arose almost invariably over matters concerning local privileges and honors, and frequently involved contests over public space. As Dubois put it in his inimitable style: "The rights and privileges for which the Hindus are ready to fight such sanguinary battles appear highly ridiculous, especially to a European. Perhaps the sole cause of the contest is the right to wear slippers or to ride through the streets in a palanquin or on horseback during marriage festivals. Sometimes it is the privilege of being escorted on certain occasions by armed retainers, sometimes that of having a trumpet sounded in front of a procession, or of being accompanied by native musicians at public ceremonies."[12] These privileges were, in fact, markers of rights that were indexed to status within and between communities, to control over public space and other public markers of position, to relations with various groups and institutions (from powerful and dominant patrons to temples), and to connections with royal families and court personages. The privilege of being escorted by armed retainers was clearly related to the kinds of political relations described above in the context of the old regime. Indeed, most of the privileges Dubois mentioned would at some point have been referenced to political authority, whether as grants from or signs of continuing relationships with kings, chiefs, and other local powers. The salience of the right-left distinction both underscores the extent to which social relations were constituted by political systems (rather than as part of some autonomous system of social and cultural relations) and the ways in which access to resources that involved land and immovable goods presented different kinds of political opportunities and struggles from control over resources implicated in trade and the artisanal production of movable goods. Disputes between right and left groups intensified in the newly created urban spaces associated with the European commercial presence; they also accompanied the breakdown of some political centers and the political transformations associated with British encroachment in the late eighteenth and nineteenth centuries. At the same time that disputes intensified, older mechanisms for dispute resolution had been severely truncated by the effects of colonial conquest and rule.

It is not altogether clear why the right/left distinction faded away, to become only a residual trace in certain parts of southern India by the midtwentieth century. The anthropologist Brenda Beck used the right hand/left hand division to organize an ambitious ethnographic study of the Coimbatore (Konku) region of Tamil Nadu, claiming that her older informants held the key to understanding the complexity of the local structures of social and territorial relations.[13] Unfortunately, this bold idea on occasion made the division seem like a procrustean bed into which her findings had to be made to fit. Her problem was not so much the small discrepancies that threatened the consistency of her interpretation as her failure to understand the historical contingence (rather than the sociological essence) of the division. Even as the components of the division were not as fixed as she insisted, the division had been sustained in relation to a specific political history.[14] The dismantling of old-regime politics enabled the formation of a new kind of unified caste system, which was facilitated as well by the changing nature of the social relations of production in the context of new forms of colonial capitalism. Although disputes between right- and left-hand groups had been exacerbated by the arrival of the British, the division itself was ultimately undermined by the longer-term effects of colonial rule. Perhaps it is not so strange, in retrospect, that the Abbé Dubois found this division irrational and bizarre, as opposed to caste itself, which he heartily approved of in principle, despite his many moral reservations.

The right/left distinction also makes sense of the very strong importance attached to territorial forms of organization and identity, as mentioned earlier. Throughout southern India, including both "poligar" areas and those in the central riverine deltas studied by Burton Stein, locally dominant groups and individuals went by the name of Nattars, or leaders of the territory, the *natu*.[15] Nattars were the headmen of villages and small territories including clusters of villages, as well as of caste groups. As Stein has suggested, "They were leaders of the major landholding people of the coast, including Vellalas, Reddis, Nainars, and Brahmans. They were the powerful big-men of any locality, and to them were conceded tasks of revenue assessment and collection under pre-British, state appointed revenue officials, amildars."[16] T. Mizushima, who studied the core revenue-producing areas of the Tamil south in the eighteenth and nineteenth centuries, has noted that caste organization was weak, in large part because Nattar authority was so powerful, and based not on caste structures but rather on Nattar control over local territories. Under such a regime, which further demonstrates the historical contingency of caste, the distinction between those who secured the major components of their identity and sustenance from a relationship to a locality and those who were not so territorially fixed would indeed have been far more important than a uniform, metonymically organized, scale of caste relations.[17]

Once again, although territory has been recognized by some as of fundamental importance to the nature of local social relations, territory itself as a significant marker of social identity was progressively deemphasized and largely lost in the understanding and explanation of caste as a historical social system in India.

## Caste as Indirect Rule

My account here is predicated on my own research on southern India, and is not intended to stand for the history (let alone the sociology) of all India. One of the problems of sociological and anthropological theorizing has been the relentless translation of the very specific to the most general, in which one experience of a single village over the course of a year becomes the basis for generalizing the experience of a subcontinent over several millennia of its history. In much anthropological writing, generalization has consisted of an effort to find a single principle to understand all caste relations. Whereas H. H. Risley attempted to explain the caste system in racial terms, W. Crooke argued instead, reviving arguments made earlier by Nesfield and Ibbetson, that caste was the outcome of a "a community of function or occupation." I have argued here against such a single theory of caste, noting, for example, that the right-hand/left-hand distinction itself underscores the difficulty of any such idea. Perhaps all that can be generalized is the extent to which caste has always been a contingent social phenomenon.

The stories I have told in this chapter refute the accounts that have become hegemonic in the West, and to some extent in India itself, in which caste is the key symbol of Indian society, and in which caste is a system of social relations in which the unvarying position of the Brahman and the untouchable confirm the spiritual basis that justifies, explains, and underlies this unique institution. Dumont's muddle in the middle is the rule rather than the exception. The positions of Brahman and untouchable are so unlike each other and are so governed by the idiosyncracies of a history that itself makes contingent the textual references that have been used to confirm a pan-Indian Brahmanic theory that a theory such as Dumont's can only gain credibility on the basis of two hundred years of colonial and Orientalist assumptions. In fact, caste neither exhausted the range of social forms, functions, and identities, nor provided underlying unity. The only common social facts of caste concerned the codification of kinship relations and, to some extent, the protocols for interdining. But even these codes and protocols yielded to larger political histories of community formation, regulation, discipline, and participation within a range of larger social and political worlds—until, that is, the larger political history became dominated by a colonial power whose interest in ruling India through an indirect logic predicated on caste changed things altogether.

If the notion of indirect rule in the princely states was in large part a fiction, sustained by a combination of nominal independence and vast ceremonial display, we should not necessarily believe that the areas of direct rule were themselves exempt from rule through indirect means in some fundamental sense. Colonialism purposefully preserved many of the forms of the old regime, nowhere more conspicuously than in the princely states, but in few respects more insidiously than in the construction of caste as the core symbol of Indian tradition. Under colonialism, the old structures were frozen, and only the appearances of the old regime, without the vitally connected political and social processes that formerly invested these structures with meaning, were saved. Colonialism thus changed things both more and less than has commonly been thought. Although it introduced new forms of civil society and separated these forms from the colonial state, colonialism also arrested some of the immediate disruptions of change by casting them as old and framing them within what looked like old-regime tableaus. But by freezing the wolf in sheep's clothing it changed things fundamentally. Paradoxically, even as colonialism worked to conflate the myriad historical particularities of social affiliation, identity, and relations under the dharmic sign of "varna," it did so in connection with the settlement of land systems that had sedimented a complex and conjunctural political history. Colonialism itself was deeply implicated in the rise of village-based systems of exchange, isolated ceremonial residues of the old-regime state, and fetishistic competition for ritual goods and privileges that no longer played a vital role in the political system. In making caste the sign for all of this, rendering it at the same time as the Indian form of civil society that would resist any modern version of social arrangements, caste could take over many of the functions of rule. Because of caste, and the colonial ethnology that constructed it as the centerpiece of Indian society, the British could rule *all* of India indirectly, as it were.

Thus the king and caste remained bound together in this perverse way. Both signs of old India, they were nevertheless separated as two distinct sides of the same traditional currency. Caste, assimilated to the principle of the Brahman and kingly authority, was subordinated both to the absolute political authority of the British state and the transcendental spiritual authority that was based in part on a fundamental civilizational disregard for the political. The king is dead; long live the Brahman. But the Brahman's immortality was as incidental as it was otherworldly, since it ultimately became appropriated by, and used for the service of, a different kind of immortality—the presumed permanence of British imperial rule in India.

# Five

## The Textualization of Tradition: Biography of an Archive

### Early Colonial Historiography

> Real history and chronology have hitherto been
> desiderata in the literature of India, and from the
> genius of the people and their past government, as
> well as the little success of the inquiries hitherto
> made by Europeans, there has been a disposition to
> believe that the Hindus possess few authentic records.
> Lieut.-Colonel Mackenzie has certainly taken the
> most effectual way, though one of excessive labour,
> to explore any evidences which may yet exist of
> remote eras and events.
> —Board of Control, East India Company,
>   February 9, 1810

History had not always been unimportant to the British in India. In the late eighteenth and early nineteenth centuries a great number of British writers—among them Dow, Elphinstone, Wilks, Malcolm, and Mackenzie—felt compelled to confront India's precolonial history. These writers often engaged a growing body of assertion and argumentation about the fundamental nature of Indian society and its civil and political institutions, in the context of extensive debates about the colonial project of conquering and ruling India. Historical questions were preeminent in the aftermath of the impeachment of Warren Hastings and the Pitt Act; in discussions around the Permanent Settlement in Bengal and modes of revenue settlement with peasants or village communities elsewhere in India; in the development of policies concerning military conquest and degrees of social and religious intervention; and in discussions of the fundamental institutions of East India Company governance. Although most British commentators saw the eighteenth century as a decadent prelude to and justification for British rule, and although they frequently disparaged Indian historical sensibilities and traditions, they nevertheless felt the need to understand India historically. And the history with which they engaged featured political rulers and institutions, warrior clans and military successes, social heterogeneity and religious admixtures—not a timeless culture committed only to "otherworldly" concerns.

The early period of colonial rule is, of course, better known for the textually and philologically trained "Orientalists" than for the "historians," given the general disparagement of Indian historical sensibilities and materials, and also the fact that historical exploration was almost entirely tied to the effort to justify land settlements and governmental regimes of one sort or another. As we have already seen, historical writing either concerned itself almost exclusively with the British in India or treated India according to stereotypes concerning village communities and oriental despotisms. Frequently, the complaint was over the lack of sources, particularly for "Hindu" histories. Well into the nineteenth century, when the administrator and historian Mountstuart Elphinstone wrote his two-volume work on the history of India, he based the authority of his scholarship on his own experience of documents concerning the Maratha kingdom, but felt the want of relevant materials for most other areas. For the history of the Deccan, for instance, he turned to an archive of historical documents that had been collected by Colin Mackenzie.[1] Mackenzie, who spent most of his long career in peninsular India as cartographer and surveyor, had given much of his time and resources to collecting every historical record and artifact he could find. By the time of his death in 1821, Mackenzie had amassed a collection that still contains the largest set of sources for the study of the early modern historical anthropology of southern India. Mackenzie's collection also represents colonial Britain's most extensive engagement with Indian history, a monument to this day of a kind of historical energy and interest that disappeared almost as soon as the concerns of colonial conquest gave way to the preoccupations of colonial rule.

Having never learned an Indian language, Mackenzie was specifically not an Orientalist. He had the peculiar advantage of being interested in sheer collection rather than interpretation and translation, tasks that could never be dissociated from colonial and missionary projects of control and conversion. Ironically, Mackenzie was perhaps more serious than any other official East India Company servant in his attempts to assemble a thick historical archive for peninsular India. In these attempts, Mackenzie not only relied almost exclusively on Indian assistants and informants, he was also forced to understand that the project of writing Indian history could be detached neither from the Indians who produced it nor from the politics of Britain's involvement in the establishment of colonial rule in India. Nevertheless, Mackenzie's collection soon fell into a growing fault line between official Orientalism and colonial sociology. On the one hand, Mackenzie's textual materials did not meet Orientalist standards for classicism and antiquity; on the other, Mackenzie's histories seemed too peculiar, too sullied by myth and fancy, and too localistic and "Oriental" to be of any real help in the development of administrative policy. But whether it was Mackenzie's ignorance or his direct engagement in colonial conquest itself that accounts for the relative transparency of his historical interest, he stands out as an extraordinary figure in the history of colonial knowledge. Largely on the side of his official employment and mostly at his own expense, he employed an impressive establishment of local scholars and agents to collect as much material as could be found concerning the political and social history of peninsular India. And he gave these local agents extraordinary latitude within the general mission of collection. As a result, the archive reflects as much a sociology of knowledge informed by the personal relations and concerns of the assistants as of the colonial "Master" and context. Despite Mackenzie's relative agnosticism, however, under the colonial regime "natives" could only be informants, "native" knowledge only the stuff of anthropological curiosity. Mackenzie's Indian assistants were not to be allowed to carry on his project after his death.

When, in the late nineteenth century, Mackenzie's collection was referred to at all, it was as a reference for the origin stories of local castes that were documented in the proliferation of manuals and gazetteers produced by and for district-level colonial administration. The fact that the Mackenzie collection had almost nothing about "caste," and reflected rather the archival survivals of an old-regime world in which social classification was invariably linked to political position, was only one part of what was overlooked. Mackenzie's collection tells the tale of the loss of the old-regime political world itself, along with the voices that struggled to translate that world in the tumultuous encounters of early colonial rule. Fragments of Mackenzie's obsessive if uncritical collection were instead used to very different ends, making the collection speak to the absence of India's history, rather than its efflorescence. The collection was catalogued by H. H. Wilson, the Orientalist who had corrected Mill's disparagement of Indian civilization but who nevertheless had little appreciation for the kinds of histories and texts collected by Mackenzie. Then the collection was hijacked by the idiosyncratic missionary William Taylor, who attempted, without success, to use the collection to predicate his own claim to Orientalist status. And finally the collection was almost lost altogether, allowed to mildew in colonial archives, appearing only as the occasional footnote for the documentation of an altogether different ethnographic knowledge under the new regime of colonial knowledge. That the Mackenzie collection could serve the ethnographic aims of Thurston and other colonial officers in the late nineteenth and early twentieth centuries only tells the story of India's loss of history under colonial rule in another register.

## Colonel Colin Mackenzie and the Surveying of India

Colonel Colin Mackenzie achieved unique fame
because he was primarily a man of action with a wide

outlook. Though by birth a highlander, by breeding a
European and by vocation an instrument of British
Imperialism in India, he was a universal man.
    —T. V. Mahalingam, 1972[2]

Born in 1754, Colin Mackenzie was a Scot from the outer Hebrides who went
out to India at the age of twenty-nine to pursue both a military career and an
interest in Hindu mathematics. Mackenzie subsequently used his mathematical
aptitude to become a skilled surveyor and cartographer, and carried out a series
of surveys in India that differed from all others in their broad range and scholarship. In 1810 Mackenzie became the first surveyor general of Madras, and in
1815 he was appointed the first surveyor general of India, a post he held until
his death in 1821.

When Mackenzie first arrived in India, he stayed for a time in Madurai,
where he was introduced to "the most distinguished of the Brahmins in the
neighbourhood," who were employed in collecting mathematical information
for his hosts. According to Alexander Johnston, the son of these hosts and
subsequently one of Mackenzie's dearest friends, "Mr. Mackenzie, in consequence of the communication which he had with them [Brahmans], soon discovered that the most valuable materials for a history of India might be collected in different parts of the peninsula, and during his residence at Madura
first formed the plan of making that collection, which afterwards became the
favorite object of his pursuit for 38 years of his life."[3]

Mackenzie was clear about his necessary complicity in the brute realities of
colonial power. His early discoveries were all made on military campaigns,
and Mackenzie himself conflated the role of the soldier and the scientist. As he
wrote, "That science may derive assistance, and knowledge be diffused, in the
leisure moments of camps and voyages, is no new discovery; but . . . I am also
desirous of proving that, in the vacant moments of an Indian sojourn and campaign in particular (for what is the life of an Indian adventurer but one continued campaign on a more extensive scale), such collected observations may be
found useful, at least in directing the observation of those more highly gifted
to matters of utility, if not to record facts of importance to philosophy and
science." Mackenzie's early years were one continuous military campaign.
And Mackenzie had no doubts about the ennobling influence of British rule,
even as his life has subsequently served to perpetuate the story of Britain's
rescue of India from its own decadent demise. As he wrote about the early
years of his Indian sojourn: "From the evils of famine, penury, and war, the
land was then slowly emerging; and it struggled long under the miseries of bad
management, before the immediate administration of the south came under the
benign influence of the British government."[4] That Mackenzie's own influence
has often been praised by historians in India can hardly obscure his full participation in the colonial conquest of India.

During Mackenzie's early years in the Army Engineers, he was frequently deputed to do survey work in those districts of the Deccan that had been ceded to the Company by Haidar Ali of Mysore and the nizam of Hyderabad. Between 1792 and 1799, Mackenzie spent much of his time engaged in a survey of the "Nizam's Territories," the area encompassing what today are the districts of Cuddapah and Kurnool in Andhra Pradesh. In the course of this survey work, Mackenzie developed a comprehensive sense of what a survey should be. As he wrote about the area he was surveying, "The Dekhan was in fact then a terra incognita, of which no authentic account existed, excepting in some uncertain notices and mutilated sketches of the marches of Bussy, and in the travels of Tavernier and Thevenot, which by no means possess that philosophical accuracy demanded in modern times."[5] Mackenzie sought therefore to make the land known, and to do so through a combination of strategies that included detailed mapping and description as well as the collection of as many local and authentic accounts as he could find.

During his surveying work in the Deccan, Mackenzie was recalled four times for military service, which consisted principally of using his surveying and engineering skills to position artillery and act as technical advisor for assaults.[6] The most dramatic of Mackenzie's military assignments was at Srirangapattinam, in the fourth and final Anglo-Mysore War that took place in 1799, where the British finally defeated a ruler who had been, with his father Haidar Ali, responsible for transforming the political and social landscape of southern India during the previous forty years, and the most formidable challenge to British military ambitions in peninsular India. During Tipu Sultan's final stand, Mackenzie was engineer in charge of the batteries to the north of the Kaveri River, "from which side the successful assault was delivered."[7]

After the defeat of Tipu Sultan, Mackenzie was commissioned to organize and conduct a survey of Mysore, in order to fix the boundaries of the newly conquered territories and to map and gain some preliminary detailed information about an area two-thirds the size of Scotland. The Great Mysore Survey, as it was called, lasted from 1799 until March 1809, during which time Mackenzie maintained nominal charge over the conclusion of the Deccan survey, as well. In his appointment letter he was told that his attention was not to be confined to "mere military or geographical information, but that your enquiries are to be extended to a statistical account of the whole country."[8] Nevertheless, his impressively conceived scheme for a survey "embracing the statistics and history of the country, as well as its geography" was constantly frustrated by a shortage of support from the Company, which wanted to do a survey on the cheap, and was less convinced than Mackenzie of the need for a comprehensive survey.[9]

The most detailed part of Mackenzie's Mysore survey was his "Memoirs of the Northern Pargunnahs of Mysore," the product of work conducted in 1800 and 1801 before the cutbacks. In addition to the usual statistical tables, called *caneeshamari*, Mackenzie collected numerous historical memoirs of the royal families of each region. As early as July of 1800, Mackenzie wrote that he was making some progress in his enquiries into that part of the history of "this country . . . which belongs to its Hindoo rulers and collecting all the materials I can get in the several districts of books, Inscriptions, and Traditions." He further noted that as he did not know the local languages, he had to employ "Native Writers and Translators of the Canara, Mharatta, etc."[10] For Chitradurga, Mackenzie's assistants collected and translated four different family histories, and then correlated the recorded genealogy of the royal family with chronological information available in local inscriptions. As he wrote in his second report, "The Historical Accounts of the Populations of Government of the Districts were compiled from creditable sources of information on the spot; sometimes traditions from registers and chequed by dates and eras, ascertained from grants and inscriptions where they could be referred to; a reciprocal correction was frequently derived from one to the other; and more satisfactory as no communication existed between the different authorities whenever a certain internal evidence arises favorable to their accuracy."[11] The royal histories, or *vamcavali*s, were received, so Mackenzie tells us, from "the official persons employed in the hereditary duties of Naadgoudes, Goudes, etc., in whose hands their records are kept." The vamcavalis frequently recorded why a particular group or family had settled in the place that subsequently became known as the base for their rule.[12] The family histories also recounted stories of the glorious exploits and courageous rule of the relevant rajas, thus ascribing special legacies and powers to contemporary rulers and places.

The rajas ("polligars," from *palaiyakkarar*) of places like Chitradurga had already been substantially subdued by Haidar Ali and Tipu Sultan in the last decades of the eighteenth century. Haidar Ali and Tipu Sultan had systematically attacked the forts of the rajas, capturing the entire royal family and carting them off to their capital city of Srirangapattinam. In their place, Haidar Ali and Tipu Sultan placed *amildar*s or managers who were charged with the task of maintaining order and collecting revenue. This administrative centralization, very different from the kind of "feudal" incorporation deployed after military conquest by the former kings of Vijayanagara, anticipated the military and administrative strategies of the East India Company. If anything, Haidar Ali and Tipu Sultan succeeded rather better than the British in dispensing with and displacing the local political elites of the Deccan, for even by the turn of the century most British officers felt the need to rule and collect revenue through local chiefs as landlords, or zamindars. Indeed, Mackenzie's studied attempt to collect the genealogical records of these displaced chiefs was due in part to the East India Company's desire to sort out claims of local political legitimacy and evaluate the nature and potential resistance of these forms of local political rule. Colonialism had to ease into the forms of direct rule that the sultans of Mysore had already deployed, as part of their own strategy of developing the administrative infrastructure that would enable them to oppose the spread of British rule in India.

Despite the clear political rationale for collecting information about local chiefs, Mackenzie's enthusiasm for assembling accounts full of what many of his contemporaries felt to be ethnographic trivia and historical fable was both boundless and peculiar. Even Mackenzie often doubted the utility and veracity of many of the texts that were faithfully reproduced, commenting, for example, on one vamcavali that "the whole of this account appears to be from tradition and very doubtful if not erroneous in dates the succession of the Polligars perhaps only excepted."[13] Other accounts were given solely "by way of specimen of what are preserved in the hands of the Natives."[14] Nevertheless, even though many accounts provided fascinating perspectives on the meaning of political authority, the categories of social identity, local textual genres, and sociologies of knowledge, Mackenzie was most interested in a fairly narrowly conceived historical record. Mackenzie clearly felt, however, that every "traditionary account" contained some potentially useful historical information, and wished to leave nothing uncollected or unexplored. Furthermore, in his 1805 annual report on the Mysore survey, he wrote that the documents he had collected consisted "not merely of a dry chain of uninteresting facts but are connected by various illustrations of the genious and manners of the People, their several systems of Government and of Religion, and of the predominant causes that influence their sentiments and opinions to this day, lights are derived on the Tenures of Lands, the origin and variety of assessment of rents and revenues, and the condition of the People, the privileges of the different classes, and the genious and spirit of the Government prevalent generally in the south for centuries." He believed that he had successfully established that there had been a political unity under what he called the "Dominion of the Carnatic," by which he meant the rule of the Vijayanagara Empire. By understanding the institutions of Hindu government that had been part of Vijayanagara rule, Mackenzie felt that the Company could gain "much useful information on many of these institutions, laws, and customs, whose influence still prevail among the various Tribes of Natives forming the general Mass of the Population at this day." But of particular concern to Mackenzie was his sense that much local historical knowledge had perished under the same conditions of instability that had led to a deterioration of the social and political life of the natives. Mackenzie declared that he felt it imperative to grasp "whatever opportunities existed for investigating what yet remained in the hands of the Natural Inhabitants of these countries which had escaped the general wrack and destruction of written records and more permanent monuments following the unsettled state of the country for so long a period."[15]

Mackenzie extended his efforts well beyond the Mysore area as he became increasingly convinced of the great importance of his endeavor. At his request, a memorandum was circulated to senior British officials in southern India in

1808 that solicited information "on the ancient history, state, and institutions of the south of India," asking specifically about "materials of various descriptions in the hands of the natives; and which from their obscurity are liable to be neglected and lost, but might be still recovered by the interposition of the Gentlemen in the Diplomatic, Judicial, Revenue, and Medical departments particularly."[16] In longer detailed memos that Mackenzie circulated to officials with whom he was acquainted, he specified his interest in materials concerning the early history of Buddhism and Jainism in the south, as well as more generally any accounts of religious "contentions" and "establishments." He was interested in coins, antiquities of any description, drawings of ancient tombs and burial mounds, and rubbings or copies of inscriptions.

Most of all, he was interested in assembling the evidentiary base for establishing the political history of the subcontinent. And Mackenzie had a critical sense of how history was constructed in relation both to cultural genre and political context. For example, he noted that "regular historical narrations and tracts are seldom found among the Natives, and such notices as exist, are generally preserved in the form of religious legends and popular poems and stories." Mackenzie went on to note that there were exceptions, listing some as follows:

> Vumshavelly, or genealogies of the several dynasties and considerable families; Dunda Cavelly, or chronological registers and records, sometimes preserved by official persons; Calliganums, literally prophecies, but sometimes really conveying under that assumed disguise, Historical information with more apparent freedom than could be addressed to Oriental Sovereigns; Cheritra and Cudha, frequently applied to tales and popular stories, but sometimes containing correct information of remarkable characters and events approaching to the nature of our memoirs; and Rakas, financial records and registers of the ancient revenues and resources of the country.[17]

Thus Mackenzie justified and explained his eclectic interests and procedures, aware all the while of the problems of textual authenticity. As he wrote to one official: "If during the Survey you can get any notices of the History of the Country in Canara, it would be preferable to a made up Persian account as being more original."[18] And, rather than despair over the ahistoricism of the oriental mind, he assumed that non- or quasi-historical genres, such as prophecies and popular stories, were less historical than they might otherwise have been in order to disguise their political and therefore dangerous nature.

Most family histories were in the genre of vamcavalis, literally genealogies, or texts recounting the line of a family (*vamcam*). Every palaiyakkarar family had at least one vamcavali telling their history, and by extension that of the kingdom as well. Most vamcavalis consisted of a succession of episodes concerning selected ancestral heads of the family. Episodes were linked by genealogical lists, which sometimes consisted of only the names of the intervening family heads. The vamcavalis were genealogies both in that they listed the entire line of the family and in that genealogy served as the narrative frame of the text. What chronology is to narrative history, genealogy is to the vamcavali: it provides sequence, relevance, and structure. It also provided the principal narrative intention of the vamcavali, which was to narrate the origins of the present palaiyakkarar and his family. The events included in some detail in the narrative seem to have been selected for two reasons: because they established the credentials of the current king and because they provided a sense of the illustrious history of the family.

Each episode typically consists of some great action performed by the hero-ancestor. For example, the hero may kill a tiger that has been plaguing villagers in the king's domain or set off to do battle against some enemy of the king's. The king then calls the palaiyakarar to court, where he presents him with gifts consisting of titles, emblems, and rights over land (sometimes the very land of the enemy who has been conquered). The basic structure of the text is repetitive, but each episode is about the establishment of a relationship. No relationship is fixed and enduring but rather must be constantly reestablished and displayed. And each new relationship transforms the position of the chief, even as it reaffirms the eminence of the greater king whose court is the center of narrative attention. Although the feats performed by ancestral chiefs appear on occasion fantastic, they suggest common epic values: bravery unto death, loyalty, and great physical prowess. And the gifts that follow these feats mark the establishment and transformation of political relationships in ways that both mirror and constitute the political landscape of the time. As we saw in the last chapter, gifts of honors, titles, emblems, and land were the principal currency of the political system. Vamcavalis were decidedly historical texts, situated as they were in a political system in which social and political relationships were marked by these same honors, titles, and emblems, in which landholding and political position were perforce part of the same relationship, and in which even social identities of the sort later captured by the single term "caste" were constituted through the kinds of narrative exchanges central to the texts read by most colonial contemporaries as fabulous and unhelpful. As in all settings, historical forms were embedded within the framework of historical context itself.

Mackenzie had a much clearer sense of the politics of knowledge than most of his colonial compatriots in southern India because he was deeply involved in the actual collection of historical information, in particular through his close relations with his assistants and his use of survey work to facilitate collection. Mackenzie was also unique in the extent to which he believed that local texts, however embellished with unintelligible fables, would afford considerable historical information if read in context, along with as many other local documents as could be found, with some attention to matters of genre, style, and rhetorical strategy. Many of the texts he collected were dismissed by his contemporaries as of little interest and even less importance for constructing an adequate account of the precolonial history of India. And among the texts that least interested other early British administrators in India were the countless family histories of the royal families that had dotted the southern Indian countryside. Although some administrators were concerned to sort out the legitimacy of certain kinds of claims to local rule, and by extension property, the growing support for a ryotwari (cultivator) settlement rather than a settlement with zamindars, following the 1793 Bengal model, meant even less interest in Mackenzie's historical findings.

It had been during his Mysore survey that Mackenzie's collection of historical materials began to gain some momentum. Mackenzie noted that while the survey work was being conducted, "the collection of materials on the history, antiquities, and statistics of the country was going on throughout the whole of the provinces, under the presidency of Fort St. George, on the basis of the information originally obtained on the Mysore survey, by natives trained and instructed by me for this purpose." Mackenzie stressed that this process had cost the government little, since "all the purchases have been entirely at my private expense, as well as the collection of MSS. throughout the Karnatik Malabar, the southern provinces, the Cirkars, and the Dekhan." Clearly Mackenzie felt that the British government should take more active interest in his endeavors; "the success of these investigations," he wrote, "justifies the hope, that considerable advantage may be derived from following up the same plan of research wherever the influence of the British government affords the same facilities, in the intervals of military occupation."[19]

During the Mysore survey, Mackenzie realized not only that his native staff was indispensable for the task of collecting and translating historical, geographic, and ethnographic materials but also that his native assistants were in a position to mediate a complex sociology of local knowledge, in situations where indigenous inhabitants often greeted British curiosity with "friendless suspicion."[20] Mackenzie was particularly concerned not to use the kind of intimidation that apparently accompanied most attempts—whether by British officials or the amildars of Tipu Sultan—to collect local knowledge, writing that "The persons and properties of the Inhabitants have been protected from all violence of any kind with me, and I have particularly attended to conciliate their minds, which was indeed necessary for easier obtaining my object."[21] But the difficulties encountered in collecting survey-related information only constituted the tip of the iceberg in "friendless suspicion." Mackenzie himself was never unaware of the potential resistance to hand over information, as also of the inverse problem that if he did not exercise scrupulous caution he would get only the kind of information that he would be understood to desire. As he wrote to P. Connor in 1816, "I presume you are yourself sufficiently aware of the Native character in general, to know that expressing any extraordinary anxiety or solicitude for any particular object is the sure way to excite suspicion, delay, and sometimes opposition—Some apparent indifference is useful and necessary and I want to recommend your abstaining from taking notes of your remarks on their answers to questions in their presence."[22] Questions of authority, and of the myriad relations between power and knowledge, as well as the usual colonial assumptions about "native character," were raised over and over again in the accumulation of Mackenzie's archive.

Some of the texts revealed their historical setting also in the sense that they became petitions to the Company for favorable consideration. The authors petitioned the Company to settle their kingdom permanently as a zamindari estate, or to reduce their tribute or, in some cases, even to release the descendant of the kingly line from prison, when one was languishing behind bars for participation in the "poligar wars" of the late eighteenth century. Most Company officers, Mackenzie and a few of his ilk excluded, were interested in these texts solely as aids to help determine if the chiefly families had been loyal enough to the British to justify any kind of favorable treatment in the deliberations over the zamindari settlement and the concluding phase of the "poligar wars."

## Collecting Caste

Colin Mackenzie—afterwards Surveyor-General of
India—drew everything he found of any architectural
importance, and was the most industrious and
successful collector of drawings and manuscripts that
India has ever known; but he could not write. The few
essays he attempted are meagre in the extreme, and
nine-tenths of his knowledge perished with him.
—James Fergusson, 1876.[23]

Mackenzie and his assistants collected every historical, ethnographic, and religious text, tradition, and document they could find; but they also collected inscriptional rubbings and copies, antiquities, coins, and images, and drew hundreds of sketches recording the scenes they surveyed. The Mackenzie collection of drawings derives from several sources, including both his own drawings and those sketched by his surveyors while on tour.[24] The 1,500 drawings range widely in subject matter. Some are careful sketches of agricultural implements, wells and irrigation devices, and other features of local agricultural technology. Others are similarly detailed sketches of sculptures from temples. Many of the pictures depict miscellaneous scenery and landscapes from Mackenzie's travels throughout the Deccan. Included are drawings of forts, ancient buildings, and local architecture, as well as some revealing portraits of the British set in the landscapes and by the buildings of the Deccan. Finally, there are watercolors of the various costumes worn by members of different castes and tribes.

Mackenzie's ethnographic drawings—pictures of "typical" representatives of different groups, types, castes, and tribes—appear to have been drawn mostly by his Indian draftsmen, in European style. One portfolio has eighty-two drawings depicting different castes in the northern Deccan—in Balaghat—drawn for the most part in the first two years of the Mysore survey, and was labeled: "Costume of Balla Ghaut, Carnatick, 1800 & 1801."[25] The principal marker for caste, indeed for all social distinctions, was costume. Costume served as the key sign and focus of ethnographic difference. Markers of hierarchy and difference in Europe as well as India, clothes were also highlighted as part of the preoccupation with the colorful and exotic aspects of the Indian social order, fostered by the cult of the picturesque. The costumes depicted in the drawings in the Balla Ghaut portfolio include those of royal and sacred personages as well as of distinct occupational categories; they sometimes marked unexplained differences within such categories as "Boya peons," and they apparently justified the inclusion of a number of drawings of Hindu dramas, where the clothes were costumes in a more modern sense of the term. Nevertheless, the drawings were clearly about far more than clothes, and portray colorful illustrations of people and customs of the Carnatic as observed in the Mysore survey.

The list of castes and groups that found their way into Mackenzie's portfolio reveals a rather different ethnographic sensibility from that which subsequently became canonized in the gazetteers and handbooks of the late nineteenth and twentieth centuries. The first drawing is of a Jain at Kancipuram, not surprising given Mackenzie's claim to have been one of the first Europeans to note the importance of Jainism in ancient India. There are two portraits of royal personages, one a sad reminder of the death of kings—a portrait of the ancient "Rayeels of Beejnagur" (Vijayanagara)—the other a fine picture of a court scene labeled "Visit from the Rajah of Goodicotta at Devasamodrum."[26] The political ceremony of the court was elegantly depicted, with the flywhisks and other symbols and protocols of the residual political authority of a Deccan chieftain prominently displayed. There is also a portrait of "A Boya of Rank," a member of the royal caste (and a relation of the royal family) in Chitteldroog.[27] Many of the earliest drawings are of "peons," the court servants and soldiers of the local chiefs, or palaiyakarars.[28] Most of these retainers were themselves attached to the court of Chitradurga, one of the first districts surveyed by Mackenzie, and a kingdom for which he collected an unusual number of royal family histories and traditions. In each picture, the caste of the peon was given, but caste identity was clearly seen as subordinate in importance to the political position of the individual. Court officials, such as one Brahman revenue officer, were also included as examples of the kinds of political personages that populated Mackenzie's Deccan. Gurus and itinerant holy men were also featured prominently.[29]

Caste as the dominant system of differentiation and identity plays a limited role in the ethnographic drawings. It appears as an important marker of difference in the context of occupational categories such as barbers, basketmakers, and palmists—when, that is, caste and occupation were interchangeable categories.[30] Caste also figures in drawings of Brahmans of various descriptions, including a number of official court Brahmans, a picture of a physician, and a lyric portrait of "Brahman women" washing clothes in the Tungabhadra River.[31] In addition, a number of miscellaneous castes were depicted, sometimes alone, sometimes in groups. One picture is of a Kurumbar, a Kanarese caste of itinerant shepherds who took their caste name from the woolen blankets they wove.[32] Another picture is a miscellaneous joint portrait of a "Comitee or Banian," a man by the name of Madaveran of the Baljawar caste, and a Canara Brahman.[33]

The drawings also provide stereotypic portraits of wrestlers, bards, and merchants.[34] The domestic household is seen as an important ethnographic unit, as portrayed in a composition of "A Family employed in their Domestic Occupations." Another picture is of two village watchmen, who had charge of protecting the property and inhabitants of a Deccan village; another two wooden, and undescribed, "figures at Jaggannath."[35] There is a rather fine portrait of a Canara Reddy, which in spite of a certain lack of proportion depicts the spare dhoti, upper cloth, and turban of the gentleman with careful detail. Yet another drawing of "Ramchurn, a Rajpoot by caste," shows rather more attention to the facial features than most others, perhaps because this is one of the few figures identified by name as well as social position.[36]

The drawings that look most typically ethnographic—by the anthropological standard set later in the century—are of tribal groups sketched in Orissa, mostly by Mackenzie's assistants in the years when, as surveyor general, he worked out of Calcutta.[37] These are drawings of such groups as Gonds, Marias, and Bhils, but interestingly there is nothing in these pictures or in their general place in the collection of drawings to reflect the early anthropological preference in India for groups separated from the mainstream of the Indian peasant population and referred to specifically as tribal. Equally "ethnographic," perhaps, is a picture of a group of young Brahman girls performing various dances at an annual festival in the northern Deccan.[38] The inscription below the picture provides details of the festival, its significance, procedures, and participants. There are also a number of scenes from Hindu dramas, as in one picture of a Hindu drama drawn from the *Ramayana*.[39]

The distribution of types and characters reveals a good deal about Mackenzie's perceptions of the social order. First, Mackenzie was aware of the importance of the contemporaneous kingdoms and their political hierarchies—the portraits of former and present rulers were illustrations of Mackenzie's sense of the political history of the Deccan. Mackenzie collected hundreds of family and local histories that documented the importance of the local chiefs, whose form of rule he obviously believed to be crucial to understanding the traditions and customs of each area as well as the disposition of rights to land and other local resources. Thus we also see court scenes, local (mostly revenue) officials, and the "peons" who were the retainers, court servants, and soldiers with whom the surveyors no doubt had a great deal of interaction. Second, Brahmans figured importantly in a number of guises. Not only were Brahmans important court officials (as well as priests) but many of Mackenzie's trusted Indian assistants were Brahmans, and when they went out collecting local texts and traditions they invariably began their search by contacting local Brahmans. The Brahman women washing clothes or bathing presented opportunities for indulgence in picturesque modes of drawing, complemented by the inclusion of light romantic poetry penned in under the pictures. Gurus and traveling holy men were not only eminently picturesque, they were also the perceived embodiment of India's spiritual wisdom. The occupational groups, from barbers to astrologers, were viewed as being particularly important to the definition and organization of the caste system, but perhaps they revealed more for the British in relation to turn-of-the-century convictions that rural India was made up of myriad village republics, each with a fully functioning and self-sufficient system of economic organization. The other illustrations documented, sometimes randomly, the kinds of groups that were identified as fundamental to the organization of Indian society, necessary to the objectives of the British in India, and/or components of the exotic landscape that made India such a compelling place in the imaginary world of eighteenth- and nineteenth-century Europeans.

Both in the absence of any kind of systematic and autonomous sense of a "caste system" and in the concentration of pictorial attention given to characters who reflected the political landscape of the eighteenth-century Deccan— the residues of India's late medieval feudal culture and society—we see major differences between Mackenzie's vision of India's ethnography and that which became canonized by the end of the nineteenth century. Mackenzie's vision may have provided some of the necessary tools of documentation and description for later colonial delineation, but his attention to individuals as well as types, political figures as well as castes, occupations as various as barbers and wrestlers—all worked to render his anthropology fundamentally different from the encyclopedic science of the Castes and Tribes Surveys. Whereas these later surveys were rigorously antihistorical, Mackenzie's ethnography was still at least in part subservient to the historically grounded contingencies of early British rule, which had not yet completely erased Indian history and replaced it by colonial anthropology.

Nevertheless, the drawings of ancient kings and royal retainers do not fully capture the vitality of these figures as they emerge in the historical documents collected by Mackenzie. Instead, the drawings make the heroes of local chronicles look like the picturesque survivals of a vanished feudal order, now metonymized in a series of ethnographic evocations of costume and color.

Even though Mackenzie's ethnographic sensibilities were embedded in his larger historical project, the drawings ironically signal the curious end of this project. For the first time, Indian history is itself made to look picturesque, an aesthetic anticipation of the ethnographic state.

## The Ambivalence of Colonial Historiography

> A collection was formed at a considerable cost of
> time, labour and expence, which no individual exer-
> tions have ever before accumulated, or probably will
> again assemble. Its composition is of course very
> miscellaneous, and its value with respect to Indian
> history and statistics remains to be ascertained,
> the collector himself having done little or nothing
> towards a verification of its results.
> —H. H. Wilson, 1828[40]

The British government was always somewhat reserved about the value of Mackenzie's endeavors. Mackenzie's allowances for the Mysore survey had been drastically cut in 1801, with deleterious consequences not only for his implementation of the survey but also for his more extensive researches. And although at various points Company and government officials expressed their approbation, Mackenzie's career prospered chiefly because of his surveying and administrative skills, as also because he was among the most dedicated and hard-working Company servants of his time. As the chief secretary of government in Madras wrote in October of 1807, "in the zealous execution of the duties of the arduous undertaking in which he has been so long engaged . . . and in honourable disinterestedness, I do not believe that Major Mackenzie is surpassed by any Publick Officer in India."[41]

There was never any doubt about Mackenzie's surveying and cartographic talent. James Rennell, the architect of the Bengal survey and the senior cartographer of the early Raj, wrote about the "masterly manner" of Mackenzie's survey: "The discrimination of the different objects is such as to render an idea of the nature of the country, perfectly clear on inspection. And I doubt not but the accuracy is equal to the execution. It is also a work of great magnitude in respect to its superficial extent; being, if I mistake not, considerably larger than the kingdom of Ireland."[42] And the Board of Directors in London received the materials of the Mysore survey with evident admiration. In their despatch dated February 9, 1810, they noted that

> It is a great pleasure to us to bestow our unqualified and warm commendation upon
> his long-continued, indefatigable, and zealous exertions in the arduous pursuits in

which he was employed, and upon the works which those exertions have produced. . . . The actual survey, upon geometrical principles, of a region containing
above 40,000 square miles, generally of an extremely difficult surface, full of hills
and wilderness, presenting few facilities or accommodations for such a work, and
never before explored by European science, in a climate very insalubrious, is itself
no common performance; and the minute divisions and details of places of every
description given in the memoirs of the survey, with the masterly execution, upon a
large scale, of the general map, and its striking discrimination of different objects,
rarely equalled by any thing of the same nature that has come under our observation—form altogether an achievement of extraordinary merit, adding most materially to the stores of Indian geography, and of information useful for military, financial, and commercial purposes.

So impressed were the members of the Board of the potential utility of Mackenzie's maps and memoirs that they declared that the survey was not to be
published, that "no copy of his map, or of the division of it, further than for the
public offices just mentioned, ought to be permitted to be taken."[43]

The Board also expressed its appreciation of Mackenzie's "superadded inquiries into the history, the religion, and the antiquities of the country," that,
admittedly, Mackenzie's "other fatiguing avocations might have been pleaded
as an excuse for not attending." Although casting some doubt on the actual
"authenticity" of the records collected, as also on the general wisdom of an
enterprise that seemed to require such "excessive labour," the Board allowed
"that this effort promises the fairest of any which has yet been made to bring
from obscurity any scattered fragments of true history which exist, and un-
doubtedly encourages the expectation of ultimately obtaining both considerable insight into the state of the country and its governments in more modern
periods, and some satisfactory indications of its original institutions and earlier
revolutions." Mackenzie himself responded quite insistently to the doubts
about the authenticity of the grants to Brahmans, which made up the subject of
most of the inscriptions as well as many of the manuscripts, noting that "not
an instance of forgery has been discovered or even suspected, save one, (and
that rather assists history)." Of particular interest in the Board's comment
about Mackenzie's historical labors was that the lack of "real history and chronology" in India was taken not as evidence of the lack of historical consciousness but rather of the "commotions and changes" that had been so "unfavour-
able to the preservation of political records." India's lack of history—and of a
sense of history—had not yet become colonial orthodoxy.

The Board's evaluation of Mackenzie's collection was based largely on earlier correspondence by William Bentinck, the governor of Madras; Mark
Wilks, British resident in Mysore; and John Malcolm, the resident of Poona,
in response to their concerns that Mackenzie was not being adequately supported and encouraged by the government. Bentinck observed that "the valu-

able collection of manuscripts and other documents of the highest antiquity which that officer has been enabled to procure, may be expected to throw useful light on the dark ages of Oriental history, and to be equally valuable as a guide in the pursuit of literary knowledge, as in the attainment of correct information with regard to the former tenures of property and the laws of the ancient dynasties of the peninsula of India." Bentinck seemed fully aware of the importance of his collection for the general project of British rule, and he feared that only Mackenzie would be able to make sense of these manuscripts, for no one else had his experience and expertise. "The object will be accomplished by him, or it will probably never be accomplished, even if his materials in their present state were to fall into other hands, they might be considered as lost."[44] He strongly recommended that London realize the importance of both the manuscripts and the man, and at the very least reimburse him for his actual expenditures.

Mark Wilks—who in 1817 published his three-volume work, *Historical Sketches of the South of India*, documented with extensive references to Mackenzie's collection—was perhaps the most enthusiastic advocate of Mackenzie's historical labors; he was nevertheless highly doubtful of the historical value of anything other than the inscriptions. "The Department of history in this country," he wrote, "is so deformed by fable and anachronism, that it may be considered as an absolute blank in Indian literature." Wilks then went on to suggest what most Indian historians since then have thought, that Indian "historical" texts and chronicles are so sullied by myth and fancy that they would be useful only to trace developments in Indian literature in late medieval and early modern times. Wilks turned, however, to the inscriptional record for southern India, to which Mackenzie had contributed so much by making rubbings of thousands of stone and copper plate inscriptions. He opined that "There is but one mode which appears to afford the most distant hope of supplying this important defect. The grants generally of a religious nature inscribed on stone and copper plates which are to be found in every part of the south of India are documents of a singularly curious texture, they almost always fix the chronology, and frequently unfold the genealogy and military history of the Donor and his ancestors, with all that is remarkable in their civil institutions or religious reforms."[45] Thus anticipating the procedures of most subsequent Indian historiography, Wilks assumed that since history is predicated on chronology, inscriptions are preferable to other texts. Inscriptions could be used to date kings, reigns, wars, and other events, whereas Mackenzie's texts—loose composites of oral and literary tradition that could rarely be definitively dated or trusted—seemed to constitute their own internal set of time referents, events, and structures, and did not succumb easily to master historical narratives and appropriations.

Wilks also shared Bentinck's official view of the value of any reliable historical information about the nature of landed property. As he wrote, "If it should be found practicable to trace by a series of authentic documents the history of landed property in the south of India, I imagine that no subject of superior interest and importance can be presented to the attention of a British Government." Wilks was "certain that the research would unfold the most useful information on many important points connected with the political economy and good Government of India." Indeed, no other subject so exercised British official opinion in the early years of the nineteenth century, particularly in southern India, where the debate was raging in those years between advocates of the Permanent Settlement with landlords (zamindars) and those, following Munro, who favored direct (or ryotwari) settlement with the "cultivators." And though Wilks was less interested in religion than in land ownership, he did note that Mackenzie had opened important new windows on the understanding of the history of Hinduism. Noting that the religion of the Hindus "is usually represented as unchanged and unchangeable," he remarked that "the religious history of Europe is scarcely less pregnant with revolutions," and that "everything in short that is usually considered most interesting and instructive in general history may be traced and illustrated" by Mackenzie's texts.[46]

Although Bentinck had clearly regretted for some years that his hands had been tied by the Board of Control from remunerating Mackenzie properly for his efforts, the final result of this correspondence was that the Company recognized Mackenzie's contribution, increased his salary by 50 percent, gave him a monthly stipend to rent a house to maintain his establishment, and endowed him with an account for at least some of his research expenses, "trusting that it will not amount to any large sum." The Board also expressed its hope that Mackenzie's new position of "Barrack-master" in Mysore, to which he was appointed at the conclusion of the Mysore survey, would afford him the necessary leisure to "digest and improve the materials he has collected." But just a few months later, at the end of 1810, the government of Madras created a position Mackenzie had long advocated, surveyor general of Madras, and appointed him to it. As Mackenzie put it, the government suddenly responded both to the increased costs of its surveys and the "unconnected confused manner in which these works were executed, without any general fixed system." However, Mackenzie's recognition and elevation made it even more difficult for him to find the time to work on his historical interests. When, a year later, Mackenzie was posted as chief engineer for a British expeditionary force that wrested Java from the French in 1811, his efforts were further set back, though he collected an extraordinary array of Javanese materials, lamenting only that "the powerful aid of the penetrating acute genius of the Brahmans which had been of such importance in India, was here wanting."[47]

In 1815, Mackenzie was appointed surveyor-general of India, the first occupant of this prestigious post. His new administrative responsibilities, and his move to Calcutta, seriously retarded his historical research. In particular, he found that it was difficult to move his establishment out of southern India: "The individuals reared by me for several years being natives of the Coast or the Southern provinces and almost as great strangers to Bengal and Hindostan as Europeans, their removal to Calcutta is either impracticable, or where a few from personal and long attachment (as my head Brahmin, Jain translator, and others), are willing to give this last proof of their fidelity, yet still it is attended with considerable expence." Without his full establishment, Mackenzie correctly worried that "most of what I had proposed to condense and translate from the originals in the languages of their country could not be conveniently, or at all, effected in Calcutta."[48]

Nevertheless, Mackenzie was determined to attempt it, planning, "in this last stage, preparatory to my return to Europe, to effect a condensed view of the whole collection and a catalogue raisonnée of the native manuscripts and books etc. and to give the translated materials such form as may at least facilitate the production of some parts, should they ever appear to the public by persons better qualified, if the grateful task be not permitted to my years or to my state of health." Mackenzie went on to suggest to his confidant, Alexander Johnston that it would, he hoped, "appear to all considerate men, that some leisure and tranquil exclusive application of an arrangement of these [materials] would be at least necessary to one who has now resided thirty-four years in this climate, without the benefits of once going to Europe."[49]

Even at this stage, Mackenzie received little support or sympathy from Company officials, who never gave any indication of their genuine commitment to Mackenzie's historical labors. In the meanwhile, Johnston advocated his friend's cause, calling on Charles Grant, the former chairman of the Court of Directors, to attempt to persuade him of "the great advantage it would secure for Oriental history and literature, were Col. Mackenzie to be allowed by the Directors to come to England upon leave, in order that he might, with the assistance of the different literary characters in Europe, arrange his valuable collection of materials." Grant apparently responded favorably, but did nothing before Johnston learned that Mackenzie had died in Calcutta in 1821, still "without having had leisure to engage in the preparation of any condensed view of his collections."[50]

## Voices in the Archive

The connexion then formed with one person, a native
and a Bramin, was the first step of my introduction
into the portal of Indian knowledge; devoid of any
knowledge of the languages myself, I owe to the
happy genius of this individual, the encouragement
and the means of obtaining what I so long sought. . . .

From the moment of talents of the lamented Boria
were applied, a new avenue to Hindoo knowledge
was opened.
    —Colin Mackenzie, 1817[51]

With Mackenzie's death, we are left with disorder and silence. For not only did Mackenzie fail to prepare a "condensed view" or a "catalogue raisonnée," he wrote little about either the collection itself or his sense of its significance beyond what I have already reported. Most of his publications were, in fact, nothing more than annotated editions of texts translated by his assistants. The only exceptions were a couple of papers on the significance of Jainism in the history of southern India, as well as a long paper submitted at a meeting of the Royal Asiatic Society in April 1815, entitled "View of the principal Political Events that occurred in the Carnatic, from the dissolution of the Ancient Hindoo Government in 1564 till the Mogul Government was established in 1687, on the Conquest of the Capitals of Beejapoor and Golconda; compiled from various authentic Memoirs and Original MSS., collected chiefly within the last ten years, and referred to in the Notes at the bottom of each page."[52] The title alone reveals the emphasis on sources, specifically on their authenticity and originality, as well as his concentration on establishing the chronology and circumstances of the principal political events of southern India's history.

Aside from these few traces, Mackenzie leaves the weight of a voluminous, detailed, and dry official correspondence, which demonstrates his attention to duty and confirms the judgment of the Company in elevating him to positions of seniority in the surveying of colonial India. And he leaves us with a much richer correspondence with the Indian assistants and agents who engaged in the actual work of collection, during the Mysore survey and after. Although Mackenzie had clear ideas about what kinds of materials and texts he wanted, and communicated these ideas in both direct and indirect ways to the people who collected things for him, he was so obsessive a collector that his principal interest sometimes seemed to be sheer accumulation. The collection—its texts, drawings, marginalia, antiquities, and diaries—is thus a sedimentation of myriad voices, some of the most prominent of which are those of the "native establishment" itself. Other voices can be heard in the texts themselves, sometimes ascribed to a village Brahman, an ancient sage, or a regional ruler. Mackenzie's historiographical concerns and modes of collection opened his archive to voices that were rarely heard. But it was Mackenzie's uncertain sense of his historical project—and his lack of training as an Orientalist, no doubt, as well—that ironically allowed other historicities to find a place, however transient, within his historical collection.

For Mackenzie, his principal assistant, Kavelli Venkata Boria, was never merely an informant. The pages of the Mysore survey in particular betray the ubiquitous and pervasive presence of Mackenzie's chief interpreter. Mackenzie met Boria in 1796, and quickly recognized the young man's brilliance as well as his potential importance to his own project of discovering India. Mackenzie wrote that Boria, "of the quickest genious and disposition," possessed "that conciliatory turn of mind that soon reconciled all sects and all tribes to the course of inquiry followed with these surveys."[53] In petitioning for government subvention of his research efforts in the Mysore survey, Mackenzie noted that Boria had formidable linguistic skills, with command of Tamil, Telugu, Kanarese, and Sanskrit, as well as considerable skill in deciphering medieval inscriptional scripts and grammars.[54] As Mackenzie's chief interpreter, he worked to collect texts, traditions, and materials of diverse kinds and also to explain and translate their contents. He prepared most of the papers on the Northern Parganas, including an extensive "Memoir on the mode of management observed in the Ballaghaat," in addition to his collections and translations "confirmed by such other evidence as leaves little room of doubt."[55] By the time of his untimely death in 1803—Boria was still a young man who had been only seven years in Mackenzie's service—he had recruited and trained an establishment of learned Brahmans, including two of his brothers and various relations and acquaintances, thereby institutionalizing what became Mackenzie's lifelong project of "collecting" India. Time after time Mackenzie professed that it was only through the merits and assiduity of his "native establishment" that he was able "to engage in those Researches into the nature and state of the country which have enabled me to collect the materials on this undertaking."[56]

Mackenzie's assistants were mostly Brahmans, although he employed a number of Christians and at least one Jain. Most research enquiries began by finding local Brahmans, as when Nitala Naina "privately made friendship with one of the learned Bramin there named Soobausaustry who had a large library of holy and pious books. . . . I gave him a one rupee present."[57] C. Appavoo wrote in a report of 1817 that "Today many Brahmans and learned people were collected by the head Hicharadaur at Caspa in Arcot agreeable to the directions of the Collector's people. They gave me many informations respecting Arcot." In another report, C. V. Ram wrote: "I was enquiring for the history of Cacati Rajaloo, who are ruled at Aunomacondah and Vorungale, I understand there was a aged learned Bramin there who knows the History of the ancient kings of the Cacati Rajaloo, who has a library of cadjan books, as it is impossible to appear myself to him at his house, I was intending to make friendship with him thro the means of his acquaintance. . . . I requested him to order the old Brahmin to give me any information of the former kings of the country, and explain me the difficult inscriptions." The subsequent information in the report was then based almost exclusively on the words of the old Brahman.[58]

Mackenzie's assistants typically reported material they collected with little editorial comment, relieved, perhaps, that they were able to document their own productive labor. Although the assistants distinguished material on the basis of whether it was copied from a book, told by a local Brahman, or written down from the remarks of a village headman or chief, only rarely did they make the kinds of comments made by British observers regarding the promiscuous admixture of "historical" and fabulous" materials. More frequently, moral tales, extraordinary stories of the exploits of kings and heroes, and attempts to date dynasties were strung together in single narratives, with occasional asides about the difficulty of collecting information. Editorial comments reflecting modern concerns about textual genre and empirical truth were made more often at the point that certain texts were copied and translated, for example when the rough translations and texts from the field were put together in a set of bound volumes during the final years of Mackenzie's life under his direct supervision.

During the first two decades of the nineteenth century, Mackenzie's assistants traveled widely throughout peninsular India, collecting, copying, and translating materials, all the while corresponding regularly with Lutchmia, who had replaced his brother Boria as Mackenzie's chief assistant after Boria's death.[59] Letters to Lutchmia often included lists of material, long synopses of particular traditions and histories, and extensive itineraries and accounts of the successes and failures of individual attempts to collect material. The letters frequently sought additional authority to enable the assistants to persuade local people to allow them access to various forms of knowledge. In areas not under direct British rule, such as Travancore, Mackenzie's men had to use their wits. According to C. Appavoo: "Mr. Ward told Mr. Turnbull that he cannot get any order to procure the histories etc. in this country. Coll. Munro told him he cannot give order to the country people to furnish any informations, but the servants may make friendships with the country people and get the old accounts of the Rajahs."[60] But in adjacent parts of British India, Thomas Munro, an influential civil servant who went on to become governor of Madras, gave written orders to the surveyors for the managers of each district, requesting their assistance. In other areas, Mackenzie's men had frequently to turn to the local British collector. When "Seenevassiah" (Srinivas Aiyar) journeyed to Tanjavur in 1809, he began copying temple inscriptions only to be told by the temple priest that he must stop: "then the Bramin of the Pagoda they prevented me and told me that they want order of the Circar, therefore next day I went to the Cachary at Caroong Cooly and acquainted with the Collector Mr. Hide, who told me now you may go, they do not prevent you, accordingly I went afternoon to the pagoda and seen all the inscriptions." Most assistants reported that before they copied inscriptions or local texts they attempted to use their own letters from Mackenzie to procure letters from the local collector. Mackenzie himself was only known in some places, and could only have authority attached to his name through the confirmation of locally known British officials.

When British authority was not absolute, there were frequent difficulties, such as those encountered by C. V. Ram, who wrote that when he was in the zamin of Calastry, he was copying certain inscriptions in the large temple, but "after we copied three inscriptions the Rajah sent for us and directed us not to copy any more stone inscriptions with an intention of exposing the secrets of their samasthanam [kingdom]."[61] "Narrain Row" (Narain Rao) wrote of similar difficulties in his visit to "Gudwall." In this case, he went directly to the local zamindar to present his credentials: a Persian letter from Mackenzie. The dewan, Narrain Row reports, "enquired of me what is the use of this books Tarraureeks and Vumshavaley [chronicles and genealogies], I replied him, My Master is very desirous of knowing the curious history of the old king for that I came here." The raja responded by preparing a letter for Mackenzie and offering Narrain Row the customary honor of betel nut.[62] He then escorted him out of the kingdom. Alas, it was not always so easy to dispense with the British.

Despite such evidence of vitality and resistance, I do not mean to suggest that the texts that were being collected and produced in the "field" were authentic survivals of a pre-British sociology of knowledge, even as they participated in complex power-knowledge relations well outside the purview of specific colonial concerns. Appavoo, one of Mackenzie's Christian assistants, was at times forthcoming about attempts by Brahmans to suppress certain kinds of local traditions: "Here, by the Bramins, the history of Jainas and Cooroombers are much concealed. As there is not a single learned Jaina and Cooroomber in the Jaghere, their written histories are very rare with the exception of some informations concerning them. . . . As Brahmans and other nations bear a great enmity at them, many refuse to give me such information in my route." And yet, despite this kind of suspicion, the collection is replete with vamcavali and other texts conveying heroic legacies of the old regime that hardly reflect what one might assume to be a Brahman preoccupation with only Sanskritic texts and traditions. Nevertheless, when local documents were collected, authority and authorship were not only affected by the interests of local agents—both the learned Brahmans who were contacted and Mackenzie's assistants who contacted them—but transferred from local to colonial contexts. The different voices, agencies, and modes of authorization that were implicated in the production of the archive became muffled and then lost once they inhabited the new colonial archive. Distinctions between types of texts (such as texts that derived from ancient authorship or the hastily transcribed remarks of a local source) and concerns about the use value of knowledge (how textual knowledge might be used to deauthorize and delegitimate), became blurred and increasingly dissolved at each stage of the collection, transcription, textualization, translation, and canonization of the archive. And the role of Mackenzie's assistants became relegated to the position of technical mediation; the diaries and letters were rarely if ever recopied and collated with the documents they accompanied. Indeed, the East India Company saw little reason other than a respect for Mackenzie's oft-expressed concerns for the welfare of his staff to maintain any of his assistants after his death. A number of Mackenzie's staff were pensioned off after Mackenzie's move to Calcutta in 1818. Lutchmia was kept on, in charge of a small residual staff, but his role was significantly reduced after Mackenzie died.

## Silence of the Archive

> For what else is this collection but a disorder to which
> habit has accommodated itself to such an extent that
> it can appear as order.
> —Walter Benjamin[63]

The collection of colonized voices in a colonial archive undermined both Mackenzie's idiosyncratic project and our capacity to hear the voices themselves any longer.[64] In the catalogues assembled by Wilson and then Taylor, and even more in the official administrative uses of and references to the Mackenzie Collection later in the century, the voices become anonymous footnotes for a new kind of colonial knowledge. Our attempt to specify and sort these voices is further frustrated by the fact that the textual traditions represented in the archive have, despite Mackenzie's own eclectic historiographical sensibility, been seen as subversive of the standards of authority, authorship, and authenticity that have motivated the last two hundred years of Western textual scholarship. The archive now known as the Mackenzie Collection houses far more than any original voices that survive from an earlier regime; it has also been the depository for Wilson's peculiar and impatient interest, more generalized Orientalist contempt, and the monumental incompetence of the Reverend William Taylor, the man who was appointed to succeed Wilson. Colonized voices have been written over even where they were most deeply inscribed in the early archives of colonial knowledge.

As much as Mackenzie was clearly an instrument of British imperialism in India, as T. V. Mahalingam so succinctly put it, his life and his collection stand at a bit of an angle to many aspects of early colonial rule. Mackenzie was not alone in his historical interests: they were certainly shared by Wilks, Malcolm, Elphinstone, Raffles, and many other British officials (many of them from Scotland) of the late eighteenth and early nineteenth centuries. But unlike these other men, Mackenzie was unable to produce a master historical narrative of his own, and he set up an apparatus of collection that turned up works even these colonial historians found difficult to esteem. The collection's first and most eminent bibliographer, H. H. Wilson, became progressively less interested in Mackenzie's project the more he worked on it, and cast doubt on the historical value of many of the texts. Bentinck's fears were almost realized when Wilson came close to abandoning the project before its completion. And the Company directors complained about the fact that they had been presented as a fait accompli with the payment of 10,000 pounds to Mackenzie's widow for the entire collection shortly after the colonel's death. They noted that the portion of materials they had seen "does not lead us to form any very favourable opinion of the value of the remainder."[65] The maps remained as proud documents of British conquest, and it is no accident that Mackenzie's name receives its fullest and most unambiguous praise in the histories of the Survey of India. But the texts—the fabulous myths, confused chronicles, and chaotic epistles from his collectors, with all that they tell us about the collisions of context and meaning, power and knowledge—have gathered far more dust than ink.

Concerns by men such as Bentinck and Johnston about Mackenzie's silence had progressively fewer echoes in the subsequent history of his collection. Wilson's catalogue was, as we have seen, ambivalent about the worth of the collection. As soon as Wilson completed his initial catalogue, published in 1828, he dropped the project completely. When Mackenzie's chief assistant, Kavelli Venkata Lutchmia, applied to the Madras division of the Asiatic Society to carry on Mackenzie's work of collection and cataloguing after the Master's death, the society rejected the application on the grounds that no "Oriental" would be able to do the managerial and critical work necessary to oversee such a project. According to the head of the Asiatic Society of Bengal, James Prinsep, "Such an extensive scheme would need the control of a master head, accustomed to generalization, and capable of estimating the value and drift of inscriptional and literary evidence. The qualifications of Cavelly Venkata [sic] for such an office, judging of them by his 'abstract,' or indeed of any native, could hardly be pronounced equal to such a task, however useful they may prove as auxillaries in such a train of research."[66] Instead, they hired Taylor, a missionary in Madras and self-professed Orientalist, who can only be judged, even in nineteenth-century colonial terms, as at best a poor scholar and more accurately as an eccentric and incompetent antiquarian.

The history of the Mackenzie Collection thus marks the emergence of a new epistemic regime, in which the enterprise of textual scholarship became progressively linked to the conventions and certainties of a British colonial sociology of India. This history of silence also tells the story of the dramatic appropriation of Indian voices, meanings, and histories by colonial knowledge. Even Mackenzie's impressive reticence in glossing and cataloguing his own collection became the pretext for the marginalization of the native scholars Mackenzie had himself seen as so instrumental in his project. Mackenzie's voice too was lost, both in his reticence and in the subsequent uses to which his life was put. In one of Mackenzie's drawings entitled "A Company Officer about to sketch a ruined temple, perhaps at Vijayanagar," Mackenzie provides, however, his own sense of his project, depicting himself in the act of record-ing.[67] In the center of the drawing stands a single structure, a temple shrine that looks like a free-standing and impressive *vimana*. The temple tower is ruined, however; the exquisite carving on all sides of the temple visibly suggests an abundance of aesthetic skill and energy, but now the temple has been left to ruin, and a single tree grows out of the center of the tower where once the deity was housed. The tree and its branches have rent the stone structure, which looks as if it is soon to collapse completely under the strain of nature's resur-gent victory over culture. At the side of the drawing a number of native assis-tants are carrying a portfolio, ink, and a chair; in front of them is a British officer in a blue coat. The officer has come to draw the ruined temple, to preserve stone on paper, to collect and protect what is being lost to nature and its seemingly inexorable process of decay.

Mackenzie was indeed enamoured of the Hindu past, seeking to recover it through his collections and, when appropriate, to sketch it before it crumbled. But herein is the paradox of his presence (and indeed of his history). On the one hand, the massive documentation of Mackenzie's empirical project was carried out with as little mediation as possible: Mackenzie deferred the writing of catalogs and annotations in favor of the need to continue collecting. On the other, Mackenzie's very absence works to legitimize his presence. The colo-nial assumption that India's histories and traditions would soon disappear if allowed to follow their natural course reminds us of the fundamental conceit of colonial representation, the notion that without Mackenzie's active efforts the process of recovery and transcription—representation itself—could not take place. Thus it is that only in his drawings does Mackenzie allow himself to appear. But he is there all along, and even his earnest antiquarian attention to historical collection works to prepare the way for the enormous condescen-sion of later colonial efforts to know India.

# *Six*

## The Imperial Archive: Colonial Knowledge and Colonial Rule

> I am a man who can recognize an unnamed town by
> its skeletal shape on a map. . . . So I knew their place
> before I crashed among them, knew when Alexander
> had traversed it in an earlier age for this cause or that
> greed. I knew the customs of nomads besotted by silk
> or wells. When I was lost among them, unsure of
> where I was, all I needed was the name of a small
> ridge, a local custom, a cell of this historical animal,
> and the map of the world would slide into place.
> —Michael Ondaatje, *The English Patient*

> It is the State which first presents subject-matter
> that is not only adapted to the prose of History, but
> involves the production of such history in the very
> progress of its own being.
> —G.W.F. Hegel, *The Philosophy of History*

### Archival Ruminations

The archive, that primary site of state monumentality, is the very institution that canonizes, crystallizes, and classifies the knowledge required by the state even as it makes this knowledge available to subsequent generations in the cultural form of a neutral repository of the past. Colonial governmentality was not merely dependent on knowledge, it was also embedded in the forms of knowledge that provided the basis for the principal practices of the colonial state. Colonial conquest made possible (even as it was made possible by) the marking of new territories with the dimensions and coordinates of colonial interest. Resources were converted into colonial commodities through a conquest based as much on knowledge as on military success. But the conquest of knowledge ran far deeper than the mere conquests of armies, for it was in the inscription of colonized spaces that colonial power was translated into useable forms of knowledge. Colonial conquest was about the production of an archive of (and for) rule. This was not an archive that was imagined as the basis for a national history, for it was only designed to reap the rewards and to tell tales of imperial interest.

Early imperial interest in India was principally concerned with commodities for trade, though the limited resources of northern Europe meant that England could only trade bullion, secured from the legacies of Spanish imperium in the new world, for the textiles, spices, and other riches of the subcontinent. Trade required not only exchange but also translation, as tantalizing in its promise of wealth as it seemed tainted by its dependence on mediation. Imperial interest in controlling the terms of trade led inexorably to imperial expansion of the theater of trade itself, from forts to factories, and then from the establishment of port cities to the negotiation of rights to collect revenue in territories surrounding those ports.[1] Even as Clive and Hastings made themselves rich nabobs by engaging in "private" trade through their "public" positions, the East India Company became increasingly restless, seeking a monopoly not only in relation to other imperial interests (within Britain and across Europe) but also to the private interests of its own servants. The Company might have professed that it was no more than a trading company, but by 1757 its enmity with the French, its alliances with some local rulers and its wars against others, and its interest in expanding trade made it look very like a full-scale imperial presence. By the end of the century, with the consolidation of the spoils of Plassey, the taming of Awadh and Arcot, the relentless wars against the southern chiefs (and even the failed efforts against the Marathas), and the final defeat of Tipu Sultan, the trading company had turned into a colonial state.

With the Regulating Act of 1784, the colonial state that was once a trading company was reined in by Parliament and brought under the direction of the "Board of Control." And it had been charged with the establishment of legitimate procedures for the delineation of revenue and property rights, on the basis of which it was to support itself not from private trade but rather from the collection of revenue. Trade was not unimportant—and the Company was ever in search of new commodities and resources it could collect on favorable terms and export for massive profit—but it became an activity of an enterprise that increasingly took on a life of its own. As the Company became like a state— albeit one at the service of and controlled by political interests in England—it developed a bureaucratic form and rationality that gave to land revenue a salience that even trade no longer had. The land that had been conquered by the military and political victories of eighteenth-century statecraft had now to be surveyed, mapped, and organized in relation to a new form of imperial interest. This interest was coded historically, for not only did the state need to assume the claims of previous (or for that matter present) rulers to own either the land itself or the right to its produce, it also needed to legitimate its assumption of these claims through historical precedent and bureaucratic management. And the state needed to fill its coffers without fomenting either revolution or massive chaos, and without occasioning the outrage of new Burkes in distant England who might conceive the greedy appropriations of the state as a new form of private corruption.

The turn of the century, then, was a time not only of major transformation but also of frenetic contradiction. Mackenzie's historical interests were rapidly overtaken by those of a new generation of colonial bureaucrats. As it turned out, Thomas Munro, the contemporary and good friend of Mackenzie who designed the "ryotwari" settlement of Madras presidency, became far more important for the production of a colonial archive than Mackenzie and his vast collection.[2] This new archive buried with astonishing rapidity the useless detritus of the age of conquest, leaving eighteenth-century history (and its historians) behind in several related senses.

## Land Is to Tax

Unsurprisingly, what survives at the center of the new colonial archive are not the myriad records and manuscripts collected by Mackenzie but rather the land records that became so fundamental to the debates over land tenure and settlement in the initial years of British rule.[3] These documents—used so extensively by historians of agrarian relations—turn out to be far more than assessments of different land parcels and their potential (or actual) productivity. They were, rather, interventions in the way the colonial state worked to constitute land relations as the basis of the state's ultimate right of ownership and, more generally, delineated relationships between state and society.

The early colonial state was chiefly an agrarian state that used various representations of "oriental despotism" to justify its legitimacy and fortify its claims to ultimate power through the bureaucratic regulation of landed property. Building on arguments between those who held that the East India Company was inheriting the king's right of ownership over all property, and those who used a Ricardian theory of rent to claim for the Company the right to set revenue rates and collect taxes as fundamental to the custodial project of the state, the British gradually established a state bureaucracy that focused primarily on land revenue. Decisions about whether the bureaucracy should accord proprietary rights to landlords (*zamindars*), village brotherhoods, or principal cultivators (*ryots*) became critical interventions in the relationship between state and society, at the same time that these decisions both produced and were produced by a variety of different histories of India that were important parts of early colonial rhetorics of rule.

When I first waded through settlement land records, I did so to determine the nature of agrarian relations in different parts of southern India, as well as to assess arguments made by different administrators about the nature of the precolonial village community. The arguments were complex and robustly documented, and always assumed that historical forms were necessary predicates for colonial policies. Intellectual histories of some of the key players of the period by historians such as Ranajit Guha, Eric Stokes, and Burton Stein have revealed how integral historical argument was to political ambition and European experience. Cornwallis was influenced by the physiocrats and driven by his ambition to recreate in India the authority and position of the landed gentry in Britain (already under major assault and in considerable defensiveness, given the events of the revolution in France); Munro was captured by Burkean rhetorics of paternalistic responsibility and a Scottish sense of the folk heroism of the yeoman cultivator; Elphinstone was enamored by Bentham but still in favor of local systems of administration based on the experience of those most grounded in Indian affairs. The discrete land records—with their plenitude of facticity—reflected these genealogies and policies, and are the result of the documentation project of the early colonial state around matters of land and revenue. Indeed, from the swashbuckling time of Clive and Hastings to the events of the Great Rebellion of 1857, conquest was the pretext not only for political control but also for revenue collection. As surely as the mercantilist logic of imperial trade yielded to the bureaucratic imperatives of the imperial state, land became what the colonial state was all about.

Edmund Burke had not only called Hastings to account during the years he held impeachment hearings, he had also questioned the very foundations of the British imperial presence in India. Part of the problem was that the British presence was not in fact imperial; it was based instead on the activities and provenance of a trading company that had managed to secure a monopoly but nothing like a charter that would justify imperial expansion across the Indian subcontinent. When Warren Hastings became governor-general of India in 1774, the position of the Company was still precarious. By making alliances with rival factions in succession disputes, choosing battles to fight in which there were high probabilities of success, and extorting massive sums of money from dependant allies, Hastings was able to secure extraordinary territorial gains. His methods were not always scrupulous; he financed his war efforts by the same combination of plunder and tax farming used by the Marathas and Mughal emissaries of the time. It is small wonder that Hastings's brilliant expansionary efforts became vulnerable to parliamentary review, which under siege by Burke's rhetorical attacks quickly seized upon both the irregularity of Hasting's successful politics and the fact that he conducted them on behalf of a trading company that had no authorization for even the most tentative imperial ambition. But there was far too much profit from the lucrative textile trade, and far too many connections between Company directors and political interests, to suspend the India operations altogether. The Pitt Act of 1784 established a Board of Control in London that was supposed to oversee the actions of the governor-general, and gave voice to concerns in Parliament that the Company either clean up its business or cede its private monopoly. And when Lord Cornwallis—who followed up his disgrace in North America with an impressive military victory against Tipu Sultan in 1792—established the Bengal Permanent Settlement in 1793, he did so in concert with a major reform in which Company servants were paid much higher wages in return for further discouragement against engaging in private trade.

The Permanent Settlement was the brainchild of Philip Francis, a lifelong foe of Warren Hastings. Hastings was by this time in disgrace, however much his actions in India had made it possible in the end for Francis, Shore, and Cornwallis to propose the comprehensive land settlements represented by the 1793 reform. Indeed, Hastings had skillfully balanced the Mughals, along with the nizams of Awadh and Hyderabad, against the Marathas and the rising power of the Mysoreans. But although he had set the stage for the Permanent Settlement by bringing Bengal under nominal British control during his rule, and had prepared the way for Britain's dominance on the subcontinent by the last decade of the eighteenth century, the Permanent Settlement was an attempt to erase Hastings's legacy in more ways than one. As formulated initially by Francis and implemented by Cornwallis, it was meant to regularize Company revenues through a steady tax rather than by extortion, to normalize administration by setting high public standards for the service of Company officers, and to create a loyal elite based on landed property rather than military alliance, by restoring the putatively traditional landholders to their rightful position. The erasure of Britain's history of Indian conquest began in the embarrassment around the aggressive expansion of Hastings, but soon took a different form under the leadership of Cornwallis, who was intent on reproducing the landed gentry of England, in a dramatic enunciation of imperial policy that seemed a denial of the entrepreneurial origins of Indian empire even as it sought to stabilize a new kind of Indian elite. But Cornwallis was also expressing his frustration about the task of knowing, surveilling, and administering India. The Permanent Settlement was in part the result of British inability to get a handle on the actual levels of production in agrarian tracts as well as on the best way to adjudicate competing claims for local-level proprietorship, tenurial right, and revenue relief. Given this level of uncertainty, it is perhaps no surprise that the settlement in fact led to many estate auctions and a high turnover in the rural elite, at least in the short term.[4] And although Francis had justified the settlement by his theory that control over profits would motivate Indian landlords to improve their properties in systematic ways, once inflation and increased agrarian productivity conspired to increase profit, most landlords became absentee, using their estates to support other pursuits in Calcutta rather than reinvesting money and energy in agrarian management.

The Permanent Settlement was bold and astonishingly simple. It entailed setting a single amount of tax for each estate that would remain the same in perpetuity, with each contracting zamindar free to alienate proprietary title and, by implication, the fixed revenue obligation. Property was introduced along with a fixed revenue demand, though the right of property was vested at a level that sometimes mimicked a feudal structure of old, and at the very least encouraged the maintenance of large estates with tenurial relations and agrarian management under the centralized control of estate managers. Francis and Cornwallis assumed that many of the assets of the estates were hidden from view, and that in any case the application of enlightened managerial attention would bring new profits to light in short order, and so the revenue demand was set at high levels. After all, once fixed it could not be changed. But the colonial interest in fixing agrarian structures and property relations misfired in serious respects. Not only were many of the contracting zamindars hardly representative of the landed aristocracy Cornwallis had hoped to identify and encourage but a great many zamindars defaulted on their revenue payments, sending virtually half of the estates to the auction block within the first twenty-five years of the settlement. In Bengal, the landed gentry turned out to be as "open," and as much part of a larger history of social transformation, as Lawrence Stone has argued was the case for the landed gentry in seventeenth- and eighteenth-century England.[5]

Despite its detractors, the Permanent Settlement was such a compelling idea, and so alleviated British anxiety about having first to determine and then to manage the microlevel details of agrarian production, that it seemed to many the only way to look after, and collect the necessary funds from, the areas over which the Company assumed direct control.[6] But as useful as the settlement was for the transition from trading company to company state, it began to incur criticism from Company officers who worked in localities where they steadily took on more direct control over agrarian affairs.[7] Among these British officers was Thomas Munro, who along with his initial supervisor Alexander Read had already begun to experiment with making direct settlements with cultivators as early as the mid-1790s. Nevertheless, the idea of the permanent settlement was still compelling, particularly in those areas where powerful chiefs—palaiyakarars as well as zamindars—made the threat of potential resistance as worrying as the difficulties that might accompany the acquisition of reliable information on agrarian matters within the countryside. Accordingly, in 1802 approximately one-third of Madras presidency was, in fact, settled under Cornwallis rules, establishing "loyal" as well as particularly powerful chiefs as the Madras version of Cornwallis gentry. But the Madras settlement tended to be in areas that were not nearly as productive, or central to the agrarian economy, as had been the case in Bengal, and was frequently contracted with local chiefs who had been loyal supporters of Company rule. Indeed, the zamindari settlement was effected in areas that had managed substantially to escape a steady process of encroachment and agrarian conversion under the combined forces of the Tanjore Marathas, the Mughal emissaries in Arcot and Hyderabad, and the especially aggressive bureaucratic policies of Haidar Ali and Tipu Sultan. The agriculturally rich riverine and deltaic regions of the Tamil and Andhra plain were kept for further revenue experimentation, and soon succumbed to the changing character of imperial rule, first enabled by the military victories over Tipu Sultan and the French, and then as a part of the general transformation of the Company state into a bureaucratic enterprise of a very different sort than that imagined even by Burke in his most imaginative renderings of the future of the British imperial presence in India.

Thomas Munro played a particularly critical role in this shift of British opinion and administration. Credited as he is with the invention of the ryotwari system, which meant "direct" revenue settlements with the cultivators, he in fact embodied in his Indian career some of the primary transformations in British rule from the late eighteenth to the early nineteenth centuries. He went to India in 1780 as a military man and spent his first four years in warfare against Haidar Ali of Mysore, not at first with any success. It was in part this early experience that made him so wary of the threat to British interests represented by Haidar Ali, and later his son Tipu Sultan. It certainly set a theme for his Indian career, for when he became a Company administrator, entrusted with the task of settling the Baramahal, Kanara, and then the Ceded Districts, he found himself often following in Tipu Sultan's footsteps. Indeed, in these assignments he often carried on Tipu Sultan's efforts to suppress the power of the palaiyakarars and to introduce in its stead regularized bureaucratic procedures designed for civil administration and revenue collection. In Baramahal he experimented with annual and individual settlements and, despite his expressed concern for the local cultivator, he set the revenue rates at an exorbitant level. In Kanara, where joint village arrangements had been even more transformed by Tipu Sultan's interventions, he developed an historical theory to justify his reliance on the idea of individual private property. And yet he also recommended that provisional settlements be made for at least five years to assure the Company that they would set their assessments on the basis of an adequate understanding of agricultural assets. In the meanwhile, he recommended lower assessments than elsewhere, no doubt in part reflecting the residual power of local interests, chiefs, and palaiyakarars prominent among them. Curiously, at the very moment that he took full responsibility for a revenue settlement of his own, he stood on considerably shakier ground than he had in Baramahal, where the palaiyakarars had already been significantly displaced and village institutions were in a stronger condition. Successful nevertheless, he was sent to the much vaster Ceded Districts in October of 1800 with the task of settling a region that posed even greater difficulties to the Madras government, which was financially in a bad way after the military campaigns of the previous decade and politically stressed by the rapidly escalating administrative responsibilities that were part of its new charge.[8]

Munro managed to pursue an aggressive policy towards the many active palaiyakarars who remained in positions of local power. He no sooner reduced many of them to pensioners than he managed to coopt them by the provision of inam benefits for those who promised loyalty.[9] Munro was frequently attacked by those who felt that he was too harsh on local chiefs—a symptom in part of his military rather than civilian background—but it was his very success in establishing local order and generating considerable revenue that convinced even his detractors and set the stage for his successful advancement of the ryotwari cause. Once again he flew in the face of considerable local evidence that suggested the institutional integrity of the village as a revenue unit, and selected dominant cultivators for proprietary title, fashioning a new system based on the isolation of elite farmers for a steadily escalating revenue demand.[10] Although he justified his policies with historical argument and precedent, he developed a method of revenue collection and local administration that was successful in large part because of a growing Utilitarian sentiment in Madras and London, as well as his evident success in raising cash and restoring order. Munro returned to England in 1807, to find a wife and advance his political fortunes. After an uncertain wait for a few years, he was vindicated when the Fifth Report of 1812, written to advise Parliament about the state of administration in India as part of the Charter Renewal debate of 1813, chose the ryotwari scheme as the revenue method of highest regard.[11] Munro returned to India in 1814 to oversee the revision of judicial administration in Madras, and went on to play a major role in the military victory against the Marathas in 1818, ultimately rising to the position of governor of Madras in 1819. Although his ascendency has been generally understood in terms of the rise of a certain kind of administrative paternalism and the canonical ryotwari system of revenue collection, I would emphasize instead the extent to which Munro played a major role in the establishment of the Company as a bureaucratic state system, which during these years developed extraordinary confidence in its capacity to know, to regulate, and to profit from local social forms. And although Munro justified his new approach through an egalitarian rhetoric that was posed against the oligarchic regime of Cornwallis in years past, the ryotwari system aided both the radical extension of Company power into the Indian countryside and the introduction of new forms of capitalist social and economic relations.

    In order for Munro's ryotwari system to work, the Company had to collect massive amounts of local information, and in the process it depended on local accountants and assistants to a greater extent than ever before. The zamindari system had been an outgrowth of an older system of tributary relations, even as it reflected a provisional compromise with the landed structures already in place. The ryotwari system—however much it was justified by resort to historical precedent—represented an unprecedented level of state governmentality, an explicit effort to engineer a new kind of political and economic elite and to micromanage a local-level agrarian economy. It involved not just the identification of individual cultivators and the adjudication of different claims to local landholding but also the periodic assessment of individual lands, rated according to soil classification, irrigational resources, and other factors that affected production such as climate, topography, and so on. Munro's success-ful advocacy, and implementation, of this system was part of a larger transfor-mation in the authoritative production of information, an imperial archive that was expanding rapidly in the early years of the nineteenth century. It was an archive that had as its principal raison d'être the collection of revenue. Accord-ingly, Munro's judicial reforms, intended as they were to unite the roles of the magistrate and the collector, organized local government within the guiding framework of a revenue state, and conferred judicial authority on those charged with the administration of the revenue system.

Munro's style of local government was both utilitarian and paternalistic, and set the stage as well for Elphinstone's pragmatic appropriation of Peshwai precedent to fashion a colonial state in western India after the defeat of the Marathas in 1818. In the colonial setting, bureaucratic state forms developed in order to enlarge the coffers of the state, balancing exploitation against po-tential rebellion by the careful manipulation of local interests and newly em-powered elites. The state forms were more intrusive and interventionist than their rhetoric made them out to be; they were also more closely wedded to colonial forms of domination than could have been possible in a metropolitan politics that witnessed at this very time new political movements and the be-ginning of serious pressure for increasing democratization, in the wake of the French Revolution. Even as the forms of state governmentality were estab-lished through the mechanisms of a revenue bureaucracy, Munro's paternalism was substituted for sovereignty and was designed to justify the transformation of the power of the colonial state.

This, then, was the emerging context in which the British state sought to know more about the social structure as well as the productive resources of the Indian countryside. This area was expanding in extent for the British by leaps and bounds, given the defeat first of Tipu Sultan and then of the Marathas, as well as the progressive isolation of the nawab of Arcot and later the nizam of Hyderabad. Officials such as Mackenzie and Buchanan had developed differ-ent forms of the survey in Mysore, where princely rule meant a fixed tribute rather than a direct revenue system and potential resources would only have tangential value. But the new generation of government servants under Munro and men like him held revenue matters as the major activity of the state and the principal purpose of collecting information. Land records of the time are punc-tuated by periodic revenue accounts that systematize new levels of detail about matters related to agricultural production. Whereas Buchanan had been chided for being too prolix in his descriptive memoir of Mysore, new surveys were increasingly statistical, constructed for ready comparison and quick account-ability. It is instructive that by the end of the first decade of the nineteenth century, when Buchanan was commissioned to undertake a new survey of the districts of Bengal and Bihar, he was himself engaged in a very different kind of survey, with extensive tables and classificatory rubrics used precisely to allow a statistical comparison across time and space for immediate administrative consultation.[12] Mackenzie's scrupulously collected and translated manuscripts concerning the histories of villages, localities, temples, kingdoms, and chiefly families might have been seen as of great (at least potential) value in the climate of the zamindari settlement and in the context of an early colonial state that was still principally concerned with identifying the proper points of mediation. But despite Munro's considerable personal support of Mackenzie's project—based in large part on his own extensive historical interest in the past of local social, political, and economic institutions—the system ushered in by Munro made this kind of information seem increasingly antiquarian. In retrospect, it should come as no surprise that Mackenzie's collection fell through the cracks of the congealing sense of a colonial archive.

## Caste and the Colonial Archive

But what did caste have to do with this new informational regime or, to put the matter more directly, how did notions of caste change in relationship to it? Very little, indeed. When Buchanan was commissioned to undertake his survey of Mysore in 1800, caste as such was not even mentioned. Instead, he was asked, among many other things, to take into account that "The different sects and tribes of which the body of the people is composed will merit your observance; you will likewise note whatever may appear to us worthy of remark in their laws and customs, and state with as much accuracy as may be in your power the nature of their common usages in matters of personal traffic at their markets their weights and measures the exchange of money and the currency amongst the lower order of people and such matters in respect to their police as may seem to you to have immediate or particular tendency towards the protection, security, and comfort of the lower orders of the people."[13] Buchanan's journal makes many mentions of Brahmans, in large part because Brahmans were contacted on a regular basis by him for information regarding the histories and customs of particular places. As was the case for Mackenzie as well, Brahmans were widely accepted as the local literati, and even when they were not the specific objects of inquiry, they were referred to by others as those who could provide reliable accounts of matters ranging from local history to sociology, from revenue systems to the existence of local texts and records. Buchanan was aware that the Brahmans had prejudices of their own, as for example in a village of Canara, where the Brahmans disparaged the knowledge of the local accountant, a non-Brahman: "These Bahudundas the Vaidika Brahmans hold in great contempt; but as the office of Shanaboga has in numerous instances continued for many generations in the same family, I am inclined to think that from this source much historical information might be procured."[14] Buchanan noted further that the Brahmans in question had contempt even for other Brahmans. But he nevertheless took for granted the role of Brahmans as an intellectual elite, if not always given to the spiritual otherworldliness that characterized them in some contemporaneous literature.

In fact, Buchanan reserved some of his sparing ethnographic comments for Brahmans themselves, struck no doubt by the contradictions attending Brahmanic status. In one case he noted that despite the obsessive endogamy of a particular "nation" of Brahmans and the prohibitions on widow remarriage, the custom of Brahman men was to take a woman who had been dedicated to the temple goddess (as a devadasi) as a "concubine."[15] Buchanan used the term "caste" only for the four varnas, and used terms such as "sect," "tribe," or "nation" for subcastes of a more specific sort. Occasionally he relayed some information about the customs of groups other than Brahmans, though with little regularity, and virtually no anticipation of any kind of colonial ethnographic interest.

In some cases, Buchanan came across statistical statements of the population, known as "kaneh shumareh," sometimes as "caneeshamari." The lists were broken into caste or subcaste groups, counted by number and gender.[16] As Buchanan noted in the case of a list he procured from southern Kanara, "The different castes are detailed in the usual confused manner, with which they are spoken of by the native officers of revenue."[17] In a population of slightly less than 400,000, divided among almost 80,000 households, there were 122 caste groups listed; they were headed by Brahmans but including such miscellaneous caste groups as Kankanies (bankers and traders), Rajputs, Muslims (exclusive of Moplays), Bhats (genealogists and poets), Marathas, Parsis, Garwadys (snake catchers), Reddis (farmers), Jogies (religious mendicants), Julais (weavers), Jettys (wrestlers), and Dhobis (washermen). The list is miscellaneous, mixing recognizeable "caste" names with occupations, religions, ethnicities, and other social categories. As Buchanan indicated here, and as is clear from records elsewhere, these population tables were produced by revenue officials (sometimes Brahmans, sometimes not) who maintained village accounts. Although they consistently break the population down into caste groupings, they do so in ways that suggest the haphazard character of caste as a marker of identity. In Mackenzie's Mysore survey, which includes a more regular compilation of caneeshamari tables than can be found in Buchanan's descriptive memoir, some of the documents attempt to group the long list into caste varna groups (Brahmans and other twice-born, Sudras, and others), but these attempts seem half-hearted and hardly helpful, when they classify the bulk of the population listed as "Soodra."

Once again, however, the Mysore survey gives little evidence of a colonial interest in caste per se, or of the prominence of caste as a social category that demanded attention except insofar as certain Brahmans were clear about declaiming their own distinct, and distinguished, position in society. As Mackenzie noted about the survey, he was successful in collecting materials and documents of different kinds, which concerned such matters as "the genious and manners of the People, their several systems of Government and Religion, and of the predominant causes that influence their sentiments and opinions to this day . . . the tenures of lands, other origins and varieties of assessment of rents and revenues, and the condition of the peoples and the privileges of the different classes."[18] But if Mackenzie collected, and wrote, almost nothing about "caste" aside from the caneeshamaris that were part of his cartographic surveys, it was both because of the relative unimportance of caste in many of the areas of British intervention and interest and because of the much greater salience of other institutions; these extended from the character of property and revenue relations to issues of local governance and political legitimacy. The relative ignorance among the British of caste matters, even concerning Brahmans, was reflected when Francis Ellis, a government servant in Madras and an eminent philologist and scholar, noted with impatience that James Mill, in his large history of British India, had failed to understand what was meant when Brahmans were designated as priests. In fact, as he observed, the lowest category of Brahmans were those who actually served as priests in temples (though those who served in sacerdotal capacities for domestic rituals of Brahman families were of a different category).[19] When H. H. Wilson edited a new edition of Mill's history, he had many occasions to correct fundamental mistakes, as well as to chide Mill for his ignorant contempt of Indian institutions. But even Wilson had little in the way of "ethnographic" knowledge of caste matters. The continued prominence of Dubois's antiquated text was the result of the combined effects of ethnographic inexperience and the fundamental disinterest in what only later became the basis for a colonial sociology of knowledge. For most of the early nineteenth century, Orientalist recodings of the increasingly reified dharma texts of Manu seemed perfectly sufficient to summarize the social forms of the Hindus. What in retrospect is most extraordinary about Wilson's edition of Mill, his substantial disagreements notwithstanding, is that such a volume was possible at all. The Anglicists and the Orientalists might have differed in the ways they viewed India's past and such Indian institutions as caste, but the two both groups shared fundamental assumptions about contemporary Indian society, and neither accumulated much in the way of empirical information about it.

What I have suggested in this chapter, therefore, is that questions of land tenure were seen as far more fundamental to the colonial understanding of rural social structure than empirical knowledge about caste. At most, caste was important in relation to debates over historical forms of land tenure. Occasionally, learned Orientalists made major contributions to this debate, as for example in the substantial treatise by Francis Ellis on *mirasi* rights in southern India. Ellis used a wide variety of historical sources to argue that the Vellalar settlers of Tondaimandalam, the area around Madras, had true property rights in the land, and were not tenants at the will of the king in the mode assumed by those holding the Oriental Despotism thesis.[20] He further argued that they all held land jointly, rotating their use of particular fields annually among the village shareholders. Significantly, his argument was solely textualist, and he used no ethnographic/administrative knowledge to support the claim. Munro argued back in part on the basis of his long experience of life in Indian villages rather than mere textual knowledge about them; he was hostile to this argument, and indeed to any notion that would suggest corporate brotherhoods among or within dominant caste groups. Indeed, Munro argued that although the village community was of primordial importance in Indian civilization, landholders always held their land directly from the state, except during moments of extreme disruption, such as when Tipu Sultan appropriated local land rights. Munro was moved most by the needs of his own ryotwari proposals. When he argued that the Indian state had been oppressive, and had engaged in excessive and capricious taxation that discouraged security and improvement, he was justifying his own revenue settlement; he was justifying, as well, his vision of a partnership between the colonial state and the dominant peasants, mediated only through a Utilitarian commitment to property. Munro was simply uninterested in caste; it served neither to explain some old system of community landholding nor to justify skepticism about the future consequences of colonial innovations predicated on ideas of individual property in land.

In retrospect, Louis Dumont argued vociferously against early colonial writings on the importance of the village community because of his sense that these writings completely ignored caste.[21] Dumont, for whom community could only be understood in relation to caste and ideas of hierarchy, was deeply concerned that contemporary anthropologists might take too seriously early colonial sources that depicted community in ways dependent on political, economic, and social modes of production and distribution. He was doubtless correct to caution scholars about the romantic character of unhistorical versions of village republics. He was unaware, however, of the extent to which his own interest in caste was dependent upon the emergence of equally romantic epistemological predispositions and an accompanying body of knowledge that was produced only during the late nineteenth century. Early colonial notions of Oriental Despotism and autonomous villages were both wrongheaded and tied to a colonial interest in organizing relations of production around new state systems and regimes; they do reflect, however, the extent to which caste relations were either subordinate to or perhaps embedded in both economic relations within localities and the political organization of relations between agrarian locales and different state units and structures.

When caste *was* singled out for empirical notice, it often appeared in awkward ways. As I have mentioned above, it occasionally appeared in lists called caneeshamaris, another example of which can be seen in the 1823 census of Tirunelveli. The Tirunelveli census provides a population breakdown by caste groups, crudely divided into eight broad categories, in rank order as follows:

Brahmans, Ksatriyas, Sudras connected to the religious establishment, Sudras of different denominations, "Muhamedans," "Christians of different castes," inferior Sudras, and the low castes (or untouchables). These macro categories reflect an uncertain marriage between the varna scale of the *Manu Dharma Sastras* and contemporaneous revenue classifications. These classifications differentiated the broad and largely meaningless group of Sudras into those who were supported by inam benefices and those who had direct revenue relationships with the state; these latter were alongside "Muhamedans" and "Christians of different castes" in the general caste scale (that is, groups placed above only the inferior Sudras and the untouchables). But the categories also make clear the limits of the varna scheme for the empirical reality of social differentiation in the far south. Ksatriyas could barely be found (and the classification of a group such as Goswamy in that group was a major stretch); Vaisyas simply did not exist. Although Brahmans were a discrete, if much subdivided, community, the appellation Sudra had meaning only in the sense of demarcating difference vis-à-vis Brahmans on the one hand and untouchables on the other. The actual subdivisions among Sudras reflect a highly differentiated social landscape, which distinguished "caste" groups such as Vellalars and Mudaliyars, occupational groups such as weavers and potters—among many other kinds of groups—all with territorial affiliations that appear every bit as significant as any other aspect of social difference. The list is not only miscellaneous, it is also unranked within categories, no doubt because of the impossibility of securing any consensus about rank outside of small localities where exchanges both established and reflected at least some of the character of local hierarchy.[22]

There is one fragment in the papers of Colin Mackenzie that sits out of place, a trace of a single ethnographic experiment that one of Mackenzie's assistants during the years of the Mysore survey must have attempted in order to understand the nature of local-level rank. On a single sheet of parchment, a curious list of caste groups was positioned on a grid, marked in such a way as to document the relationship of social rank to food exchange. Those marked N–1 were said to be allowed to eat in the houses of those under which column they are placed, and those with a blank are said to be prohibited from eating in the houses of those under which column they are placed. Anticipating by a century and a half the ethnographic proposals of McKim Marriott, the document demonstrated that within a village setting the principle and practice of food exchange—by which is meant simply whether or not one group will eat food prepared, or offered, by another group—was correlated with social rank, in this case stretching from Lingayats to "Vellauls" to Chetties, Reddys, and Coravurs.[23] What is also interesting (and in agreement with the early interactional proposals of Marriott), however, was the assumption that varna- (or any macro-) level classifications were irrelevant. The "caste" groups were highly localized and heterogeneous, including as they did families of accountants (or Kurnams), and local priests (Pundaram), as well as miscellaneous occupational groups. As in all the other documentation from the early-nineteenth-century, there was still nothing formal, or systematic, in the organization of caste categories.

Despite rare exceptions, most early-nineteenth-century catalogues of caste betray both the uncertain character of caste and the extent to which knowledge about caste was fashioned specifically for colonial interests. This can be clearly seen in one book on caste that was written by another of Mackenzie's assistants, C. V. Ramaswamy, Boria and Lutchmia's younger brother. In 1847, Ramaswamy "compiled" a book entitled "A Digest of the different castes of the southern division of southern India, with descriptions of their habits, customs, etc."[24] The work was specifically "dedicated to the British public of India, by their most obedient and humble servant." Ramaswamy began the book by noting that "According to Hindoo mythology, there were originally created by the God almighty four castes of Hindus who were placed in the land of Bharata Khanda, or India," namely, Brahmans, Ksatriyas, Vaisyas, and Sudras. But, having provided a short synopsis of their "dharmic" duties, he went on to say that it would be most useful for the British to know the actual caste groups with whom they would come into contact while in India. "Trusting that those individuals both European and Native, who may honor my humble undertaking with their patronage, particularly the former, for whom the work is principally intended, may receive that gratification and instruction which it is my anxious desire to impart," Ramaswamy went on to provide portraits, both actual drawings and short literary sketches, of the relevant caste groups. The first such category is "Butler," the second "Dubash" (meaning translator), the third "Cook."

The caste groups of Ramaswamy's book—including such categories as grass cutter and waterman, wine cooler and hookah man, horsekeeper and dog boy, dancing girl and Brahman votary, agriculturalist and accountant—reveal an inventory of service castes that put official British households and their lavish princely scale at the center of the Indian social world. A few nonessential groups were thrown in, for example the town priest and the almanac Brahman, perhaps to provide pleasing subjects for the picturesque drawings that adorn each caste type. But the book is an extraordinary artifact of its time, an archaeological finding that cannot be seen in retrospect as merely idiosyncratic. Ramaswamy was no isolated crank but rather a product of one of the most sophisticated efforts to generate local social information about peninsular India in the early nineteenth century. Although Ramaswamy's Borgesian work sits astride other more "familiar" works, from the Abbé Dubois's ramblings about Brahmanic ritual practices to the statistical lists of maps and early census documents, it sits in such a way as to disturb any effort to reclaim the early colonial period as a time when caste had the same significance that it came to have only a short time later. Caste was not a unitary signifier; there were no uniform understandings about what might be meant by a treatise on caste—or an inclusive list that might compile more than either a high textual view of some abstract order of things, on the one hand, or the actual distribution of highly differentiated social groups in some locality, or specified context such as the British official household, on the other. Caste was as variable as the Indian social world in the early, still tentative grip of colonial knowledge; it was far from being the comprehensive means for specification of the social order or for the interpretation of the cultural cartography of the subcontinent. Caste, as we have come to know it, did not yet exist.

In this context, the varna classificatory scale appeared useful, indeed necessary, for early colonial commentators on Indian society. Since so little was known about caste relations, it must have made eminent sense to fill in the blanks of ethnographic knowledge by the regular rote references to the *Manu Dharma Sastra*, as we observed so often in the accounts narrated in Chapter 2. Although the varna view of caste was not of great significance in most explanatory accounts, it served a variety of purposes and came to occupy a canonic— if only marginally relevant—place in early colonial concerns about Indian society. Thus it was that the accounts of Orientalists and Anglicists alike on the subject of caste seemed very similar, even if the emphases and judgments were as different as their respective views on the merits of Indian civilization. And thus we saw such peculiar sediments as the fragile overlay of varna categories on the territorial, revenue, and microsocial classifications of rural Tirunelveli in the 1823 census referred to above. It was not that the varna system was invented at this time but rather that its utility for explaining Indian social relations as a whole became naturalized. As we shall see, even when varna categories were most threatened by the explosion of empirical knowledge in the late nineteenth century, varna came both to signify all caste relations and to explain them in some ultimate sense.

## Governmentality and the Archive

The early imperial archive, the body of knowledge that was cross-referenced by the convictions of colonial common sense and the exigencies of quotidian state practice and concern, reflects the heavily sedimented remains of British interests in the extraction of revenue from land and agrarian regimes. The colonial state established itself in India first as the source of authority for mercantilist trading monopolies and then as an entity that had to negotiate a double legitimation crisis—in both England and India—in the late eighteenth century. Built on greed and conquest, the colonial state had now to justify itself to the interrogation of Edmund Burke, who set public standards for empire that subjected history to the scrutiny of metropolitan moral codes. Burke brought articles of impeachment against Hastings for what everyone knew was business as usual. In Burke's obsessional litany of Hastings's excess, what was embarrassing was neither Hastings's greed nor his methods so much as his manifest success in making the horrors and the pleasures of empire realizable. In the wake of Burke's attack, a colonial bureaucracy was established to monitor the greed with which all Britons went to India from the late eighteenth century on. Burke shifted the balance of power to the state rather than the mercantile elite, and it was under his scrutiny that the colonial state was born. Colonial rapacity could not be curtailed either by Hastings's recall or the India Act of 1784, however; it could only be bureaucratized through the high-minded rhetoric of the land settlements detailed in this chapter. British rule represented its interest in securing steady revenue through a language of improvement predicated on the rule of property and the benevolent intent of a new "postdespotic" state.

What Burke neglected was the other side of the legitimation crisis. All the talk of improvement notwithstanding, no Indian public was recruited by (or to) the contradictory logic of colonial sovereignty. Colonial governmentality consisted of bureaucracy without sovereignty, or rather a form of sovereignty abstracted from even the most minimal conceits of political representation. Sovereignty was to perform itself through the extension of landed property and state security. As a result, sovereignty was yoked to bureaucracy most conspicuously in the documentation project of the early colonial state, which created an archive that bears the traces of colonial failure even as it pressed down upon the lives of ordinary Indians with a rapacity that could not have been exacted through direct military or even political means without a vastly larger apparatus of colonial rule. Thus colonial knowledge was far more powerful than the colonial state ever was (a very different balance of power from that which existed in metropolitan forms of governmentality); and thus the colonial documentation project encoded British anxiety that rule was always dependent on knowledge, even as it performed that rule through the gathering and application of knowledge. As I have argued throughout the first two parts of this book, the idea of caste was not yet fundamental to either colonial knowledge or rule. But things would change, especially after the Great Rebellion of 1857 and the assumption of direct Crown rule in 1858. In the historical unfolding of colonial governmentality, caste would emerge as of fundamental importance for the colonial struggle to know and to rule India. From the crisis around state security, as well as from the direct challenge to state sovereignty, came the anthropological idea that caste could be seen as the colonized form of civil society that would both substitute for and explain away the problem of political sovereignty. Ethnography became the primary colonial modality of representation, linking politics and epistemology in a tight embrace for the last century of British colonial rule in India.

# Part Three

THE ETHNOGRAPHIC STATE

# Seven

## The Conversion of Caste

### Caste and the Great Rebellion

When V. D. Savarkar wrote his grand history of the Great Rebellion in 1909, he glossed the bloody events following the Meerut mutiny as the first Indian war of independence.[1] The national awakening that grew out of military refusal was an expression for Savarkar of the fundamental injustice of British rule in India. Savarkar wrote of the need for India to attain historical consciousness of itself as a nation, and of the importance of the rebellion for constituting a foundational moment in the emergence of a national history. Savarkar's narrative emphasized the heroic refusal of Indian heroes, ordinary soldiers as well as brave leaders, to accept British domination. He was especially critical of the commonly accepted view that the revolt had little political significance, that it was carried forward merely by the personal vendettas and interests of a few vestiges of an old regime, that indeed it was primarily about Indian concerns over caste and religion voiced in connection with the originary moment of mutiny—concerns that had clearly inflamed the passions of mutineers and rebels alike. He was referring, of course, to the question of the cartridge.

The mutiny—and for that matter the rebellion—began in the haze of alarm occasioned by the introduction of a new Enfield rifle, the cartridges for which were packed in a combination of beef and pork fat and were to be loaded by the use of the mouth as well as the hands.[2] Fears of pollution were heightened by the growing reach and influence of Christian missionaries, for it was widely assumed that pollution would be used as a technique to usher new converts into the fold. In the years before the mutiny, missionaries had been given increasingly free reign within the military as well as elsewhere; for example, Colonel Wheler, commander of the 34th N.I. at Barrackpore, openly preached the gospel to his soldiers. Missionaries had already made clear their frustration that caste was their single most significant obstacle, and spoke of the need to break potential converts of their caste in order to free their souls for possible conversion. Despite the fact that the fat-laden cartridges were speedily withdrawn and sepoys instructed to pack their own cartridges in grease of their choice, their use became the occasion for the first outbreak of resistance in Meerut on May 10, 1857. Eighty-five sepoys who refused the cartridges were placed in irons and sentenced to ten years' imprisonment. Their fellow soldiers rose up in protest, released them, and traveled to Delhi, where they fashioned the dazed and elderly Mughal emperor, Bahadur Shah, as the leader of the revolt. The fall of Delhi was followed by uprisings at many major military stations in the Northwest Provinces and in Awadh, and rebellion steadily grew, continuing through the summer of 1858 before it was finally brutally suppressed and contained by British forces.

Historians have debated the causes and ramifications of the rebellion ever since, in what has ultimately become a referendum on the beneficence of British colonial rule during its first century as well as an explanation for major transformations in the nature of that rule thereafter. Sir Sayyid Ahmad Khan wrote an account of the revolt just months after it was over, making a number of points with extreme care. Although he offered no real sympathy to the rebels, he maintained that there were legitimate issues of grievance that the British needed to understand, despite the absence of any manifest conspiracy. At the same time, he wrote to counter the charge that Indian Muslims were not only responsible but clearly shown by the events of the revolt to be disloyal. Significantly, Sir Sayyid blamed the revolt on ignorance and insensitivity rather than on more fundamental causes. He wrote that "Government has not succeeded in acquainting itself with the daily habits, the modes of thought and of life, and likes, and dislikes, and prejudices of the people." As a result, the government was ignorant not only of local modes of thought and of life but also "of the grievances through which their hearts were becoming estranged." Sir Sayyid was further concerned about the "passing of such laws and regulations and forms of procedure as jarred with the established custom and practice of Hindustan." He seemed particularly alarmed about the role of missionization, suggesting that recent events had made "all men whether ignorant, or well-informed, whether high or low, fe[el] a firm conviction that the English Government was bent on interfering with their religion and with their old established customs." Sir Sayyid noted that missionaries not only began to preach with the sanction of the government, but attacked in "violent and unmeasured language . . . the followers and the holy places of other creeds: annoying, and insulting beyond expression the feelings of those who listened to them."[3] He encouraged greater communication between rulers and ruled, and enjoined the British to pay greater attention to issues of cultural respect. For example, he suggested the institution of state darbars, and the distribution of honors to worthy subjects, as well as far more scrupulous attention to questions of prestige and status among the historically disenfranchised Muslim community.

Sir Sayyid went on to found the first Muslim University (the Muhammedan Anglo-Oriental College) in Aligarh in 1875 and bore in his title the success of at least one of his recommendations to the British; he downplayed the significance of the rebellion because of his own greater concern for reconciliation and reform under British rule.[4] Despite his symptomatic critique of the causes of discontent, he focused in particular on the outbreak of the mutiny around the refusal to bite the greased cartridges, which "did violence to the superstition of the sepoys."[5] In this, he reassured those British commentators who preferred to attribute the revolt solely to reaction and superstition, although his conservatism was apparent in early years after the rebellion even to many British, particularly those who had been participants in the events of 1857–1958, who were aware of the monumentality of Indian disaffection. Nevertheless, his gentle admonishments did not fall on entirely deaf ears. Sir Bartle Frere wrote that Sir Sayyid's essay clearly showed how "acts of our Government, well meant and well planned, sometimes do more harm than good, simply owing to our disregard for native opinion and our neglect of the maxim that our measures in India should not only be good in themselves but that they should commend themselves to the approval of the natives. We, as a rule, neither take care enough to know what the natives think of our measures, nor to explain the true grounds and objects of our measures to those affected by them."[6]

It was, in fact, widely accepted, even by the colonial historians Malleson and Kaye, that there had been serious reasons for Indian discontent.[7] In the years leading up to revolt, British policy under Dalhousie had favored annexation wherever possible. As Savarkar pointed out with particular bitterness, adoption even within royal families was frequently disallowed in order to justify annexation through the "doctrine of lapse," in which princely states without proper heirs would be ripe for colonial plucking. There were manifold political as well as economic reasons that the revolt became such a monumental marker in India's colonial history—a moment when Hindus and Muslims, Marathas and Mughals, legendary heros and yeoman farmers united with countless other unlike "conspirators" to challenge British rule and uphold the legitimate claim of the Delhi emperor. Nevertheless, the British characterized the revolt for the most part as an expression of Indian fanaticism and superstition, as colonial narratives explained the "heinous massacre of Cawnpore" and the "barbaric siege of Lucknow" through stories having to do with chapatis, pig fat, and other signs of alien alterity. And even as Savarkar, Sir Sayyid, and other Indian commentators provided alternative narratives for an event glossed variably as the first war of independence and a serious warning against colonial complacency, the revolt ended up by justifying new forms of colonial power and policy; it led in the end to greater complacency, and contempt, than had been in evidence before. The revolt was ruthlessly suppressed, while leaders of the revolt such as Nana Sahib were turned into fiends and monsters. The events of 1857 became the pretext for the transformation of religious difference into an argument about political indifference, even as it served to warn against religious interference and cultural ignorance. It served to justify the assumption of direct Crown rule over Company-controlled country, and the inauguration of new forms of indirect rule where full military conquest had left off so abruptly in 1856.

On August 2, 1858, Britain announced that India would henceforth be governed "by and in the name of Her Majesty, and all rights in relation to any territories which might have been exercised by the said Company . . . shall and may be exercised . . . as rights incidental to the Government of India." Queen Victoria followed her assumption of authority over India with a proclamation dated November 1, 1858, in which she sought to allay the concerns of her Indian subjects in matters deemed to have been of relevance to the revolt. She announced "to the native Princes of India that all treaties and engagements made with them by or under the authority of the Honourable East India Company are by us accepted, and will be scrupulously maintained." She noted that the doctrine of lapse would no longer be used as a pretext for annexation by stating outright that Britain desired "no extension of our present territorial possessions; and, while we will permit no aggression upon our dominions or our rights to be attempted with impunity, we shall sanction no encroachment on those of others." Further, she declared an end to aggressive missionization:

> Firmly relying ourselves on the truth of Christianity [this opening phrase was inserted by Victoria herself, into the text prepared by her prime minister], and acknowledging with gratitude the solace of religion, we disclaim alike the right and the desire to impose our convictions on any of our subjects. We declare it to be our royal will and pleasure that none be in anywise favoured, none molested or disquieted, by reason of their religious faith or observances, but that all shall alike enjoy the equal and impartial protection of the law; and we do strictly charge and enjoin all those who may be in authority under us that they abstain from all interference with the religious belief or worship of any of our subjects on pain of our highest displeasure.[8]

Thus Victoria put a halt to the evangelical enthusiasm that had mounted since Charles Grant had reversed Company policy earlier in the century, even as she gave voice to the growing sense among many Britons that "Christianity was . . . increasingly a mark of their own difference from, and superiority to, their Indian subjects."[9] Thomas Metcalf writes that "Despite the presence of dedicated missionaries throughout India, Christianity had become, as the Secretary of State Lord Stanley put it in 1858, to the consternation of his evangelical countrymen, 'the religion of Europe.'"[10] Liberalism did not evaporate overnight. Indeed, many liberals celebrated Britain's newfound commitment to religious toleration in the colonies, and the importance of education remained unquestioned after the rebellion. But for the most part reform foundered against the suddenly hardened shoals of cultural difference.

## Missionaries and Caste

The most common general explanation for the Great Revolt was the caste system, a marker of difference even as it was seen to harbor the ideologies of pollution and exclusion that had ignited fears around the introduction of the new cartridge. In an essay written in April 1858, the renowned Indologist Max Müller took up the question of the true meaning of caste in India; he observed that "Among the causes assigned for the Sepoy mutiny, caste has been made the most prominent. By one party it is said that too much, by another that too little, regard was paid to caste."[11] Müller noted remarks by British officers that pointed to the total incompatibility of caste with military discipline. He also reported the remarks of many civilians to the effect that "the Sepoys were driven mad by the greased cartridges; that they believed they were asked to touch what was unclean in order to lose their caste, and that, rather than lose their caste, they would risk everything." Much of the extraordinary proliferation of writing on the subject of caste was undertaken by missionaries, who felt that the time had come for an intensified assault on caste by the government. Missionaries had been complaining that caste was the largest single impediment to conversion, that the fear of loss of caste dissuaded potential converts from abandoning Hindu practice more than any other doctrinal consideration. Some missionaries had argued that caste should be broken to make conversion possible, an argument that seemed to many in government as one of the principal causes of the rebellion, in that it provided evidence for the assertion that the cartridge had been part of a deliberate strategy. But many missionaries sought to seize the moment, suggesting that Christianity should be imposed on India as a treatment, if not a punishment, for the revolt. The Church Missionary Society's Memorial to the Queen put it like this: "The Government of India has professed to occupy a position of neutrality between the Christian and false religions. Such profession, your Memorialists believe, dishonours the truth of God, discourages the progress of Christianity, and is inimical to the social welfare of the Natives. . . . [The] evils which have been fearfully exhibited amidst the revolting cruelties of the present rebellion . . . can only be effectually counteracted by recognizing the Christian religion as the basis of law and social order."[12]

Alexander Duff, the chief architect and theorist of missionary education in India, was a critic of caste from the time he first came to India with the Church of Scotland Mission in 1829. Like many other missionaries, he was concerned that his pupils were overwhelmingly from lower castes, although his opposition to caste segregation in schools clearly discouraged some upper-caste families from sending their children to him. In his early writings, he held that caste was a sacred institution: "Idolatry and superstition are like the stones and brick of a huge fabric, and caste is the cement which pervades and closely binds the whole."[13] Duff gave voice to what became missionary orthodoxy by 1850, when the Madras Missionary Conference put forward a minute in which it was held that "Caste . . . is one of the greatest obstacles to the progress of the Gospel in India . . . whatever it may have been in its origin, it is now adopted as an essential part of the Hindu religion." The Madras Missionary Conference, in fact, argued further that "Caste, which is a distinction among the Hindus, founded upon supposed Birth-Purity or Impurity, is in its nature, essentially a religious institution and not a mere civil distinction."[14] When Duff published two volumes in the wake of the rebellion, one entitled, *What Is Caste: How is a Christian Government to Deal with It?*, he continued to hold that caste was chiefly religious.[15] However, Duff also held that caste was civil, as well—that it was simultaneously a social institution and a religious doctrine. Although Duff, more moderate than many of his missionary colleagues, stopped well short of advocating "an exterminating crusade," he resolved that a Christian government should "solemnly resolve to have nothing whatever to do with caste." In the end, Duff was aware both of the limits confronting government and the reality that caste could only be exterminated by "the mighty power of the Spirit of God," though he advocated considerably greater support for missionary activity than Victoria finally would concede.

Despite dominant missionary convictions, there were occasional suggestions that the religious and civil components of caste could be separated, and that caste was in large part a social convention as well as a marker of the Hindu faith. Many thought that Indians would hold onto caste distinction far more assertively than they would to their religion. To quote Lord Stanley again: "The difference between the religion and the caste of the Hindoos was like that between the religious creed of an English gentleman and his code of honour; and that just as an English gentleman would resent any attack on his honour, and yet leave persons perfectly at liberty to attack his religion, so did the Hindoo feel with respect to his caste and religion. . . . The natives would strongly deprecate any interference with their caste, but were open to instruction and persuasion in religion, provided everything was done openly."[16] Max Müller directly dispensed with the missionary position and developed the notion that caste occupied dual domains. He was concerned that in the aftermath of the revolt and its extraordinary repercussions—such as blaming all Indians for the extreme actions of a tiny minority—most explanations of the nature and meaning of caste misconstrued both the relationship between religious and social domains, and the extent to which modern manifestations of popular religion deviated from classical Hinduism. On the basis of his examination of the ancient Vedas—the source of greatest authority for all Hindus—he held that none of the objectionable traces of caste could be found in the original constitution of Hindu thought. Indeed, Müller announced that "The Government would be perfectly justified in declaring that it will no longer consider caste as part of the religious system of the Hindus. Caste, in the modern sense of the word, is no religious institution; it has no authority in the sacred writings of the Brahmans, and by whatever promise the Government may have bound itself to respect the religion of the natives, that promise will not be violated, even though penalties were inflicted for the observation of the rules of caste."[17]

Müller was also aware, however, that caste as a social formation was little different from the racial, ethnic, religious, and class differences and prejudices that were accepted as natural in most arenas of European social life. He be-

lieved that Brahman priests had grafted religious principle onto social prejudice, thus sanctifying forms of caste exclusion in ways that made questions of
intervention sensitive at best. Fulminating against sacerdotal self-interest,
Müller nevertheless proposed that caste in many of its aspects be viewed as a
social etiquette that circumscribed marriage, dining, and other forms of social-
ity in ways that could easily be recognized, through appropriate social translation, in Europe. He was convinced that as a religious institution caste would
die away in time, though he was convinced that "as a social institution it will
live and improve." Indeed, he suggested that caste, "which has hitherto proved
an impediment to the conversion of the Hindus, may in future become one of
the most powerful engines for the conversion not merely of individuals, but of
whole classes of Indian society." But Müller argued that caste could not be
abolished in India, and that any effort to do so would "be one of the most
hazardous operations that was ever performed on a living social body."[18] He
argued that government should not actively sanction caste in three fundamental respects: first, government should not countenance the treatment of any of
its subjects with indignity on account of caste; second, government should pay
no attention to caste in any contract or employment, whether in civil or military service; and third, caste should be ignored in all public institutions. But he
strongly advocated that India must be allowed to mature in its own time. Like
earlier generations of Orientalists, his defensive understanding of India was
made at the cost of simultaneously belittling the status of modern institutions
in India and cautioning against the introduction of rapid change.

This was the dilemma of liberalism in 1858. Müller was one of the few
Orientalists who still defended Indian civilization, while the old breed of Anglicists and Macaulayan liberals was simultaneously giving way to an unholy
alliance of parliamentary pragmatists and imperial crusaders. In assuming
Crown rule, Victoria announced a new policy of noninterference, but she did
so only because of the widespread perception that imperial and missionary
interference had just about led to British defeat in India. In the late nineteenth
century, Christian triumphalism gave way to imperial ambition. The British
government shrank back from its interest in reform, as well, ploughing money
and concern instead into new technological projects of control and mastery
ranging from railways to agricultural canals. The containment of Christian
ambition within Europe and the displacement of missionary evangelicalism
onto projects of capitalist technological expansion were, of course, accompanied by the growing sense of irrevocable racial difference. The universal language family of Sir William Jones and the racial unity of Aryans posited by
Müller became the basis for race theory that cast Britons and Indians in a
relationship of absolute difference.[19] Missionary rhetoric was used to celebrate
the accomplishments of empire rather than the message of Christ. Even as the
empire took on the ideological trappings of a new crusade, missionaries were
consigned to the wings of the imperial theater.

Ironically, liberal sentiment took refuge in the margins of missionary frustration with both Indian society and colonial governmental autonomy. Or at least some liberal sentiment was reborn in unlikely encounters of a few missionaries with subaltern groups in various parts of the subcontinent. Although discourses of empire were still largely shared among imperialists and missionaries, the internal differences and debates that at certain moments animated the consolidation of imperial authority at other moments became the fault lines of other kinds of histories. When we link colonial histories to postcolonial genealogies, provisional fractures become contradictory moments, revealing unexpected affinities and peculiar alliances. The story of Robert Caldwell works both to amplify the history of missionary engagement in nineteenth-century India and to attest to the ironies of colonialism. It also allows us to begin to sense the contradictory role of caste in both colonial history and postcolonial inheritances of that history.

## Caldwell and the Limits of Conversion

When Robert Caldwell first arrived in southern India, he found "the native converts sneered at by the governing race as 'rice Christians'; and disdained by the Brahmans and educated Hindus as a new low-caste, begotten of ignorance and hunger."[20] Caldwell first went to India in 1838 as a nonconformist missionary, but after a few years he switched allegiances to the Church of England and worked for the Anglican Society for the Propagation of the Gospel, toward the end of his life becoming a bishop. Throughout his career he wrote yearly reports to the Mission Board back home, listing, as was common practice, the harvest in souls for each year—the ultimate index of missionary success. In the balance ledgers of salvation, the numbers not only remained frustratingly small and limited to specific areas but reflected the overwhelming fact that for the most part only lower-caste Nadars and even lower "untouchables" converted to Christianity in any systematic way. Caldwell thought and wrote extensively about the question of conversion, defending the Church against critics who maintained, first, that conversion by the poor and downtrodden was motivated only by material interests and was as a consequence inauthentic, and second, that the failure to convert Brahmans rendered the missionary enterprise an absolute failure.

Caldwell admitted that the lower castes initially came to Christianity for protection and material help: "the natural outcome of the circumstances in which they are placed."[21] He wrote,

> I cannot imagine any person who has lived and worked amongst uneducated heathens in the rural districts believing them to be influenced by high motives in anything they do. If they place themselves under Christian instructions, the motive

power is not their's, but ours. . . . They will learn what good motives mean, I trust, in time—and perhaps high motives too—if they remain long enough under Christian teaching and discipline; but till they discard heathenism, with its debasing idolatries and superstitions, and place themselves under the wings of the Church, there is not the slightest chance, as it appears to me, of their motives becoming better than they are.[22]

But Caldwell used this assertion to predicate a more general theory of conversion, in which he held that conversion was more than the acceptance of a new religion; it was a radical inculcation of new possibilities and predispositions, a readiness for new beliefs as well as new forms of knowledge and morality. The Church, like Christ, would take whoever would come, for whatever reason, and then endow them with the means and the conditions for a new kind of life.

Caldwell was aware that one of the principal motives for conversion, particularly among the agricultural classes, was the "desire of protection from oppression," a fact he found "natural and reasonable." But rather than alleviating the grounds for oppression, conversion often led to new forms of struggle and difficulty. Frequently, for example, landlords viewed conversion as an attempt "on the part of tenants-at-will to secure tenant right, or of people who have a tenant-right to make themselves proprietors." Newly converted Christians were accordingly often involved in long and bitter lawsuits, which steeped them "in feelings of animosity against their opponents, who are also neighbors, and whom they ought to be endeavoring to convert."[23] Not only did this render problematic the notion that conversion was desired for its own sake; Caldwell also worried that other motives could dominate the early lives of new converts, distracting both from the cultivation of Christian understanding and virtue and from the project of converting others.

Caldwell accepted the idea that the task would be easier when more educated natives became converts to Christianity, and resented the general antipathy and resistance of the higher classes. He noted that "Higher motives and a higher type of Christianity may be expected, and will be found, here and there, amongst educated converts to Christianity, especially amongst the young men that have been educated in our mission Anglo-Vernacular schools."[24] Like other missionaries in southern India, he celebrated those cases in which Brahmans converted to Christianity as instances of genuine theological triumph. But the triumph was ambivalent, their credibility compromised by the alterity of the Brahman convert on the one hand and the numerical insignificance of these conversions on the other. Through the very frustrations of the missionizing process, he developed a serious appreciation of the relation of knowledge and power, as well as of the ways in which cultural hegemony produced the terms on which knowledge and power would meet in India. In particular, he argued that despite vast differences among the indigenous population, "whatever their culture or want of culture—whether they are of high caste or low caste—the ideas and feelings of the entire mass have in the course of ages become so completely interpenetrated by the religion they all profess in common, and all classes, down even to the lowest, are so fast tied and bound by the iron fetters of caste, and so proud of these fetters, that the difficulties in the way of their conversion to Christianity are very much greater than those that stand in the way of the conversion of the ruder, but freer, aboriginal tribes."[25] Thus it was that Caldwell confronted the frustrations of his practice; and thus it was that caste was increasingly identified as the structural mechanism for, and ideological apparatus sustaining, the hegemonic sway of heathen obstructionism.

When Caldwell died in 1891, he was recognized not only for his extraordinary success in building up the Tinnevelly mission enterprise but also for his impressive scholarly writing, including ethnographic work on certain caste groups in the south, a detailed history of southern India, and a pathbreaking philological work on the history and structure of Dravidian languages. Caldwell's first major publication was an ethnographic work on the toddy tapper caste of Shanars who lived in the southern portion of the Tamil country and became one of the principal foci of Caldwell's proselytizing efforts.[26] The book provoked a largely negative reaction from the educated members of the Shanar caste, who were upset in particular with Caldwell's assertion that the Shanars were non-Aryan.

Caldwell argued that one of the principal reasons for the large number of Shanar converts to Christianity was that they were not under the sway of Brahmanical religion, an argument he felt was supported by the claim of the authentic and autonomous racial identity of Shanars as original Dravidians. He wrote that some among the wealthier Shanars imitated the Brahmanical ideas and rites held by the "higher classes of the Tamil people," but argued that for the most part "their connexion with the Brahmanical systems of dogmas and observances, commonly described in the mass as Hinduism, is so small that they may be considered votaries of a different religion."[27] He went on to anticipate the theory of sanskritization, though in a far more critical light than M. N. Srinivas years later: "It may be true that the Brahmans have reserved a place in their Pantheon, or Pandemonium, for local deities and even for aboriginal demons; but in this the policy of conquerors is exemplified, rather than the discrimination of philosophers, or the exclusiveness of honest believers." Indeed, Caldwell used this recognition to assert the fundamental autonomy of Shanar identity through religious practice and racial origin as well as philological affiliation. He betrayed the usual missionary contempt for "native" religion, writing that "the extent and universal prevalence of their depravity are without a parallel. Where else shall we find such indelicacy of feeling, and systematic licentiousness?"[28] He saved his sharpest criticism, however, for Brahmans and Brahmanism, arguing that the cultural elite of Hindu India was much more responsible for their depravity than the lower classes precisely because of their entitlement and education.

Caldwell developed a complex sociology of religion in southern India, organized fundamentally around the idea of caste difference. Although he noted that Brahmans have certain moral advantages over Shanars, he frequently condemned the effects of ritual discipline as either totally self-interested or lacking in sincerity. For example, although Brahmans have the custom of generosity, they give alms only because of the merit it accrues, not on account of compassion or brotherly love. And although Brahmans are educated and intelligent, they lack sincerity. As Caldwell noted, "The greatest of all obstacles to the spread of Christianity in India consists in the practice and love of lying which pervade all classes of the people."[29]

The authenticity of Christian conversion was judged by measures that could not be seen, perhaps more than it was in any other social process. Thus conversion was frequently evaluated in relation to the presence of possible instrumental interests, with the assumption that only when there was no interest could it be ascertained beyond doubt that there was genuine belief. Thus it was of some residual satisfaction that Caldwell found the level of deceit higher as he went up the social scale; like many other missionaries, the lack of knowledge and the dependence of poverty was offset by the simplicity and sincerity of the lower classes that did convert. As Caldwell wrote, "But the longer I have observed the characteristics of the various castes, I have been the more convinced that as regards deceit, especially deceit in matters of religion, the Shanars must yield the palm to the high castes, and the high castes and all castes to the Brahmans. . . . Their lies are never so mature, so smoothly polished, so neatly dove-tailed, or uttered with so complacent a smile." Shanars could not dissimulate as could Brahmans, and when they disappointed or deceived, they did so merely because of their "procrastination, their indolence, and fickleness," not their fundamental duplicity. The insincerity of Brahmans also extended to their religious beliefs: "The follower of the brahmanical system professes to believe in 330 millions of gods, but in the majority of cases does not care a pin about any of them. . . . He never forgets his ablutions, his holy ashes, or any of the thousand and one ceremonies which sanctify his domestic life; but ordinarily he has not the smallest iota of belief in the divinities he so elaborately worships."[30] Regrettably, Caldwell found that this lack of sincerity hindered his efforts to convert Brahmans, who cared little about religious principle and yet obsessed constantly about ritual purity.

The religion of the Shanars had little to do with the religion of the Brahmans. As Caldwell argued, "in those extensive tracts of country where the Shanars form the bulk of the population, and the cultivation of the palmyra is the ordinary employment of the people, the Brahmanical deities rarely receive any notice." Caldwell asserted that "demonolatry, or devil-worship, is the only term by which the religion of the Shanars can be accurately described."[31] Here,

anticipating his later philological work, Caldwell noted an etymological basis
for this separation: "every word used in the Tamil country relative to the Brahmanical religions, the names of the gods, and the words applicable to their
worship, belong to the Sanscrit, the Brahmanical tongue; whilst the names of
the demons worshipped by the Shanars in the south, the common term for
'devil,' and the various words used with reference to devil-worship are as
uniformly Tamil."[32] Here Caldwell went far beyond the writing of other missionaries, betraying his deep scholarly interest in origins, his Orientalist sense
that only if Shanar religion, and by implication Tamil religion more generally,
could be understood to have existed as a separate and autonomous system
could he genuinely believe that the power of Sanskritic inflection and Brahmanic belief might be undone. And for Caldwell a theory of origins could best
be demonstrated through linguistic analysis, with language as the only real
sedimentary evidence of early history. Caldwell wrote that

> The fact of the terminology of devil-worship being purely Tamil throughout is to my
> mind a tolerably conclusive argument of the Tamil origin of the system. With refer-
> ence to the social state of the Tamil people, it is clear that the origin of the words in
> common use will enable any one to determine what was introduced by the Brahmans,
> the civilizers of Peninsular India, and what existed before their arrival. All words
> relating to science, literature, and mental refinement, all that relate to an advanced
> civilization, and all words pertaining to religion, the soul, and the invisible world, are
> in the language of the Brahmans; whilst all words that relate to the ordinary arts of
> life, the face of nature, the wants, feelings, and duties of a rude and almost a savage
> people, are being exclusively Tamil, we are obliged to assign to this superstition a
> high antiquity, and refer its establishment in the arid plains of Tinnevelly and
> amongst the Travancore jungles and hills to a period long anterior to the influx of the
> Brahmans and their civilization of the primitive Tamil tribes.[33]

Thus Caldwell the scholar was able to take heart in his lifelong effort to gain
Christian converts among the lowly heathen Shanars of the southern Tamil
country.

Caldwell argued further not only that demonolatry was unconnected with
Brahmanism but also rather that it shared many features with the superstitions
of Western Africa, "as a species of fetishism." After providing an account of
devil worship (devil dancing, possession, and so on), he wrote that he had
exhausted their "scanty creed." The one thing that could be said in favor of the
bloody sacrifices that went along with devil worship, however, was that they
permitted some form of understanding of the Christian principle of sacrifice:
"the fact of the prevalence of bloody sacrifices for the removal of the anger of
superior powers is one of the most striking in the religious condition of the
Shanars, and is appealed to by the Christian Missionary with the best effect."
And yet, despite contrasting this approvingly with the incomprehension Brah-

mans exhibited toward Christian belief, he noted elsewhere that "Devil-worship is . . . not only dissociated from morality but perfectly subversive of it. If the offering of bloody sacrifices conveyed to the minds of the Shanars any idea of their own demerit or of the necessity of expiation, the rite might be productive of moral benefit."[34]

As for the progress of, and impediments to, conversion, Caldwell wrote: "It cannot be alleged of the Shanars, as of many other castes and classes in India, that they are fenced round by priestcraft and prejudice, and are apparently inaccessible to Christian influence. On the contrary, they are peculiarly free from prejudice, and peculiarly accessible. Without priests; without a written religious code; without sacred traditions; without historic recollections; without that aversion to Christianity as a foreign religion which other classes evince: the chief obstacle to their evangelization is the density of their igno-rance."[35] At the same time, Caldwell wrote that this was not an ultimate bar-rier, that Shanars could grasp basic principles, and that sometimes ignorance and illiteracy facilitated understanding, since there were fewer obstacles in the way of belief. He also noted that the Shanars were compelled to convert, in any case, because of social pressure rather than individual enlightenment:

> Partly through their indolent submission to custom, and partly through their inability to think for themselves, and their timidity, their habits of mind are "gregarious" beyond those of any people I know. Solitary individuals amongst them rarely adopt any new opinion, or any new course of procedure. They follow the multitude to do evil, and they follow the multitude to do good. They think in herds. Hence individu-als and single families rarely are found to relinquish heathenism and join the Chris-tian Church. They wait till favourable circumstances influence the minds of their relatives or neighbours; and then they come in a body.[36]

Although the mass character of conversion seemed to fly in the face of Protes-tant notions concerning the individual nature of salvation, Caldwell, like most other missionaries, was fully aware of the social character of religious affilia-tion, though once again the level of individuation and agency is correlated for India negatively against the achievements of Brahmanic civilization, and is understood in terms of a general condemnation of the intellectual and cultural capacities of the people among whom he worked throughout his life in south-ern India.

Despite his wide-ranging criticisms of Shanar religion, custom, and social position, Caldwell was taken by surprise when these same Shanars whom he sought to defend and convert reacted to his book with such vehemence that he was forced to withdraw it from publication after a series of riots against it. The reaction was principally caused by the fact that the Shanar elite did not like Caldwell's representation of their culture as so divorced from Brahmanic civi-lization. Ironically, this very point, which was once the greatest sore point, became, in the space of the next seventy-five years, the basis for Caldwell's most influential, and radical, contribution to Tamil political culture.

Caldwell did not abandon his central thesis, but instead generalized it to apply to all Tamil non-Brahmans. In his *A Comparative Grammar of the Dravidian or South-Indian Family of Languages*, first published in 1856, Caldwell predicated many of his earlier assertions on far more systematically presented historical and linguistic arguments. He had already suggested some of his fundamental philological convictions in the book on Shanars. But now Caldwell extended this argument, proclaiming in his extraordinarily learned grammatical treatise not only the antiquity and autonomy of Dravidian culture but that the Tamil language, the "most highly cultivated ab intra of all Dravidian idioms, can dispense with its Sanskrit, if need be, and not only stand alone, but flourish, without its aid." He further held that Brahmans had brought Sanskrit with them when they moved from the north to the south, along with a strain of Hinduism that emphasized idol worship. As he wrote: "Through the predominant influence of the religion of the Brahmans, the majority of the words expressive of religious ideas in actual use in modern Tamil are of Sanskrit origin."[37] Once again, the concerns of the missionary perhaps are nowhere more obvious than in this condemnation of Brahmanic religious influence, for in claiming the independence of the Tamils, he seemed also to claim their souls for Christian conversion.

Caldwell now clothed in impressive philological form his determination to prove the essential autonomy of Dravidian culture, language, and racial stock from the colonizing duplicity of Aryan Brahmans. He wrote that the Dravidians had occupied the southern portion of the Indian subcontinent sometime before the Aryan invasion. It was only well after the invasion that they were subdued by the Aryans, "not as conquerors, but as colonists and instructors." As he wrote, "The introduction of the Dravidians within the pale of Hinduism appears to have originated, not in conquest, but in the peacable process of colonisation and progressive civilization. . . . All existing traditions . . . tend to show that the Brahmans acquired their ascendancy by their intelligence and their administrative skill." Caldwell further argued that "The Brahmans, who came in 'peacably, and obtained the kingdom by flatteries,' may probably have persuaded the Dravidians that in calling them Sudras they were conferring upon them a title of honour."[38] But in fact, Caldwell continued, the Brahmans, as representatives of the Aryan race, made the Dravidian groups accept the appellation of what in the north was reserved for the servile castes. Dravidians had even, Caldwell maintained, accepted the falsehood that Tamil was inferior to and dependent on Sanskrit, the language of the Aryan race and of Brahmans in particular.

Caldwell's argument was made through a combination of historical speculation and philological conjecture. In particular, he correlated the autonomous survival of Tamil with his estimate of the limited number of Aryan colonists who actually settled in the south.

> If we should suppose that the Aryan immigration to Southern India consisted, not of large masses of people, but of small isolated parties of adventurers, like that which is said to have colonised Ceylon; if we should suppose that the immigrants consisted chiefly of a few younger sons of Aryan princes, attended by small bodies of armed followers and a few Brahman priests—the result would probably be that a certain number of words connected with government, with religion, and with the higher learning, would be introduced into the Dravidian languages, and that the literary life of these languages would then commence, or at least would then receive a new development, whilst the entire structure of their grammar and the bulk of their vocabulary would remain unchanged.[39]

Caldwell wrote that this was indeed the case, and that therefore it seemed reasonable to conclude that the Dravidians could throw off the shackles of the colonists. Here, he articulated his extraordinary recognition of how conquest and colonization could work through a subtle combination of flattery and intimidation. He also used his theories of history and language to disparage the position of Brahmans in south Indian society, directly challenging their cultural hegemony.

Caldwell's dislike of Brahmans was matched by his dislike of caste, a sentiment that he shared with almost all the Protestant missionaries who worked in southern India in nineteenth-century India. J. M. Lechler, writing from Salem in 1857, expressed a common conviction when he noted that "the greatest enemy that opposes itself to us and the gospel is that absurdity of absurdity and yet most clever masterpiece of Satan—Caste."[40] W. B. Addis, writing in 1854, noted his conviction that "idolatry will disappear from India before the system of Caste from its inhabitants."[41] Every missionary had hundreds of examples in which the appearance of conversion was sustained until caste intervened: "Caste is an evil that sometimes lies a long time dormant, but revives when the individual comes in constant contact with it, or family, or other circumstances conduce to such an effect."[42] Caste was consistently seen as the primary enemy of conversion.

Caldwell's generalized antipathy to caste, however, has been received in Dravidianist ideologies principally in relation to the general critique of Brahmans, not as applying to caste divisions among non-Brahmans. Indeed, the critique of Brahmans has elaborated another kind of assumption in Caldwell's writing altogether, namely, that Brahmans and non-Brahmans were of different racial stock, and that Dravidians were neither Indo-Aryans nor the original inhabitants of the subcontinent. Caldwell's articulation of the racial and historical basis of the Aryan-Dravidian divide was, in fact, perhaps the first European valorization of the Dravidian category cast specifically in racial terms, though Caldwell admitted the likelihood of considerable racial intermixture. At the same time, Caldwell was merely modifying conventional wisdom in his uncritical acceptance of an Aryan theory of race, in which Dravidians were seen as pre-Aryan inhabitants of India.

The Aryan theory of race, based as it was on William Jones's well-known "discovery" of the Indo-Aryan family of languages, had been developed by German comparative philologists in the 1840s and 1850s, but was articulated for the first time as a specifically racial theory by Max Müller, who maintained that the speakers of Indo-European languages in India, Persia, and Europe were of the same culture and race. Müller extended his thesis to suggest (anticipating Caldwell's argument) that the Brahmans were the representatives of the Aryan race who moved south, on their way engaging in a civilizing process through a process of peaceful colonization. However, rather than critiquing this form of colonization, as Caldwell did later, Müller praised it: "The beneficial influence of a higher civilization may be effectually exercised without forcing the people to give up their own language and to adopt that of their foreign conquerors, a result by which, if successful, every vital principle of an independent and natural development is necessarily destroyed."[43] Müller used this parable both to denigrate "the intolerant Mohammedans" and to argue against the educational policy of the Anglicists. Further, whereas most Western writers on this subject ignored the racial equality this theory afforded Asian subjects of British colonial rule, Max Müller praised this common descent. A number of Indian intellectuals used both Max Müller's praise and the general theory to claim equality and unity between Britons and Indians. Chief among these in the nineteenth century were Debendranath Tagore and Keshab Chandra Sen. Later nationalist leaders used "Aryan" less as a racial term than as a gloss for ancient Indian religious tradition. Dayananda Saraswati, Vivekananda, Ranade, and Annie Besant all urged in one way or another that the Aryan faith, which had united the north and the south in ancient times, be used once more to bring India together.

But in the Tamil country the theories of Aryanism, whether they linked or separated language and race, worked in most cases to do precisely the opposite. British writers frequently used the Aryan theory to justify a view of Dravidians as markedly inferior to Aryans. In the 1860s and 1870s, Henry Maine and Meadows Taylor emphasized the barbarity and superstition of the early Dravidians, who "had infected ancient Hindu society and destroyed its pure Aryan features." James Fergusson and R. H. Patterson took this argument one step further, arguing (in anticipation of Risley) that the caste system with its inbuilt racial suspicion and endogamous taboos made upper-caste Hindus more ambitious and progressive than they otherwise might have been, discouraging as it did intermarriage between Aryans and non-Aryans.[44] Small wonder, then, that Caldwell's grammatical writings were particularly influential, given that they were written in a spirit of praise and respect both for the Tamil language and for the cultural inheritance of the south. But Caldwell's influence has had an extraordinary career in Madras, exceeding in many ways the influence of any other European ideological formulation in the history of British colonial knowledge on the subcontinent. This was partly because of the emphasis on language, which subsequently became appropriated and inscribed in the deification of Tamil around the cult of Tamil Tay (the mother goddess of Tamil).[45] It was also partly because, as I suggested above, Caldwell was the first to argue against the dynamics and mechanisms of cultural imperialism, the operations of cultural hegemony itself. For despite his condemnations of Shanar religion in his earlier writings, he managed to suggest that the autonomy of Dravidian religious practices was part of the same history that gave Tamil its foundational originality, and Dravidian culture its civilizational integrity. But perhaps more than anything else, it was because of Caldwell's virulent anti-Brahmanism that he became an extraordinary figure in the history of the Dravidian movement.

The Dravidian renaissance entailed a multitude of intellectual, religious, cultural, and political activities from the late nineteenth century on. Although Caldwell made philology a privileged domain for scholarly investigations into the glories, and autonomous history, of Tamil, U. V. Swaminathan Iyer's "discovery" of Sangam poetic texts gave the Tamil country a classical literature of its own that could claim the antiquity, the density, and the literary accomplishment of any great classical civilization. Characteristically, some of the more dramatic activities in the "Dravidianist" movement found issues of language, and specifically Tamil, at their core. Sumathi Ramaswamy has recently argued that the importance of Tamil, and language politics more generally, to the history of Tamil cultural nationalism hinged on the capacity of language to be central to a wide variety of cultural and political movements, at the same time that language could be used to unite a wide variety of potentially divisive identities and groupings.[46] In part because she leaves the story of caste politics almost entirely out of her account of Tamil nationalism, however, Ramaswamy does not explain why the salience of Tamil also fed into the steady marginalization of Brahmans, and Aryanism more generally, from the core of the Dravidian renaissance and its associated political movements. Despite the role of Brahmans in the Dravidian movement (for example, such central figures as Swaminatha Iyer and Subramania Bharati), and despite the extraordinary raprochement between certain areas of nationalist activity in the south and the key preoccupations of Dravidianism—including the stress on Tamil literature and language, the claim of a distinguished and autonomous Dravidian civilization, and the assertion of a distinct role for the south in the nationalist career of the Indian nation—Brahmans became increasingly inscribed as outsiders to Tamil culture and civilization. Caldwell was hardly responsible for this, but he did help provide a language for the exclusion of Brahmans from the core features of a linguistically based Tamil nationalism.

If Caldwell could have had no idea that he would one day be affiliated with the rise of anti-Brahmanism on a major political scale in southern Indian politics, it was clearly his antipathy to Brahmanic accomplishment that made him so appropriate a figure for Dravidianist appropriation. But it was also his central concern with language—as the evidence for origins, as the basis for civilizational genius, as the medium for religious expression and experience—that marked him out as such a special figure. Caldwell's grammar, rather than his concerns with conversion and his dismissals of Shanar religion, survives as not only the most important missionary contribution to nineteenth-century Tamil intellectual history but the most influential of all European constructions of south Indian culture and civilization.

## Appropriations

Caldwell's fate is an illustration of how, ironically, missionary frustrations about converting Tamil souls provided considerable fuel for the most broad-based and enduring anti-Brahman (anticaste) movement in twentieth-century India. The Dravidian movement took many forms, from the elite political negotiations and agitations of the Justice Party from 1916 through the 1920s to the radical populism of E. V. Ramaswamy Naicker (E.V.R.), who formed the social reformist Self-Respect Movement in the 1930s and then established the Dravida Karakam in the 1940s. On occasion, Dravidianism exemplified the best of colonial nationalism by setting progressive social and political agendas. At other times, it popularized itself by sanctioning the dramatic rewritings of Sanskrit epics and religious traditions; it distinguished itself by advocating secularist and rationalist philosophies; it dramatized itself by pillorying Brahmans, Aryanism, Sanskrit, and Hindi; and ultimately it established itself through the consensus and patronage-building politics of modern democratic India. E. V. Ramaswamy Naicker proposed the most radical forms of critique in the history of Dravidianism, and used rhetoric that was as fiery as it was carefully modulated to suit particular occasions and concerns. He maintained friendships with individual Brahmans while railing against Brahmanism; he championed subaltern political issues, organized intercaste marriages, designed new forms of secular ritual, only to call as well for the destruction of the foreign agents of local domination: Brahmans along with their language, their religion, and their ritual conceits. And in establishing the simultaneously progressive and xenophobic terms of Dravidian nationalism, E.V.R., along with many others in the movement, cited Caldwell's work as fundamental for understanding the history of Aryan imperialism and the foundational character of Dravidian self-reconstitution.

If it seems peculiar that Caldwell's Christian understanding of southern Indian society should be adapted to the purposes of an extreme form of secular ideology, it is even stranger that Caldwell's colonial view of Aryan cultural hegemony should have been so easily converted to the uses of a xenophobic nationalism that substituted Brahmans for Britons, Aryanism for modernity, Sanskrit or Hindi for English, and northern India for Europe. Thus, too, the conversion of meanings of caste from precolonial to colonial grammars participated in extraordinary processes of translation and appropriation. Caldwell developed a particularly virulent critique of caste as a result of his frustration in confronting the apparent intransigence of caste hegemony and Brahmanical influence; in so doing, he provided the terms for a critique of caste that were as radical as they ultimately were limited by the villification of a particular social group. And this social group, namely Brahmans, could only be uniformly affiliated to the ideological apparatusses of foreign colonialism by appropriating the most specifically located critiques of Brahmanism by colonial missionaries, critiques that, as we have seen, displaced their own frustrations with conversion into a language of colonial hegemony that erased their own fundamental coloniality.

In tracing the myriad contexts, as well as effects, of Caldwell's work on Dravidian religion, language, and history, we learn about the hybrid transitivity between intention and effect, mimicry and mimesis, production and appropriation; about how the most extraordinary of all colonial enterprises—the attempt to convert the soul—can deploy philological, historical, and ethnological means that end up converting the very categories through which the soul itself can be (mis)recognized: for example, Brahmanism and demonolatry, Hinduism and popular religion, learning and ignorance, sincerity and deceit, hegemony and resistance. The crime of conversion is thus the convention of colonialism, the displacement of the logic of translation from the instrumentalities of possession to the technicalities of truth, the deferral of the adequacy of translation from the inscrutability of salvation to the intractability of sociology, the substitition of the context of conversion for the text of conversion itself. Retelling the political history of these missionary concerns thus reminds us of the violence that is done to, and in the name of, identity, about how political utopia and desire become caught up in the violence and the truths of fundamentalism and official nationalism. In other words, we are confronted with the mystery and the travesty of translation. And in the colonial context, translation is always about impossibility—or rather about the limits—of transformation across cultural, racial, and religious lines.

The story of Caldwell and his grammar is, of course, *literally* about translation. A grammar is always about translation, the production of codes that will unlock and convert the structure of a language into universal rules, forms, and features. For the British missionaries who went to India in the nineteenth century, the project of translation was fundamental, for it was the project of bringing the gospel to the natives, of writing the Bible in native languages, of conveying universal truth in the particularistic settings of heathenism. By possessing a language, one could possess a people. But for Caldwell, the project of possession and translation involved creating a set of historical identities that both explained the difficulty of his own translation—the seemingly impossible goal of significant, or complete, conversion—and was designed to create the conditions for a cultural liberation that would replace one hegemony with another, one form of flattery and conquest with his own. Caldwell's grammar was about the repossession and redeployment of language: the exorcism of certain Brahmanic religious possibilities and the celebration of new racially purified identities that could now admit the instantiation of new utopias.

Conversion itself seems to be about the project of translation, the shifting of one context to another. Context, however, is no mere ornamentation, but the ground of intelligibility, the condition of possibility, which both defines and constructs the text. Caldwell's grammar was written not just about Tamil but also about the Tamil soul, which had to be freed from its particularistic moorings in order to be accessible to the universalizing rhetorics and ambitions of Christian colonization. The Tamil soul had been defined by Orientalist scholarship in terms of Brahmanical Hinduism, which Caldwell took great care to dismantle. Hinduism was both conveyed and enforced by Brahmanical institutions, most significantly caste itself, which provided the basis for Brahmanical power at the same time that it deployed that power through the hegemonic procedures so carefully delineated by Caldwell in his characterizations of history, language, race, and religion in southern India. But the identification of one form of hegemony obscured countless others. On the one extreme, Shanar religious practice and sensibility was degraded by Caldwell in order to create the conditions under which conversion and translation (or rather, the philological constitution of a language as historically autonomous and sui generis) might be genuinely possible. On the other extreme, British colonial rule, and the relationship of the history of imperialism to the history of Christian missionization, becomes translated as the creation of conditions under which the critique of Brahmanic domination can be made. And thus the appropriation of these Christian critiques in the service of secular anti-Brahmanism and counternationalist politics becomes yet another, seemingly inevitable, effect of the history of colonial/postcolonial translation.

Although the explicit crediting of Caldwell's influence by the Dravidian movement represented a dramatic, and unexpected, outcome of missionary activity in India, it was by no means the only example of the far-reaching effects of missionary concerns about caste on social movements. Max Müller was correct in predicting caste-based conversion; in the 1860s and 1870s, missionaries reported extraordinary incidences of group conversion, though exclusively among the depressed classes. Indeed, although missionary arguments had been unsuccessful in persuading the British government to moderate their newly declared stance of neutrality and noninterference, the public visibility of these arguments in India had made clear to a number of lower-caste groups the possible alliances between movements of social mobility and Christian missionaries. In the south, large numbers of Nadars in fact turned to the Church, as did Paravar fishing communities on the Tamil coast. Virtually every region of India witnessed similar dynamics of conversion. And missionary critiques of caste spread through Christian schools, among other means. Jotirao Phule, the prime mover in anti-Brahman and anticaste movements in Maharashtra in the late nineteenth century, had been influenced greatly by missionary educators, though he never converted and was more circumspect in referring to mission influence than many Tamils have been.[47] With the rise of nationalism, of course, missionary influence waned considerably, and even for staunch critics of the nationalist movement the significance of missionary anticaste rhetoric paled before many other far more powerful influences and conjunct histories.

If missionary opinion during the nineteenth century helped put caste at the forefront of debates over social change, modernization, and the role of colonial power, it also continued to hold its own concerns with conversion as of far greater primacy than larger issues of reform. Missionaries were deeply frustrated by Queen Victoria's declaration of noninterference, but continued to work at the margins of the imperial presence in India to establish theaters of influence in which the work of the Church could go on. In doubting the ultimate possibility of the conversion of native interiority into genuine Christian subjectivity, missionaries acted out the deepest contradictions of the colonial state. And yet, missionaries railed against colonial policy either when it seemed to curtail their own activities too powerfully or when the colonial state seemed to sanction attitudes or practices that challenged the claim of Christianity to the moral charter of imperial rule. As imperium itself took on the moral character of a missionary enterprise during the late nineteenth century, it had constantly to negotiate the relationship between morality and rule. In the next chapter, we will examine how missionary agitation over the regular conduct of certain ritual practices led to further negotiation over the moral charter of the colonial state. These rituals entered the space of public and then governmental debate because they took place in public spaces rather than specifically religious sites, raised the specter of torture and mutilation, and invoked the image of the crucifixion of Christ. The "hookswinging debates," about which I write in the next chapter, also became critical in constituting the grounds for the reconciliation of received formulas of older Orientalist knowledge and new ethnographic investigations.

The fractures between missionary concerns and colonial imperatives worked in the end to provide the basis for a new anthropological imperium. Although missionaries were responsible for much early ethnographic writing, this writing came to be of special interest for the state during the years after the Great Revolt, as the colonial state realized that a simple policy of nonintervention was insufficient. Missionary concerns about conversion were dropped, of course, even as missionary interests in the relationship between religious and civil domains of social life were incorporated. The policy of nonintervention was based on the specification of autonomous religious domains that could be preserved with particular sensitivity only if the delineation of customary practice and social predisposition could proceed at a much accelerated pace. The colonial state believed that the reasons behind the revolt were less political than they were anthropological, and that the primary basis of its rule had now to be found in a comprehensive ethnographic knowledge of custom, religion, caste, and character. Caste was converted into a primary concern of the colonial state, even as missionary discourse dropped out of both colonial and nationalist registers. And the state took on an anthropological mission both as justification and as the basis for rule, in the conversion of unruly rebels into loyal subjects of the Raj, though neither as Christians nor as "citizens" of European rule.

In thus interpreting the rebellion as an anthropological failure rather than as a political or economic event, the colonial state took on an ethnographic charter in the years following the rebellion. There was an explosion of ethnographic research, collection, and writing in the last decades of the nineteenth century, as the state sought to accumulate the knowledge necessary both to explain the occurrence of the rebellion and to assure that it would never happen again. Victoria's proclamation of noninterference further necessitated a detailed catalogue of what had to be preserved and protected, even as the various agencies of the colonial state—from the magistracy and the courts to the police and the army—came to assume the foundational character of ethnographic knowledge. It is this story I shall tell in the next three chapters of this book, first through the hookswinging debates, then through the colonial anthropology of H. H. Risley and Edgar Thurston, and finally by examining the colonial census.

# *Eight*

## The Policing of Tradition: Colonial Anthropology and the Invention of Custom

### The Doctrine of Noninterference

Victoria's proclamation had announced, unambiguously, that the British would no longer seek to impose their "convictions on any of our subjects," and that she would "strictly charge and enjoin all those who may be in authority under us that they abstain from all interference with the religious belief or worship of any of our subjects on pain of our highest displeasure." She had further declared that in the "framing and administration of law, due regard would henceforth be paid to the ancient rights, usages and customs of India." But although it was clear that the British intended by this never to repeat the provocations that were seen to have led to the revolt—explicit government support for missionization, regular usurpation and annexation of ancestral and princely lands, and the introduction of military requirements that entailed choices between discipline and pollution—it was equally clear that the British had little idea what noninterference would really mean. Although colonial rule retreated from its active phase of colonizing properties and souls, it could hardly stop interfering with India during the years after the rebellion, when Britain sought to consolidate its control and make permanent the assumptions and institutions of imperialism. The notion that "religion" and "custom" could be genuinely exempted from any interference fell apart in the face of two fundamental flaws in colonial reason; the first was that the British did not know how to define either religion or custom, and the second was that the phase of high imperial rule required the state to appropriate the civilizing mission from the church, to justify itself both at home and in the colonies.

The policy of noninterference thus necessitated a new commitment to colonial knowledge about the subjects of its rule. The rebellion put an end to debates over a history that had been seen earlier to justify the state's claim over revenue and land control, but it made the anthropologization of colonial knowledge necessary for several reasons. Such knowledge could help explain why the rebellion took place, it could suggest how to avoid such disaffection in the future, it could delineate ways to claim the loyalty of subjects on the basis of custom and culture, and it could serve to differentiate the autonomous and proper domains of religion and custom. Armed with such knowledge, the British could not only avoid interference but, in time, become the primary protectors of India's tradition. Even as the history of colonial conquest could now be conveniently erased and rewritten, the primacy of history in the rhetorical debates of imperial policy could yield increasingly to other logics and imperatives. It is in this sense I have argued that colonial rule took on an anthropological cast of mind in the late nineteenth century.

The anthropologization of colonial knowledge proceeded slowly, and in the context of myriad other interests and processes in this period. It can hardly be accidental, however, that the decade of the 1860s saw a veritable explosion in the production and circulation of gazetteers and manuals that now included as a matter of course extensive reports on the manners and customs of the castes, tribes, and religions of the specific regions being studied. Colonial authors continued to write history, even as they sought with increased concern to adumbrate the moral and material progress of the imperial domains through these and other writings. For the first time, however, they began to compile ethnographic facts systematically, as if they were administrative necessities rather than antiquarian curiosities. Indeed, as this chapter will demonstrate, much of the new ethnography emerged as part of the requirements of administration rather than as independent research, at least in the early phases. Much official ethnography, later reported in manuals and then in ethnological catalogues, when it did not come from early missionary accounts emerged out of administrative and policing concerns in the late nineteenth century as the British struggled time after time with the problem of noninterference. In the story that follows, missionaries played an important role off-stage, generating sufficient publicity for a crisis to develop around the question of what the colonial state could countenance: Was colonialism on the side of barbarism or civilization, and were there occasions when the colonial power had to take a stand? Or, from our perspective more than a century later, did the policy of noninterference hold up under the demands of late-nineteenth-century high imperialism, when colonial greed and grandeur had to be clothed in the vestments of a civilizing mission, when the moral charter of Christian prosyletization had to be secularized and nationalized as the ground of and justification for imperium? Could an autonomous and sacrosanct sphere of religious belief be separated from a wide range of customs and practices that periodically leaked into public view and made imperial disinterest appear shocking, even barbaric? And what happened when Indian tradition itself became the subject of colonial discipline?

The debate that followed involved the delineation and redefinition of "Hinduism" as a religion rather than as the simple denomination of the myriad practices and customs that could be catalogued across the subcontinent. Despite the demise of Orientalism, high Sanskritic texts and Brahmanic testimonies were taken, with the help of a new generation of Orientalist administrators, as the basis on which to decide what would count as Hindu religion and what could be consigned to a world of custom. In southern India and elsewhere, Brahmans came to have particular authority as the arbiters of confessional belief. As a result, Brahmanic prejudices about local customs increasingly came to inform the administrative decisions that were made on a regular basis about questions of intereference, even when it was clear that rural Brahmans occasionally practiced these very customs. And it no longer appeared either practical or morally feasible to protect custom in the same way that was appropriate for "proper" religion. As it turned out, Victoria's proclamation was sharpened to exclude from its provisions any form of custom that seemed either dangerous to the colonial state or offensive to the various agencies—from missionaries to social reformist groups—that took on a relationship to the colonial state based on the use of petitions during the last decades of the century. In the process, Hinduism became increasingly Brahmanic, even as Brahmanic definitions of religion used Christian categories and logics to characterize the domain of belief and practice that counted as the core of Hinduism as a world religion. Such redefinitions and redeployments of religious and customary meaning would have dramatic effects, both in relation to India's modern history more generally and in the specific regional theaters where, as in southern India, an anti-Brahman movement would soon emerge.

## Colonial Subjects and Indian Traditions

In late October 1891, the *Madras Mail* brought dramatic attention to the fact that "the barbarous and cruel custom of hookswinging to propitiate the Goddess of Rain, which has been obsolete for some time, has been revived at Sholavandan near Madura."[1] The newspaper provided an account of this event in tones of scandalized disapproval. "The manner in which this horrible custom is carried out consists in passing iron hooks through the deep muscles of the back, attaching a rope to the hooks, and (after the method of a well sweep) swinging the victim to a height several feet above the heads of the people. The car on which the pole is placed is then drawn along by large ropes in willing hands. . . . Full details of this hookswinging affair are too revolting for publication." The person who is swung from the hooks was selected by lot from a larger group that represented a number of the villages sponsoring the festival. Throughout the article, he (for it was always a man) was referred to as "the victim." The newspaper explains its choice of language: "Victim he may well be called, because, though he enters upon this ordeal voluntarily, the chief reason which drives him to it is the sentiment of doing good to his village."

The questions of agency that became fundamental to the moral valuation of the custom of hookswinging were much like those raised during the debate over the abolition of sati in the early years of the century. Before the outright suppression of sati, British officials were often required to attend the "rite," to assure that the "victim" was not forced either by the compulsion of family or the mind-altering effect of drugs to jump on the burning funeral pyre of her husband. Worried commentators often wondered whether this kind of monitoring could be anything more than a periodic check on a practice that was so inscribed in custom and tradition that the voluntary participation of the widow could never be properly ascertained. Besides, the condition of widowhood was itself so deplorable that the decision to jump on the pyre could, in a perverse sense, be seen as rational. Nevertheless, voluntarism as a possibility made little sense in a context where no British official could countenance, let alone approve, such a "barbarous" custom. Sati became for the British a symbol of the backwardness of Indian civilization, even as it became an issue fraught with consequence, given the general British concern not to interfere in traditional practices and customs. As Lata Mani has demonstrated, sati also provided an extraordinary occasion for the rearticulation of tradition around the designation of, and subsequent debate over, the scriptural sanction for religious practice in early colonial Hinduism.[2] But as Mani and others have shown, the agency of women was only the pretext for other political and cultural concerns. Similarly, although the campaign against hookswinging became a symbol of British commitment to civilizational reform as well as of the crisis of enlightened colonial rule, the alleged concern about the victimization of colonial subjects worked to obscure far more salient concerns around the representation of rule and the reorganization of colonial subjectivities.

Colonial subjects, in cases such as those concerning sati and hookswinging, were constructed as victims when they were subjected to some form of custom that either threatened British rule or appeared to violate its moral foundations. Only then did their subjectivity in relation to the possibility of freedom become an issue in colonial discourse. Subjectivity presented itself as an absence; it was only there when it was totally suppressed. Many of the accounts about hookswinging suggested—against the evidence—that the victim was drugged, thus dispensing with the need to worry the issue of agency. But the newspaper account about the hookswinging episode made a far more general assertion: "It might be said that this being a voluntary act, the man submitting himself of his own free will to the torture, it does not come within the letter, and scarcely within the spirit of the law [prohibiting torture]. But it is a case parallel exactly with suttee—the victim in each case being forced to a sacrifice which the press of public opinion fixes on him or her as a duty." Even the possibility that the victim himself believes that his sacrifice is for the good of the village—specifically that it will help bring rain and prosperity—is ignored and obscured in the discursive move that subordinates his agency to the dictates of duty. Custom is enforced by the will of the mob, what is here referred to as "public opinion." And it was the public component that was particularly problematic; individual vows that involved similar forms of "self-mutilation" were not at issue.[3]

"Public opinion" seemed to the British a quality of civil society that in India was vastly underdeveloped, and yet the public domain, which was believed to exist only in the most tenuous of ways, was seen for the most part as a site of immense danger. At the very least, colonial officials worried about the maintenance of public order in public spaces: from the beginning of colonial rule, official sources betrayed consistent concern about the adjudication of competing claims among groups over rights to use public areas.[4] Frequently, colonial sources suggest that conflict developed when different religious or caste communities transgressed space, usually in some kind of ritual/religious procession, that was either claimed by another community or came too close to some other group for comfort. Indeed, much early colonial social classification emerged in such adjudicative contexts, and attempts to sort out the relations of "untouchable" and "caste" Hindus, Hindus and Muslims, and congeries of castes such as those labelled "right-hand" and "left-hand," were frequently made in relation to spatial classification and use.[5] For colonial sociology, there could be no uncomplicated designation of a public outside of its own communal categories, though in the last years of the nineteenth century, with the steady development of nationalist thought and activity, the notion of public space loomed dangerously, and was repressed seriously, for other reasons as well. It must have been a comforting thought for colonial rulers that there might be no real Indian public, and here as in other contexts the relentless anthropologizing of India served the larger purpose of misrecognizing the social and historical possibilities for nationalist awakening, even as it worked to reify categories of social classification.

If the public domain was for the British in India a contradiction in terms, public space nevertheless preoccupied colonial governance. And even when public space did not occasion the immediate threat of violence or conflict, it required colonial order(ing). It seems clear that colonial concern was immensely heightened when an event was by some definition public, and so religious functions that took place outside of the provenance of the temple or home became objects of regulation. Hookswinging was a particular problem not just because of its alleged barbarity but also because this barbarity took place in public space, with apparent governmental sanction. Missionaries viewed hookswinging as both a major distraction from their own proselytizing efforts and a public profanation of space that colonial rule should have reserved for "civil"ized purposes. Officials were horrified not only by the event itself but also by the public character of the spectacle, which was disturbing both to their self-representations and to public order. Additionally, the fact that hookswinging appealed to the baser passions of the lower groups in society—who assembled in far greater numbers for village festivals whenever rumors of hookswinging circulated—seemed every bit as troubling as the barbarism of the rite itself; civilization, in every possible sense, seemed up for grabs.[6]

Colonial power constantly sought to uncover the ways in which Indian tradition worked as a form of power; it asserted its hold on the agency of women, protected other forms of power and patriarchy, and invoked Britain's own disinterested commitment to a civilizing mission even when it claimed a policy of noninterference. Colonial power never turned its assumptions about power back onto itself, however, thus absolving itself implicitly even as it progressively found new arenas in Indian life in which to press forward its campaign of denunciation and reform.

It is impossible to date the beginnings of anthropology in India; the need to understand custom and tradition began with the first early state, and developed with renewed intensity under the British from the early days of their rule. Notions of custom were fundamental to the establishment of revenue systems and legal codes, and thus much early anthropology can be read in early settlement reports and other colonial records. Given colonial reliance on forms of knowledge, it should come as no surprise that the anthropological knowledge of India finds some of its first bearings in the files of administrators, soldiers, policemen, and magistrates who sought simply to control and order Indian life according to the demands of imperial rule and what these agents of empire considered to be basic and universal standards of civilization. But in the late nineteenth century, the efforts to understand custom and to better rule Indian society became linked to the development of official anthropology in new and important ways. Although this story has many genealogies, I will begin here with the controversies that were generated over whether or not, and if so how, to suppress hookswinging. For in these controversies we can discern many of the underlying assumptions of official anthropology: about structure and agency, custom and tradition, religion and ritual practice, as also about the objective provenance of anthropological inquiry. In addition, we will discover some of the footnotes of colonial ethnography, along with a clearer sense of the institutional links between anthropological knowledge and the apparatuses of colonial state power.

## The Hookswinging Controversies

I came across the newspaper account quoted above because it was enclosed in a file that initiated a series of governmental investigations and reports on the festival.[7] The government was clearly embarrassed by the newspaper's charge, motivated at least in part by missionary pressure, that even though it had been apprized of the event it took no steps to prevent it. The subject had come up several times before, most recently in the 1850s, but those officials who looked into it had assumed that the festival was dying out on its own, and that delicate issues such as government's declared intention not to interfere in any aspect of native religious practice would be raised.[8] As investigations in both the 1850s and the 1890s soon revealed, however, there was no clear legal mechanism to suppress the ritual on the neutral ground of physical (as opposed to moral or religious) danger. Not only did the victims voluntarily submit to the ordeal (indeed, they often seemly extremely anxious to do so), they seemed to escape the hookswinging with no grievous bodily harm. As one British official noted early on in the debate, "The fact is that the objection to the hook swinging festival is of a moral, not a physical nature, and sec. 144 C.C.P. can only be made applicable to it by distorting it from its original intention."[9] The legislation referred to was, in fact, only designed to prohibit any activity that endangered the life, health, or safety of an individual.

The intention to mount the hookswinging at Sholavandan had in fact been brought to the attention of government before it took place. The superintendent of police, the divisional officer, and an American doctor from the Madura mission had all been asked to attend and observe the event. The most that the superintendent of police could legally do to discourage the festival, in addition to expressing the moral disapproval of government, was to warn the headmen of the village that they would be held responsible for anything untoward that happened during the festival. Should the victim die from injuries sustained, or fall on top of people in the crowd, injuring them, the headmen could be booked under the provisions of sec. 144. The warning did not have the intended effect, and the festival took place without the dire effects feared (or desired) by some officials.

The district magistrate reported that

There was a crowd of about 5000 persons. Two hooks were passed through the muscles below the shoulder blades of a Kallan. This was not done in public but it is believed that the muscles were first kneaded or pounded to induce insensibility and prevent hemorrhage. The man himself says there was no pain. He was swung to a height of twenty feet by the hooks to a pole fixed in the centre of a car which was then dragged round the town. He was hung for an hour and a quarter. He was then lowered and given some arrack but says he had none previously. His voice was then full and his pulse strong. There was little or no bleeding. The hooks remained in their place and he walked about among the crowd. The holes were then large enough to admit the little finger.[10]

The account is different in tone from that in the newspaper; it is clinical rather than condemnatory. Whereas the newspaper constantly referred to the victim, we read here that the person who underwent the ordeal was a Kallan, and a man. He was also allowed to speak for himself. The newspaper had observed that "There can be no doubt that the victim of these proceedings has been heavily drugged before the hooks are passed." But here we read that the hooks were inserted with surgical skill, and that the man confessed to feeling no pain in spite of having drunk no liquor before the event.

The account becomes even more clinical when we read the inserted report of Frank Van Allen, M.D., the medical man from the Madurai American mission who had been requested to attend and report on the festival: "They were two iron hooks inserted into the skin and subcutaneous tissues, one on each side of the back bone and brought together back to back. Some blood was running down his back. I couldn't learn just how the hooks had been inserted but had heard before that a curved gouge was to be plunged into the tissues cutting down in, and then up and out and in the path thus formed the hooks were to be passed."[11] The doctor was careful to report what he had actually seen, what he had been able to surmise, and what he had only heard. Whereas the district magistrate had made the painlessness of the insertion seem irrefutable, the doctor only noted: "It is said that the parts were made somewhat insensible by slapping and pounding before the hooks were put in." The doctor reported that the man was "a splendid specimen of brute strength, though not of large frame. He was of medium or under size, stockily built and muscles markedly firm." He also observed that although the man was "evidently under strong excitement," he was "self-controlled." After describing the events of the hookswinging in terms that were clearly the basis for the district magistrate's account, he concluded by saying that "As a physician I am much surprised: that the ill effects on the man were so small. No ordinary man could pass through such an ordeal without serious danger to his life."

Colonial sources seemed preoccupied with the question of pain. As we have just seen, the man swung in Sholavandan claimed that he felt no pain, and that he was only given liquor after the ordeal. Many colonial observers insisted that the swingers were either drugged or drunk; they mistook the signs of possession for intoxication and sought evidence that the obvious pain such an experience would afford was obliterated by unnatural, even immoral, means. They assumed all the while that the infliction of pain was both the appeal of the spectacle and the underlying basis for the horror of the rite. Occasionally, men who had been swung complained that the pain had been intense (though most often, it would seem, when an official investigation would have encouraged such a response), but the issue of possession or trance, and the very stark images of what was represented as "self-torture," made colonial officials and missionaries extremely uncomfortable, particularly given the overwhelming disavowal of pain as a fundamental ingredient of the experience. Pain became an index of the barbarity of the rite, at the same time that colonial ethnography recognized (with its uneasy Christian religious sensibility) that the acceptance of pain could also be reckoned an index of devotion. Colonial ethnography also saw links between hookswinging and blood sacrifice, conjuring the horror of human sacrifice itself.[12] The determination of agency was of course inextricably mixed in with the question of pain; it seemed unlikely that any agent would willingly subject himself to extreme pain (even if now stripped away from the demand for death), thus suggesting that there were forms of coercion to be unmasked.

This issue of coercion seemed of preeminent importance. The fact that many swingers came from the lower castes suggested that the caste system itself performed the act of coercion, but in Sholavandan as elsewhere the swingers

also came from higher, locally dominant, caste groups. Although many swingers seemed to have been paid for their devotional act, thus suggesting financial
coercion, in other cases devotees actually paid so as to be able to swing. In
Sholavandan there was competition for the privilege of swinging, as evidenced
by the casting of lots. Although there were reports that some swingers backed
out at the last minute, there were many more about how swingers not only vied
for the right to perform but also collaborated with local authorities in escaping
the surveillant eyes of British officials intent on persuading the "victims" to
desist. Agency as an abiding concern had thus to be considered in light of the
more generalized tyranny of custom, the central enemy of both civilization and
Christianity in the subcontinent.

Although there was a range of opinion and commentary, no British official
was pleased that such customs survived—indeed flourished—under British
rule. Nevertheless, the district magistrate of Madurai thought that the only
sensible solution would be to downplay the festival. As he put it, "the festival
has been held for years in different places and no proof or reasonable ground
for belief that the operation of swinging is dangerous to the life, health, or
safety of the person swung or of any one else has so far as known ever been
adduced. It is no more dangerous if as much so as taking part in a polo match
or an ascent in a balloon or walking on a tight or slack rope. In all these
instances, the person or persons concerned voluntarily do an act in which a
very considerable risk of limb and life is there."[13] The comparisons are telling.
Had the hookswinging been done purely for entertainment and profit, I suspect
there would have been no serious official concern. What clearly horrified the
British (and, in particular, missionary opinion) was not just the act itself but
that it was done in the name of religion. In spite of a commitment to avoid
interference in "native religion," a commitment that had been strengthened
after the Great Rebellion of 1857, such clear examples of barbarity in religious
practice made the British uncomfortable. And one official even wondered
whether the presence of officials and doctors at the hookswinging festivals
might not be seen as sanctioning rather than discouraging the events, once
again echoing concerns that had been raised earlier in the century around the
performance of sati.

The government ignored the district magistrate's recommendation to toler-
ate the festival quietly. In fact, a number of people were worried that
hookswinging would spread all over once it became clear that government did
not intend to prevent it.[14] During the next several years, a series of investigations was conducted to determine whether there was sufficient cause to abolish
hookswinging. Each district collector was requested to forward his views on
the subject of suppressing the practice by legislation, and to base his remarks
on the opinions of local officials and citizens.[15] Although there was no specific
directive, the inquiries uniformly pursued two complementary aims: to establish first, that hookswinging did not have the proper sanction of religion at all,

and second, that in any case it was performed in the name of religion only to mislead the public and subvert religion itself—that hookswinging was done for the private profit not just of the swinger but, more critically, of the corrupt and self-serving temple priests. If these points could be established, there would be no need to confess disbelief and horror as the reasons for wishing to suppress the swinging, no embarrassment about selecting one religious truth over another.

The inquiries turned up a wide range of opinion and concern, much of it anticipated by the earlier investigations of the 1850s. In the first investigation, missionaries were particularly active in condemning the festival. For example, one G. E. Morris, chaplain of Palavaram (a village near Madras) wrote to the local magistrate that he "disclaims all intention of wishing to interfere with the religious rites and ceremonies of the Hindoos, but he asks the permission of the Government in this instance on the grounds: 1) that this particular festival forms no part of their religious system, 2) that it involves unnecessary cruelty, 3) that it militates against public order and decency, 4) that it is an infringement of the common laws of humanity, and 5) that in this particular case it disturbed the residents in the quiet and orderly observance of the Lord's Day."[16] A subsequent letter from Morris to the bishop of Madras went further: "But, my Lord, I cannot rest satisfied with a humble effort to protect only the Lord's Day from such horrible profanation, or to prevent a repetition of the inhuman ceremony only at this particular station; I feel ashamed of my own country, when I reflect that we have been for so many years Rulers of this Land, and have not yet caused such abominations to cease entirely in every corner of it."[17] Here as elsewhere in missionary commentary, it seems clear that hookswinging was a particular problem: not only did the rite frequently profane the Lord's Day, it seems to have done so especially because it drew such an intense crowd, even as it provided significant competition for proselytizing efforts among the very groups that constituted the most successful target group for conversion, the lower castes. Moveover, the rite appeared to have a horrifying resonance with the central event of Christianity, the crucifixion of Christ. A body suspended by iron hooks must have conjured another vision for European missionaries; recall the painstaking descriptions of the penetration of human flesh by the insertion of iron hooks, the repetition of the civilizational horror of the hammering of nails into Christ's hands and feet and the affixing of Christ's body to the cross. These are the sorts of stories that were used to collect funds for missionary endeavors to combat heathenism, generating as they did collective gasps, sympathy, and contributions in church halls and cathedrals across Great Britain.

Ironically, missionary pressure worked to legitimize upper-caste Hindu opinion, which ultimately sustained colonial efforts to denounce the barbarous rite and find justifications to discount its religiousity. But missionaries were horrified for distinctly Christian reasons. Not only did hookswinging raise the specter of the crucifixion and invoke the sacrilege of repeating Christ's final sacrifice, it symbolized the sins against which Jesus struggled so valiantly. The Rev. J. E. Sharkey discounted the religious character of the event in the following terms: "There are thousands around the pagoda we visited but not one professes to have come to have his sins pardoned and removed. Many have come to vend their wares, about a hundred to petition the idol for children, about seventy to offer thank-offerings for mercies received such as restoration from some illness or success in any important undertaking, and about two thirds for amusement and for the uncontrolled commission of wickedness."[18] The denunciation of popular religion here went far beyond the particular spectacle of hookswinging, and provided the basis for both a generalized dismissal of all of Hindu religious practice and the ironic collaboration of high-caste Hindus, who for reasons of their own subordinated popular practice to the more spiritual preoccupations of Brahmanic philosophy. Brahmans, many of whom had direct ritual affiliations with shrines and cults manifestly part of the mix condemned by Sharkey, were frequently eager to enunciate their own civilizational genealogy of philosophical purity, thus becoming unwitting partners of missionary discourse, at least to some extent. But in the context of the official enquiry, both missionary horror and high-caste disdain came up against British colonial concern not to agitate the natives; the government refused to prohibit the festival outright, though it expressed its strong hope that the festival would gradually die out on its own.

The inquiries of the 1890s followed the same general pattern as earlier inquiries, though the range of responses revealed greater differences of opinion, at the same time that certain anthropological assumptions about village-level ritual practice as well as the provenance of Hinduism as a religion seemed to have taken deeper root in official circles. As before, some officials echoed missionary opinion by noting their sense of scandal at the continued allowance of such a barbaric spectacle. And those opinions that justified intervention took the view that the festival had no religious sanction whatsoever. But most officials took the government's point of view that intervention would be unsupported by law and at the very least counterproductive. In 1854, before the Great Rebellion, the government had encouraged local magistrates actively to discourage the performance of the festival:

> The best method of discouraging this objectionable practice must be left to the discretion of the different Magistrates, but the right Honorable the Governor in Council feels confident that if it be properly explained that the object of Government is not to interfere with any religious observance of its subjects but to abolish a cruel and revolting practice, the efforts of the Magistracy will be willingly seconded by the influence of the great mass of the community, and, more particularly, of the wealthy and intelligent classes who do not seem, even now, to countenance or support the Swinging ceremony.[19]

Even years after the Great Rebellion of 1857, however, the government took a much narrower view of interference, and although officials sought anthropological justification for prohibition, and persevered in making a sharp distinction between religious freedom and ritual excess, they repeatedly stopped well short of definitive action.

Some of those consulted by the government in 1893 did, in fact, admit that there might be some religious basis to hookswinging. R. Fisher, a private citizen in Madurai, wrote that "The festival or practice is a religious one, and closely connected with religious ideas . . . to bring rain, and appease the goddess from bringing smallpox."[20] But this explanation was mentioned surprisingly infrequently by British officials, even though a number of other files in the Judicial Department records suggested genuine anxiety on the part of local villagers about the consequences of not performing the festival properly. For example, in 1858 the temple headmen of Abisekapuram had signed a written promise that they would discontinue the hookswinging festival.[21] In the intervening years, however, they had noticed that the festival had been held in other places, and they reported that "the goddess was angry, their cattle constantly got sick and died, they had no proper rains or crops for years and that they had their taxes to pay."[22] Indeed, there seems to have been a marked correlation between the nonperformance of the festival and the outbreak of draught. Nevertheless, such concerns found little sympathy and almost no notice in the official inquiry, except insofar as there was a tacit acknowledgement that outright prohibition might engender serious opposition.

Perhaps the most theologically speculative suggestion came from the collector of Nellore: "Fear of the unknown and timidity are almost universal conditions of thought among ordinary Dravidian natives, and consequently their first impulse to meet any difficulty is to offer a sacrifice. This is the basis of the whole of their natural religion."[23] This view seems to summarize a general nineteenth-century European view of primitive religion.[24] Some other officials tried a bit harder to understand the ritual basis and meaning of hookswinging. One reported a mythological basis in a story about Viswamitra and Vasishta, in which hookswinging took the place of human sacrifice. Another official recognized that forms of penance were regularly used in religious vows. As evidence for this view, one P. Sivaramma Ayyar, a Smartha Brahman and the deputy collector of Tinnevelly, opined that "The practice of hookswinging, no doubt, originally had its origin in that branch of the Hindu yoga philosophy named hatha yogum which was resorted to by certain Hindus with a view to acquire control over the mind by practising certain physical positions and observances causing bodily pain. . . . But like so many Hindu customs, what was once a practice of bodily torture performed in private for a certain purpose has degenerated into a public exhibition of a cruel and barbarous description."[25] He thus provides a textual gloss for the very acts of penance that elsewhere were described so disparagingly, but then dismisses the enactment of what had once been a genuine religious impulse as a degraded event now subverted by publicity stunts and profiteering.

Even if the victims of hookswinging were on occasion seen to have been motivated by the purest of religious motives, for the most part the rite was seen as barbarous and the reasons for its enactment predicated in tyranny and profit. Whatever disparate voices were collected in the investigation, it is clear that the official inquiry could not accord religious legitimacy to the ritual act. As stated by the collector of Chingleput,

> It is, in my opinion, unnecessary at the end of the nineteenth century and, having regard to the level to which civilization in India has attained, to consider the motives by which the performers themselves are actuated when taking part in hook swinging, walking though fire, and other barbarities. From their own moral standpoint, their motives may be good or they may be bad; they may indulge in self-torture in satisfaction of pious vows fervently made in all sincerity and for the most disinterested reasons; or they may indulge in it from the lowest motives of personal aggrandizement, whether for the alms they might receive or for the personal distinction and local eclat that it may bring them; but the question is whether public opinion in this country is not opposed to the *external acts* of the performers, as being in fact repugnant to the dictates of humanity and demoralizing to themselves and to all who may witness their performances. I am of opinion that the voice of India most entitled to be listened to with respect, that is to say, not only the voice of the advanced school that has received some of the advantages of western education and has been permeated with non-Oriental ideas, but also the voice of those whose views of life and propriety of conduct have been mainly derived from Asiatic philosophy, would gladly proclaim that the time had arrived for Government in the interests of its people to effectively put down all degrading exhibitions of self-torture.[26]

This statement expressed the conviction that civilization in the nineteenth century had reached such an elevated point that moral relativism of an earlier and indiscriminate kind could no longer be tolerated. Though he dismissed the motives of those involved with ceremonies such as hookswinging, the collector also appealed to enlightened Indian opinion. These are the voices to which the collector would listen; all others would be suppressed.

For the most part, the Indian voices sought and heard by the British agreed totally with them in their condemnation of ritual practices such as hookswinging, if for somewhat different reasons. These voices were mostly those of Brahmans and upper-caste Hindus who had with the British redefined a proper and autonomous domain of religion at the same time that they actively participated in governmental actions that managed this autonomy. P. C. Ananthacharlu, a prominent citizen of Bellary, directly subscribed to official opinion when he wrote to the collector to say that "As observed in para 8 of the letter of the Secretary to the Government of India, Home Department, the practice has no religious sanction or obligation among Hindus, and has almost died out in this Presidency." A. Sabapathy Moodeliar, a leading merchant in Bellary, wrote to the collector, Robert Sewell, as follows: "The individuals who promote such practices do generally belong to the backward classes and to less educated portion of the community. The advanced and more intelligent classes have no sympathy with such movements. . . . The intentions of Government in really religious matters are well understood,—and any active steps which Government may take in such matters will be rightly appreciated by the community generally." The government is here also seen as expressing the wishes and even representing the sympathies of the upper classes. And P. Rajaratna Mudaliar, deputy collector and magistrate of South Arcot, wrote that "Education has made rapid strides and even the common people have come to look upon anything that is not countenanced by Government as something which they should not take a pleasure in doing." Informed opinion thus reads rather like institutionalized sycophancy, since the government is now accorded the legitimacy and moral example of a proper Hindu state. The acting subcollector of South Arcot, Mr. Harding, was certainly correct when he wrote that "The leaders of Hindu society being the educated men would welcome the repressions of these survivals of pre-Arian savagery." After all, these leaders had provided the textual bases and moral support for these very repressions.[27]

Some officials were aware of the partial nature of the inquiry. The district magistrate of Tanjore conceded that

> It is a fact that the men whom we consult, and whom alone we can consult in a formal manner, have as little sympathy with the practice as we have ourselves, and the frequent remark that the practice has no religious sanction is only true in so far as the Hindu religion is concerned. . . . the people who attach importance to it, and the men who allow themselves to be swung, are not Hindus save in name, and as their sole idea of religion is propitiated it is idle to suppose that in absolutely prohibiting the practice we would be doing no violence to religion or, if the term be considered more applicable, superstitious feelings.[28]

But this insightful analysis—with its clear sense of Hinduism as a clearly identifiable set of religious practices and precepts—was only a preface for his condemnation of the temple priests who exploited primitive superstitions for their own gain. The district magistrate of Kurnool noted that "Although such an observance is not enjoined in the hindu sastras, yet its resuscitation appears to me to be a species of religious revival, and intended to attract large crowds and create religious enthusiasm. The victims may be drawn from the ignorant and degraded but they are not the originators of the movement."[29] Here, the generous attribution of religious meaning to the festival is again followed by an attack on the priests who took advantage of these popular religious sensibilities.

The judgments about popular religious practices were thus made together by the British and upper-caste Hindus who shared a distaste for far more than the barbarous examples of self-torture under discussion here.[30] These judgments often emerged from extensive descriptions and analyses of Indian religion, part of a developing anthropology of Indian tradition that one reads in the files of the Judicial and other departments. E. Turner, the district magistrate of Madura, wrote about hookswinging that

> As far as I have been able to ascertain, the practice has no special religious significance. It is, however, part of the Tamasha [spectacle] at certain festivals held at certain localities at certain seasons. At these festivals it is customary for the lower classes and especially the Kallers to worship the Goddess Mariyammal. The great idea is to put the Goddess into a good humour and get her to interfere in cases of outbreaks of smallpox, scarcity of rain, etc. The Goddess, it is thought, likes to have as much tamasha as possible during these festivals and as hookswinging brings together a large crowd of worshippers the Goddess is pleased with the practice and is likely to be angry if the custom is discontinued. . . . The practice has nothing to do with the hindu religion. The higher castes look at it with abhorence as a barbarous custom. But the masses in this district are Hindus only in name. What may be called Devil worship pure and simple is the real religion of the crowd."[31]

Hinduism itself is being defined as a religious system that should properly be consistent with Brahmanic beliefs and practices. Although these remarks have clearly not yet been scientized by the purer descriptive efforts of later ethnographers, they represent the mix of anthropological and official knowledge that oriented perceptions and judgments in myriad governmental interactions with Indian society.

Most of the speculations about the actual ritual basis and justification of the hookswinging festival were made in the context of predicting how much trouble would be provoked if the practice were suppressed. Aside from the pragmatics of suppression, the central justification for it—and about this official British and Indian elites were in agreement—was the assertion that the priests were manipulating the whole affair. The bias against priests (who in the case of Mariyamman goddess temples were invariably non-Brahman) was powerful and consistent, and it aligned British and Brahman sentiment at the same time that it provided an ironic basis for the antipriest arguments that were appropriated by the anti-Brahman movement only twenty years later (and used then against Brahmans as representative of the priestly class). Virtually every negative statement about hookswinging contains a critique of priests. P. Rajaratna Mudaliar of South Arcot wrote that "the only classes of people who attach any importance to this mode of worship are those that are called Poojaries in the Chingleput and South Arcot District. These generally are fond of reviving the practice because of the income they derive therefrom there being a larger gathering on such occasions than when the worship is carried on in an ordinary manner." E. Turner added, "On ordinary occasions hookswinging merely adds to the gains for the priests and the managers of the festival." P. C. Ananthacharlu of Bellary attributed the recurrence of the festival as due solely to the large annual income derived by the managers of Durga temples. And

J. Sturrock, deputy magistrate of Tanjore, wrote that "the priests and managers of Hindu temples . . . encourage the practice for the sake of gain."[32] All these statements, like some of the statements quoted earlier, are clear in ascribing the motive of profit to the priests. The attribution of the profit motive worked to discredit the priests, but it also worked to disparage local religion. Superstition, unlike genuine (or scripturally mandated) belief, was both the product of and the occasion for manipulation. The priests were seen first and foremost as manipulators, and were accorded no legitimacy. When limited attempts were made to hold certain people responsible in the event of injury, it was the priests and village headmen who were to be monitored and not the unwitting victims who were swung high on hooks. Victims were victimized not only by custom and tradition but also by the men in the middle who made money out of the naive religious sensibilities of the masses. And the linking of custom to the self-interest of priests and others who made money out of custom worked both to desanctify custom and to justify paternalistic intervention and investigation on behalf of the masses.

For the most part, British officials and Indian notables agreed that however desirable the suppression of hookswinging might be, it would be unwise to legislate its abolition; it would be better to rely instead on moral persuasion and official disapproval. Nevertheless, the Madras Missionary Conference strongly advocated outright abolition. In a memorial dated November 13, 1893, it recorded that "this practice is barbarous and revolting; and that its public exhibition must inevitably tend to degrade and brutalize the community among which it takes place."[33] The missionaries particularly cited the festivals that had been conducted in Sholavandan and written up in great detail in newspapers in Madurai and Madras. Although the government refused to abolish hookswinging, and essentially concluded that Section 144 of the Indian Penal Code could not be applied to do so, individual magistrates did occasionally use their power to prevent hookswinging from taking place, perhaps responding to pressure such as that mounted by the missionary conference. In June 1894, L. C. Miller, the acting district magistrate of Madurai, decided on his own authority to prohibit the annual hookswinging in Sholavandan.[34]

## The Meanings of Hookswinging

Miller's intervention in Sholavandan occasioned a great deal of protest from local residents. A petition with close to a thousand signatures was presented to the government, arguing that the villagers should have been allowed to conduct their normal ritual festivities.[35] The signatories included representatives of a great many castes including Brahmans (Aiyars), upper-caste non-Brahmans (Mudaliars and Pillais), as well as Kallars, Maravars, Valaiyars, Paraiyars, and Pallars. The petition was well written and argued, and appealed clearly and cogently to the concerns and assumptions of governmental officials. For example, the hookswinging festival was glossed as a proper ritual, or *ootchavam*, and thus made to look as if it had a Sanskritic genealogy and high religious justification. The petitioners went on to argue that no physical harm had come to any of the men who had been swung, "even though in the natural course of events it is impossible that the man should not be grievously hurt." Instead of arguing that the concerns about the physical welfare of the swinger were misplaced, the petitioners used the lack of injury to sustain the religious merits of the "penance." "Your humble Memorialists attribute this most remarkable state of things in the selected man coming down from the pole in full consciousness and without any serious injury whatever, to the act of the Almighty, in whom full belief is placed not only by the selected man, but by the whole mass of worshippers who attend the festival." The petitioners further reversed the arguments of the missionaries that the exhibition served only to "degrade and brutalize" the community, by suggesting that "this act is calculated to inculcate in the minds of the ignorant masses in a practical manner that firm faith in God and God alone, and full belief in his Divine Revelations, cannot but bring home to the believer the greatest amount of happiness and prosperity." The petitioners were clearly writing with full knowledge of the dominant missionary and colonial discourse, though they also invoked the more standard argument—with all of its internal contradictions—that the swinging was performed to promote the prosperity of the community at large, noting that since they had begun to celebrate the said festival in 1890 "the seasons were more favourable, the crops more abundant, the mortality less appalling, and the dire diseases less virulent."

The petition then objected to the brutal suppression of the hookswinging festival. In telling this story, the petition made a number of interesting claims. Some claims directly echoed fragments of official British opinion. For example, the petitioners noted that far more dangerous events were regularly countenanced by government, such as "balloon ascents, parachute descents, circus feats, horse racing, etc." Other claims seemed to subvert this very point, by including fire walking as well as "the compulsory shaving of a young Hindu widow's head under which other circumstances would amount to grievous hurt, being a permanent disfiguration of the face according to the I.G. code."

Perhaps the most interesting claims relate to our earlier discussion of the agency of the swinger. The petition stated that "the said Malayandi who had been worshipping in the temple having been inspired by the Goddess Mariyamman to have the hookswinging festival, and being in a state of 'Aveesam' (in a state of unconsciousness of his real self got therefrom), besmearing himself with ashes and carrying a copper plate in his hands containing bits of lighted camphor, and went round the temple to make the holy Pradakshanam, saying that Goddess has come to him and inspired him to have the hookswinging festival performed." The petition then specified that he was in an "unconscious and uncontrollable state of mind, for which he was not responsible." When he was in this vulnerable state the police arrived and carted him off to jail. What the petition had thus established was the religious character of the hookswinging; the swinger was said to be in a state resembling possession (*caamiyaattam*), which both absolves him from responsibility and sacralizes his person. Indeed, the petition implied that when a worshiper is possessed his agency becomes that of the deity itself, which clearly invokes a different discourse of victimization, agency, and responsibility than would normally be considered relevant in colonial debates. The discourse of the petition appeals both to the transvalued nature of religious action during hookswinging, and the potential liability of the swinger to police action. In more general terms, the petition intended to invoke a sense of legitimate religious practice, and in the colonial context correctly represented hookswinging as a legitimate extension of Sanskritic religion through the use of terms such as *ootchavam*, *pradakshanam*, and *aveesam*. The logic of the petition was thus multiple, employing arguments that both appealed to and no doubt mystified the British, making legitimating claims that involved a large range of religious understandings and forms, and demonstrating the strategic character of subaltern agency in the colonial situation. These subaltern petitioners, far from being paralyzed by their lack of choice under the weight of custom, could not only speak but also write. In the face of colonial efforts to anthropologize the meanings of custom, the petitioners deployed tactical appeals to colonial reason, while making strong, polyvocal, claims for their own.

The government did not intervene on behalf of the petitioners, and in the end—for reasons that had nothing to do with the arguments in this particular petition—they did decide that Section 144 provided a rather flimsy basis for outright prohibition of hookswinging. So although in an indirect sense the petitioners might be seen to have won their argument, if only for the very short term, they began to lose control over the meaning of the event in their very engagement with the official apparatus of governmental regulation. What might be called the petition wars of the nineteenth century ranged widely in subject matter; they concerned such matters as land and irrigation rights, customary law, local taxes, and management rights in temples, to mention only a few. But all these controversies worked to secure colonial discursive hegemony over the taxonomies, legitimacies, and meanings of local social action.[36] Although the petitioners did not actually use all the right forms and idioms, and clearly resisted others, for the most part they attempted to appeal to the legitimating conceits of official colonial discourse.

It is difficult to recognize some of the shifts that took place because we assume that colonial categories had always been in place. For example, the categories of, and more particularly the rigid separation between, low popular and high classical religion were in fact produced in colonial contexts such as the one described above. Indeed, the petition does not represent a more accurate or authentic understanding of popular religious practice than the colonial version, because the petition was necessarily imbricated in colonial discourse, but it can still be read as a measure of subaltern agency. After all, the petition was written specifically to persuade colonial officials to allow the hookswinging to continue. But the uncritical assumption that colonial sources can illuminate precolonial meanings when read through conventional interpretive lenses is as problematic as the faith in anthropological intuitions that confer the ring of truth to standard interpretations.[37] Colonial sources constituted a truth regime both for official knowledge and, as I will go on to demonstrate, the conventional wisdom of early professional anthropology, as well.

Nevertheless, the petition reveals certain elements of the ethnographic location of hookswinging in south Indian society, thus raising questions about colonial views and providing the basis for critical and oppositional readings of colonial sources. First, the issue of agency that was so fundamental to colonial discourse turned out to be conceptualized in terms that related to the ritual logic of divine possession and the instrumental effects of ritual action, in part because of the specific salience of possession and trance to any event such as hookswinging, and in part because of the need to argue against the criminal culpability of either the swingers or their impresarios, the priests and temple managers. The colonial obsession with agency was no doubt seen as peculiar, but the petition clearly reveals that it was also significantly connected to official attempts to find fault, round up the culprits, and assess both criminality (the significance of which we will come to later) and barbarism. Second, the clear separation between Brahmanic and non-Brahmanic domains of religious life is challenged by the fact that the petition was signed by many upper-caste members of the village, as well as by the petition's demonstration that it was clearly possible (whether or not fully plausible) to construct a Brahmanic gloss on and justification for hookswinging. Nevertheless, the clear assumption in the governmental files was that Brahmans and other members of the upper castes would have had nothing to do with such barbaric rites. The upper-caste consultants and informants for the British were, at least officially, complicit in the reading of hookswinging as non-Hindu and barbaric, even though many of these same consultants probably had multiple ritual connections to "popular" ritual practices. Indeed, as I have elsewhere demonstrated, Brahmans who still lived in rural areas in the Tamil country in the late nineteenth and early twentieth centuries often had "low" village deities such as Aiyanar and Mariyamman for their tutelary worship. Although many Brahmans would have kept some distance between their own ritual practices and popular events such as hookswinging, it was also the case that most Brahmans worshiped in temples where hookswinging was performed, and in which animal sacrifices and other "low" ritual forms were regularly practiced.

The heavy recruitment of Brahmans into colonial administration, and the not unrelated alienation of many Brahmans from their local rural roots—which had facilitated a level of tolerance for and participation in "non-Brahmanic" religious activities—created the basis for increasing collaboration between certain Brahmanic precepts and Victorian morals during the nineteenth century. Upper-caste notions of respectability and religious scruple became increasingly Anglicized, as Brahmans and other high castes were clearly incited by circumstance and conventions of colonial acceptability to define more strictly, and exclusively, the provenance of "Sanskritic" and "Brahmanic" domains. Less ironically than in the instance where Brahmans helped fuel the critique of priests, it was this very privilege that helped to create the basis for the generalized antipathy against Brahmans that fed into the anti-Brahman movements of the twentieth century.

The meanings of hookswinging were thus transformed in rather complex ways during the nineteenth century. The debates over hookswinging played an important role in constituting certain notions of agency and free will as fundamental to the evaluation of local ritual practices, and in redefining the relations between Brahmans and peasants and between Sanskritic and popular religion. And it was precisely because of the incitement to participate in these debates that upper- and lower-caste Hindus both were drafted into a colonial discourse that touched far more than the attitudes of a number of British administrators. In the past, these acts of public devotion had on occasion been supported by kings through tax-free inam land grants; increasingly in the nineteenth century the swingers were either paid by the festival organizers or were encouraged to believe that private vows would most efficaciously be fulfilled by participation in these public events. Whereas kings had once sanctioned and supported these occasions, colonial rulers now disapproved of them. Whereas agency had once been multiply constructed around notions of kingly sovereignty, collective interdependence, social forms of (often oppressive) power, and complex technologies—and social relations—of trance and possession, agency was now the index of individual criminal culpability. And whereas religious customs had been shaped by historical forces in which local power had been closely associated with institutions of local ritual, custom became now the object of new forms of knowledge, control, and classification. Even if the meanings of such intimate experiences such as fear, pain, and belief may never be fully understood, we can be sure that they, and certainly the contexts in which they took place, could not have been totally exempt from the transformations we have surveyed here.

In the end, the governmental reversal of L. C. Miller's action suppressing hookswinging was temporary. Finally, in August 1894, a hookswinging performance in the village of Bheemanaickenpolien on the outskirts of Trichinopoly led, it seemed, to a fatality; it was alleged that a fever that killed one of the swingers was the result of the suppuration of his back wounds. A report circulated in late September of the same year proclaimed that sufficient evidence had been garnered to prove that hookswinging could in fact be abolished on the basis of Section 144, given the lethal consequences demonstrated in this episode. Once a death took place, tradition could be policed effectively, in the name of the public good rather than religious interference. The hookswinging debate was over.[38]

## Custom and Coercion

When it became clear that the hookswinging victims were victimized less by corrupt managers and greedy priests than by their own belief, British officials believed in turn that tyranny resided as much in the dictates of custom as in the actions of those who manipulated it for their own ends. This is not to say that the British ever conceded very much to the world of custom—they continued to seek evidence of manipulation and oppression and sought to defend the gullibility of all who had been designated victim—but custom was the unsettling ground on which the alterity of the colonized resided. Custom also worked to resolve the issue of agency oppositionally, by creating a world in which agency, and individuals, did not exist, thus simultaneously disparaging the traditional world as uncivilized and heralding European modernity as the only haven within which agency was possible and individuals could achieve proper autonomy. Agency can thus be seen as a profoundly problematic category precisely because it disavows the possibility of consent—or anything resembling purposive individual action—outside of particular cultural worlds, at the same time that it uses this condemnation as the pretext for dismissal, surveillance, and control. Even when consent was monitored and debated, it was never really thought that sufficient evidence could exist to document it in the contexts in question: sati, hookswinging, firewalking, and so on. But the focus on consent and agency worked to mask the coercion of colonial power itself, its capacity to define what is acceptable and what is not, what is civilized and what is not, and why it is that the extraordinary burden of knowledge and responsibility is arrogated by the colonizer. Those who pursued colonial forms of knowledge continuously disavowed their own interests, while feeling compelled to enlarge the knowledge of custom as if it was a neutral mechanism for the protection of the colonized. Within a world dictated by custom, agency was held out as a tantalizing promise of freedom, but it was held out by a colonial state that used the term to adjudicate the difference between criminality and barbarism—certainly not to open up any genuine opportunities for freedom of choice.

Even as custom became the site on which the British displaced their own regulative power, custom also became something that was utterly changed and transformed when it was held to be both totalizing and invariant. In the case of the ritual forms and socioreligious categories that surrounded the hookswinging controversies, we can detect significant change that was a direct result of

colonial intervention. What M. N. Srinivas has characterized as "sanskritization," a natural social process in India that involved the emulation of Brahmans and Brahmanic social customs by upwardly mobile groups, was in fact
officially legislated over and over again in the nineteenth and twentieth centuries.[39] This legislation was the result of British officials using Brahmans as
informants and seeing Brahmans as the carriers of high culture. Not only were
practices such as hookswinging not voluntarily dropped, they were actually
constituted as examples of low ritual practice that should be prohibited if possible and at the very least officially discouraged. In certain temples in south
India, the customary practice of widow remarriage within certain castes was
discontinued after the government took over the management of temples and
outlawed the use of these temples for rituals not deemed to have support from
the sastras.[40] In myriad other examples, governmental officials—British and
Indian alike—used agencies of government that were meant simply to manage
and protect instead to legislate newly defined codes of conduct that were part
of the colonial construction of appropriate Hindu practice. The great debates
over the agency of victims in such arenas as hookswinging served not only to
miss but also to obscure a far more fundamental result of colonial intervention
in India: the continual reinvention of the subjectivity of the colonized by and
through the technologies of colonial rule.

Regulation and knowledge always went together in the history of British
colonialism in India. Forms of knowledge were produced by regulative contexts and concerns, even as the parameters of intervention and regulation were
constituted by the kinds of knowledge that were being produced under colonialism. Regulation and knowledge thus collaborated in the fixing of tradition,
by which I mean both the stabilizing and the repairing of a canonic sense of
what had always been done. The effort to fix tradition in the context of
hookswinging was certainly not a new activity. From the years the colonial
government first began to collect information about India, it was concerned to
determine how custom dictated the lives of ordinary Indians: in relation to
rights to land, labor, and agricultural resources; practices related to marriage,
kinship, and caste; and the whole array of social facts that became part of the
codification of customary as well as criminal law. Even though custom could
vary radically from place to place, even occasionally from time to time, the
essence of custom as it was constructed was that it was fixed, that it reproduced
itself through its own inertia. Although the term *custom* seemed to refer to a
single set of social practices and principles, custom steadily became a trope for
a society that was outside of history and devoid of individuals.

The specification of Indian custom was never a neutral activity, whether it
was related to the allocation of land rights or the management of a temple or
charity. Under the conceit of simply following custom, the British both
changed it and reified it. With a little help from British rule, it could now
reproduce itself through the force of law, with consequences that were as ex-

tensive as they were deep. Generally, if custom proved troublesome in the context of British rule, it was because the British thought they had not quite gotten it right, or because discrete customary practices competed against each other in new colonial contexts such as that created by the commercialized land market. But when custom appeared to challenge British rule or, less dramatically, when custom violated the general principles of civilized morality, the British then believed they had to modify the usual practice. The judgments about the authenticity of various customs were thus administrative judgments that were made in the guise of anthropological debates.

Missionaries, whose proselytizing success was confined almost entirely to the lower castes, collaborated in the reformist impulse by providing detailed accounts of local popular customs in terms consistent with their own desire to combat the residual hold of culture over the epistemic terrain of their conversion efforts. The agnostic position of many in positions of governmental authority ironically served to legitimate certain forms of intervention, since the government was adamant in representing itself as committed to a policy of noninterference. Traditions could be legitimately reformed if they were demonstrated to be inauthentic. The measures for authenticity were usually based on a set of Brahmanically defined norms, which were articulated in the context of British administrative judgments that tended to exacerbate the opposition and fixity of what subsequent generations of anthropologists labeled as great and little traditions. British rule came upon the death of Indian kings, and the ascendancy of Brahmans was predicated both on the displacement of kingly authority by the British and on the strategic alliances forged between colonizing and colonized elites.

Governmental debates about activities such as hookswinging thus sought to identify the proper place of tradition in popular social and religious life at the same time that they reconstituted the terms by which tradition was identified and evaluated. It was not so much that tradition was invented as that a new operational category for it was constructed. This new sense of tradition created a hierarchical relation between folk and classical tradition, and accorded primacy to the classical tradition in certain contexts of discomfort or dispute.

Although the British in India made arbitrary decisions about what was properly traditional or customary and what was not, they ironically shared with Eric Hobsbawm a comfortable sense of the need to differentiate between authenticity and inauthenticity, between genuine and invented tradition.[41] They even shared with him a sense of the moral implications of debating the relative plausibility of different specific customs or traditions. The nineteenth-century colonial writers whose arguments have been analyzed here debunked the priests who defined hookswinging as proper tradition in much the same way as Hobsbawm debunks states and elites. The arguments are made differently; most colonial writers used measures of universal moral sensibility as well as Brahmanic notions of how to delineate proper Hindu traditions, but they shared with Hobsbawm an outrage against the pursuit of private interests under the banner of ritual and ceremony.

My aim in making this point here is to suggest, against much of the spirit of the Hobsbawm and Ranger volume, that the effort to historicize tradition and custom is not necessarily the same as finding particular histories for traditions that we then presume to authenticate or deauthenticate, for that was precisely the kind of move colonialism enabled. When colonial discourse debated Indian tradition, it installed certain versions of custom over others, it sustained certain forms of discourse that became increasingly hegemonic (as for example in the petition wars), it displaced Indian subjectivity and agency in relation to everything but its own enlightened presence, and it concealed its construction of categories—such as those concerning low and high religion, or Brahmans and non-Brahmans—categories that in the end survived much longer and with much more important consequences for Indian social life than, for example, the specific issue of whether or not hookswinging was suppressed. In the colonial situation, moral discourse and reformist ideology thus concealed the forms (and effects) of the hegemonic power that the colonial state itself exercised.

The British displaced their own politics into such domains as custom and tradition, simultaneously endowing them with new meanings and applications, and absolving themselves from the recognition that power was being deployed by them rather than by the fixity of the hold of the past, seen as custom or tradition rather than history. But increasingly the norms of custom were established by official anthropologists who claimed the scientific status and neutrality of their discipline, while working directly for the colonial state. By the late nineteenth century, anthropology became the official discourse in which the policing of tradition was transformed into the knowledge of tradition. In the next chapter, I will examine the development of colonial anthropology in greater detail, in preparation for an examination of the census, where the effects of colonial anthropology developed their greatest impact and force in relation to the subsequent colonial, and postcolonial, history of India.

# Nine

## The Body of Caste: Anthropology and the Criminalization of Caste

### Barbarism and Its Discontents

For much of the nineteenth century, missionaries continued to dominate the production of ethnographic accounts of India through the sheer volume of accounts and reports they prepared, often to document the trials and tribulations of their labors in the midst of barbarism. Most of these writings, like Caldwell's monograph on the Shanars, concerned groups that either succumbed to conversion or were at least targeted for major missionary activity. Some writings seemed to celebrate scandal, as we have just seen in the case of hookswinging; others focused on the more exotic customs of tribal and lower-caste groups. Because missionaries had firsthand experience with these communities, their accounts were considered to have particular authority. And because missionaries frequently scripted their accounts to generate support for their conversion activities, they wrote about barbarism and scandal with a sense both of horror and exquisite detail.[1]

The *Church Missionary Intelligencer*, a journal used to report on missionary activities, ran a series of reports in 1852 on various communities in southern India. They documented animal sacrifice, speculated about human sacrifice among the tribal "Meriahs" and "Khonds," and excoriated such "revolting customs" as female infanticide and the sale of women. These last two—"both crimes closely connected, having had their origin in the heavy expenses attending marriage contracts to be paid by the suitor, which amounted virtually to a prohibition of marriage, and subjected families to the disgrace of having unmarried daughters"—were, according to the journal, "promptly abolished."[2] Missionary ethnography was always a tale of tribulation, some measured accomplishments arrayed before a proliferating tangle of barbaric customs and practices yet to be confronted, preferably subdued. Some chiefs had given up their "thieving habits" under British supervision, and a local corps of Rajmahal highlanders had been "taught habits of cleanliness, punctuality, and submission."[3] But there were long accounts of other groups who seemed to cry out for missionary intervention, nay for conversion. In "caste" areas rather than tribal belts, the usual missionary statements can be found. For example, "Brahminism is a more elaborate system of evil than the ancient demon worship; it has been more craftily and powerfully constructed. The bonds and influences by

which it holds captive the heart of man are more deeply and fearfully inter-
woven with his corrupt propensities . . . the prejudices to the reception of
Christianity were less in proportion to the diminished influence of Brahminism." As we have seen in the last chapter, it was only when missionary concerns yielded entirely to administrative ones that Brahmans came back into
ethnographic favor, if always ambivalently.

Despite the ire against Brahmans, missionaries wrote in far more detail,
frequently with the relish of the voyeur, about the extraordinary practices of
less hierarchically privileged groups among whom they usually worked. If
hookswinging had arrested missionary attention, it is hardly surprising that
reports of human sacrifice in the highland tracts of central India excited particular concern, and well beyond missionary circles. Missionaries circulated accounts from correspondents such as one Captain Crawford, who in early September 1829, noted that

> Few persons are aware, that the horrible practice of offering human sacrifices to the
> gods is of frequent occurrence in India; and many, I believe, wholly doubt the fact;
> but unfortunately it can be proved. Whilst Superintendent of the Chanda district, in
> the Nagpore dominions, I heard that such sacrifices took place every third year in the
> neighbouring principality of Bustar . . . the number of human victims ought to be
> fifteen. Should it be impossible to procure any victims by the seizure of travellers, or
> others, not inhabitants of the Bustar country, the Rajah, in that case, causes one of his
> own subjects to be seized for the sacrifice.[4]

In 1837, one Mr. Russell, who had been made superintendent of some of the
northern "tribal" districts, noted calmly that "The ceremonies attending the
barbarous rite, and still more the mode of destroying life, vary in different parts
of the country."[5] He further noted that grown men were the most esteemed for
the sacrifice, because they were the most costly. In fact, the practice of human
sacrifice had only come to the attention of the government after they developed
an interest in controlling the highland tracts of central and eastern India.
Human sacrifice became the subject of much writing during the course of the
long and difficult war against the Goomsur, in which the British brutally attacked the tribal mountainous areas where these groups lived. On September
13, 1845, the British created the office of the Agent for the Suppression of
Meriah Sacrifice, a position that was accorded administrative control over
Kond territories in the districts of Ganjam, Vizagapatam, and Rajamundry.
Captain John Campbell, who had participated in the Goomsur War of 1837,
was brought back to Kond territory in this capacity between 1847 and 1854,
and was reported to have engaged in a reign of terror.[6] Significantly, neither
missionary nor subsequent ethnographic writings noted that human sacrifice
had been used to justify merciless and violent British expansionism in the first
instance, as well as the deployment of repressive measures of administrative
control over tribal groups in the aftermath of colonial warfare.

"Tribal" groups in general, whether they were the objects of colonial conquest or not, exercised ethnographic fascination from early times, both because
they were seen as the most primitive and because missionary groups sought to
convert them with particular optimism, given the absence of caste as an impediment to conversion. The *Spectator*, a Bangalore newspaper, ran a long series
of articles on subjects such as "The Barbarism of the Todas," based on "the
rough notes of a missionary," in 1849.[7] The Todas, who later came to occupy
pride of place in the anthropological canon of "tribal" India,[8] first came to
colonial attention because of the centrality of animal sacrifices in their ritual
calendar. The *Spectator* used the articles as the basis for calling upon the government, "through their local officers, to put a peremptory stop to such savage
and brutalizing exhibitions as have this day been suffered, in the heart of this
self-styled righteous Presidency, to outrage the commonest feelings of humanity." The editorial anticipated Victoria's proclamation by noting that there was
no interest in any "violent interference with rites, to which in their way the
Todas attach a certain religious character." However, the descriptions of animal suffering were intended to evoke humanitarian outrage, and governmental
intervention on that basis.

Walter Elliot, a British official who had been posted in the Telugu-speaking
area of Madras presidency for years, becoming a respected ethnographic voice
particularly upon his return to England in the 1860s and 1870s, betrayed the
usual fascination with barbarous rites and exotic customs. He was especially
interested in the groups that would exercise particular ethnographic importance in the subsequent decades: "I will call attention to another race found all
over India, a study of which will well repay the Ethnologists. It is composed
of certain predatory tribes who have established themselves on the hills or
other places difficult of access, where they enjoy a considerable degree of
independence, furnishing contingents from their retainers or where the sovereign is weak, establishing petty principalities for themselves, and levying
blackmail from their more peaceable neighbors."[9] The groups he had in mind
were the Maravars and Kallars of southern India, as well as other groups such
as the Bhils and Goojars of the northwest, "all distinguished by the same general appearance and character, addicted to predatory habits, skillful thieves,
excellent sportsmen, unrivalled in tracking game, and unwearied in pursuing
it." Elliot noted that these groups furnished hereditary village watchman, the
very groups that had constituted the military retinues and clan networks supporting many of the smaller statements and kingdoms that had, for the most
part, resisted the extension of British rule so valiantly during the late eighteenth century. Some of these groups had accommodated themselves to colonial rule through the provisions of zamindari settlement or the provisional
alliances of princely states. Others had continued to appear resistant both to
British rule and to rural law and order. When this was the case, these "caste"
or "tribal" (in these instances, these terms were relatively interchangeable)

groups were glossed as naturally predisposed to a life of crime. The denomination of certain castes and tribes as "criminal" emerged from the various administrative depictions of groups that preoccupied military and police agencies of government, providing the ethnographic grist for much early anthropological writing and cataloguing. Colonial anthropology was preoccupied with these groups. Colonial administration was perpetually uneasy about them, as well. Elliot gave voice to general colonial anxiety when he noted about one group, the "Goojars," how the unsettled conditions of 1857 immediately elicited the return of their "marauding propensities," despite their apparent adoption of peaceful industry in intervening years. That political and economic reasons might have elicited revolt against the British, rather than simply reveal the underlying criminal character of particular groups, was of course completely missing in the account.

Not all early ethnography on Indian society was preoccupied with accounts of barbarism, whether in the form of bizarre ritual practices or as simple violence against the British. Most Orientalist accounts had, in fact, underplayed barbarism as a category in marked contrast to both missionary and official accounts. It is striking, however, how both the formal sacerdotal accounts of Abbé Dubois on the one hand—for whom the most conspicuous barbarities were often practiced by Brahmans—and the antisacerdotal reports of missionary (or missionary-influenced) observers who found nothing to commend and much to condemn in the Indian social world, combined barbarity and ethnography. Ethnography was invariably fascinated by barbarism. Missionary perspectives won the upper hand first with the demise of the Orientalists and then with the rebellion, thus catapulting the specter of caste and the horror of Brahmanism to official attention. Then, as missionary preoccupations became viewed as increasingly unhelpful in the consolidation both of the policy of nonintervention and in the accumulation of knowledge that would be useful to manage and contain the unruly social world the British hoped they could keep at bay, preoccupations with barbarism hardly disappeared. When, from the late 1860s, efforts to normalize the collection of information about Indian society began to have systematic effects on official colonial policy, information about Indian society became progressively normalized, as well—part of the everyday operations of the ethnographic state. But the tropes of barbarism were still manifest, if deployed selectively and more dispassionately. Indeed, barbarism was progressively converted into other colonial uses, as an important justification for the military and the police on the one hand, and for the new ideology of imperium on the other.

If the new imperium was increasingly predicated on an anthropological imperative in the years following the rebellion, nowhere can this be seen more vividly than in relation to two of the most crucial agencies of the colonial state: the military and the police. It was in both the army and the formalization of policing concerns that the so-called "predatory castes" became parsed into the good and loyal "martial" castes on the one side and the dangerous and untrustworthy "criminal" castes on the other. The organization of the army was an explicit outcome of mutiny considerations; the police, and the criminalization of caste, the perverse flip side of military policy. That there was an intimate relationship between martiality and criminality, the two attributes distinguished in the end only by the mysterious question of loyalty to British rule, was an issue that for the British was the most crucial one of all.

## Anthropology and the Army

The mutiny of 1857, even if it had not led to general rebellion, would have been a major crisis for the Indian army.[10] In July 1858, the British government appointed a commission under Major-General Peel (the secretary of state for war) to examine the organization of the Indian army and recommend changes in the hope that it might avoid any repetition of the events of the previous year. Many witnesses (all forty-seven of them British) suggested that the higher castes be excluded from the army; other witnesses were split on the subject of whether to rely more heavily on Sikhs and Muslims. In the end, the commission recommended a higher ratio of British troops to Indian, but no specific caste or ethnic prescription for recruitment. The commission did suggest, however, that "the Native Army should be composed of different nationalities and castes, mixed promiscuously through each regiment."[11] Nevertheless, Lord Elphinstone urged that soldiers of diverse backgrounds not be mingled in the same regiment, on the principle of "divide et impera." As a consequence, regiments were for the most part to be made up of diverse but internally homogeneous class companies, made up entirely of single caste or ethnic groups. George MacMunn, a high-ranking army officer in the early years of the twentieth century and an avid historian of the Indian army, wrote that "The object aimed at in the new construction was, to some extent, to put the races into water-tight compartments, while at the same time developing their feeling of clan emulation and martial characteristics to the full. . . . To put the analogy into English terms, it was as though a battalion should have so many English, and so many Scotch or Irish companies, or should be entirely of one race." MacMunn believed that the army had actually played a role in strengthening the Sikh faith and community; by not admitting "unbaptized" Sikhs, for example, "it is the British officer who has kept Sikhism up to its old standard."[12] In fact, British recruiting had insisted on taking only those Sikhs who looked (to the British) like Sikhs, selecting only unshorn Khalsa Sikhs for army service. And as Bernard Cohn has demonstrated, the almost canonic status of the Sikh turban owes its current importance to the development of special Sikh codes of regimental dress; the marker of an ethnic regiment became the sign of a modern religious community across the world.[13]

The principle of "divide et impera" was reaffirmed in 1879 by the high-level Eden Commission. The subsequent organization of the army into four main regional commands, recruited in different regions and serving in different regiments, put colonial sociology to work directly in the service of imperial authority. It also allowed the British to believe that any subsequent unrest could be quelled by other military units who would share neither national sentiment nor specific grievance. The colonizers saw no reason why such distant, distinct, and diverse recruiting grounds would ever provide the basis for a united front against them, convinced as they were that both the mutiny and the rebellion had been caused by retrograde and local forces of caste prejudice and ethnic pride. Besides, the British began systematically to reduce the troublesome elements in the army, and to provide pride of place to Sikhs and Punjabis generally, Muslims, and other "races" deemed loyal in large part because they had supported the British in that great test of racial and national loyalty, the rebellion. And in the meanwhile they were attempting to coopt the most worrisome of the rebels by guaranteeing security of land and title to the local magnates—zamindars and taluqdars alike—who had been most threatened by the expansionist policies of the late Company state, handsomely rewarding those groups who had backed the British during the revolt.

Concerns about military recruitment in the years after the mutiny led to a consolidation of various colonial theories about the martial races of India. Although the British had long believed, as Macaulay's florid denunciations of Bengali manliness made manifestly clear, that certain groups in India were particularly well suited for military endeavors, it was only after the mutiny that military recruiting policy became specifically tied to ethnographic classification.[14] First, the martial races were seen as devoted to military discipline and inherently predisposed to be loyal subjects of the Crown. In the wake of the rebellion, troops from the Punjab, many of them Sikh, were recruited heavily to the Indian army, in part because of their martial claims to fame in the recent past, and in part because of their historical loyalty ever since they were first defeated in 1848, and especially during the Great Rebellion. By 1875, Punjabis made up about 44 percent of the combined Bengal army and Punjab frontier force. After 1880, the balance shifted even more heavily toward Punjabis, as well as toward Nepalis (in particular Gurkhas), in part because of ever-increased recruitment in the north due to the perceived threat from Russia, in part because of the steady diminution in numbers making up the Madras army. Lord Roberts, commander-in-chief of the Indian army from 1885 to 1893 and a leading exponent of the idea of the martial races, held that the peoples of southern India were inherently unwarlike.[15] As a result of deliberate ethnographic policy, in 1882 eight of the forty Madras infantry battalions were disbanded; by the turn of the century only twenty-five battalions remained, less than half the number that had been in uniform at the time of the rebellion.

From the late 1890s, martial race theory was codified in a series of official "recruiting handbooks" for the different classes of the Indian army. These handbooks, usually written by British officers with long field experience in India, continued to appear and guide military recruiting policy until the beginning of the Second World War. Mirroring the more comprehensive ethnographic surveys of the time, these handbooks were replete with essential notions of caste character. Several handbooks opened by noting that "the dawn of Indian history discloses two races struggling for the soil. One was a fair-complexioned Sanskrit-speaking people of Aryan lineage, who entered the country from the north-west, the other a dark-skinned race of lower type."[16] The assumption was that the former group produced the most favored martial races. Other handbooks showered praise on these groups, observing, for example, that the Pathan's "proverbial hospitality, courtesy, courage, cheerfulness, and loyalty make him an excellent companion and a valuable soldier."[17] Martial races were invariably loyal: "They have a natural respect for authority, and have ever been distinguished for their military fidelity and loyalty."[18] The martial races were nevertheless characterized by "manly independence," in marked contrast to other groups said to be weak and effeminate.[19] Among the virtues of the martial races were their "thick-headedness," a virtue no doubt because it allowed the British to feel superior, and far less worried than they might otherwise have been about the spread of nationalist or anti-colonial ideologies.[20] The recruiting handbooks contained information that was meant to allow both recruiting and commanding officers a clear sense of the recruits. The handbook on Pathans enumerated every clan, division, section and subsection: "A reference to this volume will generally place a recruit. If he is unable to give a good account of himself, it is advisable to reject him."[21] Indeed, recruiters could "commit no worse crime than to attempt to pass a boy of an incorrect tribe."[22] David Omissi notes that "the handbooks were full of tips, including trick questions, which might help establish a recruit's true identity."[23] The success of the military obviously depended both on ethnographic knowledge and on the proper application of this knowledge. One false ethnographic move and the consequences could be lethal.[24]

Martial race theory was further popularized by a proliferation of military writings during the early decades of the twentieth century. George MacMunn was an especially popular exponent of the idea of the martial races; he wrote, in the midst of many other military as well as ethnographic works, a book entitled *The Martial Races of India*.[25] Published in 1933, just two years after Gandhi's salt march and the commencement of negotiations leading to two round table conferences in London, the book began thus: "Who and what are the martial races of India, how do they come, and in what crucible, on what anvils hot with pain spring the soldiers of India, whom surely Baba Ghandi [sic] never fathered?" MacMunn, who attained in 1920 the rank of quartermaster general in the Indian army (a position that involved overseeing the recruitment and organization of the army), provided an outline of Indian ethnology;

he noted that only in India do "we speak of the martial races as a thing apart
. . . because the mass of the people have neither martial aptitude nor physical
courage . . . three hundred and fifty million people, and perhaps of them thirty-
five millions whose young men are manly young man. . . . Astounding!"
MacMunn praised the martial races at the expense of the majority of other
Indians, though it is clear that his praise is mixed, given his clear avowal of the
colonial assumption that the martial races were not of marked intelligence. In
any case, intelligence in the colonized only bred disloyalty and inscrutability,
something about which MacMunn was unembarrassed to be contemptuous
even in the declining years of the Raj.

MacMunn was also unembarrassed by ethnographic doubt. He wrote that
the martial races were "largely the product of the original white [Aryan] races.
The white invaders in the days of their early supremacy started the caste system, as a protection, it is believed, against the devastating effect on morals and
ethics of miscegenation with Dravidian and aboriginal peoples."[26] In another
book on the "underworld of India," MacMunn noted further that "Caste is the
essential part of every Hindu's personal make-up, and the one thing about him
that he knows to be all-essential to him in this life and the lives that are to
follow. Like many other commentators of his kind, MacMunn was not especially critical of caste: "When we marvel at the force and rigidity of caste we
may perhaps realize that it, and perhaps it alone, has kept society in India from
entire disintegration during the centuries of conquest and invasion and has
preserved Brahminism and its popular derivatives intact for the last thousand
years, despite the onslaught of Islam."[27] Thus MacMunn, in the straight talk of
the soldier, repeated as popular wisdom the more sagacious comments of H. H.
Risley, for whom caste was the regulatory form of civil society appropriate for
India under the circumstances of its limited political and social development.

For MacMunn as for many other commentators, the most martial races of all
were from northern India, made up predominantly of Punjabis and Sikhs, Dogras and Rajputs, Gurkhas and Pathans. South Indians did not figure, and even
the halting attempts to recruit such putatively martial groups as the Mappilas
and the Coorgis failed, if for different reasons.[28] The Madras army lost half of
its battalions during the fifty years after 1857. The groups that were most often
recruited as soldiers in the south were seen as martial in character but flawed;
for the most part, their martial qualities had been corrupted by disloyalty to the
British and general disaffection toward authority. These are the groups that
tended to be classified as "criminal," a category that for the British was critically distinguished from martial.[29] Although much of the ethnographic writing
on northern India in the late years of the nineteenth century and the early years
of the twentieth was associated with the army, it is striking how the colonial
ethnographic sensibility in southern India was directed by concerns with criminality and the police.

## Anthropology and the Police

In 1893, Frederick S. Mullaly, a senior official in the Madras police, was appointed the first honorary superintendent of ethnography for Madras presidency.[30] Mullaly's principal qualification for the job was his publication the year before of a book entitled *Notes on Criminal Classes of the Madras Presidency*. This book, which borrowed heavily from standard mid-nineteenth century texts, as also from various district manuals that were being compiled from the 1860s on, was written first and foremost for his fellow policemen.[31] As he states in the preface, "These notes on the habits and customs of some of the criminal classes of the Madras Presidency have been collected at the suggestion of Colonel Porteous, Inspector-General of Police, and put in the present form in the hope that they may prove of some value to Police Officers who are continually brought in contact with the Predatory classes, and of some slight interest to such of the public who may wish to know something of their less favoured brethren." Mullaly went on to suggest his personal authority in terms that sound highly anthropological: "the facts given here have, for the most part, been verified by personal association with the people themselves."

The construction of entire castes by the British in colonial India as "criminal castes" was part of a larger discourse in which caste determined the occupational and social character of all its constituent members, though criminal castes were seen simultaneously as typical and deviant.[32] The colonial notion of caste was that each group had an essential quality that was expressed in its occupational profile and its position in the social hierarchy, as well as in a whole set of moral and cultural characteristics that adhered to each group *qua* group. In addition to those castes seen as members of the martial races, some castes were seen as specifically agricultural and others as merchant, for instance, and the British government attempted to keep these categories from getting mixed up when merchants began assuming land that had been mortgaged for loans in large quantities in the nineteenth century. Although the designation of particular qualities in relation to caste changed over time, often in response to the political evaluation of such factors as loyalty, the notion that each caste had an essence was predicated on a belief in the changelessness of caste. The theories about criminal castes also partook of a set of late-nineteenth-century notions about the genetic and racial character of criminality, characteristics that in the Indian case were always seen to apply to entire caste groups and not, as was usually the case in the West, to particular individuals.

Mullaly's book consists of a series of chapters on different criminal castes, each chapter including a large range of ethnographic detail with special attention to the kinds of crimes the group committed. Two of the most conspicuous criminal castes in his book—castes that were subsequently included in the

Criminal Tribes Act when it was extended to Madras presidency in 1911—were Kallars and Maravars. The very word Kallar has generally been translated as "thief," and there is little debate that many Kallars and Maravars had engaged in forms of predation (as well as of protection) that were part of a highly volatile political system in eighteenth-century southern India. Mullaly begins his remarks by being reasonably descriptive. He writes of the Maravars that they "furnish nearly the whole of the village police (kavilgars, watchmen), and are at the same time the principal burglars, robbers and thieves of the Tinnevelly District. Very often the thief and the watchman are one and the same individual." About Kallars, he notes that "The word 'kallan' means thief or robber in many of the languages of Southern India, and is supposed to have applied to them as indicative of their peculiar mode of earning a livelihood—their violent and lawless habits. Their profession is that of stealing with or without violence as opportunities offer."[33] Agency here is completely subordinated to the normative principles—the traditions and customs—of Indian society. In the essentialist language of the colonizer, Mullaly refers to the "profession" of these caste groups as lawlessness.

Mullaly, however, does not stop with these fairly perfunctory statements about the historical basis of the criminal castes. He uses ethnographic material not just to exemplify certain assertions but to condemn an entire caste group. For example, he writes as follows:

> The savage disposition of the Kallars appears from the following description of a custom which exceeds in atrocity almost every crime of violence of which history affords an example. The Survey Account states that—The women have all the ill qualities and evil dispositions of the men; in most of their actions they are inflexibly vindictive and furious on the least injury, even on suspicion, which prompts the most violent revenge without any regard to consequences. A horrible custom exists among the females of the class; when a quarrel or dissension arises between them, the insulted woman brings her child to the house of the aggressor and kills it at her door to avenge herself, although her vengeance is attended with the most cruel barbarity.[34]

He goes on to note that if the crime is shown to be true, then the offending husband must kill his child in public in return. "Such is the inhuman barbarity in avenging outrage which proves the innate cruelty of the people and the unrestrained barbarity of their manners and morals." Mullaly concludes this gripping atrocity story by noting casually that these customs are unknown in the present day, and he does nothing to evaluate the evidence or context of the report.

The report serves its purpose, by naturalizing the assertion that criminality and cruelty are innate to Kallars as a whole, and providing irrefutable evidence for their inclusion in the general provisions of police surveillance that consigned certain subcastes to periodic long-term imprisonment well before the Criminal Tribes Act was officially used. Mullaly also includes within his consideration of these two "criminal" castes the royal genealogies of the ruling families of Pudukkottai and Ramanathapuram, the first the only princely state in the Tamil area of Madras presidency, the other the largest zamindari in the same area. Although it seems rather extraordinary to come across a royal genealogy in a book on criminal castes, Mullaly admits neither embarrassment nor contradiction. At best Mullaly is trivializing the kingship of these groups, implying that local kings in India ruled principally by force, though he goes further and charges that the kings themselves were brigands and thieves who ruled by terror and extortion. Here colonial anthropology has displaced Indian history with a vengeance.

The post of honorary superintendent of ethnography had been instituted at the request of H. H. Risley, who in the early 1890s was the secretary to the Government of Bengal and the acknowledged expert in matters concerning Indian ethnology. In 1890 he had addressed the Government of Bengal advocating the extension throughout India of the ethnographic project he had begun in Bengal.[35] He wrote at the time that anthropological research is conducted by two methods: first, by inquiry into customs, second, by examination and record of physical characteristics. His first concern in Madras was that the appropriate castes and tribes for this kind of study be selected, and thus he was pleased with Mullaly's appointment. Risley still felt, however, that the government had not allocated enough importance, and money, for a comprehensive scheme to collect ethnographic information throughout India. In 1901 the Government of India resolved its support for a scheme to carry out an ethnographic survey of India. At that time Risley was appointed director of ethnography for India; and Edgar Thurston, superintendent of the Madras museum between 1885 and 1908, was appointed as the superintendent of ethnography for Madras presidency.[36] The replacement of Mullaly by Thurston signified the grander scale and scientific status of the ethnographic project in Madras; ethnography was now to be a general science as well as an applied form of colonial knowledge.

Thurston was the obvious and ideal choice for this position. By training a medical man, he lectured in anatomy at the medical college in Madras in addition to directing the activities of the Madras museum. He began his extensive Indian research with work in numismatics and on geology, and began his anthropological research in 1894.[37] His first ethnographic writings were on the Todas, which though superceding in "scientific importance" the earlier writings of missionaries, was itself superceded by W.H.R. Rivers's publication of *The Todas* in 1901. But by that year his "ethnographic researches in the South of India" were already "well known," and Risley in particular was delighted with Thurston's availability because of their common enthusiasm about anthropometry as the principal means for collecting physical data about the castes and tribes of India. Thurston's obsession with anthropometry was so marked that before he delivered a lecture to the Royal Society of the Arts in

London in 1909, Lord Ampthill introduced him with the following story: "A visit to the Government Museum at Madras was always a very pleasant experience, although at first alarming. Such was the author's zeal for anthropometry, that he seized every man, woman, or child in order to measure them."[38]

In the proposal for the ethnographical survey of India, the secretary to the Government of India wrote that "It has often been observed that anthropometry yields peculiarly good results in India by reason of the caste system which prevails among Hindus, and of the divisions, often closely resembling castes, which are recognized by Muhammadans. Marriage takes place only within a limited circle; the disturbing element of crossing is to a great extent excluded; and the differences of physical type, which measurement is intended to establish, are more marked and more persistent than anywhere else in the world."[39] Thus the government justified its project, and its choice of Risley and Thurston, for a survey that was specifically directed "to collect the physical measurements of selected castes and tribes." Risley's advocacy of anthropometry, and his theories about the relation of race and caste, were clearly fundamental to the definition of the ethnographic project in turn-of-the-century colonial India. The scientific claim about caste reflects Risley's justification for the ethnographic survey in terms that make India into an imperial laboratory, for Risley was confident that he could actually test in India the various theories about race and the human species that had been merely proposed on speculative grounds in Europe. Risley scripted the observation that was recorded in the official inauguration of the ethnographic survey of India, that "India is a vast storehouse of social and physical data which only need to be recorded in order to contribute to the solution of the problems which are being approached in Europe with the aid of materials much of which is inferior in quality to the facts readily accessible in India, and rests upon less trustworthy evidence." Risley added that reference to Dr. Ripley's *Races of Europe* and Professor Haddon's *Study of Man* would amply demonstrate "the extensive use that has been made by European students of the data collected in India." In advocating government expenditure even during a time of famine in India, Risley argued that "the scientific advantages [of such a scheme] are indisputable."[40]

During the 1890s Thurston lectured on the methods and claims of "practical anthropology" to Madras University students, as well as on occasion to members of the Madras police.[41] In the 1899 issue of the Madras museum *Bulletin*, Thurston published the syllabus of his course in practical anthropology, in which he stated that anthropology, which he saw as a "branch of natural history," was divided into two main divisions. First, ethnography deals with "man as a social and intellectual being, his manners and customs, knowledge of arts and industries, tradition, language, religion, etc." Second, anthropography deals with "Man and the varieties or species of the human family from an animal point of view, his structure and the functions of his body." According to Thurston, the most important division of anthropography was anthropometry, which he defined as the "measurement and estimation of physical data relating to people belonging to different races, castes and tribes." Indeed, Thurston felt that his best results came from his anthropographic labors, for example in scientifically demonstrating that the nasal index was lowest in Aryans and highest in jungle tribes, and that the index increased as body height diminished.[42] But here the underside of Thurston's scientific anthropology was revealed when he noted that one of the byproducts of his research was his discovery that "intelligence is in inverse proportion to the breadth of the nose." As he wrote in one of his many "witty" asides, "when I am investigating the claims of applicants for a clerkship in my office, I am in the habit of scrutinising the nose as well as the hand-writing, though I do not advertise the fact, in the local papers or gazette, that 'no one with a nasal index exceeding 78 need apply.' "[43]

Anthropometry included the determination of everything from average height and weight (and average weight relative to stature) to detailed measurements of the shape and size of the skull, the face, and the nasal index (breadth × 100/height); the relation of head size to body size; and the relative sizes of different body parts. For example, Thurston measured the relative length of the upper extremities, the arm span, and the distance between middle finger and knee cap, for English, Brahmans, Pariahs, Paniyans, and Negroes. As part of his lecture he compared the skeleton of a Negro with that of an orangutan, "in which hands reach far below knees." He complained about the difficulty in measuring the heads of Todas, "whose dense locks offer [an] obstacle to [the] shifting of callipers in search for [the] right spot." Elsewhere he had noted that "the measuring appliances sometimes frighten the subjects, especially [the] goniometer for determining facial angle, which is mistaken for an instrument of torture." He encouraged the offering of a two-anna piece for conciliation, "supplemented by cheroots for men, cigarettes for children, and, as a last resource, alcohol." He discussed the relative merits of gunshot or seed when measuring skull capacities. He also noted, displaying his perverse sense of humor once again, that "European inhabitants of a hill station objected to my weighing local tribesmen in [the] meat scales of [the] butcher's shop." This perversity took on even more sinister implications for the scientific aspirations of his anthropometric endeavors when he wrote that "The Paniyan women of the Wynaad, when I appeared in their midst, ran away, believing that I was going to have the finest specimens among them stuffed for the museum. Oh, that this were possible! The difficult problem of obtaining models from the living subject would then be disposed of."[44] He was only partly joking.

Thurston also noted the importance of anthropometry for criminal identification, which had been the reason for his lectures to the police. In the early 1890s, the Bertillon system of using anthropometric measurements had been adopted first in Bengal and then in Madras. The idea was to identify habitual criminals who moved from place to place and shifted their identities. In India, the Bertillon system was applied according to conventions set out by the colonial sociology of criminal castes. The basic operational principle was that "only members of criminal tribes and persons convicted of certain definite crimes" should be so measured. Since most crime was committed by circumscribed groups of people, anthropometry seemed to be the perfect means to apprehend the principal suspects. As E. R. Henry, the inspector-general of police in Bengal, put it, "With anthropometry on a sound basis professional criminals of this type will cease to flourish, as under the rules all persons not indentified must be measured, and reference concerning them made to the Central Bureau."[45]

In the early years of the 1890s, the police in both Bengal and Madras became increasingly confident that they were accumulating a central file of measurements that would help them apprehend criminals in a systematic and scientific manner. The major problem was that the measurement process turned out to be rather subjective, and required extensive training and great care. In 1893 it was announced that "no officers fit for court duties will be promoted until they hold certificates of proficiency as measurers."[46] Col C. A. Porteous, inspector-general of police in Madras, wrote in 1894 that he had earlier "expressed the opinion that the anthropometrical system for the identification of habitual offenders was too Scientific and too dependent on extreme nicety of measurement and mathematical accuracy to be suited for universal adoption in this country; a more practical acquaintance with this subject has led me to modify my views."[47] Thus experts such as Thurston were called in to train police throughout the presidency and to devise means to make the measurements as standard as possible. By 1895, police officers regularly underwent courses of training in anthropometry. And by 1897, Henry could write that the experience of the previous three years had "shown that success achieved has been progressive, and that the figures compare favorably with those submitted for Provincial France by Mons. A. Bertillon, to the Fourth International Congress of Criminal Anthropology held at Geneva in August 1896." Henry went on to note that "this outturn justifies the opinion that the anthropometric system is being worked on sound lines and effectively since, by means of it, four out of every possible ten cases were identified."[48]

Nevertheless, there was residual concern that measurements varied not only from measurer to measurer but from measurement to measurement. The instruments were costly, the course of instruction was lengthy, the statistics were hard to classify, and the measurement process itself was time-consuming. In the last years of the decade, anthropometry began to yield to fingerprinting, which in fact was initially developed in Bengal, as a means of criminal identification that had all the advantages of anthropometry with none of its difficulties. Fingerprinting was considered error-free, cheap, quick, and simple, and the results were more easily classified. By 1898, Henry wrote that "It may now

be claimed that the great value of finger impressions as a means of fixing
identity has been fully established."[49] Fingerprinting quickly established itself
as the universal system of criminal identification. In the technologies of policing, as in many other areas, empire served as an important laboratory for the
metropole.[50]

The replacement of anthropometry by fingerprinting did not lessen
Thurston's commitment to the physical measuring of Indian subjects. During
the first decade of the twentieth century, Thurston worked systematically on
his ethnographic survey along the lines set down by Risley; he collected myriad ethnographic details and extensive archives of measurements, all arranged
according to the different castes and tribes in the presidency. As suggested
throughout this chapter, Indian subjects were not only organized by but contained in their castes or tribes, which determined the cultural, economic, social,
and moral characteristics of their constituent members. Individuals existed
only as empirical objects and exemplary subjects. The ethnographic survey
ended in Madras with the completion of Thurston's encyclopedic seven-vol-
ume work on the castes and tribes of southern India.[51] Thurston was assisted
by K. Rangachari, a lecturer in botany at Presidency College in Madras, and
together they solicited the comments and observations of fellow officers and
scholars throughout the presidency.[52] Naturally, Thurston also included the
results of his anthropometric researches, which he said were "all the result of
measurements taken by myself, in order to eliminate the varying error resulting from the employment of a plurality of observers."

Within the caste entries, the material is mostly made up of quotations from
a wide variety of sources. The citations are reported cumulatively and used
comparatively, but there is no critical evaluation of the sources, even at the
level of noting the particularity of each report. Quotation marks are meant
solely for attribution, and do not in any way set anything within them off from
the authorial narration, at the same time that they accumulate an encyclopedic
sense of authority through the citation of so many authorities. For the Kallars,
as indeed for the other "criminal castes," we find citations from Mullaly's
work as well as some of the same citations used by him. For example, Thurston
reports without comment the remarks of one T. Turnbull, who in 1817 wrote
that the Kallars "still possess one common character, and in general are such
thieves that the name is very justly applied to them." Turnbull goes on: "The
women are inflexibly vindictive and furious on the least injury, even on suspicion, which prompts them to the most violent revenge without any regard to
consequences."[53] And then he repeats the same stories of revenge told by Mullaly, the same generalized indictment of Kallar character, through these reports
of the viciousness of their women and the remorselessness of their revenge.
One citation leads to the next; the writings of Mr. Nelson, a noted jurist and
one time collector of Madura district are promiscuously mixed in with articles
from the *Illustrated Criminal Investigation and Law Digest*.[54] And now,

Mullaly's disclaimer that the most horrifying of practices had not actually been known to have taken place in living memory is absent here, despite the enhanced scientific status of the account. The ultimate confirmation of Kallar criminality is the statistic that 40 percent of the people jailed in Madura were Kallars, a statistic that ignores the simple fact that whenever there was a crime a Kallar would be accused and arrested. But again, as with Mullaly's text, the ultimate charge was that the Kallars had traditionally been thieves: "The Kallans had until recently a regular system of blackmail, called kudikaval, under which each village paid certain fees to be exempt from theft."[55] In fact, this criminal system had been, through the eighteenth century, a form of local rule articulated through the institution of protection, a form of local politics that had proved particularly resistant to British colonization at the turn of the century. A precolonial system of authority in which political power was exercised through the provision of protection was taken to be the primordial sign of colonial criminality.

If one turns to the rest of Thurston's ethnographic writing, we see that the relationship of colonial anthropology to criminality is significant in other respects as well. Criminality under colonialism was about both classification and control; thus criminal castes occasioned some of the first ethnological monographs, and thus anthropology collaborated with policing to provide a scientific means to measure—and by measurement to contain the subjectivity of—persons whose identities were otherwise fluid within caste boundaries. Science worked on society at the level of the body; caste was defined as the genetic boundary of the Indian body, which was measured and explained in relation to a displaced Victorian enthusiasm for the colonized body. It is perhaps no accident that Sir Francis Galton purportedly invented regression analysis when surveying—for the greater glory of science—the naked bodies of Hottentot women in southern Africa.[56]

## The Colonized Body as Ethnographic Text

In 1906, Thurston published a long ethnographic work while he was in the middle of his labors for the ethnographic survey. Entitled *Ethnographic Notes in Southern India*, this work consisted of a series of essays, some previously published in the Madras museum *Bulletin*, on a variety of ethnographic subjects that Thurston thought held intrinsic interest.[57] Perhaps Thurston also thought that these essays could not be readily contained by the format of the ethnographic survey.

The book begins with two long essays, the first on marriage customs, the second on death ceremonies, that look like compilations of material that had been collected on a caste-by-caste basis. Caste seems slightly less important in the third essay, on "omens, evil eye, charms, animal superstitions, sorcery,

etc.," since the ethnographic material is presented as instances of a general set
of beliefs and practices. But in subsequent chapters the organizing principle is
no longer the conventional frame of caste, and the subjects seem no longer to
be standard anthropological fare. The fourth chapter is entitled "Deformity and
Mutilation," the next "Torture in Bygone Days," followed by such other chapters as "Slavery," "Firewalking," "Hookswinging," "Infanticide," and "Meriah
Sacrifice." If the caste-by-caste entries of Thurston's ethnographic survey volumes focus on the social (which for the British in India was caste), these essays
instead focus on the body.

Thurston's *Ethnographic Notes* can be seen as the critical link in the genealogy that connected official anthropology with the kinds of investigative
enquiries and reports that the British collected in their routine administration
of Indian society. These chapters are in large parts encyclopedic collections of
official material that was generated by the colonial interest in suppressing
practices such as hookswinging, slavery, and torture. In Thurston's introduction to his volumes on the *Castes and Tribes*, he had written that he had followed the scheme for the ethnographic survey that had recommended that he
"supplement the information obtained from representative men and by their
own enquiries by 'researches into the considerable mass of information which
lies buried in official reports, in the journals of learned Societies, and in various books.' Of this injunction full advantage has been taken, as will be evident
from the abundant crop of references in foot-notes."[58] But it is in the *Ethnographic Notes* that we can see the extraordinary extent of the compact between
official colonial reports and official colonial ethnography.

Hookswinging, as we saw in the last chapter, occasioned considerable official concern both in the 1850s and the 1890s, in large part in response to
missionary pressure on the government to abolish the rite. Thurston's ethnographic essay on hookswinging is in fact little more than a compilation of the
kinds of writings on the custom that were used to recommend the abolition of
what was seen as a barbaric rite by the British, and at the end of the century by
many upper-caste/class Indian officials as well. The essay begins by quoting a
government report of 1854, and notes that in 1852 two men had been killed
during the celebration of the festival in Salem district because the pole from
which they were suspended had snapped.[59] The unstated motivation for this
observation was that the only provision under colonial law that could be used
to suppress this rite was one that necessitated the documentation of actual
physical harm. Thurston does not always moderate his language, for like earlier missionary and colonial reports he refers to the ritual as a "barbarous ceremony," and quotes indiscriminately from commentators as various (and as
contemptuous of Indian customs) as Abbé Dubois and Pierre Sonnerat. Aside
from the general narrative style, and the lack of any specific argument about
suppression, there is little to distinguish this ethnographic chapter from the
accounts produced by government officials themselves. What is different, of

course, is that although there is no moral or legal argument about the suppression of hookswinging, virtually all of the material had in fact been generated out of this concern, and was initially narrated as part of an argument in the context of governmental debate. The absence of argument and contextual provenance in Thurston's account has the effect of representing the account as scientific (as do all of Thurston's credentials and the entire framework of the book), when it can be seen that this representation works to conceal the nature of the genealogical connection between the work and its sources. In ethnography, the once compelling stakes of official debate seem to disappear altogether.

I am not arguing that Thurston attempts to conceal his sources; he is far better than many colonial authors in providing footnotes and references. Furthermore, he is in total agreement with Risley that one of the tasks of the ethnographer is to digest the massive accumulation of material in governmental reports and then to present it in clear and systematic form. Thurston was himself a government servant, and saw no contradiction between science and government in the task of accumulating anthropological knowledge about India. The relation of knowledge and rule is not simply a colonial fact; it is a fact that was actively celebrated in such colonial projects as the ethnographic survey. But it is easy in retrospect to lose sight of the genealogies of the relations between knowledge and rule, and readers of Thurston's treatise on hookswinging need never know the historical context in which his footnotes were produced. The same observation applied to Thurston's essay on "Meriah sacrifice," where he made a great deal of missionary and colonial reports that the Meriah "tribe" of central India practiced human sacrifice. As is true of most such reports, they are invariably secondhand, and they become enlivened by the sheer horror of the story in ways that exercised particular forms of attention and misrepresentation—in general travel and missionary literature, in colonial documents, as well as in official anthropological writing. As noted earlier, there was of course no mention here of the relationship between these anthropological horror stories and the conquest and suppression of the Goomsurs. Nevertheless, Thurston's chapter became a primary footnote for James Frazer in his discussion of human sacrifice in the canonical text of early British anthropology, *The Golden Bough*, and thus the conduit for a major anthropological preoccupation of the late nineteenth and twentieth centuries.

Thurston's essay on torture—in retrospect, an odd focus of ethnographic scrutiny, but of considerable interest to nineteenth-century ethnographers—was similarly based almost entirely on the report of a commission that was appointed by the Government of Madras in 1854 to investigate various forms of torture employed in the Madras presidency.[60] Thurston notes that the commission used a broad definition of torture, construing it as "pain by which guilt is punished, or confession (and we may add money) extorted." Although Thurston is clear about his use of this source, he tells us nothing about the nature of the commission's task or the historical provenance of the many examples of torture. The inclusion of a series of graphic descriptions of torture under the general title "Torture in Bygone Days" suggests that torture had been a constant feature of southern Indian life, and Thurston shares with the members of the commission the belief that the examples of torture they uncovered were the traditional practices of native revenue and police officers. As the commission's report states: "knowing, as we do, the historical fact, that under the Governments immediately preceding our own, torture was a recognized method of obtaining both revenue and confessions. . . ."[61] The report also asserts that "there are many circumstances in the peculiar condition of this country which may well account for the prevalence of even a systematic and general practice of personal violence, used for the purpose of extortion among the native population," and notes the "whole of this mass of testimony emanates from parties intimately acquainted with the country, its administration, the people and their character. It cannot but afford a deep and clear insight into the actual position of matters."[62] But the report also admits that "In point of fact our investigation starts from a recent definite point,"[63] and provides no evidence other than assertion and assumption that torture, like caste and custom, is an essential component of Indian society.

I am not suggesting that torture arrived on Indian soil only with the British (any more than I have tried to suggest throughout this book that caste was invented ex nihilo by the colonizers). Here as elsewhere I mean to identify the complex relationship(s) between knowledge (in this case ethnographic categories), power (colonial governmentality), and history (as a sign of the modern). The torture report is silent about the fact that the revenue demand in the Indian countryside escalated exponentially under British rule. If torture in revenue and police matters was prevalent in the middle of the nineteenth century, as the report convincingly argues, there were other factors at work, principally the new level of revenue demand. Suddenly, dire consequences of noncompliance (loss of jobs and land), and a colonial legal structure that bestowed new powers on policemen were deeply implicated in the social fact of torture.[64] But these were not part of the commission's brief, and were absent in the commission's explanations, which depended upon a multitude of "expert" understandings of the Indian "country, its administration, its people and their character." Even more significantly, they were left out of Thurston's ethnographic account, which gave even less contextual information than the actual report about the nature of the material it provided.

It is in this sense that I assert that Indian anthropological writing was born directly out of the colonial project of ruling India. On the basis of the writings of Mullaly and Thurston, we can see that the key texts of early colonial anthropology are produced not simply in the context of colonial projects but as the culmination of what had been a long series of colonial projects (and colonial texts written) to conquer, rule, control, and reform India. It is worth reemphasizing that the pretextual field of anthropological writing includes not just the colonial reports and official documents that provide the citational basis for early colonial anthropology (and, through writers such as Thurston, canonical anthropologists such as Frazer and Rivers), but also the crimes of colonialism itself: for example, the pacification campaigns against the Kallar and Goomsur kings, the intensity of revenue collection from the countryside to finance the colonial government, and the moral reforms that highlighted and denounced the so-called barbarous practices that were always used to justify the presence of enlightened British government.

Thurston's *Ethnographic Notes* attracted considerable attention within official and scholarly circles, as well as among general readers. G. H. Forbes, the secretary to the Madras government, noted that "It is evident that the book, from its title and contents, is being bought up by the tourist, male and female; and there is certainly some matter which, though quite unobjectionable for scientific readers, is scarcely what we should put in the hands of young people who read merely from curiousity or to acquire a general knowledge of out of the way tribes."[65] Forbes did not object to the book as a scientific work, but he was deeply concerned about the ready availability of scientific detail, particularly in matters sexual. He recommended that a "bowdlerized edition . . . would be of value and use to the general public and priced low," and that a new edition of the complete work "with full scientific detail" be released at a higher price. In recommending bowdlerization, Forbes highlighted such explicit phrases as "pendulous testes" and "protuberant breasts," as also many of the most graphic examples of torture. Although most concerned about the sexual detail in the chapter on marriage, he also noted that "the subjects of hookswinging, infanticide, and meriah sacrifice are revolting though not prurient." Thus the distillation of ethnography out of government reports led not only to the advance of science but also to the production of what outside of its proper domain was seen as pornography. There was little danger that either scientists or ordinary citizens were going to sift through the mass of material that had been accumulated during British rule. This, of course, is my point; and it is important to realize that Thurston's work was generally read without any sense of the multiple readings I have provided. Instead, Thurston was read in decontextualized reference to other ethnographic notes for other areas and to other compendia on castes and tribes, sometimes even as travel literature. Although I have provided a set of genealogical readings to make my case, my argument also depends on the fact that these connections were obscured by the very project of ethnographic writing engaged in by the new generation of official anthropologists at the turn of the century.

Part of the worry about ethnographic pornography had to do with the increasing role of photographic representation during the second half of the nineteenth century. As elsewhere in the colonial world, photographers were drawn to the recording of naked bodies by the dictates of science. Photography was

seen to complement the anthropometric project, recording body types and proportions with a visual salience that highlighted the collection of dry statistics.
If number had worked to replace text, pictures were seen to provide demonstrations of the findings of ethnographic science with an immediacy, and force,
that also became privileged over textual description. Isolated photographs of
ethnographic types soon became the basis for systematic photographic surveys
of the castes and tribes of India, as in the massive eight-volume photographic
compendium put together between 1868 and 1875 by the historian John
Kaye—then serving in the Secret and Political Department—entitled *The People of India*.[66] The photographs cover the broad sweep of British India, frequently labeling caste or tribal groups with some reference to their criminal or
military characteristics (such as "marauding tribes" or "martial castes"). The
preface makes clear the relationship of the documentation project to the concerns of the ethnographic state:

> The great convulsion of 1857–58, while it necessarily retarded for a time all scien-
> tific and artistic operations, imparted a newer interest to the country which had been
> the scene, and to the people who had been the actors in these remarkable events.
> When, therefore, the pacification of India had been accomplished, the officers of the
> Indian services, who had made themselves acquainted with the principles and prac-
> tices of photography, encouraged and patronized by the Governor-General, went
> forth and traversed the land in search of interesting subjects.

The photographs consist of a mix of full-face and full-length portraits and
group shots, some more formal than others. For the south, caste types include the maharajah of Mysore in full regalia, but many more depict what were
seen as traditional caste and occupational types, with apparent efforts to represent bodies in ways that would complement the measuring of colonized
bodies.[67]

For colonial ethnography, the colonized subject was first and foremost a
body, to be known and controlled through the measurement and interpretation
of physical subjects organized in categories by caste and gender. In all this
attention to the body, there was little interest in the subjectivity, will, or agency
of colonial subjects. When colonial officials debated the nature or presence of
colonized agency, the debate was focused on the denial or suppression of this
agency, in contexts where the colonial state sought to regulate or abolish such
practices as sati, child marriage, hookswinging, and so on. Agency was an
absence, only there when it could be seen as precisely not there. On all other
occasions, agency was neither relevant nor significant, expressed as it was in
the social body of custom and tradition. Even crime was performed without
agency; crime was a function of habit, a social occupation, an effect of caste
rather than an act of will. And with the prevalence of anthropometry and ethnographic interest in bodily practices, the materiality of the text of custom, for
colonial ethnographers, was the colonized body itself.

## The Ethnographic Archive

In late colonial India, anthropology appropriated barbarism from the missionaries. Barbarism was of interest to science, its scandal as much a justification for empire as it was something that had to be controlled and periodically contained in order to celebrate the civilizing mission of empire. But by the end of the nineteenth century, the civilizing mission was less urgent, and yielded increasingly to the imperatives of a colonial science that would contain barbarism through both the regulation and the recording of tradition that so frequently emerged out of policing activities. The Victorian policy of nonintervention thus became the charter for a colonial anthropology. It involved the delineation of religion, custom, and tradition, on the one hand, and the firm maintenance of public order in an imperial regime that held the colonized in place through the knowledge and enlightened protection of tradition, on the other. Barbarism was a sign of colonial difference, producing an ever-widening chasm between the subjects and objects of colonial knowledge. And even the benign aspects of tradition, such as the caste system itself, worked both to explain how Indian society could be orderly in the absence of either political authority or tradition, and why it was that Indian society would never become mobilized around the political aims of national self-determination.

It is in this sense that early anthropology grew out of modern history, becoming the history of those without history as well as the prehistory of those now mired in history.[68] By the late nineteenth century, anthropology became literally the history of the colonized. Knowledge about India was largely produced by or in terms of the logics of colonial rule, the imperatives and institutions of the colonial state. But after the Great Rebellion, historical knowledge increasingly yielded to anthropological knowledge. Caste recapitulated the legacies of tradition, and history was perceived as absent from Indian sensibilities. Colonial historiography appropriated to itself the responsibility for antiquarian history, while conceding to anthropology the study of historical subjects who had not yet entered modernity. In this division of disciplinary labor, anthropology, whether of a physical body or a body politic, was less a complement to than an extension of modern history, spatialized by the logic of colonial conquest and rule, and linked directly to the interests and forms of the state. Colonial anthropology thus emerged out of colonial history as surely as it provided the evidence and assumption for the development of scientific anthropology, even in its postcolonial guise many years later. History was to the modern metropolitan state what anthropology was to the colonial state, reflecting both the similarities and the differences between state systems at home and in the colonies. History constructed a glorious history of the nation in which the present was the inevitable teleological frame; anthropology assumed a history that necessitated colonial rule. History told the story of the nation; anthropology explained why a nation had not yet emerged.

The archive is a discursive formation in the totalizing sense that it reflects the categories and operations of the state itself, in this case of the colonial state. The state produces, adjudicates, organizes, and maintains the discourses that become available as the "primary" texts of history. When I did the research for this book I consulted the records of the "Public" Department, the "Political" Department, the "Home" Department, among many others. I paged through indexes of documents that reflected the quotidian procedures of government, files that considered and then ruled on issues that ranged from the appointment of a particular individual to a position (such as superintendent of ethnography) to his salary and his official duties, both of which were scaled in relation to the other positions, financial needs, and political requirements of government. When I found materials about the practice of hookswinging, I read through files that responded to widespread pressure from missionaries and others regarding the suppression of an activity that brought no grievous bodily harm and little in the way of significant social unrest to the attention of district administrators, who nevertheless had to worry about the representation of governmental activities both within India and back in Britain itself. When I began to correlate the interest of official ethnography in "native" bodily practices with the Torture Commission report of 1855, I had to rely on my own long archival experience of working with land and settlement records as early as the late eighteenth century in order to dismantle the congealed character of official self-congratulation in relation to the deployment of horror stories around brutality and violence in the south Indian countryside. Each record in the archive references previous records, both as precedent and as paper trail; archival research itself invariably proceeds genealogically—record by record, decision by decision, trace by trace. Although documents are frequently scripted with posterity in mind, history is in one sense an afterthought, only incidentally related to the sources that are fetishized as so fundamental to the craft of history itself. And yet history is encoded on the surfaces of the very files—the numbering systems, the departmental structures, and classificatory rubrics—as well as in the reports, letters, decisions, and scribbles within that make up the archive. The archive contains primary sources, at the same time that it is always already a secondary trace of historical discourse.

The archive encodes a great many levels, genres, and expressions of governmentality. The records of commissions of inquiry have very different histories from routine papers that surface in the government orders of everyday official practice; government manuals and gazetteers very different uses from occasional notes or office correspondence that move in haphazard circuits of official (and semiofficial) exchange. Historical research can reveal connections that become effaced by the effects of history itself: connections, for example, between the rise of the revenue demand in the early nineteenth century (fueled by the needs of the East India Company) and the ethnographic writings of Thurston in the early twentieth century, between the dynamics of early colonial conquest and the social classifications that become hardened into late colonial views of caste, between the concerns of the police to apprehend "habitual" criminals and the early development of anthropometry (and by implication what is now called "physical" or "biological" anthropology in many disciplinary circles). Even as the connections never completely come full circle—never foreclose the possibilities of other connections and frequently displace other kinds of possible outcomes—they move us well away from the certainties of a linear and autonomous textual history of colonial anthropology, dissolving texts into contexts even as contexts constantly become reabsorbed by other texts and historical traces. Although the archive has no transparency of its own—its facts can be construed in any number of ways, and the historical record alone can by no means explain why I took the particular path I did in this chapter, or made the specific connections charted above—it is nevertheless the field within which I conducted my research, pushed by its recurrent recalcitrance, limited by its aggravating absences, and fascinated by its own patterns of intertextuality.

By establishing the colonial context for the production of the first official ethnographies of southern India, as we have done in the case of Thurston's work, we are led back to a succession of other texts that could be produced and cited only because of a complex colonial history in which certain texts secured the status of context itself. The history of the nineteenth century in India is the history of desperate attempts to fix an inchoate and uncolonizable place in textual form: texts of proprietary title, legal procedure, customary tradition, ultimately of claims to political sovereignty itself. Ethnographic citation produced colonial conviction, the reality effect of context. But ethnographic science ultimately achieved its apotheosis in the colonial census, both because of the massive scientific and administrative apparatus that the census represented and because of the way in which the census had unprecedented effects on the social realities it claimed merely to represent. It is now to the census, by way of an examination of the history of official "administrative" knowledge about colonial society in the years after the Great Rebellion, to which the next chapter turns.

The census represented not only the apotheosis of colonial science but also the final conversion of barbarism into civilized data, the transformation of moral condemnation into the moral basis of both science and state. The census exemplifies ways in which the documentation project of the colonial state attained unprecedented scope, even as the disturbing character of colonial difference became a problem only at the level of documentation. It is perhaps the greatest irony of colonial rule that the very evidence that could finally be accumulated and contained by the extraordinary apparatus of the decennial census became the basis for the colonial state's ultimate failure to contain both caste and custom. Indeed, it was in relation to the census that caste resisted the colonial idea of civil society. The census inaugurates important aspects of the history of the twentieth century around the story of this resistance, and further transformations in the political histories of caste, custom, and tradition.

# *Ten*

# The Enumeration of Caste: Anthropology
# as Colonial Rule

## Enumerative Genealogies

The Great Rebellion had made it clear to the British that they knew far too little about the colonized populations of India. Moreover, what they did know was far too unsystematic.[1] During the 1860s, a number of efforts were made to generate the basis for systematic and statistical knowledge collection and compilation. In 1862, a proposal that each district have a manual of its own was revived by the Government of Madras, which subsequently charged Mr. Carmichael, collector of Vizagapatam, and Mr. Nelson, collector of Madura, to compile model works for their respective districts. When these works were completed several years later, they occasioned considerable debate in the Madras government.[2] Although the manuals were approved, and their authors allocated Rupees 2,500 each for their labors, a subsidiary proposal that authors for other districts be found to prepare manuals along similar lines was ultimately rejected. Indeed, the government "observed that the publications were wanting in brevity and defective in statistics."[3] Nelson's work in particular was condemned for its "prolixity," which was "so excessive as to render it comparatively useless for the general public." The Governor General in Council further noted that it would be impossible for a single officer, located in the district, dependent solely on the contents of the district record room, unaware of what was being done in other districts, and without an imperial view of things, to prepare an adequate and useful statistical account.

The government was concerned that the initial experiments in the preparation of manuals and gazetteers in Madras and elsewhere failed because of defective organization and threatened to cost far more than the ensuing information was actually worth: "His Excellency in Council observes that excessive costliness is not the only unfortunate effect of the want of organization which left each Local Government to invent a scheme of its own, irrespective of what was being done in other Provinces. There was, in fact, no unity of plan or central supervision, and the results did not contain the materials required for the comparative statistics of the Empire."[4] In 1869, W. W. Hunter, a Bengal civil servant who had just published his own *Annals of Rural Bengal*, was directed to visit various local governments to "submit a comprehensive scheme for utilizing the information already collected, for prescribing the principles according to which all local Gazetteers are in future to be prepared, and for the consolidation into one work of the whole of the materials that may be available."[5] Later that year Hunter submitted a plan for an imperial gazetteer of India. His plan was accepted, and he was appointed director-general of statistics to the Government of India. Hunter centralized the activity of district statistics, directing local officers to compile statistics but to forward them to him, where at the provincial level he drew up a single systematic statistical account. When Hunter published his statistical account of Bengal in 1875, he wrote that "Under this system, the materials for the whole of British India have now been collected, in several Provinces the work of compilation has rapidly advanced, and everywhere it is well in hand. During the same period the first Census of India has been taken, and furnished a vast accession to our knowledge of the people. The materials now amassed form a Statistical Survey of a continent with a population exceeding that of all Europe, Russia excepted."[6] It was as if during these years after the rebellion the centralization of (and control over) knowledge was tantamount to the centralization of (and control over) power itself.

Hunter's enterprise did not obliterate the production of local knowledge. In Madras, for example, each district had its own manual by the end of the 1880s.[7] These manuals did not have the full "prolixity" of Nelson's work, although they did build on local records and frequently mixed long discursive accounts with statistical tables.[8] Nevertheless, although civilians such as Nelson continued to contribute to imperial knowledge concerning India at the lower echelons of colonial rule, it was clear that Hunter's project was much more attractive to the Government of India at the top. Hunter's statistical survey both revealed a new turn in imperial interest and relied upon the larger statistical enterprise represented by the census. In India as in Europe, the world came to be thought of numerically during this period. Numbers were elegant, discrete, comparable, meaningful within and across categories and units. Numbers could be manipulated in ways that narratives, however they might have always served the interests of state and privilege, could never be. Statistics could capture discrete details in ways that would best serve the state (after which, of course, the science was named), whether in metropolitan or imperial contexts.[9] In India, numbers could be readily compared and analyzed to suggest reasons for political unrest or disaffection, to demonstrate the "moral and material progress" of India under political rule, to control crime and disorder by numerical demonstration. Hunter counted roads and railways, manufactures and commerce, newspapers and famines, agricultural implements and land tenures, fruit trees and domestic animals, wages and prices, the work of the courts, the reach of the schools, the capacity of the jails, and the effects of efforts to improve sanitation and control disease. Additionally, numbers could be used to generate information concerning the caste composition of discrete areas of imperial control in relation to military recruitment, police control, land settlement operations, market intervention, and legal policy. Between 1875 and 1877, Hunter brought out twenty volumes in his series, *The Statistical Account of Bengal*. Many of his data were based on the 1872 census, particularly in his sections on caste. Hunter wrote that "The sections on castes and occupation not only dealt with the numerical strength of each caste in the district, but also gave important information about their traditional and present occupations, their customs and beliefs, as well as the regional variations in their social rank."[10] In November 1877, Hunter was named the director general of gazetteers; he was engaged to collect and digest statistics and information relevant to the ongoing project of official knowledge. These imperial gazetteers began to come out under his editorship in 1881.[11] But the task of determining what should be counted, in which categories, classes, and units, had just begun.

## The First Census of India

The base of the gazetteer project, as Hunter himself acknowledged, was the census. Although the idea of an all-India census was first seriously contemplated in the mid-1850s—before the Great Rebellion—it had a number of precedents. Many regions had records of regular caneeshamari surveys, consisting of house counts, and the Company had on occasion attempted slightly more ambitious census surveys, as it did in 1846, when it sought to test population estimates that had been derived from land settlement records.[12] Madras presidency had mounted two presidencywide censuses before 1851, when it inaugurated a quinquennial return of the population of the district, using the returns of village magistrates and accountants.[13] In 1856, the Government of India, under instruction from the Home Authorities, began to plan an all-India census to be held in 1861. However, the rebellion put the idea to rest for a time, both because of the obvious unrest and because of concerns that the interests of the census officers would be misunderstood so soon after a major military campaign. A census of the Northwest Provinces was conducted in 1865. "Oudh" (Awadh) had a census in 1869. The first census of India took place over a two-year period between 1871 and 1872, though it was not actually conducted in certain key regions and was subsequently seen as so flawed in its conception and its execution that it has never attained the status of the subsequent decennial censuses.[14]

The enumerators did, in fact, take great pains to allay concerns of the population, as they had no faith in the Indian people's capacity to understand the greater good of the census project: "The idea that the Government would incur the labour and expense of such an undertaking without having in view some direct pecuniary profit was foreign to the native mind."[15] The most obvious concern was that the British wished to introduce some kind of poll tax. Only once was there a serious riot, but that was attributed to the fact that the enumerators were specifically hired for the purpose and were not government servants. The enumerators reported rumors associated with the census as part of their enumeration. For example, in Awadh in 1869, "it was rumoured that one male from each family, or every fourth man, was to be taken as a recruit, an emigrant, or a labourer on the roads or to build an enormous fort, or that women were wanted for the European soldiers; while one report was that England had suddenly become so hot that the Queen had desired that two virgins might be sent from each village to fan her night and day, and that the census was merely a subterfuge for the purpose of carrying out her Majesty's orders." In Bengal there was a rumor that the census was in preparation for an enforced conscription of recruits to fight the Russians.[16] That the census was, of course, related in fundamental ways to imperial projects of army recruitment, policing, labor migration, emigration, and recruitment, or even the control of prostitution, was unacknowledged by Henry Waterfield, who prepared these general comments concerning the census without irony, from his position in the Statistics and Commerce Department of the India Office.[17] The British gave far more credence to rumors concerning the possible disturbance of purdah; in parts of Bengal there were rumors that the census officers wished to see the womenfolk of zamindari as well as Muslim families, an idea that according to H. Beverley, the census commissioner for Bengal, "shows how ignorant and uneducated the people of this district are, and how easily any absurd rumour can work on their minds."[18] As was now a commonplace, social phenomena that appeared to confirm the superstition and primitive character of the Indian mind were given priority in official knowledge, at the same time that there was systematic denial of the possibility that colonized subjects could have any basis for a political critique of colonial rule.

The 1871 census built on methods that had been used in previous tabulations, but for the first time sought to generate all-India procedures, standards, and categories for its enumeration. The most difficult task was the establishment of general classificatory categories for the population around the all-important issues of religion and caste. W. R. Cornish, the sanitary commissioner for Madras who oversaw the census of Madras presidency, noted that, "A Census Report is scarcely the place for a dissertation on the religious persuasions of the people; but the questions will probably be asked, what are these distinctive sects? and why is their geographical distribution in the south of India so peculiar; and to answer these a brief epitome of the Hindu religious systems is necessary." Twenty pages of discursive consideration—based on Cornish's tired and clichéd rehearsal of such texts as the *Manu Dharma Sastras* and such authors as Wilson, Dubois, Ward, Hunter, and Brown—follow, touching on such questions as the religion of the Vedas, the history of idol worship, sectarian rifts between Vaisnavas and Saivites, serpent worship, and the origin of the Lingayats, inter alia.[19]

Caste was even more vexing. Waterfield noted that "Great pains have been taken by the writers of the several reports in the classification of the population according to caste. The result, however, is not satisfactory, owing partly to the intrinsic difficulties of the subject, and partly to the absence of a uniform plan of classification, each writer adopting that which seemed to him best suited for the purpose."[20] W. C. Plowden, who prepared the general report on the census of the Northwest Provinces, wrote that "The whole question of caste is so confused, and the difficulty of securing correct returns on this subject is so great, that I hope on another occasion no attempt will be made to obtain information as to the castes and tribes of the population."[21] Plowden, whose sentiment on this score was egregiously ignored in later enumerations, was particularly hampered by the lack of official knowledge concerning the Northwest Provinces, and noted that "before the next Census is taken a series of district memoirs will probably have been compiled, in which all such matters will have been duly noticed."

The primary principle of classification used in 1872 (and again in 1881) was that of varna. The empirical project of the census was wedded to the most general of Orientalist categories for the classification of the social order, with built-in assumptions about hierarchy and precedence. Waterfield explained the use of varna in part by the uniformly high status of the Brahman, regardless of actual occupation: "In all modes of classification, the first rank is held by the Brahmin or priestly caste; but, so far from its being confined to religious duties, there are few trades in which some of its members are not engaged." Not that the category was entirely straightforward: "so minute and endless are the ramifications of caste, that, when Mr. Prinsep took a census of Benares in 1834, no less than 107 distinct castes of Brahmins were found in that one city." The fact that Brahmans were recognized as the caste of highest regard across all of India, however, conferred both pride of place and a clear sense of the utility of the category to enumerators desperate for all-India categories and measures for social order. Since he had begun with Brahmans, varna seemed to Waterfeld by far the most sensible ordering device. "Next in rank come the Ksatriyas, Rajpoots, or warrior caste. . . . They are usually soldiers, landowners, or cultivators; not merely do they in large numbers swell the ranks of the armies in Bengal and Bombay, but they are also found in the service of Native Princes, or acting as overseers or retainers of the large landlords and bankers." But Ksatriyas could not be found nearly as widely across India as was the case for Brahmans. The report noted that "there are very few of this caste in Lower Bengal or in the southern Presidencies [Madras and Bombay]; Behar, the Northwest Provinces, Oude, and the Punjab, are the homes of 85 percent of the Rajpoots." When Ksatriyas were understood to consist properly only of the category of Rajputs, it was a category that seemed regionally and socially truncated in ways that profoundly limited its utility for all-India use. "The third of the primitive castes was the Vaisyas, who were occupied in agriculture and trade." Far more than in the case of Ksatriyas, where occupation seemed a necessary but not a sufficient condition of belonging, given the particular claim of Rajputs, the Vaisya "caste" was overwhelmingly defined by occupation, especially around the category of "merchant," though this was not always an easily identifiable marker of identity. Finally, "the great majority of the Hindoo population was indiscriminately thrown together into the fourth, namely, the Soodra, or servile classes."

The limits of varna seemed clear from the start, and the difficulty and confusion increased exponentially the further one moved "below" the Brahman. Indeed, Waterfield acknowledged that the use of varna for census classification "has not, however, been maintained in more than one or two of the census reports; and, instead of attempting to keep up the old distinction, it seems better to enumerate a few of the castes which, from numbers or for any other reason, are of most importance in the several provinces." Varna was evacuated of meaning and utility even as it seemed the obvious ordering principle. In order to deal with the pitfalls of varna, Waterfield attempted a desultory inventory of different important castes in discrete regions of India. He mentions the Babhans of Behar, the Kayasths of Bengal, the Buniyas across India, the Chandals of eastern Bengal, the Aheers and Chamars of the Northwest and of Oudh, the Koormees of Bengal and the Central Provinces, the Wakkaleegas of Mysore, and, from Madras, the Vellalars, Chetties, and Vunniars. Waterfield complained that the use of occupations in Madras was invariably misleading, as it "must not be supposed that even a majority of any particular caste now follow the occupation according to which they are thus arranged." He noted that in the report on Bombay, the "primitive division of the castes" (by which he meant varna) had been retained. He also noted the sixty different tribes that were specified among the aboriginal races of the provinces of Bengal and Assam, as well as other tribes of the Northwest Provinces, Oudh, Punjab, the Central Provinces, Bombay, Madras, and Mysore. Some of these latter groups were more "Hindooised" than others. Waterfield also noted that the "caste system is, perhaps, almost as prevalent among the Mahomedans as among those professing the Hindoo religion, from which a large part of their number are probably converts, but it partakes rather of the nature of a tribal classification than of the exclusive character of what is commonly termed caste." The report considered a range of questions concerning the distribution of the population, including data on male-female sex ratios. The imbalance in the ratio in the north and west of India among the higher castes led to questions concerning the prevalence of female infanticide, a common concern for the British throughout the nineteenth century.[22]

As charged by the census commissioner, most of the regional reports began the classification of "Hindu castes" by listing the varna divisions of the community, into Brahmans, Ksatriyas, Vaisyas, Sudras, and "outcastes," although, as Waterfield had noted, there was a great deal of variability from region to region. The census for the Bombay presidency used the broad varna categories to classify the entire Hindu population without any major amendment.[23] The report rationalized the use of the varna scale in the usual functionalist manner, noting that although "the divine origin theory [is] . . . mere nonsense, it is more than probable that the first idea of CASTE was developed from the early tribal division into Priests, Warriors, and Agriculturalists, the natural classes into which their necessities would divide them"[24] The report accepted that the Brahmans were the only one of the four groups that could still boast of caste purity. Based largely on Arthur Steele's 1826 compilation of caste custom— itself largely based on the prescriptive regulations of the Brahman-led Maratha Peshwas—it provided a highly Brahmanic view of caste custom, ritual duties affecting Brahmans, and protocols concerning exchange, dining, and marriage.[25] The report from the chief commissioner for Ajmere and Mhairwara used varna categories to organize some of the caste compilations, though with rather more admixture and variability, not to mention emphasis on the subdivisions of Ksatriyas rather than, as was the case for Bombay, Brahmans. H. Beverley, the census commissioner for Bengal, was far less taken by either the Brahmanical theories or the varna system: "in attempting to classify them [the castes], we have been guided rather by the occupation of the various castes than by the stereotyped, though somewhat exploded, four-fold classification of Manu. Sub-divisions of a tribe or caste have been grouped together, no special mention being made of septs or clans which are numerically insignificant."[26] The Mysore census, like that of Bombay, used the varna categories conspicuously, and only introduced myriad subdivisions when it came to the category of Sudra. In Madras, where it had long been noticed that the varna scale was problematic, castes were divided in seventeen sets, ordered in the first instance by varna and, for the lower castes, by occupation: "priests, warriors, traders, agriculturalists, shepherd and pastoral castes, artisans, writers or accountants, weavers, labourers, potmakers, mixed castes, fishermen, palm cultivators, barbers, washermen, others, and outcastes." Indeed, it became increasingly common for varna or ritual markers to be used to differentiate and order the "higher" castes, and occupational markers to be used for lower groups; as we shall see, however, there was serious concern about how to integrate the two sets of criteria, as well as about the misleading character of many occupational classifications.

The British enumerators were manifestly aware of the limits of varna as a broad classificatory rubric, even as they came to recognize large regional differences across India. Brahmans held singular, and singularly uncontested, positions in Bombay and Madras presidencies (or so it seemed, given the extraordinary reliance on Brahmans in the civil services). Brahmans had a less preeminent position in Bengal, where a cluster of high castes made up the upper echelons of the social order, and an even more peculiar status in parts of northern and northwest India, where Rajputs and other Ksatriya castes appeared to be dominant. Aside from Brahmans and Rajputs, few actual caste groups could be readily correlated with varna distinctions and few of these castes could be found across wide parts of India. Dominant caste groups in most regions were specific to those regions, as for example the Marathas of Bombay, the Vellalars of Madras, and the Vokkaligas of Mysore. Even the assumption that occupational differentiation provided both the most ready key to caste distinction and the most usable measure of caste significance for imperial purposes flew in the face of the recognition that formal caste titles only rarely indicated true occupation. Caste enumeration was even more unhelpful for agricultural laborers, let alone a class called "indefinite and non-productive," comprising such variable groups as house or market owners, military pensioners, travelers or guests, apprentices or dependents, eunichs and brothel keepers, beggars and paupers. And then there were the women: "Very little information is given in the Census reports respecting the occupations of the women in British India. In most cases they have either been omitted from the returns, or included with the men in such a manner that the two classes cannot be separated."[27] Added to this was the difficulty of ascertaining caste status even within discrete localities in any uniform manner—given, as we shall see, the multiple and seemingly contradictory uses of titles, names, and other identity markers. Small wonder that civil servants such as Plowden recommended against the use of caste.

The Madras commissioner, W. R. Cornish, began his consideration of caste by noting that "it is a subject upon which no two divisions, or sub-divisions, of the people themselves are agreed, and upon which European authorities who have paid any attention to it differ hopelessly."[28] He held that this was in part a function of the caste system itself, which worked to isolate members of any given caste or subcaste from one another and thus to minimize general knowledge. He expressed his frustration at the outset. "To attempt to describe every sub-caste, or to trace the off-shoots in all cases to the parent stems, would be extraneous to the purpose of this report, and, I shall not attempt it. As it is, the difficulties in obtaining any satisfactory evidence have been enormous. Many learned missionaries and native officials acquainted with the habits and customs of the people have been consulted, and their opinions collated on definite questions, but the replies, as a rule, have been so contradictory as to raise suspicion in regard to the value of the testimony."[29] Cornish was especially concerned about the "almost innumerable subdivisions which still go on extending amongst the people." Faced with a proliferating array of possible social categories, he noted that he would follow the recommendations of a committee that had been constituted in Madras in 1869 to propose a system of classification. This turned out to look very like the varna scale, despite his endorsement of Nelson's observation that the code book of Manu never had any provenance in the south. Beginning with what were in effect the three "twice-born" varnas—the priesthood, the warrior castes, and the trading castes—the classificatory system then took on the problematic character of the Sudra and "outcaste" population in southern India. "But the great order of Sudras and out-castes, containing a diversity of castes, required to be shown in sub-divisions, intelligible to the general reader."[30] The categories that followed the first three accordingly were: agricultural or cultivating castes, shepherd and pastoral castes, artisan castes, writers or accountant castes, weaver castes, agricultural and servile castes, pot-making castes, mixed castes, fishing and hunting castes, palm-cultivating castes, barber castes, washerman castes, and lower races—now regarded as outcastes or pariahs.

Despite the clear order implied in his enumerative tables, Cornish did not wish to subscribe to the hierarchical implications of the varna scale. He noted that his census classification made no attempt to comment on the social position of any division of the people. "The castes are entered in the order in which native authorities are pretty generally agreed is the order of their relative importance, but there can, of course, be no unanimity on such a question, when every man thinks his own caste is superior to others."[31] Cornish went on to comment that the freedom of thought and action under enlightened British rule was manifested most of all in the claims by different caste groups for social precedence: "the lower the caste, the more it now claims pre-eminence for itself." Observing that social status in India was a social rather than an individual affair, he compared such status competitions with the attempts of parvenus in Europe to manufacture fictional pedigrees in order to sustain status claims to accompany the accumulation of sudden and unprecedented wealth. He noted that just as the census report was on its way to the press, he received a visit from "an intelligent native, whose object was to protest against the position assigned in the census classification to the Vunniar or Pully caste. . . . My visitor informed me that he had written a book to show, amongst other things, that the Pullies of the south are descendants of the fire races (Agni kulas) of the Kshatriyas, and that, the Tamil Pullies were at one time the Shepherd Kings of Egypt."[32] The census commissioners were made increasingly aware of the extent to which the census itself became a register of social precedence. As the years went by, enumerators were besieged by petitions for higher status, as the census became the official record of social status. That subsequent enumerators, in particular H. H. Risley, attempted to list castes by social rank only made matters more intense. The census incited myriad efforts to claim caste status and position through narratives about caste origin and history.

The British themselves wrote extraordinary narratives about caste origins and history. Cornish began his by disputing Manu's account as a Brahmanical conspiracy: "The whole caste system, as it has come down to us, bears unmistakeable evidence of Brahmanical origin."[33] Perhaps in part because he did put Brahmans at the top of his list, he remonstrated against the assumed status of the Brahman in particularly strong terms. "The whole system of ancient Hindu law was built up to maintain the monstrous idea that a Brahman was of a different order to the rest of created beings." But Cornish maintained that the idea that Brahmans, at least in the south, were still a pure race akin to the original Aryan conquerors of India was nothing but myth. Since by his reckoning the ancient Aryans were a white-skinned people, he suggested that the "onus remains with them of explaining how it is that in the present day the majority of the 'twice-born' castes are in no way to be distinguished as regards cranial development, physique, or complexion, from the great bulk of the people who make no pretensions to Aryan descent."[34] He feared that if the compilers of Manu's original code—for whom caste was most certainly about racial difference[35]—returned to life and saw the Brahmans of south India of the present day, they would fail to recognize in them "the haughty and exclusive Aryan people who devised the caste system." Noting that the survival of the white race was especially difficult in tropical climates, Cornish averred that a "black Brahman" would be as strange to them as "a 'black . . . Englishman' would be to us."[36] The caste system had clearly been invented to "prevent the admixture of the white and dark races." As admirable as Cornish found this goal, he not only argued that it had not been achieved in the south, but that the plains of southern India could never have actually supported a pure Aryan stock.[37] He concluded by asserting that the mixing of black and white races "has never been found to result in the production of an improved race."[38] As it turned out, Cornish anticipated the racial theories of H. H. Risley, who thirty years later came to dominate the colonial sociology of knowledge concerning caste.

## The Decennial Census

In the 1881 census, provincial enumerators were instructed to analyze only those caste groups of sufficient size to have populations of 100,000 or more. "The object of the arrangement in the Imperial form was to present to the eye the distribution of only the major castes by districts, leaving to the reporter to show in the body of his report, either in tabular shape or otherwise, so much of the information connected with the distribution and the numbers of the remaining castes as might be useful." The census commissioner, W. C. Plowden, had clearly abandoned his earlier sense of the unimportance of caste for the census project. Indeed, he now viewed the census as the "foundation for further research into the little known subject of caste, and with the object of taking full advantage of the statistics thus to be collected the Government of India has requested the local administrations to adopt certain measures for arranging, classifying, and explaining the data obtained." He recommended that a special committee, made up of representatives from each of the provinces who had sufficient local knowledge, be charged with the analysis of the data on caste collected in the census. He noted that although it was originally intended that the castes should be classified by their social position, great difficulty was experienced in carrying this out. Countless petitions had been sent to his office, as well as to the offices of the deputy superintendents of the census in the provinces, "complaining of the position assigned to castes to which the petitioners belong."[39] The issue seemed so uncertain and obscure that the original plan was dropped.

The total population was broken into Brahmans, Rajputs, and "other castes." The bulk of the members of "other castes," (143,309,046 out of 167,283,899) were enumerated as belonging to 207 castes, each consisting of the requisite minimum of 100,000. They were listed in alphabetical order. Another 65 castes were noted as of much lower population, but distributed across more than one province. The commissioner further aggregated the census data to demonstrate that there were 10 major agricultural castes (Kurmi, Jat, Koli, Kachhi, Kaibartha, Koch, Vellalar, Pulli, Koeri, Vannian), making up over 21 million, and 11 major groups of artisans and village servants (leather workers, herdsmen, carpenters, agricultural workers, sweepers and scavengers, traders, oil makers, potters, barbers, smiths, and washermen), making up over 56 million. Altogether, 37 caste groups accounted for more than half the "Hindoos" classified in the category of "other castes." The emphasis on large caste blocs suggests a colonial interest in the organization of the population by caste for administrative reasons. Large caste units, particularly when these caste blocs extended across more than one province, were seen as amenable to administrative concerns regarding military recruitment, criminal classification, social order, agricultural policy, and legal adjudication. The census enumerators were constantly frustrated, however, by the fact that statistical data revealed the importance, and preponderance, of subcaste groupings. Although enumerators were enjoined to find where different caste titles or names could be collapsed into single groups and identified by "some generally known word and not by one of merely local use,"[40] they often in fact collected data that indicated the significance of the markers of difference that produced a relentless proliferation of actual caste groups. And they also discovered that many of the so-called "great" castes by numerical distribution were in fact occupational categories, such as barbers, that produced little in the way of genuine administrative utility, let alone of socially specific knowledge.

The Madras census commissioner for 1881, Lewis McIver, noted both the shortfalls of the previous census and the difficulties in addressing them. The number of castes went up from 3,208 in 1871 to 19,044 in 1881, a clear indication of a difference in method rather than the growth of caste groups. McIver went back to the earlier census returns to discover that the number of names had been reduced by cutting all the caste names that were constructed by the addition of an affix or prefix to some well-known caste name, and "by the omission of many names which were taken, for one reason or other, to represent identical castes."[41] He noted that the earlier enumeration had followed an intelligible course, but one that favored administrative simplicity over analytic detail, and that made it difficult to assess real changes in population over the course of ten years. Such a discrepancy made clear the extent to which caste identity across Madras presidency was in large part about regional and locality affiliation, as well as other factors that modified what might have been perceived by some ethnographic purists as the real caste identity. McIver noted elsewhere in his report that "the difficulties created by the overlapping of 'caste,' 'sect,' and 'locality' have defeated the purpose of the returns."[42] He complimented Cornish's account of the origins of the caste system, but noted the increased difficulty in correlating original occupation with actual caste identity, in part because of "the modern tendency to freedom."[43] McIver noted that "The peace of British rule has turned the Caste soldier's sword into a ploughshare or a pen, the power-looms of Lancashire and the competition of other Castes will ere long drive the weaver into the fields." Thus the commissioner advised against the use of occupational criteria for subsequent caste enumerations, especially for the vast majority of the population grouped under the dubious rubric of "Sudra."

McIver was also skeptical about the interest in organizing caste groups by any hierarchical principle: "Of late years Castes have been so infinitely multiplied that, even if there were any recognised principle of precedence, the nuances of rank would be so slight, that the places of the several Castes could not be distinguished. But there is no such principle. Except the members of the admittedly degraded and depressed Castes, each Shudra thinks, or professes to think, his Caste better than his neighbour's. . . . Wealth means social pre-eminence in the India of 1881, nearly as much as it does in England." Only Brahmans, and some British officers, seemed to think that the caste system could be mapped onto some clear, and hierarchically ordered, grid. And McIver predicted that the situation would, if anything, become considerably more complex as time went on. He concluded his remarks by noting that he had sought to indicate the defects of the present classification and "its failure to cover the whole ground of the Caste System" to illustrate "the difficulties which beset any attempt to classify the Castes."[44] But he did not recommend against the enumeration of caste, instead suggesting a whole host of empirical procedures to guide subsequent enquiries. Even with all the difficulties, there seemed no way out of caste for the census.

Similar debates emerge from each of the regional census reports. For example, in the Northwest Provinces, the British enumerators attempted to devise "practical techniques for standardizing and hierarchising caste names." They standardized spelling and removed distracting "secondary" additions to caste names that were "sometimes locality, sometimes profession and sometimes ceremonial, [which] furnish prefixes to or modify otherwise an ordinary designation."[45] And they organized caste names according to hierarchical principles that were seen as providing order and stability. The only available hierarchical principle was varna, of course, though when it failed to be useful—as in other parts of India and especially for the lower castes—occupational criteria came to be used instead.

Despite the recognition of all the difficulties in the enumeration of caste, the census seemed to incite empirical confidence that a better scheme could be devised. The schemes invariably entailed the reinscription of hierarchy in enumerative procedures. Nowhere was this as clear as in the Bengal report, where the census commissioner, J. A. Bourdillon, argued that the classification scheme proposed by Plowden would do great violence to the local situation. Bourdillon proposed a category of intermediary castes just below Rajputs and Brahmans, to include groups such as Kayasthas, Khandaits, and Babhans. He based his scheme on the suggestions of Rajendra Lal Mitra, the outstanding Indian Sanskrit scholar of the time. Mitra set out an order of precedence that placed the Kayasths right below the Rajputs. The lieutenant-governor of Bengal ordered that any doubt about a caste's social position should be resolved by reference to Mitra's list.[46] Colonial reliance on Brahmanic and textual authority for the establishment of rules of social precedence only increased over the next twenty years of enumerative policy, in large part because of the ascendancy of H. H. Risley in the ethnological hierarchy of British India.

British theories of race attained their zenith in the late nineteenth century. J. A. Baines, the census commissioner for 1891, spoke for the entire census establishment when he wrote that "there is something inherent, as it were, in the conditions of life in India that fosters the sentiment of which the caste system is the expression. . . . [T]he form, or collection of forms, that this expression has taken is the outgrowth of the Brahmanic creed. . . . [I]t seems within the bounds of reasonable hypothesis to attribute to its present development an origin distinctly racial."[47] Like Cornish and myriad other late-nineteenth-century British commentators, Baines found the "germs of the caste system" in the "contact of the foreign race [the Aryans] with their late opponents, when actual hostilities had closed." Baines was struck by the extent to which the ancient colonization of India by the Aryan race was based on peaceful occupation and accommodation rather than invasion and conquest. Doubtless finding solace in the historical parallel between Aryan and British colonization, racial separation was clearly seen as the necessary and laudable basis for the genesis of an imperial social system based on separation and difference. That caste was really a way of dealing with race was further indicated by the fact that varna could be translated as color: "The question of colour was never out of mind. The gods were adjured to protect the Arya colour, and the epithet most often applied to the opposing race is that of dark-complexioned. Thus, the old name for race, or, as subsequently interpreted, caste or order, connoted, at the time it originated, that is, at the first contact of the Arya with a lower race, a real ethnic difference, as Mr. Risley has pointed out."[48] Race was thus the basis of the caste system, though it transmuted into tribal feeling as the caste system evolved into the complex structure of social relations that characterized the present age.[49] So pervasive was caste, Baines felt, that he instructed enumerators to separate questions about religion from questions about caste; in this manner the census could record caste differences among Muslims, Christians, and others, an important improvement in enumerative technique given the fact that caste extended well beyond the Hindu community.

Anticipating subsequent writings by Risley in another respect, Baines pointed out that the social system of India was antipathetic to the formation of an idea of nationality. In the opening paragraph of his comments on the ethnographic distribution of the population, he noted that "It is well to begin by clearing out of the way the notion that in the Indian population there is any of the cohesive element that is implied in the term nationality. There is, indeed, an influence peculiar to the country, but it is adverse to nationality, and tends rather towards detachment without independence." Baines puts it in these terms: "it is that of an excessive devotion to heredity and custom, manifested in the inclination to exalt the small over the great, and to exaggerate the importance of minor considerations, and thus obscure that of the more vital. . . . Rank and occupation are thus crystallised into hereditary attributes, a process which ends in the formation of a practically unlimited number of self-centred and mutually repellent groups, cramping to the sympathies and to the capacity for thought and action."[50] Thus Baines explained the incompatibility of India's social system with the homogeneity of a structure involved in any conception of a nation. That Baines was writing these words—and writing them in the preface to the huge ethnographic apparatus of the census—just a few years after the formation of the Indian National Congress can hardly be accidental. Caste was not only the central means of colonial rule, it was also the dominant reason why colonial governance could conceive of an unlimited future, unimpeded by the rise of any serious nationalist resistance. The 1891 census not only set the stage for Risley's subsequent twenty-year reign over the imperial ethnographic establishment, it also revealed the full embrace of colonial rule with anthropological authority.

The 1891 census formally abandoned varna as the central classificatory structure for enumeration in favor of occupational criteria, based in large part on the models established by Nesfield's and Ibbetson's classification of caste groups in the Punjab, the Northwest, and Awadh.[51] In part a reaction against the difficulties of ranking, in part a momentary nod toward the experience of one part of India in which Brahmanic authority was less pronounced than in others, this decision reflected the existence of serious differences among colonial ethnographers over the status of occupation.[52] Although many previous enumerators had noted the growing distance between occupational categories for caste and actual occupations, prominent civil servants such as Nesfield, Ibbetson, and Crooke advocated a functional approach to caste enumeration. Sir Denzil Ibbetson had been census commissioner for the Punjab in the 1881 census, and published his own report on caste as a separate ethnographic volume in 1883.[53] J. C. Nesfield published his *Brief View of the Caste System of NWP and Oudh*, in 1885; it consisted essentially of his examination of the names and figures shown in the 1882 Census report.[54] The 1891 census classification scheme was based on the proposals of Nesfield and Ibbetson. Nesfield suggested that tribal groups based on descent had become amalgamated into large tribal groups that were organized around occupations and specific functional affiliations. He accordingly advocated the use of broad groupings such as artisans, trading castes, serving castes, and priestly castes. In a similar vein, Ibbetson had suggested the use of categories such as minor landowning agricultural castes; religious, professional, mercantile and miscellaneous castes; and vagrant, menial, and artisan castes.

The 1891 census broke sixty subgroups into six broad categories: agricultural and pastoral, professional, commercial, artisans and village menials, vagrants, and other races and indefinite titles. In order to accommodate what was admittedly a great deal of occupational change over time, the enumerators were instructed to use the caste occupation that had been "assigned to it by tradition, and generally implied in its current appellation." As it happened, there was little contemporary utility in the occupational categories: "In fact, in all cases above those of the lowest, the members of the caste have diverged widely from the means of subsistence from which they respectively take their name."[55] Baines himself seemed uncomfortable with the result: "There are, however, obvious flaws in the grouping itself, due in great measure to the adoption of functional classification to an excessive extent." Doubtless these ruminations gave ample reason for Risley to abandon occupational criteria when he took control of the census over the next decade. And although leading figures such as Crooke continued to advocate a functionalist approach to caste, Risley became the dominant ethnological voice in India for the next twenty years.

## H. H. Risley, the Census, and the Ethnological Survey of India

H. H. Risley entered the Indian Civil Service in 1873 with a posting in Bengal, where he soon displayed an active interest in W. W. Hunter's statistical survey.[56] In 1875, he was appointed the assistant director of statistics, whereupon he compiled the volume on the hill districts of Hazaribagh and Lohardaga. Although he soon returned to regular service, he was recruited once again several years later to collect detailed information on the castes, tribes, and sociology of Bengal. It was at this time that Risley became convinced that caste endogamy had worked to preserve physical differences among castes in particularly sharp ways. Risley decided to explore whether he could apply to the leading castes and tribes of Bengal "the methods of recording and comparing typical physical characteristics which have yielded valuable results in other parts of the world."[57] Although he was also committed to collecting material about the customs and manners of each group, he felt that there had been far more cultural borrowing and exchange than there had been racial mixing. Using the methods of the French anthropologists Paul Broca and Paul Topinard, Risley began to record the anthropometric details that became the basis for his four-volume work on the *Tribes and Castes of Bengal*.[58] Risley's book was, in fact, an expanded edition of the report on the 1891 census for Bengal, of which he was the supervisor.

Census Commissioner Baines confessed that his general scheme for 1891 could not pretend even to the appearance of "ethnological order," though he argued that "in the chaotic condition of the population at the present time an attempt to achieve such would inevitably be a failure."[59] In particular, he felt that any arrangement based on the social estimation of caste position would be compromised not only by differences of opinion but also by the extremely local nature of such criteria. Perhaps a partial defense of his functional scheme, the fact remained that any effort to assess social precedence seemed irrevocably tied to the idea that the varna scale be used over other social scientific indices of caste order. As Risley took over the reins of the census and the ethnological establishment in the wake of his commanding work on Bengal, he found himself relying once again on varna, and more generally on Brahmanical measures, and opinions, concerning caste rank. Risley seemed unabashed about the scientific status of varna, given his own views on the subject of race. He opened his Bengal book with an account of a stone panel at Sanchi, in which the leader of a procession of monkeys is depicted in an act of reverence and devotion to four stately figures "of tall stature and regular features." Whereas most Orientalists had interpreted this scene as a simple act of devotion to the life of the Buddha, Risley found a deeper meaning: "if it is regarded as the sculptured expression of the race sentiment of the Aryans towards the Dravidians, which runs through the whole course of Indian tradition and survives in scarcely abated strength at the present day." Risley saw this as another expression of the true moral of the great epic, the *Ramayana*, in which the army of apes who assisted Rama in the invasion of Ceylon were clearly Dravidians: "It shows us the higher race on friendly terms with the lower, but keenly conscious of the essential difference of type and not taking part in the ceremony at which they appear as patronising spectators." Risley went on: "An attempt is made in the following pages to show that the race sentiment, which this curious sculpture represents, so far from being a figment of the intolerant pride of the Brahman, rests upon a foundation of fact which scientific methods confirm, that it has shaped the intricate groupings of the caste system, and has preserved the Aryan type in comparative purity throughout Northern India."[60] So for Risley the judgment of science confirmed the attitude of the Brahman; so for Risley race history, and perhaps as importantly race sentiment, were the keys to understanding caste.

Risley began his work with a critique of Nesfield, whose theory of caste had been foundational for the general mandate of the 1891 census. Nesfield had emphasized the importance of function: "Function, and function only, as I think, was the foundation upon which the whole caste system of India was built up."[61] Risley found fault with Nesfield in the first instance not so much because of the empirical difficulties of using occupations to classify caste groups, but because Nesfield assumed that caste could evolve as a functional system from an original unitary group. Risley quoted the words of Nesfield at length and with relish, in preparation for announcing his own diametrically opposed view of caste. "It presupposes an unbroken continuity in the national life from one stage of culture to another, analogous to what has taken place in every other country in the world whose inhabitants have emerged from the savage state. It assumes, therefore, as its necessary basis, *the unity of the Indian race*" (italics his). Nesfield held that whatever Aryan blood had entered India had within a short time mixed so thoroughly with that of indigenous groups to be unobservable through any physical means. Risley saw this as a direct challenge to his own understanding of the Indian social world, writing: "Once concede this identity of type, and the question of the real origin of Indian caste recedes into a dim pre-historic distance, where it would be waste of labour to follow it."[62]

Using the methods of Broca and Topinard, Risley took up anthropometry with a vengeance. "For our present purpose anthropometry may be defined as the science which seeks, by measuring certain leading physical characters, such as the stature and the proportions of the head, features, and limbs, to ascertain and classify the chief types of mankind, and eventually by analysing their points of agreement and difference to work back to the probably origin of the various race-stocks now traceable."[63] Risley saw India as unusually well suited to anthropometric investigation. Even putting aside his own convictions about racial origin, the "absolute prohibition" of mixed marriages under caste rules of endogamy served as sufficient grounds for his endeavor. In Europe, where anthropometry was hindered "by the constant intermixture of races," the results of this important branch of anthropology could never serve so important a scientific purpose. India was the ideal laboratory for race theory.

Risley had earlier in his preface justified anthropological research in India along administrative lines, using some of the language with which he later scripted the charter for the ethnological survey of India. He wrote that

> native society is made up of a network of subdivisions governed by rules which affect every department of life. . . . If legislation, or even executive action, is ever to touch these relations in a satisfactory manner, an ethnographic survey of Bengal, and a record of the customs of the people, is as necessary an incident of good administration as a cadastral survey of the land and a record of the rights of its tenants. . . . The

relations of different castes to the land, their privileges in respect of rent, their relations to trade, their social status, their internal organization, their rules as to marriage and divorce,—all these are matters concerned with practical administration.[64]

He noted that marriage and divorce customs were necessary knowledge for judicial magistrates in adjudicating cases concerning criminal as well as other castes. He observed that the distribution of different castes and knowledge, for example, of their food customs district by district would have a direct bearing on administrative necessities such as famine relief. And he argued that matters as various as educational policy and land issues would be affected in vital ways by caste questions.[65] And yet for Risley, unlike many in the earlier generation of colonial ethnologists, these practicalities paled before his scientific ambition: to trace the correlation between marriage customs, physical types, and the racial origins of caste.[66]

Early census officers had already recognized the extreme sensitivity of questions touching on social precedence, having received anxious petitions from different groups concerning varna identity, caste hierarchy, and social order. But despite various recommendations to curtail the collection of this kind of information in the census, and the attempt in the 1891 census to get around the problem through the use of occupational and functional classification, colonial ethnology was preoccupied by matters of relative status. Risley was perhaps more interested than any other colonial official in hierarchy, in large part because of his obsession with race. In his ethnographic survey of the tribes and castes of Bengal during the late 1880s, Risley commenced both his anthropometrical measuring of different caste groups and an extensive correspondence with local officials over questions of caste rank. Writing to deputy magistrates, subdivisional officers, inspectors of local schools, and survey directors, Risley requested local officials to provide him with detailed lists of castes in order of social precedence.[67] Risley's letter was not completely neutral, since he had formed a preliminary idea of caste rank, modeled on the varna scale but organized around the contingent specificities of different regions of Bengal. Usually based on the suggestions of local enumerators, Risley's list used the varna categories from "Manu"—Brahmans, Ksatriyas, Vaisyas, and Sudras, then moving to the "mixed castes"—as classes, adding in the specific enumerated caste groups under their proper classificatory heads. He made sure to include castes such as Kayasthas either under the Ksatriya category or, at least, high up in the scale. His boilerplate letter was as follows:

Sir: I have the honour to forward for your consideration these lists showing the chief lists of . . . arranged in order of social precedence, as stated by different authorities whom I have consulted. I shall be glad to be favoured with an expression of your opinion on the correctness of the arrangement considered with reference to your own district, or to any part of the country of which you have special experience. In order to save trouble in dealing with the lists, I would suggest that where you find the order

of precedence incorrectly given. . . . I would also ask you to state from which castes
Brahmans can take water. . . . Where, too, as in the case of the Brahmans, the main
caste group includes a number of sub-castes . . . , occupying a widely different social
position, the order of precedence of the sub-castes might be stated. . . . Interesting
particulars are believed to be in some cases available as to what castes are entitled to
claim the services of the village barber, what castes may not enter the court-yards of
some of the great temples, etc.[68]

Risley's lists were returned to him with heavy annotation, sometimes substantially revised. Rajendra Lal Mitra, one of his correspondents, noted that the list
was by no means complete, though he was obliged to confine himself to the
names he was sent. "Should other names turn up in the returns, I shall, with
pleasure, classify them, if required."

Babu Tara Prasad Chatterjee submitted his report on the castes of Bengal
based on the "Brahma Vaivarta Purana." This purana followed the authority of
Manu as regards the four original castes, and placed the Brahmans at the top
of the caste hierarchy in clear fashion. Indeed, Brahmans were always at the
top of the lists, and frequently the reports concerned the ranking of the different subgroups of Brahmans and the variable criteria to be employed to understand this ranking. Haraprasad Sastri began his list with Brahmans, followed
closely by Acharyas, or attendants on Brahmans at ceremonies; Bhats, or genealogists; Augradanis, another class of attendants on Brahmans at ritual ceremonies; and Mauriporah, performers of funeral obsequies for Brahmans. Babu
Haris Chandra listed eleven subcastes of Brahmans in order of precedence. He
also noted such ethnographic criteria as those castes from which Brahmans
take water, those castes that can claim the services of the village barber, and
those castes who can enter the courtyards of the great temples. One B. S.
Banerjee, assistant superintendent of the survey of Midnapore, listed twenty-
three castes in order of precedence: Brahman, Kayastha, Baidya, Ksatriya,
Vaisya, Satgop . . . , Sudra, Sankari, down to Peshakar. On another list drawn
up by a local pandit and transmitted directly to Risley were marginal comments of the following kind: "These were originally good Brahmans, but they
degraded themselves by accepting priesthood of Goalas, Kaiburtas, and Sub-
urnaburniks . . . their water is not taken by any other caste than that of which
they call themselves priests; for Vaidya—in Bengal there appears to be no
caste corresponding to the old Vaidya caste. The ancient custom of anuloma
marriage would place them in the rank of Brahmans but in Manu they have
been placed in the status of the mother's caste and hence they are called Anukastha." Babu Tara Prasad Chatterjee gave a long list of "mixed castes" and
noted the reasons for why certain castes had fallen in status. The carpenters, for
example, had been degraded for unpunctuality in supplying wood implements
for the Vedic sacrifice, the painters had been degraded by a Brahmanical curse
for neglecting orders to paint, and the goldsmiths had been degraded for steal-

ing gold from Brahmans. Another correspondent noted which castes could enter temples and which were not allowed to approach the idol.

Haraprasad Sastri, one of Risley's correspondents, drew up extensive comments on the structure of caste. Taking Risley's injunctions seriously, he divided Brahmans into two classes: pure and impure.[69] He then divided pure Brahmans into six classes, ranking those who refused to accept gifts from any but Brahmans in the highest class. The next class was made up of those who would never eat at the houses or officiate at ceremonies of subordinate castes, even though they would accept gifts from them. As is now clear, lower classes compromised their status by successive acts of contamination through relations of exchange and dependence. Impure Brahmans accepted prohibited gifts, and were in obvious ways far more dependent on the hospitality and employment of lower castes. He concluded his inventory of the varna scale by noting that there were very few proper Ksatriyas or Vaisyas, but that the Kayasthas had some years ago begun a movement to claim Ksatriya descent. He was clearly suspicious of such claims.

Another correspondent, the government pleader from Dacca, one Dinanath Dhar, wrote in more detail about non-Brahman twice-born castes: "On the authority of the Shastras, traditions, some of the Oriental-English scholars, and Brahmin-pundits, the Sudarna Vaniks have been proved to be Vaisyas. They are the only Vaisyas of Bengal and should therefore take the third place in the list." In a different note, he wrote as follows:

> According to the Vedas, Ramayana and the Mahabharata, Indian society has always been divided into the four castes namely the Bramin, the Kshatriya, the Vaisya, and the Sudra; or the priest, the warrior, the husbandman, and the serf. Manu also speaks of these four castes in the order in which they occur in the Vedas, and the Puranas. The classification is neither arbitrary nor whimsical but is based on considerations of rank and status which each of the castes occupied in society and is founded in ethnological, political or professional reasons. Notwithstanding the rapid spread of western ideas and influences, the Hindu still accords to the Brahman, the Kshetriya and the Vaisya, the first, the second, and the third rank respectively.

He cited Max Müller and John Wilson, among other European scholars, for vindication. Rajendra Lal Mitra contested the view of one Mr. Macaulay that the claims of the Vaidyas of Burdwan to rank with Rajputs, if not with Brahmans, should be seriously considered. "There is nothing, however, to support this claim. The Subarnabaniks, whose touch is pollution to the higher castes, now claim to be Vaisyas and some Kayasthas call themselves Kshatriyas. The Census has however nothing to do with them. Its duty is clearly to follow the text books of the Hindus and not to decide upon particular claims."[70] Mitra further noted that he drew up the subclasses under the labels of good or inferior, with sole respect to the "social position of the castes and not of particular individuals derived from wealth or influence."

Risley also collected information about the social structure of Muslim groups in Bengal, inquiring about the nature of caste divisions, marriage endogamy, and status differentials, as well as customs such as widow remarriage that marked status among Hindus. A number of commentators averred that although Muslims had none of the strict rules of pollution characteristic of Hindus, they did have status groups that were castelike, and among some, especially lower, sections of the population, caste distinctions. Indian Muslims had imbibed many of the customs and manners of the Hindus among whom they lived, as well: "Indian Moslems living under the Indian sun and breathing the Indian atmosphere have to a considerable extent departed from the orthodoxy of their faith and the customs of their co-religionists in other countries, and adopted the ceremonies of the Hindus so far as they do not directly militate against the tenets of their own creed."[71] Among lower groups, "There are certain low castes of Hindu origin that cling to their old polytheistic notions, and worship Devi and Ram Gossain, a clay idol as a tutelary deity." Although local Muslim officials were frequently asked to compile responses to Risley's inquiries, the inquiries themselves were directly drawn from a preoccupation with Hindu caste and custom.

These inquiries became the basis for much of the material that Risley assembled in his *Castes and Tribes of Bengal* as well as for the 1891 census. In retrospect, Risley's reliance on a Brahmanical sociology of knowledge is astounding. He depended almost entirely on Brahmans and other higher castes. He deferred wherever possible to the *Manu Dharma Sastras* and other puranic sources that served in part as later commentaries on Manu. And he organized his entire understanding of caste structure and rank according to Brahmanical indices such as the acceptance of food and water, the use of priests, and origin stories concerning duties and obligations toward Brahmans, as well as about degradation in relation to those duties and obligations, and ritual proximity to and functions relating to Brahmans. Because of his single-minded obsession with the racial origins of caste, he married his own late-nineteenth-century version of scientific empiricism with the powerful combination of early-nineteenth-century Orientalist knowledge and the clerical Brahmanical opinion that permeated the middle echelons of colonial administration in the localities. Caste might have been justified as a subject of study because it was seen as organizing many administrative matters from famine relief to criminality, but in the same breath it was constituted once again as a Brahmanical ritual system in which the most esoteric forms of social distinction became the basis for administrative knowledge. And despite the efforts of the 1891 census to downplay matters of social rank and to privilege functional explanations of caste, nowhere did the question of precedence take on greater force than in relation to the census of 1901.

In 1899, Risley was selected as commissioner for the 1901 census. In 1901, he was appointed the director of ethnography for India, both because of his acknowledged preeminence as an ethnographer and because the Ethnographic Survey was designed to be conducted in connection with the census of 1901. In 1899, when the preliminary arrangements for the census of 1901 were under consideration, the British Association for the Advancement of Science had recommended to the secretary of state that certain ethnographic investigations be undertaken in connection with the census operations. These included an ethnographic survey—"or the systematic description of the history, structure, traditions, and religious and social usages of the various races, tribes and castes in India"—and an anthropometric survey, which would entail the measurements of castes directed at determining the physical types characteristic of particular groups. The association placed its full faith in H. H. Risley:

> The results of the census itself constitute, of course, by their very nature, an ethnographical document of great value; and my Council feel that, without overburdening the officers of the census or incurring any very large expense, that value might be increased to a very remarkable degree, if to the enumeration were added the collection of some easily ascertained ethnographical data. They are encouraged to make this suggestion by the reflection that the Census Commissioner is an accomplished ethnographist, well known by his publication on the Tribes and Castes of Bengal, the valuable results of which would be supplemented by the inquiries now proposed.[72]

Risley's acclaim can be seen in the attention paid to anthropometry in the proposed survey. The secretary of state noted that "It has often been observed that anthropometry yields peculiarly good results in India by reason of the caste system which prevails among Hindus, and of the divisions, often closely resembling castes, which are recognised by Muhammadans. Marriage takes place only within a limited circle; the disturbing element of crossing is to a great extent excluded; and the differences of physical type, which measurement is intended to establish, are more marked and more persistent than anywhere else in the world." And so Risley's racial theory and anthropometric preoccupations were endorsed by the British government, as they appointed Edgar Thurston to assist him in Madras and empowered Risley to oversee the survey across the rest of British India.

In authorizing funds both for the director of ethnography and for the various surveys contemplated over and above the census operations, the secretary of state commented on the importance of these investigations, noting that "The entire framework of native life in India is made up of groups of this kind, and the status and conduct of individuals are largely determined by the rules of the group to which they belong. For the purposes of legislation, of judicial procedure, of famine relief, of sanitation and dealings with epidemic disease, and of almost every form of executive action, an ethnographic survey of India and a record of the customs of the people is as necessary an incident of good administration as a cadastral survey of the land and a record of the rights of its tenants." Using language that was a direct quotation of Risley, the secretary of state added that "The census provides the necessary statistics: it remains to bring out and interpret the facts which lie behind the statistics."[73] No clearer statement could be made of the colonial uses of anthropology, of how by the late nineteenth century the British in India recognized that the task of colonial rule was essentially ethnographic. Virtually no area of governmental policy or activity could be conducted without benefit of extensive anthropological knowledge. The late colonial state was genuinely an ethnographic state.

Risley did not rigidly separate the ethnographic survey, which in the end was never formally completed, from the census, which stands to this day as a monument to Risley's general influence on colonial anthropology and administration.[74] And although Risley scripted much of the above justification for the conduct of ethnography, his interests were relentlessly "scientific" rather than attuned to the needs of practical administration. With Risley, ethnography simultaneously informed and escaped the province of statecraft, and in the end it unleashed a political revolution that the British could neither understand nor control. Predictably, his commentary on "Caste" in the 1901 census was dominated by his interest in race.[75] He began his chapter on caste by repeating his anecdote about Sanchi and racial consciousness, before moving quickly into an impassioned defense of the importance of anthropometry. Demonstrating the terrific strides made over craniology by developments within anthropometry, Risley noted that he had introduced scientific anthropometry to India seventeen years before in the ethnographic survey of Bengal. He explained the significance of this scientific revolution in part to counter Nesfield's "uncompromising denial of the truth of the modern doctrine which divides the population of India into Aryan and aboriginal."[76] He then turned to a criticism of the 1891 census, for not altogether unrelated reasons. He averred that the functional grouping of the census accorded "neither with native tradition and practice, nor with any theory of caste that has ever been propounded by students of the subject."[77] He was particularly exercised at the classificatory patchwork that led to such strange affiliations as the grouping within single categories of "Brahman priests, Mirasi musicians and Bahurupia buffoons," or of the Dravidian Khandaits of Orissa with Rajputs, Jats, and Marathas.

Risley insisted upon the principle of "social precedence as recognised by native public opinion." He was convinced that distinctions predicated on the centrality of Brahmans and involving matters of rank on the basis of ritual distinctions would be far more helpful in understanding the nature of the caste system as a whole. He prepared criteria for understanding caste distinction that could have served as research guidelines for the latter-day students of Louis Dumont or McKim Marriott:

> that Brahmans will take water from certain castes; that Brahmans of high standing will serve particular castes; that certain castes, though not served by the best Brahmans, have nevertheless got Brahmans of their own, whose rank varies according to

circumstances; that certain castes are not served by Brahmans at all but have priests of their own; that the status of certain castes has been raised by their taking to infant-marriage or abandoning the remarriage of widows; that the status of some castes has been lowered by their living in a particular locality; that the status of others has been modified by their pursuing some occupation in a special or peculiar way; that some can claim the services of the village barber, the village palanquin-bearer, the village midwife, etc., while others cannot; that some castes may not enter the courtyards of certain temples; that some castes are subject to special taboos, such as that they must not use the village well, or may draw water only with their own vessels, that they must live outside the village or in a separate quarter, that they must leave the road on the approach of a high-caste man or must call out to give warning of their approach. In the case of the Animistic tribes it was mentioned that the prevalence of totemism and the degree of adoption of Hindu usage would serve as ready tests.[78]

That Risley was so invested in the minutiae of caste status, to the point of certifying practices such as infant marriage or the prohibition of widow remarriage at a time of active social reform movements across India, and that Risley's investment was in the context of the administrative enumeration of the population of India, suggests both the extent to which caste had been naturalized as the colonized form of civil society, and the way in which an anthropological imaginary dominated colonial knowledge at this time. Anthropology was no longer merely an administrative tool but was now an administrative episteme.

Risley returned to the use of varna as the basis for enumeration and classification, as befitted both his resort to Brahmanical opinion and his interest in social rank. He clearly believed that present-day castes were the "modern representatives of one or other of the castes of the theoretical Hindu system." Accordingly, "In every scheme of grouping the Brahman heads the list. Then come the castes whom popular opinion accepts as the modern representatives of the kshatriyas, and these are followed by the mercantile groups supposed to be akin to the Vaisyas." As always, Risley was on less sure ground when he left "the higher circles of the twice-born," for it was here that the difficulty of classification by rank was legion. Thus his seventh category, after the three twice-born castes and the castes "allied" to them, was "castes of good social position distinctly superior to that of the remaining groups." The degree to which Aryan blood was retained by a group was marked by the direction in which women were exchanged—hypergamously or endogamously—and by exchanges of food, water, and services between caste; thus the eighth category was made up of castes from whom some of the twice-born would take some kinds of food and water. For these "Sudras" and other mixed castes, Risley was aware that the criteria for social precedence varied considerably by region. Not only did the Sudra category vary greatly in social status, it included the dominant groups in most parts of western and southern India, where in any case Brahmans would only take food and water from their own caste or sub-caste. In many parts of north and northwest India, exchanges with Brahmans among other castes were possible and determined ritual status among high castes, but strangely it was in these very areas that the status of Brahmans seemed less secure than where no exchanges were countenanced.

Varna seemed of little value for non-Hindu populations, but Risley—once again using his extensive research and correspondence of earlier years—noted that, "In India, however, caste is in the air; its contagion has spread even to the Muhammedans; and we find its evolution proceeding on characteristically Hindu lines."[79] Risley also contemplated the extent to which caste might be breaking down as a consequence of new ideas and institutions, and determined that technological change such as the introduction and extension of the rail-ways was having a paradoxical effect. Railways worked to diffuse Brahmani-cal influence, as education worked to expand the reach of Hindu scriptures. Although greater "laxity" in matters of food and drink might be observed in some cases, Risley noted that he observed "a more rigid observance of the essential incidents of caste."[80] And Risley repeated his critiques of other theo-rists of caste (most especially those of Nesfield), reiterating his own view that the dominant factor in the formation of caste was the conquest of one race by another. Marriage restrictions developed around the two races, and then were further elaborated around the groups that were born of mixed unions. The principle of the caste system rests on the distinctions of race.[81] "Once started in India the principle was strengthened, perpetuated, and extended to all ranks of society by the fiction that people who speak a different language, dwell in a different district, worship different gods, eat different food, observe different social customs, follow a different profession, or practise the same profession in a slightly different way must be so unmistakeably aliens by blood that inter-marriage with them is a thing not to be thought of."[82] And for Risley, the principle was enshrined in the person of the Brahman and the doctrine of karma.

The ultimate proof for Risley of the wisdom of his system was the great number of petitions and memorials to which it gave rise. Census officers had received similar petitions and representations since the first census, but the announcement by Risley that the census would be reorganized on the basis of social precedence made the census into a political instrument in a way it had never been before. Risley noted several major struggles, including an attempt by Khatris of the Punjab and United Provinces to be classified as Rajputs that was ultimately successful, asserting that these efforts vindicated his belief that "the sole test of social precedence . . . was native public opinion."[83] For the most part, of course, Risley used the opinion of just a small group of "natives," overwhelmingly from the class of official Brahmans and higher castes with whom he had a regular ethnographic correspondence over the years, to develop the textual and ethnographic parameters for the assignment of social status and the determination of categories. And yet he had no real conception that the list of social precedence could become a political document rather than a detached scientific survey. He was unable to respond to the politics his system unleashed.

In Madras, a caste group once vaguely denominated by the title of Palli, or Vanniyar, had organized as early as the time of the 1871 census, when they petitioned to be recognized as Ksatriyas. In 1891, T. Ayakannu Nayakar wrote a learned treatise about the status of the Vanniyars, including a detailed list of answers to questions commonly posed by the census concerning matters of caste origin and identity. In 1901, the Madras census commissioner noted that "they claim for themselves a position higher than that which Hindu society is inclined to accord them," adding that they were working to achieve this status through "a widespread organization engineered from Madras."[84] The Madras census commissioner in 1911 wrote about the "irritation produced by the social precedence tables of 1901, which has found vigorous expression on the part of many, no longer willing to admit their polluting abilities in black and white. . . . Thus the Shanans of Tinnevelly, no longer content to 'pollute without eating beef,' claim to be Kshatriyas; as do the 'slightly' polluting Pallis. . . . Kammalans are suspected of an evolution into Brahmanhood."[85] The census commissioner for 1911 began his report on caste by complaining that "No part of the census aroused so much excitement as the return of the castes. There was a general idea in Bengal that the object of the census is not to show the number of persons belonging to each caste, but to fix the relative status of different castes and to deal with questions of social superiority. . . . The feeling on the subject was very largely the result of castes having been classified in the last census report in order of social precedence."[86] The commissioner reported that hundreds of petitions were received from different caste organizations, their weight alone amounting to one and a half *maund* (about 120 pounds), claiming changes in nomenclature, demanding a higher place in the order of precedence, and emphasizing affiliation to one of the three twice-born varnas. Sekhar Bandopadhyay has noted that "At the local level, these movements of lower castes sometime involved hostility against the higher castes, and sometimes the action of the lower caste leaders led to annoyance and opposition on the part of the higher castes."[87]

Ironically, Risley's presumed success in tapping into concerns about social precedence led to the abandonment of his scheme. Although the 1911 census continued to collect caste information, it was decided from the outset not to classify castes by status. And yet the petitions did not cease. The first two decades of the twentieth century saw an explosion of writing on the subject of caste, much of it around claims by specific caste groups for higher status in the context of varna classification. In spite of the official decision to cease ranking castes in the census, Risley's influence was long-lived. Risley had lasting influence on British caste literature, since most of the provincial compilations about castes and tribes, as well as many of the district gazetteers, were compiled during the time of his superintendence of the census and the ethnographic survey. And Risley had dramatic influence on the rise of caste organizations and the exploding production of literature about the caste system and its principles of order by Indians from all over the subcontinent. In 1931, the census commissioner, J. H. Hutton (later the Cambridge professor of Anthropology), wrote that "All subsequent census officers in India must have cursed the day when it occurred to Sir Herbert Risley, no doubt in order to test his admirable theory of the relative nasal index, to attempt to draw up a list of castes according to their rank in society. He failed, but the results of his attempt are almost as troublesome as if he had succeeded, for every census gives rise to a pestiferous deluge of representations accompanied by highly problematical histories, asking for recognition."[88] And when castes asked for recognition, they did so in the vexed Brahmanical language of varna that Risley had done so much to revive and racialize.

## Caste, Nation, Empire

Risley's ethnological report on the 1901 census of India was republished, with some additions and revisions, as *The People of India* in 1908. The most significant revision was the addition of a single concluding chapter entitled "Caste and Nationality." Risley wished to address in this chapter the effects of recent social and economic change on caste, as well as to speculate about whether caste would be "favourable or adverse to the growth of a consciousness of common nationality among the people of India," perhaps in response to the clear indications of a developing nationalist movement that had erupted after the partition of Bengal in 1905.[89] Risley obviously believed in the importance of caste; he wrote that it was the cement that held Indian society together. And he had little but scorn for those "philanthropic" Englishmen who, on the basis of their experience of presidency towns, predicted the immediate demise of caste. He wrote that "anarchy is the peculiar peril of a society that is organized on the basis of caste," noting that ancient Indian monarchy had functioned well precisely because it could control caste antipathies, at the same time that it could take advantage of the exclusion of most castes from politics. But for the same reason, caste hardly contributed to the formation of an idea of common nationality. "So long as a regime of caste persists, it is difficult to see how the sentiment of unity and solidarity can penetrate and inspire all classes of the community, from the highest to the lowest, in the manner that it has done in Japan where, if true caste ever existed, restrictions on intermarriage have long ago disappeared."[90] British influence, both through the common study among Indian elites of English history and literature and through the "consciousness of being united and drawn together by living under a single government," has begun to suggest the possibility of change.[91] For Risley, however, change would have to occur through traditional means, both because the vast majority of Indians were yet untouched by the idea of nationality and because the construction of an idea of nationality would best be built on the foundation of traditional institutions such as the village community and the village council, "the common property of the Aryan people both in Europe and in India." Thus Risley's racial theory predicated his hope for India's national future, even as he cautioned Indian nationalists against the temptation of sudden change. In the most paternalist of ways, he concluded his chapter by advocating the "orderly development of the indigenous germs of such institutions," warning at the same time that progress would in any case be slow.[92]

Risley's final ethnographic contribution to colonial knowledge thus reiterated the divisiveness of caste, as well as its fundamental compatibility with politics only in the two registers of ancient Indian monarchy or modern Britain's "benevolent despotism."[93] He warned Indian nationalists and European liberals not to give in to either "impatient idealism" or a belief in the force of modern change in India. And he did so by invoking the full authority of an anthropological view of India that reckoned India as fundamentally apolitical and caste as essentially divisive. Indeed, caste was the basic obstacle to change. Change could only be gradual, the introduction of something akin to representative politics could only be the eventual outcome of the cultivation of village forms of political representation and activity. Risley's own antipathy to change, expressed either in relationship to his implicit advocacy of Brahmanic customs in the face of pressures for social reform or in his consternation that the enumeration of caste by rank would unleash a politics that his own social theory could not explain, was of course profoundly mired in his commitment to race science. It is hard to think of another "impartial" observer of society in the Indian context with so profound an impact on the very society he observed. It is also hard to imagine another figure who so admired India's ancient constitution precisely because of the ways it enshrined, so he imagined, a late-nineteenth-century European conception of race.

If Risley's views on caste clearly marked his imperial conceit, they also reflected a curious conjuncture in the history of empire. Risley, whose advocacy of race science was akin to that of Galton and other late-nineteenth-century eugenicists, fashioned a peculiar symbiosis between the racial anxieties of imperial Britain and the ritual anxieties of Brahmans and other higher castes at the turn of the century. He was obsessively committed to the measuring of skulls and bodies and the appropriation of the enumerative project of the census by his zeal to prove a racial theory of origins; and he found a strange kinship with his interlocutors in the imperial theater of India. Brahmans used their late imperial access to political privilege to deny the political character of their influence. Meanwhile, the British relied on Brahman knowledge at the same time that they denied Brahmans any real relation to the racial privilege they sought, despite all the claims about Aryan affinity, to preserve for themselves. All this was accomplished with the putative authority of ancient Brahmanic knowledge, both textual traditions that had been authorized by Orientalist knowledge and ethnographic assumptions that were confirmed by "native" informants. And so the British enumerators kept returning, despite all the manifold difficulties, to a reliance on the old varna scale for their all-India enumerations, even as they maintained a keen interest in caste as fundamentally about rank and social precedence.

At the end of a century that had seen Indians from all across the subcontinent unite in various social reform efforts to combat Brahmanic privilege, Risley directed the full apparatus of colonial power to the task of using India to prove the truth of racial difference. In his enterprise, he accepted Brahman claims about the superiority of such customs as the prohibition of widow remarriage or the importance of infant marriage, even as he rejected the claims of manifestly non-Aryan racial groups to twice-born status. One imagines that Risley would have set himself up as an ancient Indian monarch if only he could have, adjudicating competing claims over status with calipers in one hand and statistical tables about nasal indices in the other. In his last work on caste, he effectively denied that Indians had the capacity to develop an idea of nationality, let alone to rule themselves. At a time when India had already witnessed the agitation over the partition of Bengal and growing nationalist activity across the presidencies, Risley used his racial theory of caste to vindicate his views that nationality would be unable to release the tenacious grip of caste feeling. Race could simultaneously explain Britain's imperial role in India and India's inability to contest it. And although race justified Risley's imperial project, it also became the unfortunate wedge by which Risley's considerable influence on the subsequent careers of both imperialism and nationalism, would be felt in the years to come. As I shall argue in the final section of this book, the combined forces of Brahmanic privilege and racial theory provided major obstacles to the unfolding of nationalist ambitions in the twentieth century—one of imperial Britain's most venal legacies to India.

But if Risley's racial vision gave the census an especially significant role in the production of modern caste identities in India, it also provided the ideological basis for an even more dramatic contribution to the modern rise of communalism. As home secretary to the Indian government, a position he assumed after his stint as director of ethnography, Risley played a key role in the 1903 proposal that Bengal be partitioned into two provinces, in large part because of the political benefits thought to attend the separation of the politically threatening Hindu minority from the majority of Muslim population.[94] A few years later, Risley argued strongly against the view of John Morley, secretary of state for India, that serious political reforms were necessary in the wake of the agitation over the 1905 partition, in particular the Swadeshi movement of 1905–

1907. Risley was against territorial representation and parliamentary government for India, and used the demand of the newly formed Muslim League for separate electorates to make his case. In the end, the award of separate electorates for Muslims in the Morley-Minto reforms of 1909 was in large part the result of the energetic role played by Risley, who used his ethnological view of India to make one of the most influential, and deadly, decisions of Britain's colonial era.[95] It was this award of separate electorates in 1909 that set the stage for the demand for Pakistan and the eventual partition of the subcontinent.[96] Risley's anthropology worked not so much to retard nationalism as to render it communal. In so doing, it also left a bloody legacy for South Asia that continues to exact a mounting toll.

# Part Four

RECASTING INDIA: CASTE, COMMUNITY, AND POLITICS

# *Eleven*

## Toward a Nationalist Sociology of India: Nationalism and Brahmanism

### Social Reform and Colonial Rule

Risley was by no means the only observer to suggest that caste opposed nationality. This view found a steady refrain among colonial voices, for whom such an analysis was deeply comforting in its projection that Britain's empire would not be threatened by a genuine nationalist movement for many years to come. Although the putative divide between Muslims and Hindus became the more dominant colonial charge, caste division had been used throughout colonial history to explain India's "lack" of politics, and when that did not work, to trivialize its politics as localistic, particularistic, and inherently divisive. Indeed, the antipathy of caste to nationhood was also a common assumption among Indians, that motivated many aspects of social reform from the early nineteenth century on and produced many a disagreement about the relationship between caste politics and nationalist politics as the twentieth century wore on. For many nationalists, caste had either to be discarded altogether or acknowledged as a cultural inheritance that could be seen as another glorious, if frequently degraded, aspect of Indian civilization that had to be returned to its original religious and cultural form. In recent years, the structure of this debate, though for the most part not its ideological entailments, has resurfaced in the charge by Hindu nationalist voices that caste politics is antinationalist. This chapter will begin by noting the place of caste in social reform movements, before turning to the place of nationalism in the development of dominant, and professional, discourses on caste in India in the twentieth century. This discussion, along with some anticipation of the contemporary relationship of caste and politics, will set the background for the subsequent two chapters. The first of these chapters is on the rise of caste politics, first around anti-Brahman movements in Madras and Maharashtra, then around the figures of Periyar and Ambedkar, the latter in the context of the emergence of Dalit politics. The second of these chapters is about the eruption of violence around the use of caste as the basis for reservations in independent India. Gandhi will play a critical, if shadow, role in all of these chapters, and I shall return to the role of Gandhi in contemporary social and political theory in the concluding chapter.

Increasingly, caste came to preoccupy Indians as it had Britons in the nineteenth century, if in different ways. It could be used to explain exotic customs to foreigners and to defend against rampant misunderstanding and negative judgment—even to advocate the essential social significance of Indian civilization. Caste could also be used to decry the backwardness of Indian society, particularly when it was seen as a force impeding social equality and the better treatment of women in Indian society. Caste could occasion defenses of Brahmanism and critiques of Brahmans, as well as calls to revive older and worthier forms of custom, tradition, and duty against the decadent forms caste had assumed in modern times. In retrospect, however, it is striking that most explicit critiques of caste condemned it for its divisiveness, portraying it as a barrier to the gradual unification of the Indian people under the essentially beneficent, modernizing rule of the British. Sumit Sarkar has observed that "the social injustice argument, while not absent, remained secondary."[1] Although major social reform initiatives addressed matters related to gender injustice in the context of upper-caste practices and beliefs, caste privilege itself was rarely addressed. No doubt this was related to the preponderance of upper-caste members in these reform movements, though it was also because of the colonial context.

It was impossible to write or speak about caste without making reference, implicit or explicit, to a general colonial climate in which caste had become a sign of Indian civilization—at best the object of relentless colonial critique, at worst a general trope for barbarism. Given the hegemony of European discourses and the centrality of British colonial power, writings on caste seemed implicated in colonial struggles from the beginning of colonial rule. This produced a defensive cast of mind, a concern about unity that had as much to do with the desire not to appear either divided or backward to the British as it did with genuine concern about the essential shortcomings of caste. If, as Partha Chatterjee has suggested, the "women's question" thus disappeared from nationalist discussion, the same was true of the "caste question." Indeed, in some ways caste was an extension of the "women's question," given the extent to which caste values—in particular upper-caste values—were implicated in the issues that were targeted by social reformers concerning the treatment of women, such as sati, widow remarriage, and the age of consent. By the early twentieth century, a growing number of nationalist figures were less concerned that caste might be antipathetic to nationalism than they were with the possibility that a preoccupation with caste reform would retard nationalist mobilization, or give moral support to Britain. Either nationalism itself would transcend caste identities, they thought, or caste problems would be addressed later, after independence.

The exception here was Gandhi, for whom nineteenth-century commitments to social reform could be, indeed had to be, harnessed to nationalism both as an ideal and as a practice. When Gandhi returned to India for good from South

Africa in 1915, Gopal Krishna Gokhale, political moderate and avid social reformer, and Bal Gangadhar Tilak, political extremist and communalist, defined the antipodes of political opinion for the time. The time was politically quiet, as England was at war, and the Indian political movement was still reeling from the conflicts that had developed over the swadeshi movement on the one side and the Morley-Minto reforms on the other. Gandhi tried in different ways throughout his life to wed social reform issues with nationalism, though at times he also alternated his emphasis on the two concerns with great strategic skill, for example to distract attention from necessary political retreats (after 1923 and 1932). But Gandhi never formally abandoned his absolute commitment to certain kinds of reform, most saliently the questions of "harijan" uplift and communal harmony, though his concerns also ranged widely from issues of village development and women's equality to caste prejudice and discrimination. We shall consider in a later chapter the epic struggle between Gandhi and Ambedkar over the representation and mobilization of "untouchable" politics, particularly in the negotiations over questions of joint or separate electorates and electoral quotas in 1932, as well as the pronouncements by Gandhi on caste that so antagonized E. V. Ramaswami Naicker (Periyar). For the moment, however, let us turn briefly to Gandhi's own attitudes toward the institution of caste.

Despite his early denunciation of the treatment of untouchables by caste Hindus, Gandhi was reluctant to blame the caste system as such. Initially, he idealized the varna system as well as the Brahmanic principles underlying it. As he noted in a speech in Madras in 1921, during a time when the non-Brahman movement was gaining considerable support in the Tamil country, "I have not a shadow of a doubt that Hinduism owes all to the great traditions that the Brahmans have left for Hinduism. They have left a legacy for India, for which every Indian, no matter to what varna he might belong, owes a deep debt of gratitude. . . . I would therefore urge—a non-Brahman myself—all non-Brahmans to whom my voice may reach that they will make a fundamental error if they believe that they can better their position by decrying Brahmanism."[2] Gandhi had earlier noted in his newspaper, *Young India,* that he was "inclined to think that the law of heredity is an eternal law and any attempt to alter that law must lead us, as it has before led, to utter confusion. I can see very great use in considering a Brahman to be always a Brahman throughout his life. If he does not behave himself like a Brahman, he will naturally cease to command the respect that is due to the real Brahman."[3] Gandhi defended the caste system for a variety of reasons. He was in favor of hereditary occupations, which worked against competition and class warfare and provided efficient means for the reproduction of traditional skills. He also accepted the doctrine of rebirth and the law of karma, which made each individual's occupation conform to his or her actual ability. Further, as noted by Bhikhu Parekh, Gandhi saw caste as "a self-governing social unit performing legislative,

executive, judicial and other quasi-governmental functions. . . . As such, it reduced the role and the power of the state, fostered habits of self-government
and nurtured the spirit of democracy."[4] Additionally, caste had preserved
many elements of Indian culture and civilization in the face of foreign invasion
and rule over the centuries.

However, Gandhi modified his views of caste over the years, advocating
reform at times in more radical ways than others did. Although Gandhi defended the ideal varna system of varnashramadharma (social and religious
duties tied to class and stage of life), he also defined morality in terms of
self-purification and social service. Some have argued that Gandhi so radically
redefined the varna system that it bore no relationship to any textual precedent.[5] However, Gandhi defended a notional idea of the varna system in part
in relation to an idea of tradition that was meant to be ambiguous. When, years
later, Gandhi defended himself against attacks by Ambedkar over his views on
caste, he wrote that "Caste has nothing to do with religion. It is a custom whose
origin I do not know and do not need to know for the satisfaction of my
spiritual hunger. But I do know that it is harmful both to spiritual and national
growth." At roughly the same time, he stated that "Caste Has to Go."[6] Arguing
that the ancient sastras could not be held in higher esteem than the universal
dictates of reason and morality, he frequently would observe that caste itself
was not the problem, only its degradation in modern India. And yet Gandhi
made efforts to justify his interpretation of the ancient truths of India by reference to specific texts and traditions, and in different contexts he both defended
the ideals of an Indian civilization, which included Brahmanic trusteeship and
occupational differentiation, and suggested that the solution to the "untouchable" issue was to include "harijans" within the caste system (as he wished to
include them within Hinduism and its institutional practices) rather than exclude them from either caste or the temple. Gandhi's textual tactics were never
accepted by orthodox elements within India, who mounted major critiques of
his presumed authority, particularly around his transactions with Ambedkar.[7]
And yet Gandhi's views were seen as traditionalist apologetics by Ambedkar,
Periyar, and many other twentieth-century reformers (including, to some extent, Nehru).

Gandhi did not comment on the British manipulation of caste, worrying as
he did much more about the views of orthodox pandits. And although he
blamed the British for a great deal in India, he was concerned to take national
responsibility for the mistreatment of untouchables and the pride and prejudice
of upper-caste Hindus. But despite his lack of interest in either scholastic debates or colonial genealogies, he articulated positions on caste, and specifically
untouchability, that became increasingly canonic within the scholarly domain
as debates mounted over electoral strategies and policies from the early 1930s
on. Gandhi's attempt to reform caste attitudes while embracing a general notion of varnashramadharma, coupled with his opposition to what he saw as the

divisive strategies of anti-Brahman movements and untouchable agitations and conversions, became increasingly important for many Hindus, for whom Gandhi represented a responsible rapprochement between social reform concerns and the colonial ambivalence they engendered. Gandhi may have been unique in his political capacity to maintain equally strong commitments to nationalist objectives and social reform during the twentieth century, but he did speak for many in his attempt to fashion a middle ground between revivalist traditionalism and reformist modernism. As Indian intellectuals began increasingly to respond to British colonial sociology, both in academic debate and in the context of designing institutions of governance, Gandhi's positions—variably defined as they were—became a benchmark. As a consequence, Nehru's own ambivalence about the place of traditional charters and templates for political and social theory—using a syncretic Hindu idea to characterize India as a civilization even as he sought to secularize his sense of India's present and future—hardly challenged Gandhi's canonic status for debates around caste and tradition.[8]

Gandhi had formulated his views in relation to specific debates and issues, rather than proposing any general theory. Although he wished to defend Indian civilization against the colonial charge that it was barbaric, he also wished to restore those aspects of this great civilization that had been corrupted by venality, self-interest, and prejudice. When he defended Brahmanism from the charges emanating from the non-Brahman movement in Madras, he meant to defend the true principles of Brahmanism but not its political privilege nor its social investments in ritual purity and precedence. When he responded to Ambedkar's charge that untouchability was at the core of what caste was all about, he meant that the original idea of caste was incorporative of the whole Hindu community, and was about interdependence rather than either exclusion or domination. And when he was critical of caste, he was critical in relation to the reactionary claims of orthodox pandits who opposed Gandhi both because he was not a Brahman scholar and because they recognized in him a dangerous modernizer rather than an exponent of caste privilege. If in the end Gandhi was hardly a social radical in matters relating to caste, it was in large part because the politics of caste appeared to him, as they appeared in different contexts to the British, as divisive and antinationalist. And here again, the colonial context conditioned the available options for any nationalist sociology of India.

## Caste Politics: The Background

We noted in the last chapter that the emphasis on caste in the decennial census had given rise to increasing agitation over caste denomination and the assignment of social status by caste groups. The colonial census might have reinscribed a Brahmanic ideal of caste but, ironically, in doing so it gave rise to a

competitive politics that began to make caste the basis for political mobilization on a new scale.[9] Indeed, political movements based on caste mobilization
developed across India, in the first instance as a direct response to census
enumeration, and over time expanding in provenance and context as well as
constituency. Sekhar Bandopadhyay has written about the mobilization of a
congeries of lower-caste groups who joined together under the title of Namasudras. They began their social advocacy through petitions submitted to the
census commissioner for 1891—a process that inaugurated years of protest
and caste struggle.[10] Caste mobilization across Bengal can be seen dramatically in figures collected by Sumit Sarkar: "One rough indicator of changing
times are the classified catalogues of printed Bengali tracts in the India Office
Library. Only 24 entries are listed under the "Castes and Tribes" heading for
the entire period up to 1905; the years from 1905 to 1920, in sharp contrast,
include 140 titles, the vast majority of them written by, or in support of, lower-
caste claims." Caste had become a significant social focus for narrative as well
as politics, congealing in large part around fifty years of the colonial constitution of caste as the fundamental basis of the Indian social fabric, expressed
most proximately, and saliently, in the census. Thus caste became the primary
mode for the textualization of social identity in the last years of the nineteenth
and early years of the twentieth centuries, the census providing a primary illustration of the extent to which textual politics were as much about political
struggle as about narrative form. Speaking about the local politics of Bengal,
Sarkar notes that this explosion of caste politics alarmed the upper classes,
frustrating their developing nationalist aspirations by providing "ample indications that the British would seek to balance any political concessions (like
expansion of the sphere of representative government) with safeguards for
'backward' groups; initially Muslim, but capable of extension to lower
castes."[11] From a nationalist perspective, Sarkar noted that caste politics
ceased to have major significance in Bengal after 1920, unlike the situation in
neighboring Bihar.[12]

Similar developments took place in Maharashtra, as well, where various
caste groups sought to be recorded as Ksatriya or Vaisya during the censuses
of 1891 and 1901.[13] The census commissioner for 1911 described this part
of his task with frustration, even after the effort at social precedence was
abandoned:

> Brahmans and Vanis have been correctly classified as a whole, and various preten-
> dants to Brahmanical dignity such as the Sonars and Panchals have been rejected:
> Kunbis have been carefully differentiated into their widely divergent groups, and
> Kolis have been probably more accurately distinguished from Bhils and mixed
> castes than would have been possible had the term Koli been accepted *tout court*. . . .
> In the Deccan and Konkan our task is easier, but where the Rajput and the Bhil
> combine to resist the application of Brahmanical standards, we are confronted

with a perfect welter of mixed endogamous groups masquerading under fancy titles and concealing an entirely different or similar origin under the same or varied appellations.[14]

But in Maharashtra, caste politics developed with a particular vengeance, and not only around the claims of individual castes for higher status. As early as the 1850s, Jyotiba Phule had begun writing impassioned treatises against Brahman privilege and domination. In his writings, Phule rejected the process of sanskritization—the emulation of Brahmanic custom as a strategy of upward mobility—breaking with the usual ritual idiom of caste movements that had "worked within the parameters of Brahmanic ideology."[15] Phule was directly critical of Brahmans; he argued that they had come to Maharashtra as Aryan invaders, conquering the local inhabitants by force. However, "the Brahmans had been able to conceal this original act of usurpation, and to perpetuate their social privileges and religious authority." Indeed, Brahmans were able to do this "by their invention of the caste system," giving their invidious social distinction the force of religious law through the dharma texts.[16] Phule was perhaps the first to develop this kind of critique, which viewed caste as entirely unacceptable for the lower castes, in marked contrast to the views of most upper-caste reformers. Appearing before the Hunter Commission in 1884, Phule argued that it was the ignorance of the British government that allowed it to give in to Brahmanic strictures and laws, conferring on them even more authority than they had before.

In 1873, Phule established the Satyashodhak Samaj, which, according to Gail Omvedt, contained both "an elite-based conservative trend and a more genuine mass-based radicalism."[17] The first developed along sanskritizing lines, occasionally claiming a Ksatriya origin for the marathas, and from the 1890s received the patronage of the Maharaja of Kolhapur. The second worked in villages rather than towns, staged politically and culturally subversive tamashas (dramas), and attacked the caste system as a whole.[18] Phule's movement set the stage for the rise of a sustained anti-Brahman movement in Maharashtra in the twentieth century, which always seemed characterized by a similar split. The Maharaja of Kolhapur continued, with occasional support from the British (particularly when Tilak and the Tilakites were on the other side), to be an active force in anti-Brahman politics during the early twentieth century. Tilak's strong opposition to Phule's movement and to any anticaste rhetoric endowed nationalism with stronger and stronger Brahman associations, and Bhaskarrao Jadav's non-Brahman party after 1919 was strongly anti-Congress. Nevertheless, after the noncooperation campaign of 1919–1922, the non-Brahman movement in Maharashtra was progressively absorbed by the local Congress organization, which managed to recruit prominent non-Brahmans and direct non-Brahman concerns into the larger nationalist cause, especially in the 1930s, in marked contrast to what happened in Madras. The fact that anti-Brahmanism grew first in western India was due not just to Phule's extraordinary political mobilization but also to the extent to which Brahman hegemony had been installed by the Peshwas and then continued by the British in their accomodationist social and cultural policies. Phule was particularly perceptive in his analysis of the Brahmanic sympathies of British rule in western India in the nineteenth century. But in the twentieth century, western India became better known for the genesis of "untouchable" caste politics than anti-Brahman caste politics, as we shall explore in the next chapter.

Anti-Brahman movements also sprang up in parts of the south of India, in Mysore state as well as the Tamil area of Madras presidency, where they became critical to the development of Tamil politics in the twentieth century. The philological and racial theories of Robert Caldwell had become completely naturalized in both local political discourse and in colonial sociology by the late nineteenth century. As the 1891 census report put it,

> With the exception of the Brahmans and the Marathi and Musalman immigrants, the population of Madras is usually considered to be entirely Dravidian, though it has been contended that many of the lower servile castes belong to a pre-Dravidian people. The arguments for and against this theory are carefully stated by Dr. Caldwell, and the conclusion he arrived at is that these lower castes are also Dravidian and that they were reduced by conquest to the condition of serfs and wandering jungle tribes. Dr. Caldwell's opinion has been adopted by the compiler of the Manual of the Administration and by Dr. Gustav Oppert, and, although it is a question on which the last word has not yet been said, there is at present but little to add to the arguments stated by Dr. Caldwell.[19]

The census commissioner continued, "It is hardly necessary to explain that the caste system as expounded by Manu, is altogether foreign to the Dravidian races. Prior to the introduction of this Brahmanical institution the people of Madras were divided into tribes, but the tribe was not the close community that the caste has now become. Nor had the line of division anything to do with occupation; the connection between caste and function is, in my opinion, entirely a non-Dravidian idea."[20] The census commissioner appeared as skeptical and critical of Brahmans as many of the ideologues of the Dravidian movement.

He also noted that there was an increasing number of claims for Vaisya and Ksatriya status, anticipating the caste movements that preoccupied the census commissioners in the subsequent two censuses. In Madras, castes such as the "Pallis," or Vanniyars, responded to the census by producing tracts and various kinds of arguments to assert Ksatriya status, as well as by the establishment of a caste association, which had appeared as early as 1901. In that year the Madras census commissioner noted that "they claim for themselves a position higher than that which Hindu society is inclined to accord them," adding that they attempted to achieve this status with the aid of "a widespread organization engineered from Madras."[21] Although initial efforts to attain appropriate recognition in the census were unsuccessful, by 1921 pressures from this community led the Madras census to drop caste occupations. By 1931, the Pallis had disappeared altogether from the census, and only the Vanniya Kula Ksatriyas, a new honorific title, remained. The caste organization did not disappear, however, but developed into a major local-level political organization as the century provided more and more political opportunities. In 1935, the Vanniyakula Ksatriyas petitioned for proportional representation in backward-class reservations for Madras.[22]

Success of this kind was also, though after a violent history, attained by the Nadars, a traditionally "toddy-tapping" caste group that had previously been labeled Shanars. In response to a series of petitions from the Nadar caste association, the Madras census commissioner noted in 1891 that they were "usually placed a little above the Pallars and Paraiyans, and are considered to be one of the polluting castes, but of late many have put forward the claim to be considered Ksatriyas, and at least 24,000 of them appear as Ksatriyas in the caste tables." The commissioner held their claim to be absurd, but it was not abandoned, and in 1897 fifteen Nadars entered the Minakshi temple in Kamudi and precipitated a major legal battle. The courts upheld the claim of the temple managers, led by the Maravar raja of Ramnad, that the Nadars should compensate the temple for necessary purification rituals. The courts invoked Brahman law and the testimony of Brahman witnesses, and ruled that since the Nadars' claim to be Aryans could not be sustained, their status as Ksatriyas could not be accepted. Major riots followed the court case in parts of Tirunelveli district in 1899. But by 1921, the census recorded Shanars as Nadars. G. T. Boag wrote that "the Shanar of 1911 now appears as a Nadar; this is done under orders of the Government of Madras, that the word Shanar should cease to be used in official records, . . . in deference to the wishes of the Nadar community."[23] Nadars and Vanniyars were not unique. Across Madras, caste associations grew up virtually overnight, demanding entry into temples, prestigious caste titles, honorable occupational designations and histories in the census, heightened respect in matters of dress, local rights, and traditional roles, and, increasingly, representation in new administrative, political, and educational institutions.

Conflict between caste groups increased significantly in the first decades of the twentieth century, not least because of the growing attention to questions of precedence and issues of respect. These eruptions were hardly all caused by the census. Throughout the nineteenth century there is persistent evidence of caste conflict, for example in missionary records (which reflect both the role played by missionaries in fomenting caste rebellion and the concern of missionaries to decry the role of caste in Indian society). However, records from Madras presidency suggest that conflict between upper and lower castes—

between Brahmans as well as landed upper-caste Sudra groups on the one hand and either lower-caste Sudra groups or depressed-caste groups on the other—rose dramatically in the early decades of the twentieth century.[24] And conflict emerged with special force in the wake of the politicization of caste around the census, as well as in relation to the rise of anti-Brahman movements and the growing agitation—both from within Congress and outside it—concerning the rights of untouchables. The Kamudi conflict between Shanars/Nadars and Maravars was a signal example, and interestingly was followed in the 1930s by a series of conflicts between Nadars—by then an economically prosperous community—and Muslims over the use of certain streets for ritual processions.[25]

In the 1920s there was a series of disputes between barbers (Maruthuvars) and high peasants (Vellalars) in the towns of Tirunelveli district of Madras. Problems arose after the barbers formed an association and decided, as a gesture of protest against various forms of ill treatment suffered at the hands of their upper-caste patrons, to stop performing the ritual service of cremation. Perhaps the principal concern of the barbers, at least as expressed in their petition, was the degrading nature of the cremation service, something the caste group claimed had only been added to their ritual service duties in recent years. But the barbers were treated very badly by their upper-caste patrons in other respects, as well, and decided to try to teach them a lesson. Some members of the patron caste proceeded to terrorize the barbers by boycotting their services, appropriating their customary shares and benefits, and on occasion making examples through beatings and the burning of houses. Although there was manifest concern about the level of everyday oppression in the legislative debates that considered this issue, concern in Madras (about this as well as other similar cases) was especially heightened by worry that the barbers might convert to either Christianity or Islam.

There were other disputes between depressed class groups (Pallars and Paraiyars) and upper-caste groups, including Brahmans, usually over the use of public streets for ritual processions (including cremation). In each case, the upper-caste group claimed that custom had dictated that the lower groups use other streets, and objected to what they saw as new, unsanctioned notions of public rights. Disputes frequently turned violent, often on ritual and festival occasions. Many of the new claims were clearly the result of a changed political atmosphere, in which the depressed classes successfully claimed in 1922 official sanction for the title of "Adi-Dravida," or "First Dravidians."[26] In 1929, a group of Adi Dravidas in Chidambaram paraded through an upper-caste neighborhood carrying a photo of the King Emperor in a bullock bandy, accompanied by music and drums, thereby clothing their provocation in a public act of loyalty to the Raj.[27] Another dispute in Coimbatore district, which involved the passage of Adi Dravidas through Brahman streets on their way to take their children to a new school, was attributed to a decision in the previous month to hold a conference of the depressed classes in a nearby town, occasioning both increased boldness on the part of Adi Dravidas and heightened resentment from upper-caste groups.[28] A major dispute broke out in Ramnad district over the wearing by Adi Dravidas of shirts while performing ritual duties, such as pulling temple cars, sweeping streets, beating drums, and blowing trumpets at festivals. The adjudicating magistrate noted that "The genesis of the trouble seems to be the new ideas of civilised life imbibed by the Adi-Dravidas, who went to Burma and other places, and came back with notions of refinement in matters of dress and living. They began to shake off subservience to Nattars, and to put on decent dress. The Nattars naturally resented the innovation as it was looked upon by them as an invasion upon their rights and customs maintained for a long time to preserve the distinction between the Nattars and the Pallars."[29] In another region of the same district, Adi Dravidas complained that the upper-caste assembly had made a series of codes and declared that they would henceforth enforce them; among these were decrees that Adi Dravidas would not be allowed to wear ornaments of gold or silver; that men should not wear clothes below their knees or above the waist, and that they should use neither umbrellas nor sandals; and that women should wear neither upper-body clothes nor flowers and saffron paste.[30]

One case was brought to the government after a young untouchable boy was beaten nearly to death after inadvertently touching a young upper-caste girl; such cases were hardly new, though the possibility of redress from government clearly was.[31] Numerous petitions began to surface in government records, telling stories such as this: "Generous Sir, still we humbly explain the difficulties caused by the caste Hindus of our village we are fined heavily for nothing at all putting some blame on the poor Adi Dravidas of the Cheri. All the Cheri people and even our cattle fear to travel out of our Cheri, for some way or other they create some fault on us and compelled us to pay heavy fines they levy; or else we are beaten to death. Our position now is very miserable Sir, as we are depressed very much."[32] Most such cases never surfaced anywhere near a place of possible redress, and very often they were suppressed locally. The submagistrate of Tiruvadanai, one Periasamy Thevar, attempted to do this to a meeting of Adi Dravidas in the town of Devakottai in 1931. Thevar noted that A. S. John, president of the Adi Dravida Mahajana Sabha of Ramnad, was causing communal tension by traveling from town to town and holding public meetings, and thus banned such a meeting in his town "in the interest of the peace and to avert a disturbance of public tranquillity."[33] Efforts to contain the political organization of depressed classes have continued to the present day, but it is ironic that the very upper-caste non-Brahman groups who contested Brahman privilege were the ones who sought to keep the depressed classes in their ritual position of inferiority and subservience.

The anti-Brahman movement in Madras had itself only developed major political importance with the establishment of the Justice Party in 1916. Founded by a group of upper-caste non-Brahmans, the movement derived much of its momentum from the overwhelmingly Brahman character and constituency of the Home Rule movement, which was spearheaded in Madras by Annie Besant. The leaders of the non-Brahman group, most prominent among them T. M. Nair and Tyagaraja Chetti, published a "Non-Brahman Manifesto" on December 20, 1916. The manifesto began by asserting that "The time has come when an attempt should be made to define the attitude of the several important non-Brahman Indian communities in this Presidency toward what is called 'the Indian Home Rule Movement.'" It went on to say that the apparent unity of the Home Rule League was in fact a Brahman conspiracy, and that non-Brahmans had no place in the nationalist movement as it was at present constituted. Non-Brahmans supported British rule, not least because the British were committed to justice for all castes and creeds. This was of particular concern in Madras, where Brahmans, though making up only a bit more than 3 percent of the population, dominated the universities and the administrative cadres. "But it passes our understanding why a small class which shows a larger percentage of English-knowing men than their neighbors, should be allowed almost to absorb all the government appointments, great and small, high and low, to the exclusion of the latter among whom may also be found, though in small proportions, men of capacity, enlightenment, and culture." The manifesto committed itself to the advocacy of non-Brahman issues, and pressed for greater educational, social, political, and economic development. It ended by noting that when "the rigidity of class and caste begin to disappear, the progress toward self-government will unquestionably be more satisfactory."[34]

The Justice Party was remarkably successful in attracting political support during a period of Congress mobilization, particularly in years dominated by Gandhi's noncooperation movement. In disavowing non-cooperation, it was able to contest the 1920 municipal elections successfully, and used its position to bring before the Legislative Council in Madras a series of resolutions designed to give non-Brahmans a greater proportion of government jobs. The promulgation of what came to be known as the First and Second Communal Government Orders, in 1921 and 1922, represented a great victory for the Justice Party in its efforts to provide a greater distribution of government jobs to non-Brahmans. The First Order directed that collectors and other local officials be attentive to the subject of the distribution of appointments among various castes and communities; the Second Order strengthened the resolve of government to give priority to non-Brahmans and other "backward" communities in their recruitment policy, not only for new appointments but for all government employees, including personnel in permanent, temporary, or acting appointments, and those appointed either for the first time or promoted from subordinate grades. For the first time, official government records were to be scrupulously kept to record the communal distribution of government appointments and promotions. Despite this great success, it became clear that the Justice Party leaders were less committed to the support of "untouchables" and the more "backward" non-Brahman castes than was desired by many of their supporters, and with the abandonment of noncooperation by Congress, the Justice Party began to lose influence and power. By 1925, it was yielding its position on the one hand to the nationalists, and on the other to inheritors of the non-Brahman movement such as E. V. Ramaswamy Naiker, to whom we shall return in the next chapter. Nevertheless, the short but successful history of the Justice Party demonstrated both the extraordinary reserve of anti-Brahman sentiment in Madras and the inextricable association of certain forms of nationalism with complicity in caste privilege and power.

If the first few decades of the twentieth century demonstrated the potent role of caste in political mobilization, it showed both the power of Brahmanic ideology and the growing resentment against Brahmans, particularly in western and southern India. Even though caste politics frequently led to antinationalist outcomes, the British experience of the census, combined with the frustration they felt when they were asked to adjudicate struggles over caste rank, led to increasing pressure to deemphasize caste for official purposes. In large part because of the clamor and contest over issues relating to caste rank, the British therefore decided to discontinue the use of caste as a category for enumeration in the census after 1931. Such a decision was recommended by none other than J. H. Hutton, the census commissioner for 1931, who had been so frustrated by Risley's legacy. But even as the decision came as a result of dissatisfaction on the part of particular groups with their enumerated denomination and rank, it was also related to pressure from those who objected for various principled reasons to the use of caste in any form. Pressure came from many groups who claimed the status of twice-born castes, at the same time that it mounted from groups such as the All India Hindu Mahasabha, which petitioned for Hindus to be registered first as Hindus, or from the International Aryan League, which complained that census officers refused to enter "Vedic Dharma" in the caste tables. Many notable individuals also put pressure on government to suspend the use of caste. S. Satyamurti, a leading Congress figure in Madras, spoke out in the Central Legislative Assembly in March 1939 to the effect that public opinion in India was united that "we must not divide up the country into these castes."[35] It is not irrelevant in this context that Satyamurti was one of the most vigilant opponents of caste politics—which for him meant non-Brahman politics—in Madras presidency. In Madras as in other parts of India, a commitment to nationalism often entailed the deemphasis of caste. Nationalism and Brahmanism became increasingly linked. And if this was so in the thick of the political strategies and struggles of nationalist mobilization, it was also so in the theorizing of Indian society by intellectuals and scholars committed to the national cause.

## Brahmans and the Nation

S. V. Ketkar, a Maharashtrian who went to Cornell in the early years of the twentieth century to study for a Ph.D. in political science, published his *History of Caste in India* in 1909, just a year after the publication of Risley's *The People of India*. He began his work by noting that "The mystery of caste is a hard problem for a foreigner to understand." He was sure that caste was the most inscrutable aspect of India, and it became clear that he felt this chiefly because of the common condemnation of Brahmans by foreigners. "Some feel," he wrote, " that the unscrupulous priesthood have led their countrymen into this snare of folly to maintain their own supremacy." He said that he wrote this book in part to attempt to recuperate the position of the Brahman, although he was not optimistic about the capacity of non-Indians to develop either understanding or empathy. "It is quite natural that no other feeling than that of amusement should occur to the English mind. He can afford to laugh at the absurdities and contradictions in such an antiquated and complicated institution."[36] Writing from America, he did not restrict his concerns to the English: "An American missionary," he wrote, "finds the subject very useful to induce his countrymen to subscribe money to save the souls of two hundred millions of people from heathenism." Ketkar did not go on to apologize for caste, or to suggest that foreigners misunderstood caste out of malice, but rather proposed that, as a Hindu who could not remain unmoved and uninvolved in the face of such a momentous topic, he was well placed to propose the methodological guidelines for a scientific study of caste. But he was obviously writing for Americans and Britons, as well, and he made frequent allusions to the caste system in America, both the racial hierarchy between blacks and whites and other ethnic divisions, to relativize the study of caste and assert its fundamental universality.[37]

Ketkar was especially concerned that the suspicion about Brahmans held by his contemporary colonial commentators on caste stood as a major obstacle to scientific understanding. Whereas early colonial writers had relied on Brahmans and on their texts, later writers had not only replaced a textual with an empirical approach but also often accused Brahmans of writing texts—and organizing the caste system—in order to maintain their superior position. Ketkar wrote that "The thankless task of guiding the people and of preventing them from doing wrong fell, to a large extent, on spiritual authority, as the political authority was unfit for their share of the burden. . . . But with such a huge task before the Brahmans what power did they have? All that they had to rely on was their knowledge of the sacred literature, for which all people had high respect."[38] Indeed, Brahmans effectively had to use their sacred authority and law to compensate for the weakness of the Indian state and its moral capacity. In countering colonial disregard for India's sacred traditions, Ketkar subscribed directly to colonial disregard for India's political past.

Ketkar's text is primarily an explication of the *Manu Dharma Sastra*, which he saw as foundational for understanding caste in contemporary India, not to mention a brilliant document written to order and explain a complicated but logical system of social relations. Accordingly, Ketkar understood caste as predicated in the varna system, itself organized—as were the internal subdivisions of jatis—on the basis of relations of purity and pollution. Strongly committed to a belief in the centrality of social precedence, Ketkar argued against the idea that public opinion was a reasonable arbiter of precedence, at least in the absence of traditional rulers. "The country is now fallen into the hands of 'casteless barbarians,' and only formal precedence has remained."[39] Ketkar explained the gradations of social rank through distinctions based on a logic of pollution—where the acceptance of water, differentiation between cooked and uncooked food (including distinctions having to do with the media of cooking, the composition of the vessels, the context and venue of exchanges, and so on), as well as rules of ceremonial purity—provided the logic of calibration. Brahmans were clearly at the head of the caste system, though distinctions among Brahmans too could be explained by the rules of pollution. Ketkar accepted the truth of origin stories and affiliated narratives in which castes could be degraded by changing dietary customs, loosening commitments to caste endogamy, and allowing various kinds of unacceptable exchanges with members of other, lower, castes. When in doubt, the sacred texts were to be consulted by learned pandits. "When a question of precedence between two castes came before the colleges of Pundits in Benares, or Poona, it was decided, not by the observation of actual social conditions, but by the authority of old books. . . . The underlying theory was that the laws which define caste status are fixed and known. They are given by the gods. It is the duty of the Pundits to explain the laws."[40] One can sense Ketkar's horror that men like Risley (a casteless barbarian par excellence), using empirical, ethnographic, and physical measures rather than the authority of priests and texts, was adjudicating social precedence at that exact time.

Although Ketkar did not address Risley's adjudication of social precedence, he did add an appendix to his work in which he argued specifically against the claims of colonial ethnology on the subject of race. In particular, he argued against Risley's sevenfold classification of the races of India, and claimed that all Indians—Aryans as well as Dravidians—were of the Caucasian race. Earlier in his text he had expostulated about the colonial claim that "Arya" meant a race of invaders, preferring the idea that Arya referred to "properly qualified people." He did concede that there might have been a Vedic meaning of the term that had racial connotations, but he believed that well before the time of Manu "the descendants of the invading tribes had forgotten where they came from, and thought themselves to be autochthonous and men of noble qualities and culture," a sentiment he shared.[41] Ketkar's book, cited in all subsequent major works on caste and one of the principal influences on G. S. Ghurye, expressed the author's frustration with and disappointment in the demise of Orientalist interest in texts and textual authority and the more recent rise of administrative prejudice and empirical predilections.

Ketkar was concerned both about the rise of empirical social science and the increasing politicization of caste during late colonial times. A less embarrassed plea for Brahmanic authority is hard to find. Ketkar was right for all kinds of reasons to question the capacity of Westerners to understand caste. But he was right in particular for underscoring the question of the stakes of writing about caste. The stakes for Westerners, when there were any besides amusement, were governed either by the administrative necessities of colonial rule or the potential uses of heathen institutions for missionary fundraising. It was clear that Indian social scientists would write from very different positions and concerns. If Ketkar's defense of Brahmanism was problematic, the reasons leading to his defensiveness were hardly parochial. At the same time, Ketkar's work anticipates a peculiar conjunction in the history of a national sociology of India. Concerns about Brahmans, and Brahmanic authority, played an important role both in the modern history of Indian nationalism and in the modern career of professional discourses concerning Indian society.

G. S. Ghurye was the most influential among Indian academics to write about Indian sociology during the colonial period (as well as after). Born in Maharashtra in 1893, Ghurye did his Ph.D. at Cambridge in social anthropology under the supervision of W.H.R. Rivers and A. C. Haddon, and returned to India as head of the Department of Sociology at Bombay University in 1924. He trained many of India's most prominent sociologists until his retirement in 1959,[42] and exerted tremendous influence on the sociology of India through his myriad writings, most importantly his *Caste and Race in India*, first published in 1932. Ghurye's text went through five editions, each with new sections that addressed contemporary issues in the study of caste, such as the rise of interest in the study of class (one edition was entitled *Caste and Class in India*) and the strong emergence of non-Brahman politics in Tamil Nadu in the 1960s (the fifth edition, published in 1969, carries a final chapter on this subject).

Ghurye began his study with a line that echoes Ketkar, yet is vastly different in tone: "A foreign visitor to India is struck by the phenomenon known as the caste system."[43] He outlined six major features of the caste system: the segmental division of society, hierarchy, restrictions of feeding and social intercourse, civil and religious disabilities and privileges of the different sections, lack of choice of occupation, and restrictions on marriage. Ghurye attempted to weld empirical description and conceptual unity. On the one hand, he noted that in each linguistic area there were about two hundred groups called castes that fixed the limits of marriage and effective social life. On the other, he noted that the major groups "were held together by the possession . . . of a common priesthood." For Ghurye, the caste system was made up of many parts, but it was characterized throughout by harmony:

> Common service to the civic life, prescriptive rights of monopolist service, and specific occasions for enjoying superiority for some of the castes, considered very low, made the village community more or less a harmonious civic unit. Complete acceptance of the system in its broad outlines by the groups making up that system and their social and economic interdependence in the village not only prevented the autonomous organization of the groups from splitting up the system into independent units, it created a harmony in civic life. Of course, this harmony was not the harmony of parts that are equally valued, but of units which are rigorously subordinated to one another."[44]

Ghurye's emphasis on harmony was not unrelated to his textualist interpretation of caste. He devoted two long chapters to textual accounts of caste from the Vedas to the *Manu Dharma Sastras*. Although these texts privileged varna rather than jati, they provided ample room for the derivation of the contemporary array of regional caste denominations. Having surveyed literary references to texts from classical sources to Abu'l Fazl, he then turned to an examination of the relationship of caste to race. Ghurye was especially concerned to evaluate the claims of H. H. Risley about the racial origins of caste as well as his use of anthropometric methods and data. He was extremely critical of both the data and their uses, and ultimately determined that only in the Punjab and parts of the United Provinces was there a correlation between race and caste, in which Brahmans betrayed physiognomic indications of their hereditary connection to the Aryan invaders of the subcontinent. Everywhere else, and for all other groups, general miscegenation had eroded any racial distinctness to caste. Ghurye emphasized the mixing of castes particularly in Maharashtra and Madras, where he believed that caste, in the form of anti-Brahman movements, had become dangerously politicized (and erroneously supported by racial justification).

Ghurye was also directly critical of Risley's role in the politicizing of caste, particularly in relation to the census. Although Risley was not the first to use the decennial census for collecting and presenting material about caste, Ghurye noted that "This procedure reached its culmination in the census of 1901 under the guidance of Sir Herbert Risley of ethnographic fame."[45] Risley had assumed that the only intelligible picture of social groupings in India could be gained by using a classification of "social precedence as recognized by the native public opinion." Ghurye complained that Risley adopted this procedure despite "his own clear admission that even in this caste-ridden society a person, when questioned about his caste, may offer a bewildering variety of replies," according to whether he chooses to emphasize his sect, subcaste, exogamous section, titular designation, occupation, or region. Ghurye lamented the growth of caste sabhas organized expressly around the attempt to press forward claims of higher status in the census. He quoted with approval the remarks of a Mr. Middleton, one of the two census superintendents in 1921, to the effect that the so-called occupational castes "have been largely manufactured and almost entirely preserved as separate castes by the British Government"; and that "Government's passion for labels and pigeon-holes has led to a crystallization of the caste system, which, except amongst the aristocratic castes, was really very fluid under indigenous rule."[46]

Ghurye also felt that the apparatus of the census, along with various decisions of government, had encouraged the anti-Brahman movement. In particular, he criticized the use of quotas to restrict government employment for Brahmans in Maharashtra and Madras. Ghurye, a Maharashtrian Brahman and a staunch nationalist, was skeptical from the start about the rhetoric of the Maharaja of Kolhapur, who spearheaded the Maharastrian non-Brahman movement and was given to requesting "the protection and guidance of the British Government until the evil of caste-system becomes ineffective" in connection with the early implementations of home rule.[47] Ghurye acknowledged Brahman dominance in administrative positions, but noted that the initial complaints of non-Brahman activists had been addressed by non-Brahman political mobilization alone: "An analysis of the membership of the various local bodies in the presidencies of Bombay and Madras clearly proves that the non-Brahmans know their rights and are generally keen to conduct a strong campaign against any measure which they feel unjust to them." Ghurye argued very strongly against the policy of reservations, which he viewed as "opposed to the accepted criteria of nationality and the guiding principles of social justice." And he accepted that non-Brahmans might have legitimate grievances, and exist as a single class in structural terms, in relation to social matters, "because the attitude of the Brahmins as regards food and social intercourse, and religious instruction and ministration towards them, has been uniform." But he strongly opposed the notion that legislative sanctions or reserved posts would address this issue: "Whatever liberalizing of the Brahmin attitude in this respect has taken place during the last forty years is mainly due to education and social reform campaign and not to the very recent reserved or communal representation."[48] Indeed, Ghurye argued that the "restriction on the numbers of the able members of the Brahmin and the allied castes, imposed by this resolution of the Government, penalizes some able persons simply because they happen to belong to particular castes," at the same time clearly abandoning "the accepted standard of qualifications and efficiency."[49] Ghurye believed that reserved representation was not only not necessary, but actually harmful "in so far as it tends to perpetuate the distinction based on birth," something he felt was both counterproductive and antinational: "To harp on the caste differences and to allow special representation is to set at naught the fundamental condition for the rise of community feeling."[50] Given the collaboration between the non-Brahman movement and the British, Ghurye's argument was not altogether far-fetched, even if his own sense of caste identity, and more general commitment to a Gandhian injunction for national unity and Brahmanic trusteeship, doubtless generated no small measure of his concern.

Ghurye may not have been the first to argue against the policy of reservations and the effects of politicizing caste, but he made the most eloquent, and academically sound, critique of the contemporary relationship of caste and politics in the decades surrounding independence. Further, Ghurye was perhaps the first serious scholar to suggest that the politicization of caste was not merely a natural outgrowth of the traditional institution but a conscious design of British colonial policy. The principal colonial lesson of the Great Rebellion of 1857, according to Ghurye, was that the "safety of the British domination in India was very closely connected with keeping the Indian people divided on the lines of caste." Ghurye quoted James Kerr, the principal of the Hindu College of Calcutta, as having written that the spirit of caste "is opposed to national union," and argued more generally that a policy of divide and rule on caste grounds influenced the policy and conduct of many British officials.[51] He further suggested that the British were so receptive to the arguments on the part of leaders of the non-Brahman movement in favor of reservations and caste quotas precisely because "as a logical development of the attitude of the Government . . . [reservations] nursed, rather than ignored, the spirit of caste." And so, when writing against the non-Brahman movement in his own Bombay presidency, Ghurye used an anticolonial argument to support his concern that national life, due to the rise of caste enmity and conflict, could "be reduced to an absurdity."[52]

Ghurye thus anticipated by years the critical historical anthropology of Bernard Cohn and others who have, in turn, anticipated and influenced the argument of this book. He was certainly the first anthropologist to turn his attention to the dangerous effects of colonial discourse and colonial institutions. Indeed, much of the critical thrust of the present work can be found in his early writings, predicated as they were on a careful dissection of the ways in which colonial preoccupations with caste and race contributed to the reification of caste as a single system characterized by separate identities and competing political agendas. His critique of colonialism was both prescient and profound, for he understood the hidden and dispersed effects of colonial policy on Indian society in the grip of nationalist mobilization. His nationalist agenda, however, was mixed, for although non-Brahmans were recruited to a Hindu community, little mention was made of Muslims in Indian society.[53] And his greatest concern seemed to be the loss of Hindu community in the face of attacks on the sacred charter of Brahmans and Brahmanism. He concluded his chapter on the effects of British rule on caste by noting that "Even the apex of the ancient scheme, the priesthood of the Brahmin, which has been the great bond of social solidarity in this finely divided society, is being loosened by caste after caste. At about the end of the British rule in India, caste-society presented the spectacle of self-centred groups more or less in conflict with one another."[54] His argument against colonial policies of divide and rule, eloquent and persuasive though there were, stood side by side with his nostalgia for an age in which the otherworldly prestige of the Brahman could be acknowledged for its innocent capacity to hold Indian society together. Ghurye did not apologize for all aspects of the caste system. Even though he lamented the decline of the "priesthood," and was particularly worried about the rise of prejudice against Brahmans, he clearly supported Gandhi's attempts to ameliorate the conditions of the untouchables (even as he disapproved of Ambedkar's attempt to politicize caste to that end). But he was resolutely opposed to the politicization of caste, whether by the British or by forces in the anti-Brahman movement. And his greatest concern in the politicization of caste seemed to be the generation of bad faith around both Brahmans and Brahmanism, the latter being for him the font of principles that were fundamental to Indian civilization.

Ghurye's complex position reveals more than the specific conjunctures of his own time and place. Influenced by the Hindu revivalist Vishnu Krishna Chiplunkar as well as other major figures in early twentieth-century Maharashtra, he was, in the words of A. R. Momin, "steeped in ultra-nationalism and revivalism." Additionally, his specific scholarly investment in Indology as well as anthropology sustained his understanding of the ideal of caste harmony. As Momin has put it, "Ghurye's early background in the classics and his life-long preoccupation with textual and scriptural sources led him to adopt the Brahmanical model of Indian society, which is too idealistic and overarching."[55] Additionally, Ghurye was a young nationalist academic at a time when the anti-Brahman movement in Maharashtra appeared to many to be collaborating with British rule and organized around antinationalist principles and alliances. And yet his pathbreaking analyses of caste anticipate other conjunctures as well: between anticolonial nationalism and social conservatism, between a critical relationship to colonial transformations of caste and a newly revitalized commitment to an idea of caste as fundamentally harmonic, between a critical reaction to the colonial denunciation of Indian society and the idea of Indian civilization as essentially Hindu. In the present age, more than fifty years after the successful outcome of anticolonial nationalism in India, these conjunctures have not lost their force, and if anything lurk with growing danger.

Ghurye was a particularly important figure in these growing conjunctures, as he both made an early, and forceful, argument against the social effects of British rule and correlated his sociological theories with contemporary political predicaments. Indeed, in each new edition of his major work he took on new issues, though always with his sense that the politicization of caste was part of the problem, not part of the solution. But the influence of his work was soon superceded by that of his most celebrated, if somewhat rebellious, student, M. N. Srinivas, who during his distinguished career changed our understanding of caste.[56] Srinivas's work has in particular raised new questions about the relationship between caste and politics. Although he made many important contributions to the study of Indian society, his most original idea was in his characterization of social change in India under the rubric of "sanskritization." Srinivas defined sanskritization as "the process by which a 'low' Hindu caste, or tribal or other group, changes its customs, ritual, ideology, and way of life in the direction of a high, and frequently, 'twice-born' caste."[57] In other words, sanskritization involves claims for upward social mobility through status emulation, with Brahmanical codes for conduct setting the standard for status. Srinivas gave many different examples, from his work in Coorg and Mysore to ethnographic reports across the subcontinent, of how caste groups would become vegetarian, prohibit the remarriage of widows, become far more exclusive in relation to exchanges of food with other proximate castes, worship different kinds of gods and employ different kinds of priests—in order, eventually, to press claims for higher positional status. Sometimes these groups would change their behavior one or two generations before claiming higher status. Some of his most compelling examples came from the history of the census. Srinivas believed that sanskritization occurred whether or not Brahmans were dominant; he also believed that sanskritization occurred in every part of the Indian subcontinent, and that although it has been more active at some periods than at others, "the process has been universal."[58] Srinivas viewed sanskritization as the principal modality of social mobility in India, and stressed that throughout Indian history castes had been able to convert secular power and wealth into status precisely in this way. In pre-British times, Indian monarchs would play an active role in these struggles for mobility by conferring perquisites and titles on castes that attained particular political importance. And although Srinivas felt that the varna scale itself had in all probability become unusually significant only during British rule, he felt that the abstract character of status attached to varna did provide salient opportunities for caste groups to change their standing in society over time.

Srinivas's picture of the Indian social order was much more dynamic than most previous colonial and sociological views, and his ethnographic speculations were invariably situated in historical contexts. He was also on occasion critical of his own work, as when he chastised himself for focusing exclusively on a Brahmanic model for the possibilities of status emulation. He wrote that in his early work, he "emphasized unduly the Brahminical model of Sanskritization and ignored the other models—Ksatriya, Vaishya, and Shudra."[59] In his later writing, he attended far more to the importance of Ksatriyas, noting that there were times when there were "declarations to the effect that the Ksatriya had no superior and that the priest was only a follower of the king."[60] Srinivas further affiliated the traditional process of sanskritization to more modern processes of Westernization and secularization. He wrote extensively about the movements by backward castes to press for greater equality, attempting to understand these movements and their sociological implications with far more sympathy, and complexity, than had Ghurye before him. And yet Srinivas never came to terms with the extent to which the theory of sanskritization was not merely exemplified by struggles around the census but was also in large part produced by them. The significance of a single, "universal" Brahmanical scale for upward mobility was clearly the result of the new colonial sociology of knowledge, not an expression of a fundamental principle in Indian civilization. When in earlier days kings had adjudicated and mandated questions of social precedence and prestige, they had done so according to very different principles and concerns than those suggested by the theory of sanskritization (even when modulated by formal distinctions among varna categories). Furthermore, Srinivas had serious difficulties appreciating the rise of backward-caste agitations in more recent days. He noted that that such agitations were typically antinationalist and counterproductive. Srinivas, like his teacher Ghurye before him, worried as well about the effects of quota systems, as had been introduced in Madras presidency: "A system of caste quotas was established; this often resulted in better qualified Brahmins being rejected in favor of less qualified non-Brahmins."[61] Srinivas's progressive and historically textured view of social mobility appeared, even by his own admission, to favor a Brahmanical view of India, as well as to register concern about the effects on Brahmans of social legislation (and to agree with the widely held view that reservations for non-Brahmans naturally increased the level of administrative inefficiency).[62]

Srinivas was rare among social scientists working on India for his subtlety and insight, as well as for his self-reflexive candor. As an epilogue for his book *Social Change in Modern India*, he wrote a chapter entitled "Some Thoughts on the Study of One's Own Society."[63] He began by noting, wryly, that his work had been repeatedly evaluated outside of India in reference to his being "an Indian sociologist engaged in the study of my own society." Although many observed that this gave him a great advantage, there were those who asked "how far can any sociologist understand his own society," as well as others who felt he was at his best when he forgot the technical apparatus of social anthropology in writing about India. Srinivas decided to take these questions seriously, without raising obvious questions about the relationship of Western anthropological views about India to colonial concerns and the difficulties of proper sociological analysis in the face of what was usually massive ignorance about language, history, and culture—let alone the fact that such questions had never been posed to Weber, Durkheim, or any other major Western sociologists of the West. Indeed, he used the opportunity of this essay to raise critical questions about his own positionality, noting for example that his views on the effects of reservations could not but be related to his sensitivity regarding the distress of many Mysore Brahmans, many of them his friends and relatives, over the "steady deterioration in efficiency and the fouling of interpersonal relations in academic circles and the administration—both results of a policy of caste quotas."[64] But he sought to defend himself in particular against a charge that came from the renowned British social anthropologist E. R. Leach, in a review of his earlier book, *Caste in Modern India*. Leach had complimented Srinivas for his insider's knowledge of India, but had questioned whether this was fully an advantage or not "from the viewpoint of sociological analysis." Leach went on to suggest that the basic theme of the concept of sanskritization was that "there is a long term tendency for caste groups which are low in the social hierarchy to imitate the style of life of high caste Brahmins, thus introducing a certain fluidity into the total hierarchy of castes." He continued: "That such fluidity exists has been clearly demonstrated, but that it should be seen as arising from an emulation of the Brahmins seems to me odd—a specifically 'Brahminocentric' point of view! If Professor Srinivas had been of Shudra origin would this have coloured his interpretation."[65] Rather than taking umbrage—as surely he could have—over the patronizing character of comments from one who had directly inherited an imperial perspective from his national culture as well as his discipline, Srinivas wrote to say that Leach had gotten it wrong. In his book on Coorg he had observed that Lingayats rather than Brahmans had been the agents of sanskritization, and he now argued that this should have made it clear how sanskritization was not about emulating Brahmans per se.[66]

My argument in this chapter has been about the relationship between nationalism and Brahmanism, a problematic connection hardly discounted by the suggestion that non-Brahmans could be the agents of Brahmanism. But I hasten to note that my point here is not that Ketkar, Ghurye, and Srinivas were all Brahmans (any more than my concern about the propriety of Leach's critique is due solely to the fact that he was English). I assuredly do not wish to affiliate myself to the critical tone—let alone position—of an Edmund Leach. I have sought to make the point that sanskritization—both its historical reality, as it was exemplified with particular intensity during late colonial rule, and its conceptual celebration of the force of Brahmanic hegemony, is an idea that is inseparable from colonial history. Sanskritization became the pervasive idiom for social mobility as the result of the transformation and legitimation of Brahmanic values in relation to colonial rule as well as nationalist resistance. And in this last regard, it is hardly surprising that a nationalist critique of caste felt the need to revive and celebrate values of a different kind from those used in colonial critique, values that could be seen to undergird the moral commitments of a transcendent Brahmanism and the spiritual disposition of an entire social system.

My account of colonial forms of knowledge in this book points to the contingent and necessarily compromised character of all social scientific knowledge, especially in colonial contexts. Nationalism had to rail against colonial structures even as it was embedded in them, as these suggestions about the rise and place of Brahmanism make clear.[67] Ketkar had been right to suggest that Indians had different stakes in the study of caste from those of foreigners: "But the sons of India would have to think on caste with quite a different feeling. They cannot afford to enjoy the absurdities as an Englishman would. . . . A Hindu cannot be so unmoved. The more he thinks on the caste system, the better he understands his own burden." Ketkar went on to suggest a textual view of caste, but he did so in the more general context of suggesting that the ancient sages were mere mortals, and that "if they have erred, it is neither a sin nor an impossibility to correct them."[68] Under the conditions of colonialism, internal critique was very different from external condemnation. But this is not the end of the story. For sanskritization was not only a description of a natural social process that valorized Brahmans and Brahmanism across India, it also entailed the naturalization of a specific history in which colonial transformations displaced themselves onto (even as they relied upon) "native" sociologies.[69]

Despite Srinivas's serious attention to the role of political authority and recent history in his understanding of social change, the theory of sanskritization worked to consolidate the relationship between social ideology and sociological analysis in ways that necessitate other kinds of critique and forms of resistance. In late colonial and postcolonial India, the most insistent resistance to social and cultural privilege has come in the form of caste politics. In sociology as well as in nationalist politics more generally, the conditions for resistance against colonialism and for the realization of a historically valorized national project seem forever mired in the limits imposed by colonial history. The next two chapters will seek to historicize the conditions of knowledge and truth further, within the context set by previous chapters. But despite the move into a critical consideration of nationalist ideology and postcolonial politics, the burden of this argument throughout is to insist that we once again acknowledge the special burden carried by any nation that has been colonized by the West, in the name of modernity.

# *Twelve*

## The Reformation of Caste: Periyar, Ambedkar, and Gandhi

### Hindu Nationalism

There is nothing new in the phrase "Hindu nationalism," even if it has come to be associated with the recent emergence of political movements expressing Hindu rather than secular ideology. Nationalism in India emerged under colonial conditions, conditions that put Indian civilization itself on trial as the principal impediment to modernity and self-rule. We have traced parts of the process whereby India was consigned to an otherworldly and decidedly premodern position, and have pointed out moments when reactions to colonial and Orientalist characterizations led to other versions of Hinduism as the indigenous cultural repository of identity and value. This process led, as well, to a variety of attributions related to Islam, as a foreign presence and a colonizing power that had subdued a Hindu nation and prepared the way for British colonial rule. As much as Muslims were targeted both as scapegoats and as outsiders, they were not the only ones to worry about the formation of dominant nationalist ideological formations in which new and quintessentially Hindu self-representations became increasingly taken for granted, even in avowedly secularist formulations. And as Muslims became figuratively reincorporated in the nationalist consensus as minorities that needed protection as well as representation as an effect of difference, other cracks in the nationalist body politic became visible, as well.

One of the major consequences of the census was the denomination of "Hindus" as the majority group in India, with "Muslims" as the dominant minority, atop groups of other, progressively smaller, discrete religious communities. It was not just the idea of a majority community that was new but also the use of a single term, "Hindu," to designate a population that ranged so widely in belief, practice, identity, and recognition. "Hindu" began as a general designation for the people of a place, but little by little it was affiliated to normative conditions that were oppositional (to Muslims, or Christians), exclusive (of tribals, or untouchables), and confessional (in the sense of a single world religion). If one of the most dramatic effects of colonial history has been the denomination of Hindus as a majority community made up of the adherents of a uniform religious system, this history has been neither straightforward nor uncontested. Even as upper-caste Hindus only came to relax the exclusionary concerns of ritual propriety in the face of demographic pressures and the onset of democratic institutions, the troubling character of the homogeneous monolith was apparent both for designated "minorities" and for a host of other groups. The phantasmatic nature of the Hindu whole worked ironically to constitute its reality even as it made contestation and critique more urgent than ever. New voices emerged as representatives of sociopolitical constituencies that saw the Hindu whole as hierarchical, oppressive, and graded, the precipitate of a politics of exclusion that endangered groups "within" as much as outside. And in this respect, the majority was an effect of the idea of the minority, even as the exemplary minority of Muslims created the terms of and models for other minority groups. Minority languages of dissent emerged as a consequence of the general discourse of the minority, even as they were necessarily tied to and dependent on the majority languages of national, religious, regional, and ethnic unity.

The constitution of minorities in colonial India served both to justify the colonial state, which legitimated itself in part through its claim to offer protection to minority groups that were seen as endangered, and to fashion the majority as a homogeneous group. The majority not only was represented through colonial lenses; it also congealed as a single community in nationalist reaction to colonial rule. Even the most secular elites fashioned rhetorics of Hindu majoritarianism when engaged in social reform; they called simultaneously for the reform of caste and gender relations within the Hindu fold and urged social and legal autonomy for different communal—read religious—groups. These same elites accepted colonial policy and practice concerning civil and personal law, maintaining faith in the secular mission of the colonial state even as they gave administrative support to the fashioning of a distinctive set of compromises motivated by the general understanding of Hinduism as an unusually all-encompassing way of life as well as a religion.[1] Although social reform agendas in the nineteenth century often focused on Brahmanic practices, with only a few exceptions (such as with Phule's movement in Maharashtra) they worked to assert the primary importance of Brahman customs for the definition of the Hindu community. And although the salience of social reform activities waned considerably in the twentieth century, there was in fact a growing consensus in favor of the regulation of civil domains and public spaces. The management of temple trusts, the abolition of devadasis (temple dancers), and the legislative efforts to promote temple entry for untouchable groups were all pitched in terms of principles having to do with fundamental human rights, but not only singled out Hindu institutions for state reform but also enshrined enlightened Brahmanic opinion as the basic arbiter of Hindu practice. Even when legislation such as that which established the Hindu Religious and Charitable Endowment Board in Tamil Nadu in 1927 was mobilized ostensibly in order to control Brahman power, the net effect was to broaden Brahman control and further establish the hegemonic authority of certain textual traditions and interpretations that could only be described as Brahmanic. In fact, the Hindu Religious and Charitable Endowment Board had the effect of "sanskritizing" ritual practices and procedures and "Brahmanizing" managing boards in many temples that had earlier been controlled by non-Brahman caste groups such as Chettiars, Maravars, and Valaiyars.[2]

This chapter concerns the emergence of minority and majority languages, and movements, around caste (a marker in any case of Hindu identity) in relation to two extraordinary individuals, E. V. Ramaswamy Naicker and B. R. Ambedkar. Eloquent spokesmen for and organizers of social and political movements through much of the twentieth century, these two individuals fought for minority rights while they also contested the ideological charter of the majority. Both, in their own ways, fought as much against "Hinduism" as they did for political rights, revealing in their particular ways the extraordinary tyranny of nationalist ideology as it became tied to late colonial Hindu self-representations. Both, as well, became obsessed with the role of Gandhi in the formulation of Indian nationalism, and their lives, and struggles, inevitably shed a great deal of light, and some darkness, on the saintly father of the Indian nation himself (as well as on recent appropriations of Gandhi). Both, in the end, help us to anticipate the current crisis around Hindu nationalism, and call into question the ideological uses that have been made of the idea of a tolerant majoritarian religion in India today.

## Periyar

Periyar, a title meaning "Great Man" that was conferred on him by many Tamilians during the political struggles, was born E. V. Ramaswamy Naicker in 1879. Also known as E.V.R., he entered nationalist politics as an enthusiastic supporter of Gandhi and the Congress movement shortly after the satyagraha of 1919, and rose quickly to be elected president of the Tamil Nadu Congress in 1920. He became a critical figure in the mobilization of political agitation in Madras around Gandhi's noncooperation campaign, and was imprisoned by the British in November 1921. After his release several months later, he took up various Gandhian causes, from prohibition to the popularization of khadi. In the spring of 1924, he entered the campaign at Vaikkam, a temple town in the princely state of Travancore. The campaign concerned the issue of temple entry for the "untouchable" caste of Ezhavas. Temple entry had become an important concern of Gandhi and of Congress, as an extension of reform activities around the plight of untouchable groups, and perhaps also as a reaction to the difficulty of relations with Muslims after the troubled Khilafat alliance. Gandhi had long decried the sin of untouchability, but only after 1920 did untouchability become defined formally by Congress as a "reproach to Hinduism." T. K. Madhavan introduced a resolution to the 1923 Kakinada session of the All-India Congress which stated that temple entry was the birth-right of all Hindus. The next year, Madhavan and other local leaders inaugu-rated untouchable marches to and around the Vaikkam temple, provoking mul-tiple arrests. Gandhi followed the movement closely, intervening when a Syrian Christian assumed charge of the satyagraha. Gandhi wrote to say that the Vaikkam satyagraha was not a Christian concern and that "Hindus [should] do the work."[3]

In saying this, Gandhi gave implicit voice to one of the central concerns that motivated Congress support for Gandhi's position on untouchability, namely, the inclusion of untouchables within the Hindu fold for reasons of number. Rather than constituting another minority, untouchables were to help Hindus constitute the majority. Untouchability was a reproach to Hinduism rather than to the nationalist movement. The campaign to force temples to allow entry for untouchables thus occupied a contradictory position for both Gandhi and Con-gress. Although he advocated Congress involvement in temple entry, Gandhi wished that Hindus alone be involved in what he felt was a cause for Hindu shame in the context of an exclusively Hindu quarrel. And Congress took up a Hindu cause as a national issue (which, unlike most other social reform issues, specifically concerned questions of religious worship). Perhaps it is no surprise that temple entry had an ambivalent career in the nationalist move-ment, both in the early twenties when it was first undertaken, and later in the thirties when it became an important plank in Congress's constructive pro-gram. Although the Vaikkam satyagraha managed to bolster "the spirits of a demoralised [Kerala] Congress . . . after the shock of the Mappila Rebellion of 1921," it did so at the cost of further communalizing local nationalist politics.[4] It also had an unintended effect: E.V.R.—one of the heros of the Vaikkam agitation—left the satyagraha assuming that systematic reform of Hindu insti-tutions had become Congress's main ambition, only to discover soon there-after that social reform had very limited scope for both Congress and Gandhi.

E.V.R. quarreled with Congress and Gandhi very soon after the Vaikkam affair over the question of separate dining for Brahman and non-Brahman stu-dents in a Congress-sponsored school (Gurukkulam) near Madras. The school was set up by the nationalist leader V.V.S. Iyer with the aim of imparting traditional religious education in the larger context of a commitment to patriot-ism and social service. After several complaints, it became clear that Iyer had arranged for separate dining facilities for several Brahman students at the request of their parents. Although Gandhi attempted to intervene through a compromise resolution, the controversy split a number of Brahman and non-Brahman Congress leaders and led to a great deal of bitterness on the part of E.V.R. and several of his principal associates. While this controversy raged, E.V.R. further attempted to interest the Tamil Nadu Congress to support a resolution for communal representation. At the same time that E.V.R. met failure in this attempt, he found that his efforts to expand non-Brahman representation on the Tamil Nadu branch of the All India Spinner's Association (of which he was then president) were frustrated, as well. Once again, E.V.R. found himself locked in bitter dispute with some of the same Brahman leaders who had opposed him over both the Gurukkulam school issue and the communal resolution. In late 1925 E.V.R. decided to leave the Congress. After this break, he declared his political agenda to be: "no god; no religion; no Gandhi; no Congress; and no brahmins."[5]

The year 1925 was a time of turmoil in south Indian politics. Coming in the midst of the period when Gandhi had consigned Congress to a preoccupation with social reform activity rather than direct or constitutional political action, at this time the moderate "Swarajists" came to dominate the national political agenda. In the south, the Congress had to usurp the reformist momentum from the Justice Party, which from its position in the Legislative Council had successfully mobilized non-Brahman opinion and pushed through the first communal legislation mandating non-Brahman participation in government service. Meanwhile, Congress efforts were compromised both by some of the conciliatory social gestures of Gandhi and its initial difficulty—given the prominence of Brahmans in the local organization—in pressing home its own charge that the non-Brahman movement was narrowly self-interested. The Justice Party had originally been formed in 1916, in part in reaction to Annie Besant's alliance with Brahmans in her Home Rule League, around the concern to advance non-Brahman interests in public and government domains. The Justice Party achieved its greatest success through its role in the two "Communal G.O.s" of 1921 and 1922. The Communal G.O.s (Government Orders) established new guidelines to increase the proportion of government offices held by non-Brahman communities in Madras Presidency; the population was classified into the following groups: Brahmans, Non-Brahman Hindus, Indian Christians, Muhammadans, Europeans and Anglo Indians, and Others. These classifications were used to measure and press for greater proportional representation in new government appointments, as well as in promotions and other personnel decisions.[6] Although the Justice Party could take major credit for the implementation of these new policies, its constitutional collaboration with the British during the period of the noncooperation campaign set the limits of its political success. By 1925, the Swaraj Party, licensed to engage in electoral politics during the period of Gandhi's political retirement and commitment to constructive activity, was showing signs of eclipsing Justice, which received little support from E.V.R. despite his break with Congress.

For a man with the political ambitions of E.V.R., constitutional collaboration was an inadequate political goal, to say the least. E.V.R. was regularly critical of the way Brahmans continued to conflate ritual scruple and national

principle, and at the same time he genuinely felt the slights Brahmans routinely offered to non-Brahmans in the newly emerging public spheres of Madras. But he never seemed content with the normal procedures of minoritarian
politics, and he recognized many of the compromises and problems such a
politics necessarily implied. Indeed, one of his stated reasons for leaving Congress in 1925 had been his concern that Gandhi had given too much credence
to the Swarajists, who were allowed to engage in Council elections and politics. Ironically, E.V.R. felt that Gandhi had not sufficiently emphasized the
importance of the constructive (social uplift) program. Despite E.V.R.'s osten-
sible agreement with Gandhi in not supporting direct political activity, he
seemed particularly bitter when Gandhi undertook political retirement during
the late 1920s. At one point he wrote, "The reason why Gandhian Constructive
principles have lost all value is because, in the name of a fraudulent unity, they
were abandoned and in their place a Gandhi Mutt established. Since madness
is characteristic of all mahatmas, our own is no exception to the general rule."[7]
E.V.R. was preoccupied with Gandhi's personal authority, while at the same
time he seemed especially concerned to challenge the way Gandhi formulated
national political goals, and dissented with manifest bitterness over the definition of political communities, social reform issues, and religious questions and
identities. Indeed, E.V.R. was most enraged by Gandhi himself, whose involvement in Tamil Nadu Congress matters seemed invariably conservative.
For E.V.R., Gandhi represented a Brahmanic position on the question of reform. To be sure, Gandhi's statements about caste in response to the non-
Brahman movement in Madras were defensive on the subject of Brahmans and
hardly designed to suggest sympathy with a full-scale critique of caste.

In April 1921, addressing a public meeting in Madras, Gandhi had said that
Hinduism "owes its all" to the great traditions established by Brahmans. He
noted further that Brahmans "could pride themselves on taking the first place
in self-sacrifice and self-effacement and that they should remain the custodians
of the purity of our life." In obvious reference to the non-Brahman struggle in
Madras, Gandhi admonished non-Brahmans not to attempt to "rise upon the
ashes of Brahmanism."[8] In a later speech in Madras in 1927, Gandhi upheld
the fourfold classification of caste and the duties appropriate to each stage of
life (varnashramadharma), though he firmly rejected the notion that caste had
anything to do with high or low status. Further, he maintained that a ban on
intermarriage or interdining was essential to the ideal system.[9] E.V.R. responded to Gandhi by arguing that support for the principle of varnashramadharma in effect relegated all caste Hindus to the position of Sudras,
which implied for him that they were "sons of prostitutes."[10] If Sudras were to
follow Gandhi's advice, E.V.R. said at a public meeting in Tinnevelly, they
would end up only serving Brahmans.

E.V.R. met with Gandhi in September 1927 in an encounter that resolved
none of their differences. E.V.R. reportedly told Gandhi that he believed true

freedom for India would only be achieved "with the destruction of the Indian National Congress, Hinduism, and Brahminism."[11] These exchanges were widely covered in the Tamil press, and were critical in the legitimation of E.V.R.'s break with Congress. For most non-Brahman political activists—including those for whom the Justice Party had been tainted from the start by its antinationalist position—support for *varnashramadharma* was support for Brahman hegemony. For E.V.R., this was to be his last meeting with Gandhi: "Though the public believes that Mahatma Gandhi wishes to abolish untouchability and reform religion and society, the Mahatma's utterances and thought reveal him to hold exactly the opposite views on this matter. . . . We have been patient, very patient and tight-lipped but today in the interests of abolition and self-respect we are, sadly enough, forced to confront and oppose the Mahatma."[12]

In 1926, E.V.R. established the "Self-Respect Movement," an organization that set for itself a very different task from that of the Justice Party, even though its rhetoric built on that of the early non-Brahman movement. Whereas the Justice Party had been principally concerned about proportional representation, the Self-Respect Movement advocated the overthrow of caste and instituted new forms of marriage and other ritual practices designed to encourage intercaste associations. The movement further engaged in a radical critique of religious belief and practice. At various points and in different ways, the movement attacked the Brahman priest and the whole Brahmanic ideology of privilege, scriptural authority in general, and religion either as general ethos or as theological doctrine. Periyar himself advocated outright atheism as the only rational worldview. Periodically, the movement organized dramatic assaults on religious symbols; its members burned sacred texts such as the *Manusmriti*, proclaimed that the *Ramayana* was an Aryan myth designed to denigrate Dravidians, beat priests and idols with shoes, and marched on temples and seminaries in mass demonstrations. During this time, E.V.R. used his newspaper, *Kudi Arasu*, as the mouthpiece for a series of radical critiques of Congress and Brahmanism; he reached new audiences well beyond the more elite-based Justice constituencies, at the same time as he countered the dominant role he felt Brahmans had accumulated in mainstream newspapers such as *The Hindu*. Especially in the period following Gandhi's 1927 visit to Tamil Nadu, E.V.R. engaged in a number of provocative activities that became the hallmark of the Self-Respecters' style of social activism, distinctive acts of social protest that fashioned E.V.R. as a counterforce to Gandhi in symbolic as well as political domains. E.V.R. was particularly critical of the Brahman priesthood, and used the racial and linguistic theories of Caldwell and others to proclaim a new form of Dravidian national pride.[13] By the early 1930s, when E.V.R. had to escalate his rhetoric to capture attention in the period of national civil disobedience, the Self-Respect Movement officially took up a "rationalist" position, debunking all religious belief as superstition and upper-caste propaganda. As E.V.R.'s political rhetoric evolved over the years, constantly engaging the issues of the day, he enunciated an essential relationship between Hinduism and Brahmanism, and vowed to work steadfastly against them both.

E.V.R. continued to press for the right of temple entry for Adi Dravidas through the decade of the 1920s and well into the thirties. As Gandhi and Congress took up this cause once again after the Poona fast of 1932, however, he seemed to lose interest in the goal, despite his argument that the temple was a civil space as well as a religious one. He also became skeptical about the possible role of the Hindu Religious and Charitable Endowments Board in either controlling Brahmanic power in temples or seriously reforming the ways in which developing distinctions made between religious and secular activities might work to redress Brahmanic authority over symbolic capital.[14] Indeed, although S. Satyamurty, a leading political figure in the Madras Congress, lamented that the state was grabbing the sacred wealth of temples in the manner that Henry VIII confiscated the wealth of monasteries, the history of state control over temples and other charitable endowments makes it clear how the domain of religion itself was reconstituted through developing agreements between upper-caste Hindus and British Christian administrators. Under such a general regime, temple entry meant simply buying in to a Brahmanic dream, which for E.V.R. always had a hallucinatory power.

During these years E.V.R. began to up the ante increasingly in his criticisms of Brahmans. He blamed them for duping non-Brahmans into believing that Hinduism was a reasonable religious system and attacked them for the ritual privileges they encoded as fundamental precepts of the Hindu fold. E.V.R. suggested that Brahmans would do anything to maintain their ritual status, by dominating secular as well as sacred activities through their preponderance in the British civil service, as well as by their control over educational institutions and their dominance in public media. "When it comes to seeking alms and practising their priestcraft, brahmins feign ignorance of politics, but when it comes to securing high positions for themselves in government, they tell the white man that brahmins alone are eminently suited to man these posts and that they alone qualify as good political leaders and reformers."[15] E.V.R. argued that Brahman interest in Tamil studies (as in the example of U. V. Swaminatha Aiyer's scholarly rediscovery of the Sangam classics) as well as their controlling interest in the Indian nationalist movement were further illustrations of Brahman treachery. There were times when his rhetoric became particularly offensive, as when he accused Brahman women of immorality, and on more than one occasion he implied that Brahmans should be murdered. He also accused Hindu gods in coarse language of acts of sexual perversity in a variety of writings. His vulgarity and excess were calculated to shock, and often landed him in trouble with antisedition laws, both during the colonial period and afterward. There was also a time in the thirties when he embraced Russian communism and preached against Brahmans and Britons as agents of world capitalism, in language that was sure to attract colonial concern. But through many changes of emphasis and influence, he maintained throughout his life a sustained critique of Brahmanism, Hinduism, and nationalism.

Nationalism was for E.V.R. "an atavistic desire to endow the Hindu past on a more durable and contemporary basis."[16] He was as contemptuous of the religious fervor used to animate nationalist goals as he was convinced that the underlying interest for both religion and nationalism was Brahmanic privilege. Thus he never worried about being branded antinationalist and, despite his disinterest in the quasi-religious cult around the Tamil language, saw the Congress imposition of Hindi in government schools shortly after it came to power in 1937 as a further illustration of the oppressive character of nationalist ambition in India. Imprisoned for a time because of his vociferous critique of Congress on the subject of Hindi and what he saw as an Aryan conspiracy, he increasingly advocated the creation of a separate Tamil Nadu. His call developed in time into a demand for an autonomous Dravida Nadu. By the early 1940s, he supported the claim for a separate Pakistan, and argued for a separate Dravidistan as well.[17] In 1944, E.V.R. established the Dravidian Party (Dravida Kazhagam), which had as its central aim the establishment of a separate non-Brahman or Dravidian nation. Significantly, when Ambedkar met Periyar in 1944 to discuss joint initiatives, Ambedkar noted that the idea of Dravidisthan was in reality applicable to all of India, since Brahmanism was a problem for the entire subcontinent.[18] E.V.R. wrote a unique obituary for Gandhi in 1948, condemning his murder but also noting that Godse was not an isolated bigot or madman but rather an expression of the very forms of Hindu nationalism that Gandhi himself had done so much to cultivate, and that had become pervasive in India at large. Gandhi, he writes, was struck down by a cancer within, a scourge that E.V.R. saw as fundamentally about the cloying connection of Brahman privilege to Hindu ideology.

But although he was a secular rationalist, E.V.R. was obsessed with religion and ritual (read Hindu religion and ritual). And he was a figure as contradictory as he was flamboyant. He was a social radical who genuinely championed egalitarian social relations across caste and gender lines, but he was so consumed by Brahamanic ritual privilege and its role in the local nationalist movement that he often appeared to be a reactionary in both national contexts and more local ones. Refusing the role of minority activist, he sought to critique the ideological and social constitution of the majority, even as he attempted to expel it from his own national project. Although he was an iconoclast in many things, his major concern was always caste; for E.V.R. the minority was figured in relation to caste rather than religion. Except for a brief moment in his early career, his interest was far less in the representation of non-Brahmans in numerical terms than in the representation of non-Brahmans in symbolic terms; non-Brahmans were to be seen both as the majority and as the principal modality of social value. His use of the transformed idea of *varnashrama-*

*dharma* as a way to forge a new egalitararian majority rankled non-Brahmans for obvious reasons, but it was also the case that E.V.R. shared with Gandhi the conviction that caste was deeply anchored in the social conventions of the subcontinent. Indeed, E.V.R. shared a great deal with Gandhi—in his reliance, for example, on the symbolic character of politics, on the necessity of social reform, and in his overriding interest in ideology rather than political process. He even set himself up as a kind of Rabelasian alter ego to Gandhi, wearing black rather than white, indulging his appetites rather than curtailing them, and establishing a personal cult that was nevertheless based on social service, among other things. But for a variety of reasons E.V.R. was always positioned on the margin—of the nationalist movement, of social reform, and of symbolic access to the national pool of ideological possibilities that were cultivated within colonial nationalism. The margin became a space where all action was reaction—spectacular at times, utopian as well, but driven by forces that were always elsewhere. When E.V.R.'s own movement began to enter the mainstream of Tamil political life in independent India, E.V.R. seems to have had no choice but to stay in the opposition. He agitated against the compromises of normal politics, provoked Hindu and Brahman sensibilities, and echoed Gandhi's own profound unease about the inexorable tyranny of social hierarchy. He occupied a space of radical critique that is as impressive today as it was always a sign of the contradictions of the position of minority in a caste hierarchy. And yet E.V.R. was ultimately trapped by his own critical language, in a syntax that could never transcend its oppositional character.

Ironically, E.V.R.'s last political battle, in alliance with the ruling DMK party of Tamil Nadu, makes clear once again what he had been up against all of his life, and how little some things had changed under the secular postcolonial regime. In 1970, the chief minister of Tamil Nadu signed into law a new amendment that did away with the practice of appointing hereditary priests, thus opening the way for persons for all castes to be eligible for the priesthood. But the constitutionality of the amendment was challenged, and the Supreme Court of India reversed it. Although the bench upheld the DMK's argument about the appointment of non-hereditary priests, it refused to accept the idea that priests could come from any caste. Such a policy would interfere with the Hindu worshiper's practice of faith, stipulated by Agamic textual precepts and injunctions. According to the Supreme Court, "any State action which permits the defilement or pollution of the image by the touch of an Archaka not authorised by Agamas would violently interfere with the religious faith and practices of the Hindu worshipper in a vital respect and would therefore be prima facie invalid under the Constitution."[19] For the Supreme Court, the ultimate authority was P. V. Kane's interpretation of the Brahma Puranas. For the court, the protection of religious freedom "had to be decided . . . with reference to the doctrines of particular religion." Thus Hindu tradition was to be upheld and preserved in textual terms, exactly as had been established by colonial practice. That the old texts were themselves to be interpreted by Brahmanic standards of Orientalist knowledge only sealed the equation of Brahmanism and Hinduism. Under the circumstances, E.V.R. chose a form of iconoclasm that was neither religious nor "secular" but strategically oppositional. An extraordinary figure who resisted Brahmanism and nationalism through his entire life, his life's struggle puts in bold relief the problematic history, and bequests, of Hindu majoritarian nationalism.

## B. R. Ambedkar

Although E.V.R. was preoccupied throughout his life with matters of caste, his position was always that of the "Sudra." He seems rarely to have addressed the question of untouchable rights or concerns. After 1930, E.V.R. was little interested in politics beyond the borders of the south, so perhaps it is no surprise that he paid no attention to B. R. Ambedkar in Maharashtra. But even if he had been interested in building alliances across the subcontinent, it is unlikely that he would have reached out to Ambedkar. Ambedkar, who went on to become the "father" of the Indian constitution, had a Ph.D. in political science from Columbia University and was deeply Western in outlook. Rather than modeling himself in some oppositional way on Gandhi, he was a figure much more like Nehru, except that he could never get beyond his caste origins and the political sensibility that the daily insults of untouchability engendered in him. And yet, despite the many differences between these two figures, they were startlingly similar in some respects. Both E.V.R. and Ambedkar were keenly aware that caste was the principal impediment to social justice, equality, and reform; and they were in agreement that caste could not be separated from the beliefs and institutions of Hinduism more generally. Where they differed most was in their relationship to politics. Ambedkar not only relied on constitutional issues, he made one of his most important marks through the constitution, and he was convinced that untouchables could only thrive through constitutional negotiation around their status as an oppressed and disenfranchised minority. And yet, in the end, Ambedkar was not content with politics as usual. In the most dramatic political statement of his career, he announced his intention to leave Hinduism through conversion to Buddhism. Despite his deep and abiding secularism, he could only counter religious prejudice with religious conversion. And he did this despite the threat that reservations for scheduled castes had been established as an incidence of unequal treatment within the Hindu fold. This meant that it was by no means a foregone conclusion that Buddhists would benefit from the very constitutional provisions Ambedkar had so strenuously fought for throughout his life.

Born in 1891 into a Maharastrian Mahar untouchable family, Ambedkar studied in army cantonments and then in Bombay, graduating from

Elphinstone College in 1912. His educational attainment and social background gained the recognition of the Maharaja Gaekwad of Baroda, who gave him a scholarship for travel to Columbia University in New York, where he earned his Ph.D. as well as to do further advanced work in law and economics at the London School of Economics and the London bar. After an unsuccessful attempt to practice as a lawyer in Baroda—his caste status earned him steady insults and made it impossible for him to rent rooms in town—he went to Bombay to become a college lecturer and practitioner before the Bombay High Court. As early as 1927, Ambedkar was officially nominated to the Legislative Council as one of two representatives of the depressed classes. During the next two decades Ambedkar maintained a role as a prominent figure in official circles as well as in government, at the same time that he took up a series of political and social struggles on behalf of untouchables.

Ambedkar first took up the cause of educational access for untouchables, turning as well to three major issues: the abolition of the traditional duties of Mahars in village society, the campaign to gain access to common water, and the movement for temple entry for untouchables. His public notoriety began with the issue of temple entry. He greeted the untouchable victory in Vaikkam, which had been spearheaded by E.V.R. (Periyar), with great enthusiasm, and subsequently he led a campaign to open up the Thakurdwar temple in Bombay in 1927. This was followed by struggles around the Parvati temple in Poona in 1929, and around the Kalaram temple in Nasik beginning in 1930. Ambedkar was conspicuously unable to gain the support of more than a few caste Hindu reformers, in large part because of his confrontational style and rhetoric. He led the Mahad satyagraha of 1927, in which speeches were delivered about such things as the need for Mahar women to wear their saris in the manner of the upper castes. He concluded the rally by marching to the high-caste tank and drawing water to drink. Orthodoxy claimed to be outraged, the tank underwent ritual purification, and the municipal council withdrew its support for Ambedkar's efforts. He performed his most dramatic act in December 1927, when in a public gathering he set fire to a copy of the *Manusmriti*, a gesture that outraged many a sympathetic social reformer.

Ambedkar's symbolic assault on Hindu scriptures illustrated his general sense that caste had become an integral component of the Hindu religion. His first systematic critique of caste had been made in a paper he presented while a graduate student at Columbia, in an anthropology seminar in May 1916. He argued that caste was first and foremost the imposition of the principle of endogamy, a social system of exclusion that began with Brahmans and was imitated by other groups both because of the prestige accorded by Hinduism to Brahmans and because of the social logic of exclusion ("Some closed the door: Others found it closed against them").[20] Even if Brahmans did not impose caste as a system by strict force, they nevertheless invented caste to suit their own concerns and predilections: "These customs in all their strictness are obtainable only in one caste, namely the Brahmins, who occupy the highest place in the social hierarchy of the hindu society. . . . [T]he strict observance of these customs and the social superiority arrogated by the priestly class in all ancient civilizations are sufficient to prove that they were the originators of this 'unnatural institution' founded and maintained through these unnatural means." But neither Brahmans as a class nor the great lawgiver Manu could have manipulated social forms to produce caste as a social system; rather, Ambedkar suggested that Brahmans set the ball rolling, and that Manu worked to provide spiritual and philosophical justification for the conversion of a class structure into a system of endogamy. Ambedkar dispensed with prevailing European theories of caste, noting that Nesfield's suggestion that caste was really about occupational differentiation was as obvious as it was unsuited for providing any kind of social explanation. Ambedkar implicitly critiqued Risley and all those who provided racial explanations for caste by noting that "European students of caste have unduly emphasised the role of colour in the Caste system. Themselves impregnated by colour prejudices, they very readily imagined it to be the chief factor in the Caste problem. But nothing could be further from the truth." He quoted Ketkar to say: "Whether a tribe or a family was racially Aryan or Dravidian was a question which never troubled the people of India, until foreign scholars came in and began to draw the line."[21]

Ambedkar expanded his critique of caste and transformed an academic argument into an explosive political intervention in an undelivered address for the 1936 annual conference of the Jat-Pat-Todak Mandal of Lahore. Invited to the conference by a group of social reformers who wished to honor Ambedkar's lifelong struggle against caste, he wrote an address that led some of his most avid supporters to back away from him. Ambedkar apparently went over a line when he wrote that the annihilation of caste required an assault on Hinduism itself. "People are not wrong in observing Caste. In my view, what is wrong is their religion, which has inculcated the notion of Caste. If this is correct, then obviously the enemy, you must grapple with, is not the people who observe Caste, but the Shastras which teach them this religion of Caste. . . . The real remedy is to destroy the belief in the sanctity of the Shastras." Ambedkar noted further that "Brahminism is the poison which has spoiled Hinduism. You will succeed in saving Hinduism if you will kill Brahminism."[22] Ambedkar was told that he could not deliver his address without modulating the language of his attack on Hinduism, in particular exempting the shastras from any criticism. Refusing to do so, he printed the address at his own expense and entered into a public debate with Gandhi.

Gandhi responded to his address by insisting that "Caste has nothing to do with religion." Noting that caste was harmful both to spiritual and national growth, he also argued that "Varna and Ashrama are institutions which have nothing to do with castes."[23] He went on to say that "The law of Varna teaches

us that we have each one of us to earn our bread by following the ancestral
calling. It defines not our rights but our duties. It necessarily has reference to
callings that are conducive to the welfare of humanity and to no other. It also
follows that there is no calling too low and none too high. All are good, lawful
and absolutely equal in status. The callings of a Brahmin—spiritual teacher—
and a scavenger are equal, and their due performance carries equal merit before
God and at one time seems to have carried identical reward before man."[24]
Gandhi continued to hold to the views that had so exercised E.V.R. in Madras
the decade before, when Gandhi had responded to the rise of non-Brahman
politics. He felt that caste as a ranked structure of groups was bad but that the
principles of varna and asrama (stage of life) on which caste was based, and of
which caste could be seen as a degraded form, were noble and well worth
reviving as ideals. Ambedkar took Gandhi as his most significant rhetorical
adversary. Whereas he seems to have written his address in part as criticism of
Gandhi's views on social reform, he jumped at the opportunity to debate
Gandhi directly about these views when Gandhi reviewed Ambedkar's address
in his newspaper *Harijan*. Ambedkar wrote that "what the Mahatma seems to
me to suggest in its broadest and simplest form is that Hindu society can be
made tolerable and even happy without any fundamental change in its structure if all the high caste Hindus can be persuaded to follow a high standard of
morality in their dealings with the low caste Hindus." In perhaps the most
scathing of a series of rebuttals to Gandhi, he wrote that the Mahatma "has
almost in everything the simplicity of the child with the child's capacity for
self-deception. Like a child he can believe in anything he wants to believe. We
must therefore wait till such time as it pleases the Mahatma to abandon his
faith in *Varna* as it has pleased him to abandon his faith in Caste." For Ambedkar, the disagreement with Gandhi was fundamental. He was not, as he
said, quarrelling with Hindus, and Hinduism, because of "imperfections of
their social conduct." No indeed; his quarrel was "much more fundamental. It
is over their ideals."[25]

Ambedkar's fundamental quarrel with Gandhi had, in fact, begun in earnest
in relation to the question of separate representation for untouchables in the
wake of negotiations with Britain after the civil disobedience campaign of
1930–1931. Indeed, the quarrel took on epic proportion in 1932, when Gandhi
announced a fast unto death over the establishment by Ramsey MacDonald of
a separate electorate for untouchables, in large part as a consequence of Ambedkar's advocacy of untouchable interests at the Round Table Conference.
Like E.V.R., Ambedkar grew increasingly suspicious of Gandhi's defense of
the caste system as an organic, unifying, and inclusive system that could divest
itself of all hierarchical traces. Ambedkar saw caste as part of the problem, not
part of the solution, and rejected Gandhi's call for untouchables to be included
within the compass either of the caste system or of Hindu society. In the actual
negotiations, the most heated issue concerned the classification of the elector-

ate. Gandhi, who was opposed to separate electorates for any group, grudg-ingly accepted them for Muslims, Christians, Sikhs, and Anglo-Indians but, in what was clearly his commitment to the unity of the Hindu community, drew the line when it came to untouchables, whose interests he claimed to represent. The Communal Award of August 17, 1932, granted untouchables Ambedkar's demand for separate electorates in areas of their largest concentration. Gandhi responded to the award by announcing that he would fast unto death, a deci-sion that Nehru, among others, thought was disastrous, since it elevated what for him was a side issue in the nationalist struggle to center stage and threat-ened the Mahatma's health and life once again. Nevertheless, many in Con-gress supported Gandhi, some because of their concern to protect the great Hindu base of Congress in the face of other communal interests. Ambedkar was unable to withstand public pressure to defer to the force of Gandhi's fast, and in the resulting compromise, known as the Poona Pact, the electorate was maintained as joint while the numbers of seats specifically reserved for un-touchables was doubled.

A conference of Hindu leaders was convened in Bombay in September 1932 to ratify the Poona Pact, and they unanimously adopted a resolution in effect outlawing untouchability. The resolution not only stipulated an end to discrim-ination in the use of public wells, schools, and roads, it also advocated temple entry for untouchables. Gandhi covered the ensuing temple-entry movement in his weekly paper, *The Harijan*, with regular reports of new temple openings, as well as of protests performed to press for other temples to open their doors. Congress supporters proposed a series of temple-entry bills in various legisla-tive councils. Ambedkar was bitter about Gandhi's sudden advocacy of temple entry and his effort to make it into a central plank of the constructive program at this point. He believed that Gandhi's object in joining the temple-entry movement (which he claimed Gandhi had earlier opposed) was "to destroy the basis of the claim of the Untouchables for political rights by destroying the barrier between them and the Hindus which makes them separate from the Hindus." He also believed that Gandhi was manipulating the issue for his own fame and glory. In February 1933, Ambedkar came out against the Temple Entry Bill, arguing that by this time, although he had supported it in the past, temple entry was a side issue. Not only was it less important than higher edu-cation, higher employment, and economic advancement, it appeared to be the only public issue related to untouchable social status that had attained support by Congress (and that too only after local referendums called for temple open-ings). Ambedkar further believed that temple entry conferred additional sym-bolic capital on high-caste Hindus, thus suggesting a level of disgust with Hinduism that anticipates his later interest in conversion. Finally, Ambedkar wrote that he had no interest in joining Congress on the issue of temple entry if they did not join him in his effort to destroy the caste system itself.[26]

For both Ambedkar and E.V.R., temple entry was a goal that lost its appeal once it was generally shared, not least because of the shame that the religious politics of exclusion had produced during invariably disheartening struggles for recognition and respect. From 1933 on, Ambedkar took a relentlessly oppositional stance to Gandhi and Congress, as he became suspicious of all majoritarian politics. Although he had been forced to back away from the idea of separate electorates—confronted as he was with apparent responsibility for the Mahatma's life—he nevertheless pursued constitutional measures designed to protect depressed classes from either limited representation or misrepresentation. At the same time, he continued to defend separate electorates on the grounds that he did not trust the majority to elect minority representatives who would genuinely represent minority interests. Indeed, Ambedkar's aim was for untouchables to be treated as minorities in the same terms as other groups, especially Muslims. And yet, Ambedkar cultivated an ambivalent sensibility about the politics of the minority, distrustful of any effort on the part of the majority to incorporate the minority, and all the while harboring a growing sense of bitterness at the social and religious system that conferred on untouchables such a pathetic fate. Even to accept minority status on the basis of caste position was to accept some residual taint of the hegemonic system of caste prejudice.

Indeed, both E.V.R. and Ambedkar seem to have become even more embittered with Brahmans, and Brahmanism, as a result of their experience working within the framework of Hindu social reform, whether in the advocacy of temple entry or the common pursuit of social aims that were ultimately designed to give greater credibility to the Hindu fold. When Ambedkar wrote *The Untouchables* in 1948, he noted that the cause of Hindu civilization was itself at fault. As he wrote, "The Hindu does not regard the existence of these classes [untouchables, etc.] as a matter of apology or shame and feels no responsibility either to atone for it or to inquire into its origin and growth." The primary reason for this, he claimed, was the undisputed position of the Brahmans as the learned class. "The power and position which the Brahmins possess is entirely due to the Hindu Civilization which treats them as supermen and subjects the lower classes to all sorts of disabilities so that they may never rise and challenge or threaten the superiority of the Brahmins over them. As is natural, every Brahmin is interested in the maintenance of Brahminic supremacy be he orthodox or unorthodox, be he a priest or a grahasta [householder], be he a scholar or not."[27] Although in 1916 Ambedkar had been calmly analytic about the relation of Brahmans to the caste system, thirty years later he saw them as a scourge, and as the basis of a religious system that he had announced he must abandon.

If Ambedkar felt disillusioned by his experience of working with Hindu social reformers, his defeat by Gandhi over the issue of separate electorates left him permanently disillusioned, as well, with the possibility that democratic institutions would allow adequate self-representation on the part of untouchable constituencies in India. But as several commentators have noted, Ambedkar's career reflects an extraordinary ambivalence about politics. On the one hand, Ambedkar went on to become the architect of the Indian constitution, and it was he who set the legal guidelines for reservations and positive discrimination for postindependent India. It was clear from this extraordinary investment and legacy that Ambedkar never gave up entirely on the state as the ultimate seat of justice. On the other hand, he announced his intention in 1935 to leave the Hindu fold, doing so finally twenty years later, shortly before his death.[28] And in his studies of and searches for a new religion, as well as in his final conversion to Buddhism, he gave voice to his conviction that even as untouchability was not simply a political (or social, or economic) problem, the stigma of untouchability could not be erased simply by political means. If caste was so fundamental to Hindu society, it could only be annihilated by abandoning Hindu society altogether. A nationalist to the end, he chose a religion that was as Indian as Hinduism.[29] As a secularist, he chose a religion that could be conceived as rational, ethical, and unburdened by sacerdotal hierarchy. But the conversion of this secular constitutional lawyer into a neophyte Buddhist was more than either a strategic political move or the outcome of basic philosophical frustration. Rather, Ambedkar's conversion was a poignant illustration of the contradictory position of caste in colonial and postcolonial India. Müller and Gandhi both could argue that caste and Hinduism were distinct, but for an untouchable, such distinctions seemed irrelevant, wrong, and ultimately impossible. For Ambedkar, the use of a religious idiom to make his final critique of caste—a critique far more powerful than all his extraordinary essays, speeches, and political interventions over his long career—was forced on him by his recognition, as an untouchable, that he could neither undo nor escape the horrible embrace of Hinduism and caste society. Conversion, for Ambedkar, seemed the only way out. When, in the last year of his life, he converted to Buddhism and advocated the mass conversion to Buddhism of all untouchables, he performed what he considered to be the final and most decisive rejection of the claims and hegemonic character of caste Hinduism.

## Caste in a Minor Key

E.V.R. and Ambedkar began their political careers advocating communal representation. They both claimed the need for non-Brahmans and Depressed Classes to attain rights and redress through proportional (and thus necessarily affirmative) representation in the emerging electoral bodies of late colonial India. In this process they were required to fashion their political constituencies as minorities, accordingly deploying critiques of the majority while at the same time issuing a range of appeals to the majority for recognition. Significantly, these claims for recognition betrayed the peculiarity of the language of the minority for the communities in question. Non-Brahmans were numerically minor only in the context of public bodies and institutions that were dominated by the numerically minor but socially, culturally, and politically major Brahmans. Any significant extension of the franchise entailed the promise of growing power and influence for non-Brahmans, who claimed to represent all non-Brahman classes (including by default the depressed classes, who were largely neglected by the non-Brahman movement). The non-Brahman movement was based in part on the claim for proportional representation and in part on anti-Brahman sentiment. Although these two trajectories were synergistic in the early years of the Justice Party, they began to split off from each other by the middle of the 1920s, as non-Brahmans began to play an increasingly important role in the Congress and the nationalist movement more generally. The depressed classes were a classic example of the minority, dominated by the upper castes in every sense, even as they were always doomed to numerical minority with no natural social or political allies. Even the depressed classes, however, were not a minority in the same sense as Muslims were, despite the efforts of Ambedkar to model untouchable politics on the strategies of the Muslim League.

In the initial stages of political mobilization, the depressed classes sought both protection and inclusion, the latter through the extension of rights to political representation, economic benefits, and religious participation. However, protection and inclusion turned out to be contradictory aims, since the development of minoritarian politics in India around the Muslim question led to an expectation that protection was necessary only when communities were committed to the maintenance of difference and separation. Certainly Gandhi's desire for untouchables was that protection be predicated on the paternalism (he used the phrase trusteeship) of the upper castes. At the same time, untouchables were to be incorporated into the Hindu fold in such a way as to render the protection of difference, rather than simply the protection of weakness, unnecessary. In this way untouchables and Muslims were themselves fundamentally different (and the possible conversion of untouchables into Muslims was protected against at all costs). Indeed, Muslims were never offered the option of (re)conversion; protection was the flip side of a coin that was minted in the service of the ineradicable nature of religious difference. In part as a logical extension of the Muslim position, Ambedkar realized that in his rejection of the hegemonic condescension of caste Hinduism he also needed to refuse the incorporative strategy of the majority. Ambedkar's ultimate conviction that he needed to convert to another religion was a tacit acceptance of the minority model of the Muslim, a tragic sign of the limited conditions for recognition in a nation that had been constituted around a peculiar form of secular majoritarianism. It is not unimportant, of course, that he seems never to have taken seriously the idea that he might convert to Islam. And I can only mention here the lack of interest among most backward-caste leaders in making strategic alliances with Muslims, who in most rural situations shared structural (often castelike) conditions with backward and depressed classes.

Both E.V.R. and Ambedkar rejected the hegemonic claim of the majority community, even as both of these figures developed radically different political ideologies and strategies. And yet even in rejection, the power of the majority asserted (indeed constituted) itself. In particular, E.V.R. and Ambedkar were ultimately unable to think themselves out of what they themselves diagnosed as the conspiratorial and quintessentially Hindu embrace of religion and politics. E.V.R.'s secular rationalism could never transcend its strategic iconoclasm, one that in the end produced both mythologies and rituals of its own. And Ambedkar's constitutional secularism never made it possible for him to accept either that caste was only an index of material relations or that Hinduism could be transcended (or simply defeated) without conversion. Ambedkar shared with Gandhi a fundamentally ritualistic view of caste, even as he shared with E.V.R. an incapacity ever to get beyond the insults of Brahmanic Hinduism. Both of these figures, and the movements they spawned, simultaneously tell the stories of minority impossibility and of majority intolerance. They serve, additionally, to caution against some of the current uses of Gandhi to help us think beyond the contemporary crisis of secularism. And even as they highlight the modal story of Muslim exceptionalism in modern Indian history, they remind us too that the minor is the necessary other of the major, whether the major dominates through logics of exclusion or inclusion. They reflect the peculiar contradictions that are still very much a part of the colonial inheritance for the nation, and that still work against most progressive postcolonial politics in India today, however they might be positioned in the contest with Hindu majoritarianism. And they demonstrate that caste is still very much a part of the communal problem in the political struggles over recognition, identity, and rights.

E.V.R and Ambedkar were both seen as antinationalist figures, though Ambedkar was more easily folded into the nationalist apparatus and became a key figure in the drafting of the Indian constitution. Both figures split with the canonic nationalist cause centered on Gandhi's role in defining Indian nationalism. It is ironic in retrospect to see Gandhi in this light, given the extent to which we are now being told that Gandhi was the nationalist figure who managed most successfully to negotiate the pitfalls of colonial mimesis. Gandhi was opposed both to the efforts of various non-Brahman groups to challenge the role of a broadly Hindu ideological structure for national unity and to the concerns of other non-Brahman and untouchable groups to challenge the representational character of national politics. E.V.R. and Ambedkar represented different groups as well as different oppositional strategies, but they both bring into relief the incorrigible relationship between certain caste constituencies and assumptions, on the one hand, and the ideological charter of the anticolonial form of nationalism that emerged in the Indian case, on the other. Clearly they tell a different story from the one that would be conveyed had this book focused on religious communities rather than caste. But the stories converge in important ways, as well. And in this convergence, they also remind us of the extent to which the most pernicious inheritance of colonialism may be the colonial role—persisting long after direct colonial rule—in fashioning the oppositional terms for the construction of the idea of a national community. If it is the case that the postcolonial state has been relentlessly seen as threatened by communitarian forces, it is also the case that these forces have been fundamental to the formation of this state—and the presumed nation it represents and governs—in ways that have worked both to mask and to justify oppression. And as the lives of E.V.R. and Ambedkar have both made manifest, oppression has been enclosed within the Brahmanic fold of Hindu civilization.

# *Thirteen*

## Caste Politics and the Politics of Caste

### The Mandal Crisis and Its Background

On September 19, 1990, a student from Delhi University poured kerosene over his body and set himself on fire. According to some accounts, Rajeev Goswami had initially only intended to stage a mock self-immolation; as soon as he struck a match his friends were supposed to have doused him with water, waiting only for a few photographs to be snapped. These photographs and the attendant press coverage would be used to draw dramatic media attention to the protests against caste reservations that had been mounting over the previous six weeks. But in the heat of emotion, in the context of an impassioned protest against a government decision that was seen as taking all future prospects of respectable employment away from young people with upper-caste backgrounds, Goswami set his body alight without checking to see whether his friends were anywhere nearby. Photographs were taken; his burning body could be seen on the front page of every newspaper and the cover of every glossy magazine in India over the next few days. But Goswami was by that time in the critical care ward of Safdarjang Hospital, struggling for his life with 50 percent of his body burnt. And his photograph gave way to other, similar, terrifying images. In quick succession, youths in a series of cities across northern India, from Ambala to Lucknow, followed Goswami's example and set themselves on fire, as well. Within the next month, more than 159 young people also followed suit, attempting suicide by self-immolation; 63 succeeded. Another 100 people were killed in police firings and clashes that accompanied the widespread protest.

Quite apart from the horror of the fiery protest, the discomfort felt by many had more to do with the reason for the spectacle than the spectacle itself: in the burning of Rajeev Goswami's body, caste leaked simultaneously out of the traditional worlds of the subaltern and the village and into the middle-class enclaves of new India. Modernity confronted the uncanny double of its traditional other, and found that it had never really left the horrors of the past behind. Rajeev Goswami and his tragic train of followers engaged in these desperate acts as part of a protest by students against Prime Minister V. P. Singh's decision to implement the recommendations of the Mandal Commission, which introduced quotas for "backward castes" for recruitment to central and state government, to private undertakings receiving financial assistance from the government, and to all government universities and affiliated colleges. Supplementing constitutional reservations for scheduled castes and tribes already set at 22.5 percent, the Mandal Commission recommended proportionate representation to the level permitted by the constitution (50 percent), which entailed the reservation of 27 percent for the backward castes not included under the earlier provision. Although the actual number of young people affected by this decision was relatively few, government education and employment had always enjoyed high prestige and the promise of financial security; the prospect of losing these opportunities obviously seemed for many insecure youths more than they could bear.

The uproar that attended V. P. Singh's decision was, of course, not about traditional anthropological questions of caste hierarchy, purity and pollution, residential location, occupational specialization, and access to the village well; in the wake of Mandal's announced implementation, upper-caste students feared that they would be denied even the slim chance they already had for acquiring educational credentials and government employment. But the debate, in fact, brought the anthropology of caste out of the academy and into the forefront of public discourse. This chapter uses this uproar, and the anthropological debate it occasioned, to point both to the contemporary crisis around caste politics and to suggest the extent to which contemporary public debate around caste has been shaped by the colonial past described in this book.

At the same time, the debate renders any simple critique of the role played by colonialism in the politicizing and reifying of caste deeply problematic. It makes clear the stakes of arguing that caste was never merely a religious institution but was instead inscribed by relations of power through and through; that caste was converted by colonial history into a special kind of colonial civil society, which both could be seen as India's special religious form of social self-regulation and the reason for India's unsuitability for modern political institutions; and that many of the current excesses of caste politics were the inevitable consequence of continuing colonial contradiction. But it also suggests that a blanket condemnation of colonial history can now be affiliated in peculiar ways to a critique of the postcolonial state for allowing caste to leak mischievously into the political world, as if it had never been there before. The often abstract and academic writings about caste by eminent anthropologists as varied as G. S. Ghurye, Iravati Karve, M. N. Srinivas, Milton Singer, McKim Marriott, Louis Dumont, and T. N. Madan, to mention just a few, have found their political apotheosis in Mandal (often without explicit reference to reservations or Mandal). Further, caste has become the ghost hovering over many contemporary discussions about nationhood, citizenship, and modernity. Despite the pressing and at last much discussed dangers of Hindu fundamentalism, right politics, and communalism across India, it is necessary to remember the role played by the controversy over Mandal in generating the political consensus that made Hindu fundamentalism more acceptable. It was in the wake of the politicization of caste over Mandal that calls for Hindu unity over caste division began to be made by the political leaders of the BJP. In addition, caste violence is as virulent as ever, in certain areas of India more than ever before, which suggests yet again that caste continues to haunt not just the modern self but the national project of India.

The debate over Mandal goes back in some ways to the quarrel between B. R. Ambedkar and Gandhi, that embarrassing rupture in the smooth history of nationalism that prefaced the long debate over issues of political representation and constituency within the so-called Hindu community. In so doing, it raises the larger question of how to classify traditionally disadvantaged groups in Indian society, and the extent to which caste is about something called Hindu society at large. Were untouchables really a mix of caste groups or, as "outcastes," were they in fact groups that had been placed outside the pale of both caste and Hindu society? The term "caste Hindu" has been used in more than just redundant ways, even as untouchable groups have often been characterized as non-Hindu. Despite these pervasive uncertainties, there was general agreement about what constituted an "untouchable caste" in most parts of Madras and Bombay presidencies and in the Central Provinces, thus making the classificatory dimension of reservation policy (as well as concerns about the separate identities of these groups) fairly straightforward. Matters were less clear in northern and eastern India, however. Given this lack of clarity, the debate over classification revolved around the question of whether to identify groups on the basis of their depressed status (which could be established by their social, economic, and cultural backwardness) or in reference to the specific criteria of ritual and social exclusion. In what was perhaps the most elaborate attempt to define untouchability, J. H. Hutton, the 1931 census commissioner and author of the influential monograph *Caste in India*, established a set of indices, including whether "the caste or class in question can be served by Brahmans . . . [and] by the barbers, water-carriers, tailors, etc., who serve the caste Hindus," "whether the caste in question pollutes a high-caste Hindu by contact or proximity," and "whether the caste or class in question is merely depressed on account of its own ignorance, illiteracy or poverty and but for that, would be subject to no social disability."[1] In other words, the question was whether to use "class" (that is, general social and economic criteria) or "caste" (which in this case, ironically, referred to groups traditionally referred to as noncaste, or as outside the pale of caste) as the basis for classification.

If Gandhi and Ambedkar struggled throughout their lives over the definition of the caste system and the ultimate authority of Hinduism, they agreed about the fundamentally ritual character of the social. Thus Gandhi saw untouchability as a Hindu crime to be absolved by the folding of harijan communities into the main fabric of Hindu society, and Ambedkar ultimately saw religious conversion as the only way out of Hindu hierarchy; they both agreed with Hutton,

who stressed the ritual exclusions shared by all untouchables in his classificational schema. As a result, there was general agreement about the classification
of scheduled castes, the newest and most neutral euphemism for untouchables,
as the basis for reservations in independent India. In the delineation of the
scheduled caste category, there has been no single connotative definition or
principle, but selection has nevertheless proceeded primarily on the basis of
ritual "untouchability," though according to Galanter this has been "combined
in varying degrees with economic, occupational, educational, and . . . residential and religious tests."[2] In the final determination of scheduled castes for the
constitutionally mandated reservations, Hutton's criteria and Ambedkar's general classificatory guidelines prevailed, proceeding primarily on the basis of
ritual criteria.

Although Gandhi and Ambedkar shared a fundamentally anthropological
view of caste, they had, as we have seen, very different ideas about politics.
Although Ambedkar was committed to the need to politicize caste, using it as
the basis for organizing political constituencies and waging political battles,
Gandhi was perhaps more concerned than any other major nationalist leader
about the possibility that caste would become the basis for political and social
conflict. Thus Gandhi felt the need to minimize caste difference and underplay
caste identity, although throughout his life he was convinced that this would
be best accomplished by emphasizing an ideal of caste that stressed organic
unity and harmony rather than hierarchy. Gandhi used much the same definition of an ideal originary caste system as had been deployed by such earlier
Hindu social reform figures as Dayananda Saraswati and Vivekenanda, who
defined the Sanskrit term *varnashramadharma* to mean the ideal order of
things (around caste, stage of life, and the performance of duty), shorn of any
hierarchy or power. Despite the serious exception taken to these political and
rhetorical strategies by leaders such as Ambedkar, Gandhi saw the flip side of
his nationalist struggle to be his effort to contain the growth of communalism,
the growth of conflict between groups defined by the categories of caste and
religion.[3] Ambedkar, on the other hand, was convinced that caste (or, rather,
untouchable) identities had to be fostered in order to combat centuries of oppression by collective organization and political struggle. In a curious way, the
debate between Gandhi and Ambedkar continues to rage to the present day,
though the terms of debate have changed in critical respects.

Although Ambedkar lost the political struggle with Gandhi in the early
1930s, by the time of India's independence, and certainly after Gandhi's death
in 1948, he won after all. Ambedkar, in fact, went on to draft the terms by
which reservations were established for scheduled castes and tribes. Despite
concerns of a variety of kinds, from the difficulty of imposing time limits; to
the kinds of arguments that are used in affirmative action debates in the United
States (namely, that quotas stigmatize designated groups), the debate over
these kinds of reservations subsided quickly. The widespread concern that led

to the Mandal Commission had instead to do not with scheduled castes and tribes but with the intermediary groups, marked less by clear ritual markers than by murky socioeconomic ones, that have been increasingly labeled as the backward castes.

Despite continued resentment and debate on the part of some, there has been general unanimity about the importance of constitutional provisions and guidelines concerning reservations for scheduled castes and tribes. There have been concerns, however. Some academics within India argued, for example, that caste reservations have "affected the morals, the administration and the society adversely"; "imped[ed] the development of secularism," "perpetuated and accentuated the caste consciousness," and promoted "vested interests in backwardness."[4] G. S. Ghurye was always very careful to distinguish his arguments against the politicization of caste from his acceptance of the need to use extraordinary measures to combat the problem of untouchability; only in the case of scheduled castes did Ghurye approve of reservations and positive discrimination, though he disapproved of Ambedkar's attempts to politicize caste around the untouchable movement and strongly supported Gandhi's nonconfrontational and assimilationist ideals. But Ghurye was also concerned that reservations be a short-term remedy, and was sharply critical of the automatic extensions granted to constitutional provisions that he felt were originally intended to be provisional.[5] And some American academics, echoing the debates about affirmative action in the United States, have endorsed concerns by many in India that reservations promote a sense of second-class citizenship and accomplishment: Lloyd and Susanne Rudolph wrote that "The price of discrimination in reverse has been a kind of blackmail in reverse; in return for access to opportunity and power the untouchable is asked to incriminate himself socially. This is not only profoundly disturbing but also an important source of alienation and rebellion," though it would appear in fact that the great locus of rebellion was among caste Hindus, not untouchables.[6]

The subsequent history of reservation policy for scheduled castes has not always been smooth. Ironically, Ambedkar's move to encourage untouchables to convert to Buddhism created problems for the classificatory guidelines related to reservations. The ritual definition of untouchability assumed that the issue of discrimination was a Hindu problem, and untouchables were categorized as Hindus, despite their exclusion from Hindu temples and their marginal, if according to some anthropological accounts necessary, role in Hindu ritual. When petitioned by Buddhist converts to extend reservations to them, some courts held that conversion from Hinduism to religions that do not recognize caste, specifically Buddhism, led to their loss of caste identity and their attendant eligibility for reservations.

Although this problem was resolved by state decree in Maharashtra, where most converts lived, the courts have routinely maintained that caste is a religious rather than a secular identity.[7] Nevertheless, the question of time limits for reservations has been even more intractable. After considering the recommendations of a special committee set up to evaluate reservations, the Lokur Committee, the government pledged to begin dealing with the issue of descheduling, first by taking the relatively advanced caste groups off the reservation roles, then by descheduling the entire list of castes and tribes by the end of the sixth five-year plan, in 1981.[8] But the fears of Ghurye have been vindicated, at least in the sense that it has proved difficult to stop reservations once they have begun. At the same time, those who argued for the cessation of reservations on the grounds that untouchability was disappearing as a social problem and ritual evil—some suggesting that the only thing that maintains the institution has been the schedules themselves—have had to confront the fact that since the mid 1960s there has been a dramatic rise in caste violence against untouchables, particularly in rural areas. The annual report on the scheduled castes and tribes began routinely to list and measure the terrifying rise in "atrocity," which included outright murder and the causing of grievous hurt, rape, and arson, among other things. In 1978 it was decided that a commission with much greater legislative and juridical power needed to be appointed specifically to deal with the reports of atrocities committed against scheduled castes and tribes. By the early 1980s, when descheduling was to have been completed, the number of atrocities was constantly on the rise, particularly in Madhya Pradesh, Uttar Pradesh, Bihar, and Rajasthan.[9] Although the causes for violence were usually said to concern land disputes, the preponderance of cases carried the full signature of caste and power. As M. J. Akbar has written, "In the autumn of 1981, Harijans were killed in several villages in Uttar Pradesh. Two of these massacres—one in Dehuli, followed by another a few days later in Sarhupur—received widespread publicity. The killers, who were Thakur Rajputs, had just one message to send through murder—the untouchable Jatav cobblers had to learn their place in society and the caste hierarchy."[10] And in the mid-1980s, serious antireservation riots and attacks on harijans in the city of Ahmedabad and throughout the state of Gujarat put to rest the notion that untouchables were only afflicted in the countryside or in the Hindi heartland. Although there are those who would argue that reservation policy has exacerbated caste tension, no responsible observer today could claim that untouchability has disappeared. In the present climate, there seems to be little legitimate concern about the continuation of reservation policy for scheduled castes.

## Backwardness and Reservations

The widespread concern that led to the Mandal agitation was, of course, not about changes for scheduled castes but rather about the extension of a similar reservation policy to other backward classes; it occurred well after the drafting of the original constitutional provisions that empowered the president to appoint a committee and take measures to better the conditions of the socially and educationally backward. The president, in fact, had appointed such a committee well before the Janata government recruited Mandal to this task; in 1953 Kaka Kalelkar was asked to head the Backward Classes Commission to investigate the possibility of establishing reservations for Other Backward Castes (or OBCs). The first task was to determine how to identify the backward classes. Whereas there had been widespread agreement about the classification of the Scheduled Castes and Tribes before independence, there had been no such consensus or precedent, at least at the central level, for the backward classes. The constitutional mandate had used the term class rather than caste, concealing what were already massive differences about the role of caste in postindependent India, not to mention the difficulties experienced by the British over the use of caste for any all-India enumeration and classification. Nehru was particularly reluctant to acknowledge the role of caste in India's new social policy, but at the same time he was especially concerned to break the hold of the past on vast sections of the population: "We want to put an end to . . . all those infinite divisions that have grown up in our social life . . . we may call them by any name you like, the caste system or religious divisions, etc."[11]

Part of the difficulty later confronted by the commission in finding adequate data to draw up their lists of backward groups was due to the fact that the British, to allay what they saw as the hyper-politicization of caste through the census, had ceased using caste categories after 1931; part of the difficulty was that Sardar Patel, home minister until 1950, had rejected caste tabulation as a device because he did not want to confirm British characterizations of India as caste-ridden. The embarassment had contradictory expressions, as in the case of the anthropologist N. K. Bose, who saw the specific purpose of the Backward Classes Commission to lessen the hold of caste: "It is . . . the desire and will of the Indian nation to do away with the hierarchy of caste and of its consequent social discrimination, and prepare the ground for full social equality."[12] Like Ambedkar, Bose argued for the use of pollution and exclusion indices in assigning backward class status. And Ambedkar himself clarified his wording in the constitutional mandate when he observed that "what are called backward classes are . . . nothing else but a collection of certain castes."[13] If there was major concern about linking backwardness and caste, there was at the same time a consensus among many of independent India's founding fathers that the backwardness of India was itself in large part about the continued hold of caste; colonial shame, as well as colonial discourse, was writ large upon the initial social ventures of the new Indian state.

Although the category of backwardness was both vague and unprecedented at the central level, certain states had developed clear ideas of the salience of the category well before independence, most significantly in conjunction with the development of anti-Brahman movements in Mysore, Maharashtra, and Madras. The term "backward classes" first acquired a formal significance in the princely state of Mysore, where in 1918 the government appointed a commission to consider the problem of disproportionate Brahman participation in public service. In 1921, preferential recruitment of "backward communities" was instituted; all communities aside from Brahmans were classified as backward. Reservations for backward communities were instituted in Bombay after 1925, when a government resolution defined backward classes as all except for "Brahmins, Prabhus, Marwaris, Parsis, Banias, and Christians." As we have already noted, the most important precedent in the prehistory of the backward class movement was established in Madras Presidency, where the non-Brahman Justice Party was formed in 1916 specifically around a platform of addressing the preponderance of Brahmans in colleges, universities, and government service.[14] The success of the Justice Party in enacting communal orders that dictated quotas for caste recruitment was later codified through a roster system that operated until 1947, providing a precedent for strong backward class legislation around reservations in Tamil Nadu after independence.

The anti-Brahman movement also provided an organizational impetus for the development of legislative interventions to address issues of social justice and access to power for so-called backward communities; it certainly had dramatic effects on Brahman hegemony in colonial administration and postcolonial politics. This particular genealogy also raised questions, however, about the instrumental appropriation and political entailments of the backward classes category. The Justice Party hardly represented a fringe collection of lower-caste groups wedged uneasily between untouchables and dominant castes, whether Brahman or non-Brahman. The classificatory breadth of the backward category in Mysore, Maharashtra, and Madras, no matter how dominant Brahmans had become in the previous hundred and fifty years of British rule, suggests the tenuousness of the rhetoric behind much backward class legislation. And the history of the Justice Party provided ample evidence of the relationship between reservation politics and complicity with British colonial rule.

The connection between anti-Brahman movements and backward class mobilization helps to explain why the eminent sociologist G. S. Ghurye was so adamantly opposed to the use of caste for reservations. Ghurye believed not only that reserved representation was not necessary but also that it was harmful "in so far as it tends to perpetuate the distinction based on birth," something he felt was both counterproductive and antinational: "To harp on the caste differences and to allow special representation is to set at naught the fundamental condition for the rise of community feeling."[15] Given the collaboration between the non-Brahman movement and the British, Ghurye's argument was not altogether far-fetched, even if his own sense of caste identity, and more general commitment to a Gandhian injunction for national unity and Brahmanic trusteeship, doubtless generated no small measure of his concern.

The intellectual and ideological background of backward class legislation was thus complicated by its connection to non-Brahman movements that had not always established secure nationalist credentials. As we have seen, objections to this legislation ranged from concerns that the economic conditions of backwardness were being obscured to the kinds of concerns raised by Ghurye. But there was still strong political pressure to do something about the condition of the backward classes—from figures such as Ambedkar who played significant roles in the drafting of social policy, from the redistributional ideology of the new socialist state, and from the effects of developing forms of electoral democracy. Nevertheless, the provisional decision to use caste groupings as the basis for assembling a roster of disadvantaged communities invoked the colonial contradictions involved in any use of caste classifications in postindependent India. When the Backward Classes Commission released its report after two years of work, it presented a list of 2,399 backward groups and recommended various measures for their advancement.[16] The commission was deluged, both before and after the release of its report, by communities claiming to be backward; it was also seriously hampered by the lack of good data reflecting all the caste groupings across the subcontinent and their social and economic standing. The problems that earlier generations of British census officials encountered were experienced all over again. Caste turned out to be a very loose category; there was tremendous variation across India in the size, extent, and autonomy of classificatory rubrics around caste, and despite the best efforts of British officials and ethnographers, caste was still not a uniform system of reference across India. Further, many caste groups had large internal differences in their social and economic standing. And since the political consequences of classification had by now far exceeded those occasioning many of the political battles over census designations in earlier decades, the commission found itself in the thick of political battle.

## Caste and Class: The Political Stakes of Sociology

The chairman of the commission himself virtually repudiated the report, concluding at the end of his deliberations that "it would have been better if we could determine the criteria of backwardness on principles other than caste."[17] Nehru was also unhappy with the commission's criteria: "the Commission had to find objective tests and criteria by which such classifications were to be made; they had to find indisputable yardsticks by which social and educational backwardness could be measured. The report . . . has not been unanimous on this point; in fact, it reveals considerable divergence."[18] As the decade wore on, these reservations found increasing consensus. When the report was submitted to parliament in 1956, it carried with it the negative evaluation of the minister of home affairs, who thought that the emphasis on caste demonstrated "the dangers of separatism." The minister added that the caste system was undeniably "the greatest hindrance in the way of our progress toward an egalitarian society, and the recognition of specified castes as backward may serve to maintain and perpetuate the existing distinctions on the basis of caste."[19] The minister requested each state government to undertake ad hoc surveys to determine the numbers of backward classes, at the same time affording them all possible consideration in local government schemes. In the meanwhile there was growing criticism from academics and public intellectuals about the reliance on caste; significant here was the presidential address by M. N. Srinivas to the anthropology section of the Indian Science Congress in 1957, in which he suggested that it was time to give serious thought to evolving "'neutral' indices of backwardness. . . . The criteria of literacy, landownership and income in cash or grain should be able to subsume all cases of backwardness."[20] As a consequence of growing negative opinion and the negative reception accorded the commission report, it was not actually taken up by parliament until 1965, by which time there seemed even greater antipathy to the use of caste categories to alleviate the social distress of backward communities; between the early fifties and early sixties the tide seemed to have turned entirely. When the report was presented in parliamentary discussion, the central government's spokesman reiterated his opposition to communal criteria, arguing that they "were contrary to the Constitution, would perpetuate caste, and would create in the recipients both vested interests and a sense of helplessness."[21] The report was dropped, despite some agitation from various backward classes organizations, and individual states were advised to use economic criteria in their own redistributional and reservation policies.[22]

It may therefore appear odd that the very issue that seemed to have died so convincing a death would have been resurrected more than a decade after what seemed the final chapter in the debate. Indeed, the Mandal Commission was convened by Morarji Desai, a staunch Gandhian who would hardly have been ideologically in favor of politicizing caste per se. But the 1977 election manifesto of the Janata Party, drafted under the influence of populist rhetoric that hearkened back to Jayaprakash Narayan's challenge to Congress and Indira Gandhi, promised the establishment of an independent and autonomous civil rights commission "competent to ensure that the minorities, scheduled castes and tribes, and other backward classes do not suffer from discrimination or inequality." The manifesto specifically pledged that it would work to "reserve between 25 and 33 per cent of all appointments to Government service for the backward classes, as recommended by the Kelkar [sic] Commission."[23] Desai accordingly appointed a five-member commission in December 1978 under the chairmanship of B. P. Mandal, a member of parliament from Bihar, with a charge that was largely the same as that which had been used for the 1953–1955 commission. But by the time the report was ready, Janata had lost its mandate and Mrs. Gandhi was ready to come back to power. The Mandal Report was set aside, and though vague references were made to it by different parties, usually positive, it awaited the return of Janata rule. But even when a Janata victory brought V. P. Singh into power in the autumn of 1989, along with a platform commitment to the implementation of the Mandal Report, the actual decision to institute reforms in August 1990 took most observers by surprise.

I have already rehearsed the reaction to this decision—the fact that scores of young people attempted suicide to protest what they felt to be the loss of any chance at all to secure government employment, the most prestigious and secure form of general employment in India. The protest turned out to be the undoing of V. P. Singh. Within a matter of months he was forced out of office after a vote of no confidence in parliament, and although the Janata Party held onto power a bit longer, the Mandal issue appeared to sink the entire party, as well. At the same time, the furor over Mandal fed into BJP attempts to gain increased legitimacy and popularity during this time. If Mandal was one of the two big political issues of this period, Mandir (temple) was the other, namely, the BJP call to replace the Babur Mosque (Babri Masjid) in Ayodhya with a temple to Lord Rama. The agitation over Mandal was certainly behind the development of a new political rhetoric by the BJP, which stressed that Hinduism was a much better focus for social identity than caste; from 1990 onward the BJP, and many other forces on the right, have not tired of stressing the way in which emphasis on caste identity works against the spirit of national unity, in language reminiscent of that mobilized around reservation politics by commentators such as G. S. Ghurye in the context of the nationalist movement, and in ways specifically calculated to take advantage of public reaction against Mandal. The debate over Mandal brought together strange allies and arguments, complicating the politics of position and renewing the centrality of caste in public debate. Once again, as had been the case in the debates over reservations in the first years of Indian independence, academics took a variety of positions, and technical anthropological arguments developed national prominence and revealed at least some of their political entailments. But the arguments were different now, and revealed as well the myriad complexities circulating around the status of caste in a political climate vastly changed from that of the more optimistic 1950s, when secular and socialist dreams were widely shared and little contested.

## The Backlash against Caste

The mainstream English-language press was predominantly negative in its initial reaction to and treatment of V. P. Singh's decision to implement the recommendations of the Mandal Commission, sometimes aggressively so. Inderjit Badhwar began the cover story in *India Today*, India's leading fortnightly news magazine (published in English as well as in a number of regional languages), by writing that "as events unfolded during the fortnight it became clear that what Singh was trying to reap was a harvest of shame. He had been reduced, like all power-hungry politicians before him, to a vote-hungry power broker shamelessly using the two elements that have ever bloodied and divided this nation—religion and caste." Using extraordinarily strong language, Badhwar characterized the antireservation protests as completely spontaneous, and suggested that the "Government would even back a caste war for narrow partisan gains."[24] *Frontline*, the news magazine run by *The Hindu* newspaper group but reflecting the Marxist intellectual commitments of its editor, was much more supportive of Mandal, but in a long feature article by Anand Sahay noted that the really radical recommendations of Mandal, which advocated serious land reform and economic redistribution, were naturally left completely aside in the Mandal wars. Sahay quoted Mandal with approval as having noted that "reservations in government employment and educational institutions, as also all possible financial assistance, will remain mere palliatives unless the problem of backwardness is tackled at its root."[25] The *Economic and Political Weekly*, a serious intellectual journal with solid leftist credentials, published a number of exchanges on Mandal that reflected general agreement about the importance of reservations for backward groups. But for the most part, *India Today* set the tone of elite public debate. K. Balagopal, in a review of some of this debate, complained that "There is perhaps no issue on which we are such hypocrites as caste. Nor any other which brings out all that is worst in us with such shameful ease. The moment V. P. Singh announces the decision to implement the Mandal Commission's recommendation of reservations for the backward castes, an avalanche of obscenity hits the country. It carries before it the Press, the universities, and opinion-makers of all kinds."[26] Balagopal was unapologetic in his defence of Mandal, noting that "so long as caste remains one of the determinants of property and power, so long as it is used by the rich and the powerful as a means of maintaining and strengthening their domination, it remains the moral right and indeed the political duty of the poor and the deprived to use their caste identity in the struggle for their liberation."[27]

Rajni Kothari, one of India's leading political scientists and editor of the influential book *Caste in Indian Politics*, wrote an assessment of the reservation debate in relation to his earlier theoretical arguments about the politicization of caste.[28] Kothari had earlier argued that "casteism in politics is no more and no less than politicisation of caste," a process that he felt played an important role in the facilitation of democracy and the growth of social awareness. Kothari held that Mandal reforms would continue this process in useful ways.

He wrote that "caste formations are at once aggregative and dis-aggregative, emphasizing the secular dimension of a plural society. Caste, indeed, is the great secularizer in a society being pulled apart by convoluted religions bent upon tearing apart the social fabric." Kothari noted that caste was an indigenous institution that was playing a modern democratic role, "something that social anthropologists should have noticed long back, but given their class background, they have been unable to."[29] Kothari continued to see evidence of the formation of class configurations out of "dispersed and fragmented caste identities," but in ways that reflected regional differences and specific political movements. He further argued that the work of the Mandal Commission was built on the recognition of the salience of these movements, not on any attempt to exacerbate the pernicious influence of caste: "It is the backlash from the upper and 'foreward' castes against the upsurge that is casteist, not the upsurge itself." Finally, Kothari was adamant about the secularizing function of caste in contemporary India: caste is a "bulwark against religious fundamentalism and its fascist overtones. It is caste playing a secular historical role that we are witness to in the growth of social mobility that the Mandal Commission and its various antecedents have given rise to." This was perhaps the strongest argument made in defence of Mandal by a leading, mainstream academic figure.

Kothari's article occasioned a strong letter from three other prominent Indian social scientists, M. N. Srinivas, A. M. Shah, and B. S. Bavaskar.[30] Although they took care to praise his earlier scholarly work, they disputed his claim that when castes grouped themselves together for political purposes they lost the quality of being castes. They then argued that the political process not only failed to erase divisions within caste/class groupings but actually provided new opportunities for exploitation and the enrichment of elites, a process they claimed would be further enhanced by implementations of Mandal reforms. They concluded their letter by noting that "the ploy of caste-based reservations, encouraging caste-based politicisation, is not the solution to these problems. For all we know, this will benefit only the rich and the influential in all the castes and leave the poor and weak where they are. All in all, in his passion for creating a political order of his choice, Dr. Kothari has ignored the ground realities of the social order. We hope he is not one of those intellectuals who place the state before the social order." This was a rather ominously phrased concern, given the extent to which the social mandate of the Indian state has come under criticism in recent years. For these authors, the politicization of caste would have only negative consequences, though they stressed the lack of fit between caste and class rather than the pernicious character of caste itself.

Other authors responded to the Mandal debate by suggesting various ways in which caste would be hardened and rendered even more divisive a force within the Indian nation. In another letter to the *Times* responding to Kothari,

one Dr. Harendra Mehta noted that "the menace of the Mandal recommendations is that it would further the imperial designs of the British by the caste
based reservations of public posts."[31] Veena Das and André Beteille also noted
that reservations effectively reproduced colonial policies of divide and rule,
and Dharma Kumar specifically argued that the colonial construction of castes
as essentializing identities that work to displace notions of civil society from
the political to the religious (and then perversely back again) provided the
unfortunate precedent for the architects of reservation policy.[32] All these scholars echoed (and sometimes cited) the eloquent critique of colonialism by G. S.
Ghurye, which prefaced his own critique of reservation policy. The affiliation
of postcolonial reservation policy with colonial attempts to play the caste card
to antinationalist ends has become almost an accepted litany, thus betraying
some of the fundamental contradictions in Indian nationalist ideology.[33]
Ashok Guha wrote that "in its tenure, the V. P. Singh government's most
conspicuous success has been the restoration and solidification of the caste
barriers that time and change have been slowly eroding. In the process it has
accomplished the permanent division of the Indian polity—an achievement
that eluded the British in their efforts to divide and rule India on the basis of
caste and religion."[34] Indeed, I have found that my own arguments on the
colonial transformation of caste have been used to document the pernicious
effects legislative (or juridical) reifications of caste might have in the postcolonial period. Much to my regret, work that was motivated by a particular critique of colonial history has been aligned with and used to support serious
critiques of Mandal.[35] In the case of the Mandal debate, the politics of position
have had the effect of making the position of politics particularly contradictory, critiques from the left and the right mixing promiscuously in ways that
allow charges of retrograde politics and casteism from virtually all sides.

Ashok Guha argued strongly that the effect of Mandal would be to harden
caste identities and conflicts further. He wrote that "The defenders of reservations argue that Mandal did not invent the caste system, that caste is a fact of
life. . . . The charge against them is only of fortifying it by rewarding membership in certain castes. But this is no less serious a charge. . . . Reservations then
are sociologically archaic and politically divisive."[36] Dharma Kumar suggested that the frequent use by Mandal defenders of the long experience of
caste reservations in southern India and the fact that they have not been correlated with disproportionately high levels of communal or caste violence
missed some fundamental points, in particular the fact that in the south it was
very largely the small minority of Brahmans who were affected by reservations, and most of them have migrated either to the private sector or outside
southern India. Kumar noted that the threatened groups in northern India
tended to be more extensive, more tied to rural landholding, and more likely
to engage in violence and political reaction. She was correct in noting why

Mandal occasioned such protest in the north, though her argument if anything might be used to justify reservations rather than argue against them. Kumar further argued that caste consciousness in India had been on the increase, and directly correlated this fact with political mobilization around reservations.[37]

André Béteille, whose writings on caste inequality have been especially influential, also addressed the issue of the relevance of the history of reservations in southern India for the debate on the pros and cons of Mandal.[38] He noted the colonial character of reservation policy: "The circumstances under which caste quotas were imposed in south India in the high noon of colonial rule were totally different from the ones under which they are being sought to be instituted today after more than 40 years of national independence. . . . It will not do to erase from our collective memory the fact that caste quotas, like communal electorates, were inventions of colonial times."[39] Béteille went on to detail the southern experiment, noting like Kumar the very different circumstances of the non-Brahman movement from the movements on behalf of backward castes in the north. He further argued that the southern experiment was not at all the raging success it was held up to be, noting that caste quotas in southern universities had worked against intellectual excellence, and that the question of relative efficiency could hardly be answered in the context of the vastly different administrative histories of north and south ("All that we can say perhaps is that there are many ways to ruin the administration, and not just through caste quotas").[40] Béteille noted that the only clear lesson from the southern experience was the permanence of caste quotas once implemented; though always justified as provisional measures, they developed political constituencies and dependencies that would not let them disappear. Béteille concluded his observations with the extraordinary claim that

What has sustained the movement [against Mandal] and given it its peculiar intensity is not any kind of political organisation, but a certain sense of moral outrage. It is this sense of moral outrage and not any political force that has unsettled every political party. It is true that the British policy of pitting caste against caste, and community against community in the name of justice and fairplay, aroused widespread resentment and hostility, but it did not create the kind of response that has now come to the surface. Perhaps Indians of an earlier generation could never feel towards their alien rulers the sense of outrage that their descendants now feel towards the leaders they have themselves freely chosen.[41]

Quite apart from the curious suggestion that outrage in the context of democratic rule can far exceed that of, or directed toward, colonial rule, Béteille here clearly shared the sense of outrage that reservation policy, a policy that was irrevocably tied to colonial rule, special interests, and undemocratic outcomes, had been restored by responsible government forty years after independence. A group of social scientists from the Madras Institute for Development

Studies, which was exempted from Béteille's critique of southern Indian institutions of higher education (though on the grounds that caste quotas were not
enforced there), replied in the pages of the same newspaper that: "It is not self
generated 'moral outrage' but callous anti-reservationist bystanders who have
egged on the Sati-like 'self-immolations.'"[42] Neither side in this argument
could actually begin to explain the enormity of political suicide, but each
sought to appropriate irrational sacrifice to the rationalizations of their political
position.[43]

Not all contestants in the Mandal debate were quite so partisan. Veena Das,
though she argued elsewhere against Mandal, came out in favor of an American style of affirmative action as against the use of quotas.[44] Ashis Nandy was
far more ambivalent than usual; while sympathizing with the protesting students, and wishing that some political party would show the moral courage to
come out against the Mandal Commission, he said that he was "close to being
a supporter of the Mandal commission . . . because I think caste does play a
role and irrespective of your educational and economic status certain things are
not available to you."[45] Upendra Baxi, then vice-chancellor of Delhi University, spoke eloquently about how both the protest and the debate tended to miss
the basic issues, some of which concerned the need to begin reservations far
lower down in the system if they were to do any good, and others had to do
with the necessity to recognize the technical nature of the judicial and legislative process.[46] P. Radhakrishnan, a social scientist at the Madras Institute of
Development Studies who had done extensive research on the history of reservation policy, wrote that "while the decision to implement the Mandal report
itself is of an extreme nature, the reactions to it have also been so. . . . Since the
Constitution has provisions for reservations for the OBCs, it is the government
of India which has to be blamed for its failure to implement these provisions
for about four decades now and having allowed the state governments to politi-
cise the matter."[47] Radhakrishnan was one of many who expressed support for
the idea of reservations but argued the need for much better criteria and classificatory guidelines in the establishment and implementation of genuine social reform.

## The Embarrassment of Caste

Despite much muddiness in the general debate, what did become clear was the
extreme ambivalence surrounding caste, and the accompanying crisis on the
left when matters of caste were involved. Aditya Nigam argued, against the
spirit of much of the debate, that "A left position need not necessarily be
identified either by its crusading ardour against merit and efficiency or by its
messianic zeal for reservations. What it certainly needs to recognize, in no
uncertain terms, is that merit and efficiency are largely socially determined and

therefore, any consideration on merit alone works inherently against the under-privileged."[48] This moderate position seemed welcome, given the polarized character of the debate. But the sorest spot in the debate, again, had to do with the position of caste itself. Shiv Visvanathan characterized the problem with particular clarity:

> For years a whole generation of sociologists talked of caste as a fundamental reality. We talked of the vitality of the caste system and how it adapted to industry and the city. We boasted about the modernity of tradition. M. N. Srinivas made his reputation with concepts such as sanskritisation and westernisation. His epigoni added to it in innumerable ways writing about caste associations and caste rituals. The literature of this generation provided the framework of many reports and many of these luminaries served as consultants to commissions on reservation. . . . Instead of condemning . . . [caste] as a parochial structure, they spent hours portraying it as a protean system quite at home in office and the city. They celebrated the grammar of purity and pollution, heralding the sheer geometry behind it. This was the world that the doyens of the era, Srinivas, Shah, Karve, Dumont, MSA Rao, gave us. . . . Marxists attacked such a view but only succeeded in reducing it to a caricature. Now suddenly caste has become threatening, stifling, even worse than communalism. It is no longer protean; it is Procrustus, terribly constricting, absolutely threatening to a way of life. . . . Caste is now casteism and everyone has reservations about it.[49]

Visvanathan saw the ambivalence around caste as reflecting a whole series of contradictions at the core of the lives of Indian intellectuals, beginning within the university but permeating the abstractness of intellectual engagements with social and political realities. In making this argument, he identified the contradictions around caste itself, the way the anthropologization of the Indian social imaginary had run aground against the specter of caste politics. Although others argued that the Indian elite always felt a certain civilizational embarrassment about caste, Visvanathan asserted that caste became a marker of a certain kind of identity, simultaneously belonging to the private sphere and affiliating the most modern (and Western) of spirits with the domesticating comfort of tradition. Thus the appeal of Srinivas et al., whose notions of westernization, sanskritization, and compartmentalization—the latter meaning the capacity to situate caste solely within the domestic sphere, the home, frequently as a matter of fashion and family—became the happy pieties of the secular elite; thus the establishment of a certain anthropological orthodoxy that resolutely resisted serious engagement with history and politics.[50]

When analyzing the changing character of caste in contemporary India, G. S. Ghurye had observed that the interdependence of caste groups was being replaced by caste solidarity, what he also called "caste-patriotism." Ghurye lamented that "Conflict of claims and oppositions has thus replaced the old harmony of demand and acceptance," noting later in his argument that "caste-solidarity" has now "taken the place of village-community."[51] He also

commented that the modern phenomenon of marriage among different subcastes was further contributing to the growth of this phenomenon of caste
patriotism, thus anticipating other arguments about the increasing ethnicization of caste. M. N. Srinivas wrote in a similar vein that "In general it may be
confidently said that the last hundred years has seen a great increase in caste
solidarity, and the concomitant decrease of a sense of interdependence between different castes living in a region."[52] Srinivas was less directly critical
of caste solidarity than Ghurye, though he shared Ghurye's concern about the
rise of conflict between caste groups and the politicization of caste in relation
to the non-Brahman movements of Madras and Mysore. Edmund Leach formally theorized what both Ghurye and Srinivas were addressing when he
wrote that the caste system was changing fundamentally when it shifted from
interdependence to competition; for Leach, invoking Durkheim, this meant
that the caste system was dying, at least as the traditional system it had always
been.[53] Both Ghurye and Srinivas agreed with Leach, though they stressed the
way in which caste was not so much dying as being reborn, if now in increasingly sinister ways. Louis Dumont had noted that Ghurye and Srinivas were
both referring to the process he dubbed "substantialization." Ironically,
Dumont, despite his overt Brahmanical perspective on caste and the conservatism of his general theoretical views, actually welcomed these changes: "Anti-
Brahman schemings, although they have a demagogic and somewhat violent
side, are a positive aspect in the struggle against caste."[54] But Dumont also
agreed that this meant the effective death of the real caste system, a system that
in its classical form had been free from political strife and struggle.

Whether caste is dying off or being reborn as a monster, the political entailments of these theoretical positions have been clearly revealed over the years
in the debates about reservation policies and the politics of caste more generally. Outside of India, the debates over caste have raged free of an immediate
political terrain, though with all sorts of implications for the instantiation and
naturalization of Orientalist perceptions about the character of tradition and
modernity in India. The debates within India, however, have taken place not
only in academic corridors (which themselves have not been autonomous—as
Visvanathan noted, not only did anthropologists play important roles in the
making of policy, they set the questions about Indian society that all Indian
civil servants and academics had to answer on standard competitive examina-
tions) but also in public debates over the nature of history, the character of
society, the changing meanings and relations of tradition and modernity, and
the responsibilities and risks of redistributive policy decisions that would use
the category of caste. If caste has been taken as the inevitable category to
define minorities in need of positive discrimination, it is perhaps equally inevitable that many have reacted to these measures by decrying not just the politicization of caste but the tacit acknowledgement that caste, interdependent or

competitive or both, seems destined to stay on as fundamental in India's social and political life.

Despite Risley's failure to establish his views about the fundamentally racial character of caste, caste has become like race in its contradictory positionality. On the one hand, caste is the fundamental determinant of privilege in a society that is still bound by histories of prejudice and exploitatation; on the other, caste is the only natural way to make social distinctions, even granting the extent to which economic markers would be generally accepted as the most scientific way to consider the problem of redistribution. This is to suggest neither that caste is a natural category nor that it is seen by most social scientists as one (it is of course, like race, a social construction). Ironically, in a modern world where the economic is increasingly naturalized as the fundamental condition not just of the human but of freedom, the natural distinctions of the social order around notions such as race and caste have become deeply inscribed as the signs of modernity, the necessary exceptions that prove the truth of the rule.

In the case of India, the history of colonialism plays a fundamental role in the elaboration and naturalization of these contradictions. Although there is a general consensus that caste is a retrograde force, there is also widespread acceptance of the social fact that caste is the natural focus of political mobilization and economic redistribution, as well as the somewhat illicit marker of cultural identity and traditional pleasure. Indeed, caste identification is a form of pleasure that negotiates the contradictory faultlines between embarrassment in the face of colonial criticism and nostalgia over the comforts of home. An uncanny alliance has developed between critiques of colonial history and denunciations of reservation policy, in what is surely a curious disavowal of the way caste is still the most conspicuous marker of social privilege in India, even as it is genuinely hardened by reservation policy now as it was by colonial classificational regimes earlier. But it must be recognized that the power of colonial history was precisely to complicate the politics of modernity in colonial places. Colonialism worked to affiliate progress and reason with domination and humiliation, to demonstrate that the modern was always an argument for British rule rather than Indian independence, to naturalize the necessity that tradition would raise its head time after time to announce both the perils of the modern and the contradictory allure of the old. If it is no longer easy for a critic such as myself to excoriate the colonial construction of Indian society without worrying that I will play into anti-Mandal forces (or worse, Hindu fundamentalist ones), it may be because I have necessarily affiliated myself with the rationalizing conceits of demystifying critique and assumed that one can fight reason only with reason—that one can dispel the enchantment of a certain kind of history only with a powerful account of the same kind of history.[55] For reasons I have suggested in this chapter, the contradictions of caste may stay with India for a very long time, outliving both colonial critiques and various forms of substantialization and politicization. Caste may be the most telling reminder of the postcolonial character of India's contemporary predicament, the chilling sign that India's relationship to history and tradition will necessarily continue to be mediated by the colonial past. Even as caste and colonialism in India could not, it seems, have done without each other, they will survive together in India for a long time to come.

However, the affiliations of caste with colonial history notwithstanding, caste has come to occupy a very specific position in the nationalist social imaginary. Caste, as long as it can be safely consigned to the private, the personal, and the domestic, is not a source of danger, nor is it hugely problematic for the self-representation of Indian modernity in the context of the new nation state. In part, as I just suggested, we can see this as a reaction to the history of colonial discourse and colonial anthropology, not unlike the story told by Partha Chatterjee, in which the women's question dropped out of the nationalist reform agenda around the end of the nineteenth century because it was a sign of the inherent failure of Indian tradition. The retreat from earlier commitments to social reform, women's worlds, and domesticity more generally was affiliated to an effort to find a space outside of the colonial sphere, shielded from the colonial gaze, where nationalist Indians could retreat from the harsh and hegemonic modernity that was both the domain of political action and the constant reminder of Indian lack. By the same token, caste too became an embarrassing sign of failure/lack/tradition, of the incapacity of India to free itself from medieval preoccupations with prestige and with everything from insidious forms of social hierarchy to the contamination of any possibility of a public sphere/public domain/public politics that could be free, open, and progressive. Within the nationalist social imaginary, only two options have presented themselves: the first that of Ghurye and Gandhi, the second that of Ambedkar and Nehru. Caste must be idealized in essentialist nostalgia and domesticated in relation to a newly sheltered private sphere, or disavowed through retreat or rejection.

The debate over Mandal has also demonstrated how uncertain the political entailments of either of these political positions might be. On the one hand, the conservative and anti-nationalist Justice Party's use of caste for positive discrimination had a continuous history/politics with the progressive backward class movement; on the other, the evidently nationalist commitments of figures such as Gandhi and Ghurye had an equally continuous history/politics with the current opposition to Mandal. The postcolonial condition—the myriad, contradictory, frequently displaced legacies of colonial rule for postindependent politics—cannot be allowed to serve as a license for the erosion of the progressive narrative of the postcolonial state, despite the manifest crises of a post-Nehruvian secularist politics. Only by recognizing the thoroughly political character of caste identity (whether in precolonial, colonial, or postcolonial times—

however much the terms and regimes of both politics and caste have shifted) will it be possible to interrogate the continuing slippage between nostalgia for some "traditional" idea of caste and the multiple concealments of caste power. If caste can be comfortably imagined as something that can be genuinely "compartmentalized" and "contained" (worn on the body in the privacy of the domestic sphere), we must remind ourselves of all the critiques that have been mobilized in recent years, from critical as well as feminist theory, about the myriad conceits enabling such a bourgeois dream world. Bourgeois social theory must be exposed for what it sets out to do, even within the permissive parameters of a postcolonial alternative modernity.

All this is not to argue either that caste has not been further hardened and reified by its current round of politicization, or that Mandal itself had any real likelihood of making a manifest difference in the social distribution of economic opportunity. But the debate over Mandal has heightened concerns among many that the legitimacy of state intervention in areas related to social justice has been further eroded, compromised in part by the resurgence of caste privilege and efforts to naturalize that privilege through the ideological linkage of communalism and nationalism. Thus I have focused not on the redistributive potential of Mandal but rather on its discursive and political implications. In particular, I have been interested in the history of concern about the politicization of caste. It is, I think, as impossible to return to a (neo)traditional view of caste that can escape either critiques of privilege or concerns that caste is concealing the accumulated violence both of old India and new—traditional as well as modern operations of domination, exploitation, exclusion, and erasure—as it is to suggest any longer that caste is nothing but class, that it is likely to die a quick death under the pressures of the modern, or that it might be reborn as a straightforward clone of some Western sociological category (as substantialized ethnicities, bloc political voting groups, and so on).

Caste should no longer be disavowed, however, or critiques of colonial history licensed to wish it away. I would suggest that caste might even provide an ambivalent vehicle for charting out new ways of thinking about Indian modernity, secularism, and nationalism. Caste has the dubious advantage of signaling class privilege, highlighting sociohistorically determined modes of access to and exclusion from resources and opportunities, and calling attention to the differentiated and particularistic forms of relationship to other social collectivities and religious beliefs and practices. In many ways like the category of gender, caste both interrogates and acknowledges difference. If Mandal has worked to elicit embarrassment and contradiction, we need not follow the path of conservative forces that would seek to erase or silence caste (in the name of religion) as a site of identity and power. And so I would argue that caste is the form of community that most effectively occupies the space of political society proposed recently by Partha Chatterjee.[56] The genealogy of caste politics (in its modern form) in the agitations over rank and status around the census need not compromise contemporary possibilities for political mobilization that work to transform the postcolonial relations of state and society. Caste in its present form may indeed be a colonial hangover, but the challenge of the postcolonial predicament is to find other ways to transform history, while always acknowledging the barbaric hold it has on us all.

# Fourteen

## Conclusion: Caste and the Postcolonial Predicament

> Hegel remarks somewhere that all facts and
> personages of great importance in world history
> occur, as it were, twice. He forgot to add: the first
> time as tragedy, the second as farce.
> —Karl Marx

KANCHA ILAIAH begins his remarkable book entitled *Why I am Not a Hindu* by saying, "I was not born a Hindu for the simple reason that my parents did not know that they were Hindus." He goes on to make clear that this was not because his parents belonged to some other religious identity but rather because his "illiterate parents, who lived in a remote South Indian village, did not know that they belonged to any religion at all." Members of the Kuruma caste, breeders of sheep, his parents brought him up in a world in which Hinduism was clearly the province of the upper castes—Brahmins, Baniyas, Ksatriyas. "We knew nothing of Brahma, Vishnu or Eswara until we entered school. When we first heard about these figures they were as strange to us as Allah or Jehova or Jesus were."[1] According to Kancha Ilaiah, the cultural life of Hindus, determined in large part by protocols of hierarchy, ritual, and purity, steeped in beliefs that were seen as inaccessible and foreign, was not something he shared. Only in recent years, under the sway of a Hindu fundamentalist movement that has sought to recruit Dalits and other low-caste groups to a generic confessional idea of Hinduism, has he experienced any intimations of a possible connection. And yet, as a political activist and theorist, skeptical of a movement that seeks to build new conditions for the hegemony of an upper-caste Hindu chauvinism, he has written a book to reject the right of Hindus, and Hinduism, to claim him. Now, basing his autobiography and his political identity in his lower-caste origins, he champions caste mobilization as both a progressive political force and as antithetical to Hindu nationalism.

That caste might have nothing (or, rather, everything) to do with the idea of Hinduism as either a religion or a community is of course hardly a new thought, or condition, for Dalits across India. But the resistance to a new incorporative Hinduism that began with Ambedkar in the early years of this century reflects the changing claims of Hinduism itself during the last century. From the textual discovery of "Hinduism" in the eighteenth century, through the various institutional methods deployed by colonial rule throughout the nineteenth century in which Hinduism both as doxa and as praxis was defined by an upper-caste elite in relationship to colonial and national contexts and imperatives, to the birth of a new postcolonial Hindu nationalism, the relationship of religion to society has undergone massive redefinition. Whereas those colonial Orientalists who, like Max Müller, argued for the distinction between the religious aspects of caste and its social manifestations had to resort to Vedic texts and interpretations, now Hindu nationalists who seek to submerge caste difference in religious unity echo these older arguments in new contexts. The intellectual genealogies are complicated by the changing nature of the categories of religion and society, even as it is clear that colonial history has produced the conditions for latter-day appropriation. Caste represented different kinds of life worlds and different kinds of threats in the nineteenth century, but the fact that the current resurgence of caste has sometimes occasioned a debate with the idea of Hinduism itself is surely rooted in the long history of debate about whether caste was civil or religious, or both.

In many current debates, Gandhi is credited with anticipating the problems of postcolonial secularism. Gandhi is correctly seen as the most eloquent and progressive spokesperson for an idea of religion that could not be separated from politics. Gandhi concluded his autobiography by writing that it was his devotion to truth that drew him into the field of politics, "and I can say without the slightest hesitation, and yet in all humility, that those who say that religion has nothing to do with politics do not know what religion means."[2] For Gandhi, the idea of truth could be used to make other kinds of distinctions—between, for instance, good religion and bad. But it also allowed him to make what in other contexts might appear as new separations between religion and politics, as when he distinguished between caste as a system of social discrimination and *varnashramadharma* as a principle of value and order. In a famous speech given in Tanjore in 1927, Gandhi reiterated a position that had landed him in serious trouble in Madras throughout the decade of the twenties. "I still believe in *varnasharma dharma*. . . . *Varnashramadharma* is humility. Although I have said that all men and women are born equal, I do not wish therefore to suggest that qualities are not inherited, but on the contrary I believe that just as everyone inherits a particular form so does he inherit the particular characteristics and qualities of his progenitors, and to make this admission is to conserve one's energy." He went on to address the implications of his position for the debate in Madras Presidency over the non-Brahman movement.

> And if you accept what I have ventured to suggest to you, you will find that the solution of the Brahmin and non-Brahmin question also, in so far as it is concerned with the religious aspect, becomes very easy. As a non-Brahmin I would seek to purify Brahmanism in so far as a non-Brahmin can, but not to destroy it. I would dislodge the Brahmin from the arrogation of superiority or from places of profit.

> Immediately a Brahmin becomes a profiteering agency he ceases to be a Brahmin. But I would not touch his great learning wherever I see it. And whilst he may not claim superiority by reason of learning I myself must not withhold that meed of homage that learning, wherever it resides, always commands.[3]

Gandhi articulated here a position that was similar in many respects to those of earlier Hindu social reformers, Dayananda and Vivekenanda among them, even as he stretched the distinction between Brahmanism and social (or economic) privilege in order to claim an uncompromised commitment to equality. And yet despite Gandhi's careful effort to separate principle from practice, he angered E.V.R. and Ambedkar, among many others, precisely because his principles seemed to them irrevocably connected to the dominance of the upper castes in Indian social, political, and religious life. It also struck them as disingenuous, for they believed that Gandhi used these principles to attract multiple constituencies for whom his distinctions were hardly relevant.

Religion and politics could only be separated, or combined, once they were constituted in modern registers as discrete fields of belief and action. My argument throughout this book has been that the registers of modernity in nineteenth- and twentieth-century India were colonial ones, which compromised both the promise of modernity and the possibilities of resistance to it. Gandhi might well have been responding in creative and compelling ways to the mutual inheritance of colonial Orientalist and anticolonial nationalist concerns about the denigration of Indian civilizational values, but he could hardly exempt himself and his words from the colonial contradictions that constituted both the threat and the limit of his formulations. Although I have suggested ways in which Gandhi must be read against the grain of caste, in particular through my treatment of E.V.R. and Ambedkar, I am also proposing here that Gandhi's critique of secular concerns about the reach of religion into politics was undermined both by the ambiguous relationship of caste (as a social and political fact) to religion and by the fundamentally ambiguous nature of Hinduism as a modern religious form. Even as caste could only be justified through an appeal to religious principle, Hinduism could only mobilize itself in political terms by constructing boundaries and making exclusions. Thus I argue not only that tradition was produced under the sign of colonial modernity but also that it was irrevocably tainted for political purposes precisely because of this colonial history.

Ashis Nandy has argued that Gandhi was an arch antisecularist because he "claimed that his religion was his politics and his politics was his religion."[4] Nandy, like T. N. Madan and a number of prominent Indian social scientists, has sought to recast Gandhi's position as one that was predicated neither on a modern style of cultural relativism nor on his efforts to mobilize political support for the struggle against colonialism. Madan has asked, for example, whether "men of religion such as Mahatma Gandhi would be our best teachers

on the proper relation between religion and politics—values and interests—
underlining not only the possibilities of interreligious understanding, which is
not the same as an emaciated notion of mutual tolerance or respect, but also
opening out avenues of a spiritually justified limitation of the role of religious
institutions and symbols in certain areas of contemporary life." In assuming an
answer in the affirmative, he goes on to write, in near apocalyptic language,
"The creeping process of secularization, however, slowly erodes the ground on
which such men might stand." And Nandy sees Gandhi's religious tolerance as
rooted in his "anti-secularism, which in turn came from his unconditional rejection of modernity."[5] Nandy states his case clearly and powerfully: "Religious tolerance outside the bounds of secularism is exactly what it says it is. It
not only means tolerance of religions but also a tolerance that is religious. It
therefore squarely locates itself in traditions, outside the ideological grid of
modernity." Nandy goes on to note that traditional Hinduism (or, rather, *sana-
tan dharma*) was the source of Gandhi's religious tolerance. Although I would
hardly argue against Nandy's, or Madan's, plea for religious tolerance, let
alone criticize either for suggesting that tolerance be made into a religious
value, I fear that this position is not merely unhistorical but also out of step
with contemporary critiques of Gandhi by those who understood his message
in very different ways. To dismiss Gandhi's position as only politically manip-
ulative is no doubt wrong. But to argue that Gandhi's sense of the relationship
between religion and politics was not situated in complex relation to colonial
modes of knowledge, the formulations of Hindu social reformers, and the contingencies of political struggle and support is disingenuous, as well. Leaving
aside his polemical style, Nandy fails to grapple with the extent to which the
kind of antisecularism he espouses is implicated in the same problematic contradictions as the secularism he so passionately attacks. If Nandy is justifiably
concerned by the misuses of Gandhi made by those who controlled Indian
statecraft in the years of Nehruvian secularism, surely he must recognize how
his reading of Gandhi could be used to justify the kinds of religious tolerance—read intoleration—that are promulgated by Hindu nationalists in more
recent times, as well.

Ambedkar and E.V.R. found it impossible to separate Gandhi's defense of
religion from his defense of caste, and as a result made extreme attacks on both
caste and religion, if in rather different ways. When their critiques, and lives,
are read into Gandhi's own extraordinary political and intellectual struggle, it
is possible to appreciate the contradictory bequest of colonial rule for contemporary social and political life, even as it is necessary to recognize that all of
these struggles must be understood as part of the history of anticolonial nationalism in India. If I have suggested that an uncomplicated resort to tradition can
no longer be seen as either innocent or authentic, I have also tried to suggest
that the recognition of the power of modernity need not preclude the celebra-

tion and deployment of contradiction. Caste in its present form(s) may be the precipitate of a tragic history, but it is now, for better and for worse, a fundamental component of political struggles that seek to redeem that same tragic past. But that is only because caste has been part of the same history that has transformed the terms both of the traditional and of the modern in the postcolonial world in which we live today. New traditions will continue to be invented, even as tradition as an idea—sometimes an inspiration and other times a phantasm—will hardly yield its power to increasingly stale and scary visions of the modern. But the purpose of this kind of postcolonial critique is to suggest that even as tradition has never been like this before, it will, perforce, continue to be rooted in the very history that it seeks to precede or transcend. And the purpose of bringing Ambedkar and E.V.R. into conversation with Gandhi is in part to suggest that nationalist ideology can only move beyond the stifling conditions of colonial production by reclaiming the histories of caste mobilization, religious critique, and political struggle that these profoundly national figures represent.

There is no end to history. And now, at the dawn of the new millennium, it returns with almost farcical vengeance in the form of the census. After a decade that began with the convulsions surrounding the implementation of the Mandal Report, it has been proposed that caste be reintroduced as an enumerative category in the 2001 census. A recent symposium at the Institute for Economic Growth in Delhi brought together distinguished social scientists to debate the issue. The conveners of the symposium began their summary article by noting that "The controversy around the proposal to reintroduce caste returns in the Census of 2001 provides yet another instance of our deep-seated ambivalence towards the most distinctive institution of Indian society. As liberal-modern intellectuals and citizens, we would like to reject caste altogether, to consign it to the dustbin of history. But we are also forced to acknowledge its continued relevance as a contemporary form of discrimination and inequality, and therefore also as an axis for mobilisation or avenue for advancement."[6] The article goes on to adduce more reasons for ambivalence, including a suspicion of the state's intentions in making this move, and uncertainty about the role of caste in an age of liberalization and globalization. Among the most compelling arguments in favor of reintroducing caste in the census are the sense that caste is as important a variable in contemporary Indian society as language, religion, or region, that the inclusion of caste in the census will facilitate the social scientific study of changes in the morphology of the system as a whole, and that such a move is necessary so long as recent legislation mandating various types of legislation for the backward castes is on the books. Among the arguments against the use of caste are the belief that the inclusion of caste would intensify divisive caste identities and could lead to violence, that the use of caste would be abhorrent given the constitutional vision of a casteless society, that given the nature of caste the data would be faulty and difficult to collect, and that in the end such a policy would continue British colonial policies of "divide and rule" through caste.

Has colonial tragedy now returned as postcolonial farce? When critiques of colonialism can be used to argue against what many commentators agree are progressive, if flawed, measures to pursue a constitutional commitment to social and economic equality, is it time to put historical concerns with the colonial past back on the shelf of academic historiography? The purpose behind a postcolonial historiography of colonialism is to come to terms with the weight of the colonial past without turning our backs on that past. This must entail yielding neither to the misuses of the colonial critique nor to the argument that colonialism did not, in the end, matter. Many historians, as I demonstrate in the Coda to this book, now suggest that an emphasis on colonialism effaces both the ancient reality of India and the contemporary agency of Indians, as if the bad faith—and tragic fate—of colonial history might now be simply wished away. Alas, colonialism not merely happened, it continues to haunt the postcolonial nation. That colonial history can now be used to undermine progressive politics, even as that same history produced the conditions for a nationalist ideology based on social and religious inequality as well as prejudice, is only the most recent illustration of the powerful, and contradictory, legacy of the colonial interlude in India. If caste returns as a critical enumerative category for the Indian state in the new millennium, it both carries the enormous contradictions of this legacy and points to new possibilities for social transformation and political citizenship. Caste, in these terms, is neither tragedy nor farce, but history itself.

# Coda _____

## The Burden of the Past: On Colonialism and the Writing of History

> History is the work expended on material
> documentation (books, texts, accounts, registers,
> acts, buildings, institutions, laws, techniques, objects,
> customs, etc.) that exists, in every time and place, in
> every society. . . . [I]n our time, history is that which
> transforms documents into monuments . . . in our
> time history aspires to the condition of archaeology,
> to the intrinsic description of the monument.
> —Michel Foucault, *Archaeology of Knowledge*

WHEREAS the nineteenth century was the great century of imperial power, the most astonishing accomplishment of the twentieth century has been the struggle to consign colonial rule to the past tense. Although that struggle has been successful, it has not only been drenched in violence but it has also led to the general recognition that the effects of imperialism have by no means disappeared with the demise of formal colonial regimes of rule. Colonialism lives on in the massive disparities of wealth and control over capital between north and south, in the contradictory institutional legacies that inhabit political, juridical, educational, and economic systems, and in the differential manifestations of cultural entitlement and social capacity that characterize a world of ethnic dispute and national dislocation. Even as the colonial past was written into every aspect of the early consolidation of Western metropolitan economic and political domination, it continues to be written into the new world order—in subnational ethnic violence, in national debates over immigration and identity, in the postimperial positioning of the United States after the end of the cold war, in postnational developments around liberalization, globalization, and the late twentieth-century triumph of capitalism, and in worries that the specter of future cataclysm resides not in communism but in other civilizations. Colonialism may be dead, yet it is everywhere to be seen.

Colonialism was fundamental to the origins of capitalism in England and the West, the rise of European and North American political domination, the acceptance of an anthropological vision that conferred cultural explanations on the colonized world, and the emergence of basic assumptions of historical thought that were enshrined by Hegel and expounded by Macaulay, Mill, Seeley, and many others.[1] In this book I have sought to demonstrate these larger propositions in the light of specific examples in the history of caste in India. I have also attempted to show in detail how colonialism was served by, even as it produced the conditions of possibility for, forms of knowledge that, in the wake of Said's extraordinary challenge, can be characterized under the single term of "Orientalism." But I have sought to go much further than Said (whose project was admittedly limited to texts of Orientalism and their relations to sites of colonial power in the West), even as I have taken seriously his claim that the Orient was produced as the "Orient" by the historical power of Orientalism, defined both as specific bodies of scholarship and as colonial knowledge writ large. In doing so, I have acknowledged the power of colonial formations, power that was both concealed and displayed through the transformations and effects of colonial rule in India. I have attempted to demonstrate how knowledge and power were entangled in an unsteady and often unstable history of institutions, representations, legislation, policies, and rhetoric, how power was realized through the incitements of colonial modernity as well as the confusions of colonial rule. The colonized as well as the colonizer participated in power, enhanced by moments of failure as well as by the complicated logics of contradiction, displacement, and deferral, and ultimately overdetermined both by the historical outcome of high imperialism and by the multiple imperatives that sustained the European commitment to it. The story is neither simple nor straightforward. Embedded in historical process, it has necessarily been changed by different historical forces at different historical moments. But it is a story that insists on, and demonstrates, the overriding significance of colonialism in the making of modern India.

This is not a story that colonialism told about itself. The British, of course, took credit for all that was good and modern in India, but they also underestimated the impact they had, even as they complained about their weakness, ignorance, and lack of real power. J. R. Seeley, who assumed the chair in modern history at Cambridge in 1869, gave a series of lectures in 1881 and 1882 that became the basis for one of the best-selling history books in England in the late nineteenth century (the book was, in fact, in print until 1956, the year of Suez). Seeley was in some ways a liberal, critical of certain aspects of colonial policy at the same that he warned against imperial complacency in India; he was respectful of Indian accomplishment even as he suggested that once Indians united the empire would fall. He was also critical of Britain's enclosed sense of itself and its history, and criticized English historians for making "too much of the mere parliamentary wrangle and the agitations about liberty, in all which matters the eighteenth century of England was but a pale reflexion of the seventeenth. They do not perceive that in that century the history of England is not in England but in America and Asia." But he acknowledged that this amnesia was itself a reflection of the general tenor of the earlier centuries of imperial expansion, in which England did not so much conquer its colonies as stumble into them. "There is," he wrote, "something very characteristic in the indifference which we show towards this mighty phenomenon of the diffusion of our race and the expansion of our state. We seem, as it were, to have conquered and peopled half the world in a fit of absence of mind."[2] By this now famous phrase, Seeley reiterated earlier colonial views of the eighteenth century in India, in which English traders simply filled the vacuum left by the collapse of the Mughal state. "We shall see that nothing like that what is strictly called a conquest took place, but that certain traders inhabiting certain seaport towns in India, were induced, almost forced, in the anarchy caused by the fall of the Mogul Empire, to give themselves a military character and employ troops, that by means of these troops they acquired territory and at last almost all the territory of India, and that these traders happened to be Englishmen, and to employ a certain, though not a larger, proportion of English troops in the army."[3] And so the story that had been sold to Parliament throughout the eighteenth century, at least until Burke called Hastings to account, is transmuted here into an authoritative history of the origins of imperial rule in India.

Seeley's history both informed and was informed by his sense of the contemporary conditions of colonial rule. He wrote, "For we are not really conquerors of India, and we cannot rule her as conquerors; if we undertook to do so, it is not necessary to inquire whether we could succeed, for we should assuredly be ruined financially by the mere attempt."[4] By this he meant that India was governed in the same way it was conquered, through the complicity, and lack of any unified resistance, of the governed. For Seeley the liberal (of the same liberalism as that of Mill and Macaulay), this was not because of "some enormous superiority on the part of the English race," but rather because of the lack of any national feeling in India. "There is then no Indian nationality, though there are some germs out of which we can conceive an Indian nationality developing itself. . . . If there could arise in India a nationality-movement similar to that which we witnessed in Italy, the English Power could not even make the resistance that was made in Italy by Austria, but must succumb at once." Seeley acknowledged the role of the British government in suppressing the rise of national resistance, as when he noted that "the mutiny was in a great measure put down by turning the races of India against each other."[5] And yet, his prediction that English power would collapse in the face of nationalist mobilization was clearly refuted during the next sixty years. Even as he was correct to observe, if only in an aside, that the British played a role in the arrested history of nationality, the fact was that British rule in India was not as fragile as Seeley thought. Colonial history was colonial fiction.

That colonial history is fiction has been a major part of the argument of this book, even as I have argued that fiction makes history happen. I have

suggested this through my interrogation of the colonial archive, the histories
behind and beneath the production of the kinds of primary sources that have
represented colonial knowledge even as they have been used to determine and
justify colonial policy. The archive has enshrined, in Foucault's sense, this raw
material for subsequent historical representation. In the Indian case, the archive is both the precipitate of the history of conquest and rule and the basis
on which that history has been written by colonial administrators like Mill and
Risley and by colonial historians like Macaulay and Seeley. And it is in large
part because of the uncritical acceptance of the archive as a primary source
rather than itself an historical document, that colonial power has been so good
at dissembling. In the historical literature, colonial power, at least in forms that
were not cast solely in economic or political terms, escaped serious interrogation outside of the specific contestations of the nationalist struggle until the
new critical imperial history inaugurated by figures as various as Bernard
Cohn, Edward Said, and Ranajit Guha. Despite differences within this tradition of critical history, about which I will say more below, much recent work
has addressed the extraordinary role of colonial knowledge in facilitating empire and in producing the very categories used to understand the effects of
empire in postcolonial societies. But it has by no means supplanted scholarship in imperial history that continues to take the sources of colonial history
itself, as well as the colonial historiography of so canonic a figure as Seeley,
as the basis for its own understanding of colonialism. Indeed, there has been
remarkable continuity between the historical proposals of Seeley and the
latter-day "Cambridge school" of Indian historians, not to mention the recent,
and massive, five-volume historical encyclopedia, *The Oxford History of the
British Empire*.[6] Like the aftermath of colonialism itself, colonial history
lives on.

Anil Seal laid out the basic theme of early Cambridge school historiography
when he asserted that colonialism could be described as "British rule through
Indian collaboration."[7] Early work by members of this school focused on the
nationalist movement, debunking claims about the ideological motives of nationalist leaders, and arguing that Indian politics emerged as a direct reflex of
administrative initiatives set in motion by colonial rule. Seal himself wrote
about the relationship between English education and Indian nationalism,
though his students concentrated much more on the factional affiliations and
structures that characterized the often nasty and always self-interested world of
Indian political struggle. The basic argument was that local elites, the very
groups that had been the collaborators for British rule, turned nationalist—in
the context of participation in the progressively enlarged electoral arenas of
provincial and municipal politics—when they realized that more of the pie
could be obtained through autonomous political institutions than through colonial ones. Nationalist ideology was shown to be hollow, even as colonial rule
was viewed as completely dependent on elite complicity. Seeley's sense that

British colonialism was a mere veneer was thus reborn in Seal's insistence on the logic of collaboration. The Cambridge school proved its arguments by using colonial sources—frequently police records and confidential files—that documented the spurious activities of nationalist figures in what was a large-scale colonial effort to track, contain, and debunk the very politics that sought to overthrow colonial rule.

Whereas the early work of this influential group of historians first concerned nationalism—earning thereby considerable notoriety, and ire from historians in India as well as in North America and Australia—Cambridge historiography has in recent years been far more trained on the eighteenth century and questions around the transition to, rather than from, colonial rule. Christopher Bayly has now produced three weighty and important volumes that have given empirical density to an argument that, along with the work of many others, has seriously modified Seeley's characterization of the eighteenth century as one of Indian decadence. Bayly has advocated Seeley's basic view, however, that "conquest" is the wrong way to conceive of the rise of the British presence in the subcontinent. As he wrote at the beginning of his 1983 work, *Rulers, Townsmen and Bazaars*, "Even though the late Victorians tended to see 'native' society as a static backdrop to British exploits, Sir John Seeley in the 1880s warned his audience against the chauvinistic belief that Britain had conquered India in any simple sense. The East India Company, he said, had merely taken advantage of the disturbed conditions after the end of the Mughal empire in 1707, and that was mainly by dint of the support of important groups of Indians. This change of perspective was slow in establishing itself."[8] Bayly's own history has emphasized continuity, Indian "agency," and British weakness. As he wrote in a later reflection about his own historical corpus, he stressed "continuities even across the ruptures created by the coming of colonial capitalism. It was the fact that even under British colonialism, Indians recruited from precolonial service and commercial communities continued to control the bulk of mercantile capital and title to land and to populate the lower ranks of the army, judiciary and police, which informed the theme of continuity in *Rulers, Townsmen and Bazaars*."[9] Guided by Ronald Robinson's insistence on the "non-European foundations of European imperialism," he sought to locate the "central mechanisms of imperialism . . . in the systems of collaboration set up in preindustrial societies which succeeded, or failed, in meshing the incoming processes of European expansion into indigenous social politics and evolving a balance between the two."[10] In the process of documenting this claim, Bayly both emphasized the force of Indian social and economic politics and suggested that the British only succeeded in their project of expansion, and the consolidation of colonial rule, through the desires, actions, and agency of Indians.[11]

Curiously, however, Indian agency becomes a way of suggesting that colonial rule itself was an Indian project more than it was a European one. Bayly has updated Seeley's account of passive conquest, but in using the same language as his Cambridge predecessor he seems to substitute disavowal for chauvinism. He writes that "The British were *sucked into* the Indian economy by the dynamic of its [India's?] political economy as much as by their own relentless drive for profit. In turn, the Company was *forced* to build an army and develop new administrative methods."[12] Bayly notes, like Seeley before him, that the British were not entirely passive: "The Company was able to play off one state against another and offer its own formidable services for sale in the all-India military bazaar." But Bayly is more impressed by the fact that imperial ventures were financed by Indian capitalists, despite the fact that these capitalists were often short-lived and that indigenous capital was soon subordinated entirely "to the vast system of British peculation and inland trade." And he makes little of the fact that the Bengal revenues, secured by force after the Battle of Plassey, financed the army and made up for shortfalls in income from trade (mostly due to the fact that British traders skimmed off Company profits by indulging in lucrative private trade). Instead, Bayly focuses on the indigenous role in colonization and the indigenous forces of change that "continued to flow strongly even after the fuller incorporation of the subcontinent into the capitalist world system."[13] His position complements that of David Washbrook, who has written that "the indigenous logic of military fiscalism and commercial expansion led on to the conjuncture which produced colonialism as much as did that logic of European history, which pushed its sailors out into sea." Indeed, Washbrook has put the issue very clearly: "In a certain sense, colonialism was the logical outcome of South Asia's own history of capitalist development."[14] So much for Indian agency!

Washbrook has made the same argument as Bayly, though he has taken it further, and made it with rather more polemical fervor. The polemic is partly enhanced (and on the surface distinguished from Bayly's) by Washbrook's rhetorical endorsement of a Marxist-inspired approach to issues of class and capital, but Washbrook's delight in charging Indian capitalism with full responsibility for British colonialism undermines not only his Marxism but also his historical credibility.[15] He delineates recent research that strongly suggests the indigenous roots of capitalism in South Asia (much of it Bayly's) and then asks why, "after a few early misunderstandings, South Asia's capitalist social classes became the most loyal supporters of the British Raj and sustained it throughout the middle and later decades of the nineteenth century." His answer is clear. "Subordination to the dominance of British capital and loss of control over the central institutions of the commercial and fiscal systems meant the reverse of any inability to make and accumulate 'private' wealth."[16] In short, the new magnates made out like bandits, and expressed their own interests by accumulating private wealth rather than working toward the development of India.[17] These processes allowed capitalists, "whatever their ethnic origins," to take "an increasingly dominant and privileged position over producers and labourers."[18] Indeed, many Indian capitalists—such as "the celebrated Brahmin bureaucrats (more properly bankers, commercial agents and landowners) of Guntur who ran the district under the British; . . . [or] the six leading mirasidari families of Tanjavur who ran the Collectorate office and, between 1819 and 1835, 'acquired' land rights in about one-third of all the villages in the district"—not only rubbed salt "into the wounds of the Company" but also illustrated "which was dominant in the relation between capitalism and colonialism."[19] These capitalists manipulated formal legal and administrative mechanisms under the Company to allow them to accumulate, and hold on to, huge hoards of wealth. This, Washbrook argues, was the basis for the great success of capitalism in India, for he notes that "India, by the middle of the nineteenth century, must be regarded as one of the most successful of all contemporary capitalist societies."[20] Capitalism, in this case "Indian" capitalism, underdeveloped India through the logic of its own success (or, perhaps, the success of its own logic). Colonialism, in this case "British" colonialism, was incidental.

If colonialism was indeed epiphenomenal, so superficial a cover for Indian agency in the spheres of capital and accumulation, it should perhaps be of little surprise that Bayly and Washbrook both have scoffed at assertions such as mine that colonial forms of knowledge were critical in the establishment and maintenance of colonial rule in India. For Washbrook, such work at best simply exposes the mystifications of the working of capital, reifying both colonialism, and the importance of culture, in the process. But Bayly has taken great pains to counter this "fashion" in Indian historiography. In a chapter of the *Oxford History of the British Empire*, Bayly noted that historians began, in the wake of the force of Said's work (Cohn's influence is strangely ignored), "to argue that Indian caste, African tribe, 'Islam', or 'native polity'—the basic building blocks of the subject—were inventions of the colonial power in the early nineteenth century."[21] Bayly has called this work "retrogressive," not only because it ignores the great body of work in British intellectual history that has traced the complexity of imperial ideas, but because "histories in this vein tended to deny Asians, Africans, or Polynesians 'agency' in their own histories more thoroughly than had the nineteenth-century Imperial writers."[22] In Bayly's recent *Empire and Information*, a book written largely to dispute work of this kind, he has given full vent to his unease "about the assumption that the 'learned' ideas of orientalism played a consistent or determining part in the process of governing and exploiting India."[23] Bayly's book is characteristically rich with documentation and erudition, but it is riddled with internal contradictions, and strangely crippled by its insistence that knowledge is really nothing more than information.[24]

Bayly has argued that Orientalism, in Said's sense, was in any case "hardly a coherent system of thought," remaining, even after 1820, "self-contradictory, fractured and contested." Stereotypes of India as "ruled by fanaticism and caste" were only in evidence at moments of panic, and were in any case "a

product of the weakness and blindness of the state at the fringes of its knowledge rather than a set of governing assumptions at its core." Indeed, far from
being "the property of a domineering European government in Asia," these
ideas were a reflection of Europe's "weakness," and of the "fear, bafflement
and guilt of its expatriate citizens."[25] Over and over again we are told of England's weakness, how "Orientalist fantasy flooded into gaps left by the decline of pragmatic information," how knowledge was based on fundamental
ignorance, that stereotypes came from European experience rather than from a
deliberate "attempt to create a stereotyped Orient," that knowledge was not
only unreliable, unstable, and ambiguous, but virtually entirely dependent on
Indian sources.[26] Blame the victim again! Bayly notes that "The British understanding of Indian society—as opposed to its trades—may have been extraordinarily defective, but this was more the result of a lack of reliable informants
than the consequence of orientalist stereotypes," though elsewhere he notes
that the "social and religious values motivating" Indians were often "mysterious to Europeans." When Bayly asserts that colonial knowledge was "far from
being a monolith derived from the needs of power," he is simply restating his
conviction that the colonial state was weak, dazed, and confused.[27] And once
again Indian agency—simultaneously decisive, unreliable, and unknowable—
emerges triumphant through the flaccid superstructure of colonial rule, a tribute to the heroic Indian role in the making of the British empire.

Bayly's now clichéd insistence that colonial knowledge was not a monolith,
that it was unstable, contested, and in constant tension with a larger world of
uncertainty and unease, fails to do the rhetorical work he intends. The scholars
to whose work I have affiliated my own have all been aware of the fractious
and at times precarious nature of colonial knowledge. Few scholars have taken
Said's general propositions about Orientalism as a single formation of knowledge as literally as Bayly suggests, at the same time it has been widely recognized that what might in reality have been internally riven often appeared, at
least to the colonized under the conditions of colonial power, as monolithic.[28]
To argue this is also to argue against the self-representations of colonial authors, for whom weakness and ignorance were rhetorical as well as political
conceits. It has been the argument of this book that the success of colonial
discourse was in any case dependent on the contradictions and apparent open-
ness of colonial knowledge, certainly up until the middle of the nineteenth
century.[29] And yet the argument favored by Bayly, Washbrook, Frykenberg,
Irschick, and others that early colonial rule was a "dialogue" seems as mis-
guided as Seeley's assertion that the British would pack up and leave once a
nationalist movement appeared.[30] Dialogue is not an appropriate way to characterize the transactions of imperial power, even when it fails to have either the
full control or knowledge that it would invariably claim as its right. And,
whereas colonial hegemony continued even at its peak period during the nineteenth and early twentieth centuries to secure its power in part by such hetero-

geneous methods and institutions as rule by law, even David Washbrook has argued in a different context how legal institutions in the nineteenth century were steadfastly controlled by colonial interests.[31]

I have demonstrated how colonial power became both more secure and more ambitious as the century wore on. The shift from historical to ethnographic preoccupations—and the shift in turn from military conquest and soon thereafter revenue collection to concerns about political loyalty—changed the character of colonial knowledge in fundamental ways. There is no doubt that colonial domination became increasingly racialized, and stark, in the years following the suppression of the Great Rebellion. But this too is either denied, or at the least made light of, by Cambridge historiography. Indeed, the conviction that colonial conquest and rule were fragile at best and at the service of Indian agency at worst is what enables Bayly to argue that neither colonial power nor colonial knowledge was really so bad. He protests that "It was difficult to sustain an 'apartheid' ideology stressing ineluctable racial difference in a subcontinent where Indians continued to control—albeit under severe constraint—the vast bulk of capital and almost the whole means of agricultural production. Colonial officials, missionaries and businessmen were forced to register the voices of native informants in ideology and heed them in practice *even if they despised and misrepresented them.*"[32] Racism, in other words, was as epiphenomenal as colonial rule itself, hardly fundamental to the "continuous" historical experience of empire over the last three centuries. Small wonder that Cambridge historiography had difficulty understanding the force of nationalist ideology.

Bayly's disavowal of colonial power and prejudice is thus the predicate for his own historiographical conferral of agency onto the colonized subjects of Indian history. Washbrook, whose sense of structure makes his own rhetorical embrace of Indian agency seem especially paradoxical, seeks to dissolve the idea of colonialism entirely in the world soup of capitalism, even though in India capitalism takes on a distinctly national flavor. Washbrook's own position becomes clearer when he argues, in a variety of polemical attacks, that the attention given to colonialism works only to mystify the class interests of multicultural adherents or fellow travelers in the American academy. Both Washbrook's polemics and Bayly's rebukes lump together all of Said's "disciples," an extraordinary locution that seems to include Cohn (who wrote much of his early critical work on colonialism before Said's entry to the field) and his students, as well as scholars who have been associated with Subaltern Studies.[33] Although it is true that all of these miscellaneous scholars take colonialism seriously and have been critical of Orientalism, these polemics have tended to obscure the significant differences in recent writing on colonialism. A recent review by William Pinch follows Bayly in affiliating Cohn, represented as a postmodernist and deconstructionist (!), with the Subalternist historians on the grounds of their common commitment to the idea of cultural difference.[34] In his preference for Bayly's tacit "humanism"—he writes in favor of a history of the British in India that includes Britons "interacting materially, biologically, socially, and emotionally with Indians (and occupying the same cognitive world as Indians)"—he joins the ranks of many latter-day writers for whom any attention to questions of difference provides potential fodder for religious fundamentalism. Although Pinch's critique would seem appropriate for Dumont and others who traffic in Indological and essentialist anthropological ideas of India, he not only misses the fundamental point about recent critical studies of colonialism, he also echoes concerns of a wide number of recent critiques in which the emphasis, indeed any emphasis, on colonialism is seen as dangerous.[35]

Why, indeed, has colonialism become so bad a thing "to think," for so many different voices in the academy today? Bayly and Washbrook find themselves joined by a steadily growing group of historians, anthropologists, and cultural critics who view the connection between critical colonial history and postcolonial critique as a new form of academic terrorism. Indeed, colonialism has become a problem precisely because of the connections made between colonial history and postcolonial concerns, whether they focus on the status of postcolonial historical writing or on the epistemological and archival problems of reading colonial sources. Figures as different as the culturalist Marshall Sahlins and the materialist Aijaz Ahmed join forces when railing against the assertion of native agency in the writing of a different kind of contemporary history. Too much emphasis on colonialism is seen to license everything from too much stress on the role of Europe in the history of the "third world" to too much stress on issues of race rather than questions of class. Rosalind O'Hanlon and David Washbrook, in a recent critique of post-Orientalist fashions in the writing of Indian history, included in their sweeping denunciations not only an essay by Gyan Prakash but the historical anthropology of Cohn and his students as well as the writings of the subaltern school. They referred only once to the historical question of colonialism, to disparage the writing of James Clifford about the colonial entailments of British anthropology.[36] In this lone reference to colonial history, the authors suggest that their greatest concern about colonial history has nothing to do with India but is rather about the production of the idea of culture, now used to mystify social relations that are really about class and capital. The problem of colonialism, in other words, is located in the American academy, and has to do with the use of colonialism as a significant category of historical analysis. Historiographical attention to colonialism, rather than identifying key political dynamics behind the exercise of capitalist domination in India, is now accused of merely licensing postcolonial anxiety about cultural rather than economic matters, allowing a postcolonial elite to masquerade as the oppressed rather than the oppressors.[37] A history that focused on world capitalism would instead underscore the weight of global forces that in fact differentiate peoples on the basis of access to the means of production rather than the epiphenomenal questions of cultural (racial, or national) identity. And here is where Cambridge school history masquerades as Marxist history, using networks of materialist analysis and so-called class analysis to disparage anticolonial nationalism and to deny the historical reality and lasting effects of colonialism. Surely this is not what Marx had in mind by the historical analysis of class.

## Toward a Postcolonial Historiography

The polemics discussed above not only work to separate histories of colonialism from histories of capitalism, they also obscure the very real differences within histories of colonialism. I trust that it is clear that my emphasis on colonialism has not been meant to elide capitalism, but rather to suggest that the modern history of capitalism in India has been conducted under the auspices of the political economy of colonial rule. The salience of the historical structures of colonial rule cannot be trivialized by pointing to a handful of Indian "capitalists" who managed to secure wealth for themselves during colonial times. Further, I have taken for granted in this book that colonial preoccupations with economic wealth and political power provided the conditions for cultural engagement that ultimately worked to legitimate the colonial presence in India through cultural means, even as that colonial presence became dependent on cultural technologies of rule. I have also viewed culture principally as an effect of power, insisting that contemporary assumptions about cultural difference have been largely produced out of the long history of colonial domination. In this sense I have drawn on the work of Partha Chatterjee, who has used an idea of culture to delineate the particular strategies of nationalist resistance to colonialism, and has shown how cultural difference was a situated tactic, a colonial strategy, rather than an expression of essential incommensurability. That being said, I worry that Chatterjee underplays this historical dynamic in some of his writings on the "inner sphere" of Indian nationalism.[38] And I do not share all of the proposals of Ranajit Guha, whose resort to Sanskritic sources for indigenous political theory and historical consciousness seems to betray a general commitment to writing subaltern history against the grain in most other contexts.[39] More fundamentally, Guha's sense of the autonomy of nationalism has led him to argue that colonial rule was merely about domination rather than hegemony. This sense of the illegitimacy of colonial rule produces a different reading of the complex effects of a colonizing power that, in my reading, had such a profound impact on India precisely because of the kinds of mechanisms that produced a new form of caste in modern India. The refusal to accept the hegemonic character of colonial rule in India restricts

the use of the category of hegemony too resolutely within the space of a narrowly defined civil society, rendering the national subaltern autonomous, and
the difference between India and Britain as absolute.[40]

And yet Guha's insistence on the significance of racial, cultural, and political exclusions in the foundation of colonial governmentality provides the basis
for my own argument about the apotheosis of the ethnographic state in late
colonial India. It also allows us to see that imperial societies were useful laboratories for metropolitan experimentation—in spheres as various as cartography, epidemiology, penology, anthropology, and military science—precisely
because of the way imperial concerns with legitimation always referred to
metropolitan constituencies rather than colonized ones.[41] But far from being
entirely separate, it was the very connection between metropole and colony
that made the practices of governmentality so similar, and so mutually rein-
forcing. Indeed, I have suggested in this book that the formation of the metropolitan nation-state was itself as much a product of imperial expansion as of
domestic consolidation, and the same is true for many of the ideological cove-
nants of the metropolitan state, as well—from the idea of a liberal democratic
government to notions of religious toleration and secularism.[42] And yet this is
not to return the historical gaze entirely to Europe.[43] This book has made clear,
I trust, that attention to the wide historical provenance, not to mention the deep
historical force, of colonialism is neither to deny the rule of colonial difference
nor to lose sight of the specific histories and subjects of colonized lands.

I have focused on caste to establish the salience of the imperial archive and
the extraordinary impact of colonial rule, to the point that both the sources for
the understanding of tradition and the terms of reference for tradition are implicated in colonial history. But if tradition itself has been in some fundamental
sense produced through the history of the colonial modern, it is this same
history that so problematizes both tradition and modernity in the context of
postcolonial India. Caste can only be embraced ambivalently; although it is
impossible to treat caste as the object of nostalgia, it can hardly be the marker
of a satisfactory present. Inasmuch as caste is a sign of the past, it is also a
vehicle for the construction of a different future. The history of the production
of colonial difference does not license all expressions of nativist fundamentalism, even when it helps to explain their rise. Similarly, the writing of the
history of nationalist mobilization and resistance in colonial conditions need
not celebrate the promotion of an increasingly Hindu nationalist ideology that
excludes women, Muslims, and lower-caste "others" from the inner circle of
the national "we." Finally, a critical history of the colonial role in the production of caste does not justify the use of this critique to argue against caste just
at the point when it becomes the vehicle for the mobilization of an oppositional
politics.

These are only some of the reasons that the writing of colonial history in a
postcolonial time is so fraught. Writing has never been a neutral activity, but

the brief critique above, and the critical sensibility that has animated this book, should show at least some of the specific histories that have inflected the conditions for the writing of colonial history today. In the last fifty years we have learned anew how much it matters from where we write, to whom we write, and more generally how writing is positioned: geopolitically, sociohistorically, institutionally. The crisis of writing has been ushered in by many forces, among them decolonization, a rising chorus of new nations, the reemergence of new kinds of colonial relationships in the unequal distribution of global wealth and operations of global capital, and the dispersal through phases of migration and relocation of once colonized peoples. Postcolonial critiques have been necessary, if contentious, features of all the new landscapes we inhabit or survey. Postcoloniality in this sense is neither some new, faddish, trend nor an abandonment of the real, whether postulated in positivist or materialist language. And although postcoloniality is related to current developments in identity politics, multiculturalism, ethnonationalism, and even postmodernism, it is both far more and far less than these terms imply.

I have suggested here that postcoloniality might be used to signify those places and histories, rather than either specific identities or theories, that resist the universalization of position and perspective, even as they underscore the power of the forces of universalization. Postcoloniality might then remind us of the fact that history, culture, and modernity have always been corrupt, invariably predicated on violence and domination, the terms of conquest for colonization itself. Postcoloniality both embodies the promise of the West—a promise that flows from the enlightenment and the birth of nations—and reminds us that the promise is always flawed, the present always an impossible time and place in which to live. Postcolonial history is the epic story of seduction and betrayal, destined to repeat itself again and again, even as it seeks to put the colonial past behind, for all time. But it also teaches us that there is no going back, to a time when tradition, or identity, or civilization might be recuperated whole. To think otherwise would be to open history to other forms of seduction and betrayal. And that would leave us all without any of the lessons history might still be able to teach.

# Notes

## Chapter One
## Introduction: The Modernity of Caste

1. "Speech on the Opening of the Impeachment of Warren Hastings," 15 February 1788 in P. J. Marshall, ed., *The Writings and Speeches of Edmund Burke*, Vol. 6 (Oxford: Clarendon Press, 1991), pp. 302–3.

2. Jawaharlal Nehru, *The Discovery of India* (1946; reprint Delhi: Oxford University Press, 1985), pp. 245–46.

3. Louis Dumont, *Homo Hierarchicus: The Caste System and Its Implications*, translated by Mark Sainsbury et al. (Chicago: University of Chicago Press, 1980), p. 5. Italics in original.

4. Ibid., pp. 18–19.

5. Ibid., p. 20.

6. I use governmentality here in Foucault's sense. "To govern a state will therefore mean to apply economy, to set up an economy at the level of the entire state, which means exercising towards its inhabitants, and the wealth and behaviour of each and all, a form of surveillance and control as attentive as that of the head of a family over his household and goods." In "Governmentality," in *The Foucault Effect: Studies in Governmentality*, edited by G. Burchell, C. Gordon, and P. Miller, (Chicago: University of Chicago Press, 1991), p. 91. When I refer to "colonial governmentality," I mean the specific forms of governmentality deployed by the colonial state, in which the relationship between sovereignty and bureaucracy is necessarily different from metropolitan forms. For debates over the definition of this term, see David Scott, "Colonial Governmentality," *Social Text* 43 (Fall 1995), pp. 191–200; Gyan Prakash, *Another Reason: Science and the Imagination of Modern India* (Princeton: Princeton University Press, 1999); Partha Chatterjee, *The Nation and Its Fragments: Colonial and Postcolonial Histories* (Princeton: Princeton University Press, 1993); Ann Stoler, *Race and the Education of Desire: Foucault's History of Sexuality and the Colonial Order of Things* (Durham: Duke University Press, 1995); and Paul Rabinow, *French Modern* (Cambridge: MIT Press, 1989).

7. Gyanendra Pandey, *The Construction of Communalism in Colonial North India* (Delhi: Oxford University Press, 1990). Pandey's work was the first to argue systematically that colonial history played a foundational role in the communalization of religious identity in India.

8. Nehru, *Discovery of India*, p. 247.

9. See Ranajit Guha, *A Rule of Property for Bengal: An Essay on the Idea of Permanent Settlement* (Paris: Mouton and Ecole Pratique des Hautes Etudes, 1963); idem., *Elementary Aspects of Peasant Insurgency in Colonial India* (New Delhi: Oxford University Press, 1983); idem., *Dominance without Hegemony: History and Power in Colonial India* (Cambridge: Harvard University Press, 1997).

10. For my appreciation of the importance of these thinkers, see my foreward to Bernard Cohn's *Colonialism and Its Forms of Knowledge* (Princeton: Princeton Uni-

versity Press, 1996), pp. ix–xvii; and also N. B. Dirks, ed., *Colonialism and Culture* (Ann Arbor: University of Michigan Press, 1992), especially my introductory essay, pp. 1–25. As I note in the Coda of this book, Guha does not in fact accept the hegemonic character of colonial rule, though he writes about its cultural effects. And although Cohn assumes the cultural effects of colonial forms of knowledge, he writes far less about them than about the modalities of colonial rule itself. This book takes up Said's challenge to document the colonial role in the actual constitution of the Orient, something Said himself has not done.

11. For an extraordinary study of the cultural and political effects of colonial rule in Africa, see Mahmood Mamdani, *Citizen and Subject: Contemporary Africa and the Legacy of Late Colonialism* (Princeton: Princeton University Press, 1996). For other comparable views of colonial history, see the essays in Dirks, ed., *Colonialism and Culture*; Gyan Prakash, ed., *After Colonialism: Imperial Histories and Postcolonial Displacements* (Princeton: Princeton University Press, 1995); and Frederick Cooper and Ann Laura Stoler, eds., *Tensions of Empire: Colonial Cultures in a Bourgeois World* (Berkeley and Los Angeles: University of California Press, 1997).

12. Cohn, *Colonialism*, p. 162.

13. See Edward Said, *Orientalism* (New York: Random House, 1978).

14. Chatterjee, *The Nation and Its Fragments*, p. 20.

15. For an evocative and nuanced account of this problematic in the context of the history of scientific thought in modern India, see Prakash, *Another Reason*.

16. G. S. Ghurye, *Caste and Race in India* (London: Routledge and Kegan Paul, 1932).

17. N. B. Dirks, *The Hollow Crown: Ethnohistory of an Indian Kingdom* (Cambridge: Cambridge University Press, 1987; 2nd ed., Ann Arbor: University of Michigan Press, 1993), pp. 4–5.

18. Seeley completely disavowed the idea of a colonial conquest, writing that "Nothing like that what is strictly called a conquest took place." John Seeley, *The Expansion of England* (Chicago: University of Chicago Press, 1971), p. 165. See the Coda below for an extensive discussion of Seeley's argument, as well as its more recent manifestations.

19. Shakespeare, *Richard II*.

20. See, for example, M. N. Srinivas, *Social Change in Modern India* (Berkeley and Los Angeles: University of California Press, 1966).

21. Chatterjee has defined political society as a space between the state and the people that was produced by governmentality in a register different from the normative sphere of civil society. Although political society emerged out of a form of colonial rule predicated on the cultural difference and political insufficiency of an Indian public—the invidious terms setting the parameters for civil society—it is a space of mediation that for Chatterjee carries the promise of political transformation in a postcolonial setting. See Partha Chatterjee, "Two Poets and Death: On Civil and Political Society in the Non Christian World," in Timothy Mitchell, ed., *Questions of Modernity* (Minneapolis: University of Minnesota Press, 2000).

22. Thus it is that this book uses the history of caste to stand in for the history of colonialism more generally, in part to follow through one particular story, in part to demonstrate analogues for other similar stories that could be told about the construction of Hinduism, ethnic identity, or the rise of the nation itself.

23. For a provocative study of the relationship between Dalit politics and the gen-

dered character of caste in western India, see Anupama Rao, "Undoing Untouchability? Violence, Democracy and Discourses of State in Maharashtra, 1932–1991," Ph.D. Dissertation, University of Michigan, 1999. For some important contributions to our understanding of the relationship of caste and gender, see the work of Lata Mani, *Contentious Traditions: The Debate on Sati in Colonial India* (Berkeley and Los Angeles: University of California Press, 1998); Mrinalini Sinha, *Colonial Masculinity: The "Manly" Englishman and the "Effeminate Bengali," in the Late Nineteenth Century* (Manchester: Manchester University Press, 1995); Janaki Nair, *Women and Law in Colonial India: A Social History* (New Delhi: Kali for Women, 1996); Uma Chakravarty, *Rewriting History: The Life and Times of Pandita Ramabai* (Delhi: Oxford University Press, 1998); Tanika Sarkar, "A Book of Her Own: Autobiography of a Nineteenth-Century Woman," *History Workshop Journal* no. 36 (1993), pp. 35–65.

## Chapter Two
## Homo Hierarchicus: The Origins of an Idea

1. Louis Dumont, *Homo Hierarchicus: The Caste System and Its Implications,* translated by Mark Sainsbury et al. (Chicago: University of Chicago Press, 1980), p. 347.

2. *The Book of Duarte Barbosa: An Account of the Countries Bordering on the Indian Ocean and Their Inhabitants, Written by Duarte Barbosa, and Completed about the Year 1518 A.D.* Translated and annotated by M. L. Dames (London: Printed for the Hakluyt Society, 1918), pp. 212–13.

3. Ibid., p. 217.

4. Bernard S. Cohn, "Notes on the History of the Study of Indian Society and Culture," in *An Anthropologist among the Historians and Other Essays* (Delhi: Oxford University Press, 1987), p. 140.

5. Quoted ibid. See Jean-Baptiste Tavernier, *Travels in India by Jean B. Tavernier,* edited by Valentine Ball, 2 vols. (London: Macmillan, 1889).

6. Abu'l Fazl'Allami, *A'in-i-Akbari* (Calcutta, 1786), vol. 3, pp. 82–84.

7. Alexander Dow, *The History of Hindostan, Translated from the Persian.* 3 vols. (London, 1768–1771).

8. Abbé J. A. Dubois; translated, annotated, and revised by Henry K. Beauchamp, as *Hindu Manners, Customs and Ceremonies* (1897; Oxford: Clarendon Press, 1906).

9. Sylvia Murr, "Nicolas Desvaulx (1745–1823) veritable auteur de oeuvrs, institutions et ceremonies des peuples de l'Inde, de l'abbé Dubois," in *Purusartha* 3 (1977): 245–67; Murr, "Les conditions d'emergence du discours sur l'Inde au Siècle des Lumières," in *Purusartha* 7 (1983): 233–84; also see Murr, *L'Inde philosophique entre Bossuet et Voltaire,* vol. 2, *L'Indologie du Père Coeurdoux: Strategies, apologetique et scientificité.* Publications de L'Ecole Française d'Extrême-Orient 146 (Paris: Ecole Française d'Extrême-Orient, 1987).

10. Mark Wilks, *Historical Sketches of the South of India, in an Attempt to Trace the History of Mysore,* 2 vols. (1810, reprinted with notes by Murray Hammick, Mysore: Government Press, 1930).

11. Mark Wilks, Preface to first edition. Jean Antoine Dubois, *Description of the Character, Manners, and Customs of the People of India; and of Their Institutions, Religious and Civil,* by the Abbé J. A. Dubois, translated from the French manuscript (London: Printed for Longman, Hurst, Rees, Orme, and Brown, 1817). This was the

first English edition, translated from the original French manuscript; the first French edition, from a later manuscript, revised and much altered by the author, was published in 1825 under the title, "Moeurs, institutions et cérémonies des peuples de l'Inde." The first English edition of this later enlarged manuscript was first published in 1890.

12. Beauchamp, Introduction to Dubois, *Hindu Manners* (1906), p. xv.

13. Ibid.

14. Extract of Public Letter from Fort St. George, dated 25 January 1816, Board's Collections (BC), No. 541, Indian Office Library (IOL).

15. Ibid. It is likely that A. D. Campbell's request for revisions would have been deeply worrisome to Dubois, knowing that he had plagiarized the text and that scholars such as Campbell would have had access to Coeurdoux's text. F. W. Ellis, also attached to the college, had just published what T. Trautmann has called a "blockbuster exposé" of the "Ezour Vedam," a "fifth" Veda that turned out to have been forged by a Jesuit. See Thomas Trautmann, *Aryans and British India* (Berkeley and Los Angeles: University of California Press, 1997).

16. BC No. 541.

17. Prefatory Note to new edition by Beauchamp, in Dubois, *Hindu Manners* (1906), p. vii.

18. Abbé J. A. Dubois, "Letters on the State of Christianity in India" (London: Longman, Hurst, Rees, Orme, Brown, and Green, 1823).

19. Letter from Abbé Dubois on the state of the missions, Erskine Manuscripts, Eur. MSS D. 30, IOL.

20. Rev. James Hough, *A Reply to the Letters of the Abbé Dubois on the State of Christianity in India* (London: L. B. Selley and Son, 1824).

21. Dubois, "Letters on the State of Christianity in India."

22. Dubois, *Hindu Manners* (1906), pp. 28–30.

23. Duncan B. Forrester, *Caste and Christianity: Attitudes and Policies on Caste of Anglo-Saxon Protestant Missions in India* (London: Curzon, 1980), pp. 14–16.

24. Dubois, *Hindu Manners* (1906), p. 33.

25. Ibid., p. 37.

26. Ibid., p. 97.

27. R. Suntharalingam, *Politics and Nationalist Awakening in South India* (Tucson: University of Arizona Press, 1974), p. 34.

28. Antony Copley, *Religions in Conflict: Ideology, Cultural Contact, and Conversion in Late Colonial India* (Delhi: Oxford University Press, 1997), p. 5.

29. Forrester, *Caste and Christianity*, p. 26.

30. Ibid., p. 34.

31. Ibid., p. 37.

32. Ibid., p. 39.

33. Ibid., p. 42.

34. Report from the Select Committee in the House of Commons, Evidence, III Revenue, Appendices, minute dated November 7, 1830.

35. Quoted in Wilks, *Historical Sketches*, vol. 1, p. 139.

36. Walter Firminger, *Affairs of the East India Company: Being the Fifth Report from the Select Committee of the House of Commons*, July 28, 1812 (Calcutta: R. Cambray, 1917–18), vol. 3.

37. Mountstuart Elphinstone, *Report on the Territories Conquered from the Paishwa* (Calcutta, Government Press: 1821), p. 17.

38. Ranajit Guha, *A Rule of Property for Bengal: An Essay on the Idea of the Permanent Settlement* (Durham: Duke University Press, 1996).

39. For the apotheosis of the place of the village in nineteenth-century colonial policy, see the study by Richard Saumerez Smith, *Rule by Records: Land Registration and Village Custom in Early British Panjab* (Delhi: Oxford University Press, 1996).

40. H. H. Wilson, *Catalogue of Oriental MSS. Col Mackenzie* (Calcutta: n.p., 1828).

41. The Mysore Survey Documents, SIR.

42. Mackenzie's drawings are in the Map Library of the India Office Library and catalogued in Mildred Archer, *British Drawings in the India Office Library*, 2 vols. (London: H.M. Stationary Office, 1969), see pp. 534–38.

43. James Mill, *The History of British India*, 8 vols. (London: James Maddon, 1820).

44. See Ronald Inden, *Imagining India* (Oxford: Blackwell, 1990), p. 45.

45. Javed Majeed, *Ungoverned Imaginings: James Mill's The History of British India and Orientalism* (Oxford: Clarendon Press, 1992), p. 127.

46. James Mill, "Voyage aux Indies Orientales," *Edinburgh Review* 15 (January 1810): 369. Majeed argues that Mill was concerned that the riches of India had been vastly exaggerated due in part, at least, to an Orientalist imaginary, and that British policy was both more expansionist, and extractive, than it should have been under the circumstances.

47. Mill, *History of British India*, p. 24.

48. Ibid., p. 456, 458. For an incisive analysis of the peculiar limits of Mill's liberalism, in relation to a more general critique of liberalism and utilitarianism in the context of British imperial blindness, see Uday Singh Mehta, *Liberalism and Empire: A Study in Nineteenth-Century British Liberal Thought* (Chicago: University of Chicago Press, 1999).

49. Mill, *History of British India*, pp. 471–72.

50. Hastings had laid down in 1772 that "inheritance, marriage, caste and other religious usages or institutions" were to be administered in different ways for Hindus and Muslims, according to the sastras and Islamic jurisprudence, respectively. "But by far the greater part of litigation was never brought before Muslim officials, but was settled by recourse to traditional methods of resolving disputes, which differed according to the caste, the status in society, and the locality of the parties." J.D.M. Derrett, *Religion, Law and the State in India* (London: Faber and Faber, 1968), pp. 229, 233.

51. Charles Grant, *Observations on the State of Society among the Asiatic Subjects of Great Britain, Particularly with Respect to Morals*. Written chiefly in 1792. Excerpted in Martin Moir and Lynn Zastoupil, eds., *The Great Indian Education Debate: Documents Relating to the Orientalist-Anglicist Controversy, 1781–1843* (London: Curzon Press, 1999), pp. 82–83.

52. Mill, *History of British India*, p. 472.

53. In Sanskrit, the text is properly titled either *Manavadharmasastra* or *Manusmriti*, and informally known as *Manu*, though it is also frequently referred to as the *Manu Dharma Sastra*. Sir William Jones's translation was published under the title of *Institutes of Hindu Law, or the Ordinances of Menu According to the Gloss of Culluca, Comprising the Indian System of Duties, Religious and Civil* (Calcutta: 1794).

The canonic English translation of the text for the twentieth century was George Bühler, *The Laws of Manu* (Oxford: Clarendon Press, 1886). For the most extensive English commentary on the text, see the classic work by P. V. Kane, *History of Dharmasastra*, 5 vols. (Poona: Bhandarkar Oriental Research Institute, 1930–1962). For a more recent assessment of the text and its history, as well as a new translation, see Wendy Doniger and Bardwell Smith, eds. and trans., *The Laws of Manu* (New Delhi: Penguin Books, 1991).

54. Doniger and Smith, *The Laws of Manu*, p. xviii.

55. Ibid., p. lxi.

56. Mill, *History of British India*, p. 48.

57. Ibid., pp. 50–51.

58. Ibid., p. 66.

59. See the argument in Gauri Viswanathan, *Masks of Conquest* (New York: Columbia University Press, 1989).

60. Mountstuart Elphinstone, *The History of India*, 2 vols. (London: J. Murray, 1842), p. xvii.

61. Ibid., p. 108.

62. Ibid., p. 99.

63. Ibid., p. 368.

64. Significantly, when Elphinstone turned to an inquiry into early Indian history outside the purview of the Orientalist canon, in particular in his chapter on the early history of the Deccan, he relied upon the manuscript material collection by none other than Colin Mackenzie. Mackenzie's collection did provide an abundance of local historical material, but as we have seen, little in the way of help for opening chapters on the general character of Indian social organization. But the kind of material collected by Mackenzie was in fact of great interest to Elphinstone, who as a practicing administrator was far more concerned than Mill with the establishment of precedent for the reforms he was undertaking in the Maratha country.

65. James Mill, *The History of British India*, fifth edition with notes and continuation by Horace Hayman Wilson (London: James Madden, 1858), preface, pp. xii–xiii.

66. Max Müller, "Caste, 1858," in Müller, *Chips from a German Workshop* (London: Longmans, Green, 1867), pp. 297–356.

67. The general explanation for the outbreak of hostilities in Meerut had been the use of the new Enfield rifle and the rumor that the cartridges were to be loaded with animal fat and that a new method of loading required the use of the mouth. There was imperial convenience and self-delusion, to be sure, in the British belief that the rebellion was caused solely by atavistic superstition and terrified/terrifying alterity—there were many other issues ranging from disciplinary procedures within the army to the annexation of Awadh and the fact that what developed was a general revolt designed to reinstall the power and authority of the Mughal emperor—but there was also genuine concern about the relationship between missionary proselytization and official policy. And there were many missionaries who felt that the "mutiny"—with the horrible images of British women and children attacked by Indians promulgated in myriad genres across India and Britain—afforded an opportunity to win their argument and establish a guiding ideological relationship to the colonial state. See Chapter 7 below.

68. Müller, "Caste, 1858," p. 300

69. Ibid., p. 301.

70. Ibid., p. 300.

71. Quoted in Forrester, *Caste and Christianity,* p. 64.

72. See Talal Asad, *Genealogies of Religion: Discipline and Reasons of Power in Christianity and Islam* (Baltimore: Johns Hopkins University Press, 1993); Gauri Viswanathan, *Outside the Fold* (Princeton: Princeton University Press, 1999); and Peter van der Veer, *Imperial Encounters: Religion and Modernity in India and Britain* (Princeton: Princeton University Press, 2001).

**Chapter Three
The Ethnographic State**

1. Rudyard Kipling, *Kim* (New York: Dell, 1959), p. 113.

2. Much colonial historiography makes a lot of the supposed ignorance of the British about India, without ever confronting the extent to which the professed ignorance was itself a conceit of a certain kind of epistemological regime. As I will demonstrate in later chapters, the uncritical reading of colonial sources invariably excuses the British in relation to explicit alibis of their rule.

3. See for example, Bernard S. Cohn, "The Census, Social Structure and Objectification in South Asia," in *An Anthropologist among the Historians* (Delhi: Oxford University Press, 1987), pp. 224–54; Anand Yang, ed., *Crime and Criminality in British India* (Tucson: University of Arizona Press, 1985); David Washbrook, "Law, State, and Agrarian Society in Colonial India," *Modern Asian Studies* 15, 3 (1981): 649–721; A. H. Bingley and A. Nicholls, *Brahmans: Caste Handbook for the Indian Army* (Simla: Government Press, 1897); P.H.M. Van Den Dungen, *The Punjab Tradition: Influence and Authority in Nineteenth-Century India* (London: George Allen and Unwin, 1972).

4. Madras: Government Press, 1868.

5. Home Proceedings, Public Department, February 12, 1870.

6. Public Proceedings, Nos. 32 & 33, March 7, 1870.

7. Public Proceedings, Nos. 144 &145, September 30, 1871.

8. C. D. Maclean, ed., *Manual of the Administration of the Madras Presidency*, 3 vols. (Madras: Government Press, 1892), p. 29. Italics added.

9. M. A. Sherring, *Hindu Tribes and Castes*, 3 vols. (1872; reprint New Delhi: Cosmo Publications, 1974), Preface, p. iii.

10. Ibid., vol. 3, pp. 218–19.

11. An Anglican minister, the Rev. Sherring noted that he had no admiration or respect for caste. He noted that his intense conviction was "that, next to the universal prevalence of the Christian faith, the greatest boon to India would be the absolute and complete renunciation of caste. The author has portrayed the institution as a phase of humanity, and because he considers that every aspect of human society, even the most distorted and ugly, should be fairly represented and fully understood"; ibid., Preface, p. iv.

12. Ibid., vol. 3, pp. 220, 225, 226, 231.

13. Ibid., p. 231, 235, 245.

14. Ibid., pp. 274–96.

15. Ibid., p. 280, 296, 292.

16. H. H. Risley, *The People of India* (1908; 2nd ed. London: W. Thacker, 1915).

17. H. H. Risley, *The Tribes and Castes of Bengal* (Calcutta: Secretariat Press, 1891).

18. W. Crooke, *Tribes and Castes of the North-Western Provinces and Oudh*, 4 vols. (Calcutta: Office of the Superintendent of Government Printing, 1896).

19. Risley, *The People of India*, p. 278

20. Public Department, Madras, Government Order No. 647, June 26, 1901, Tamil Nadu Archives, Madras.

21. Risley, *The People of India*, p. 282.

22. Ibid., p. 291.

23. G.W.F. Hegel, *The Philosophy of History* (1899; reprint London: Dover, 1956), p. 113.

24. Ibid., p. 142

25. See J. H. Hutton, *Caste in India: Its Nature, Function, and Origins* (London: Oxford University Press, 1946).

26. McKim Marriott, ed., *Village India: Studies in the Little Community* (Chicago: University of Chicago Press, 1955).

27. See Wolfgang Sachs, ed., *The Development Dictionary: A Guide to Knowledge as Power* (London: Zed Books, 1992).

28. Louis Dumont, *Homo Hierarchicus: The Caste System and Its Implications*, translated by Mark Sainsbury et al. (Chicago: University of Chicago Press, 1980).

29. The key text for this breakthrough was in fact the *Manu Dharmasastra*. In my first graduate seminar, we spent the first four weeks reading Bühler's translation of *Manu* as if it were the source of all true knowledge about the essential structure of caste relations.

30. These were also heady days in American anthropology, when the idea of culture flowered and seemed to make possible an interpretive methodology for cracking and understanding cultural codes with many of the conceits, if not always the full-blown theoretical commitments, of the structuralism of the time.

31. McKim Marriott and Ronald B. Inden, "Caste Systems," in *Encyclopedia Britannica* (Chicago, 1974). Some time between 1969, when Marriott critiqued Dumont in an important review of Homo Hierarchicus from the perspective of empirical social science, and 1971, when he coauthored the first draft of the Encyclopedia Britannica article with Ronald Inden, Marriott underwent a sea change in his intellectual style and perspective.

32. Ronald Inden has subsequently written an important book about colonial ideology that seeks in part to disavow his role in the "ethnosociology" of India. See Inden, *Imagining India* (London: Blackwell, 1990).

33. Ronald B. Inden and McKim Marriott, "Interpreting Indian Society: A Monistic Alternative to Dumont's Dualism," *Journal of Asian Studies* 36.1 (November 1976): 191.

34. Ibid., p. 193.

35. "For a Sociology of India," *Contributions to Indian Sociology*, 1 (1957): 7, 9. Italics in original.

36. See, for example, symposia edited by T. N. Madan in *Contributions to Indian Sociology* 5 (December 1971), and by J. F. Richards and R. W. Nicholas in *Journal of Asian Studies* 35.4 (August 1976).

37. Edmund Leach, "Hierarchical Man: Louis Dumont and His Critics," *South Asian Review* 4.3 (1971): 233–37.

38. Stanley Tambiah, review of Dumont, *Homo Hierarchicus: An Essay on the Caste System*, in *American Anthropologist* 74.4 (August 1972): 832–35.

39. Ravinder Khare, "Encompassing and Encompassed: A Deductive Theory of Caste System," *Journal of Asian Studies* 30.4 (August 1971): 859–68.

40. McKim Marriott, review of Dumont, *Homo Hierarchicus*, in *American Anthropologist* 71.6 (September 1969): 1166–75.

41. Dumont, *Homo Hierarchicus*, p. xxxiii.

42. Ibid., p. 74.

43. Ibid., p. 234

44. Dumont, "For a Sociology of India," p. 9.

45. Ibid., p. 21.

46. Dumont, *Homo Hierarchicus*, p. 235.

47. Jan Heesterman, *The Inner Conflict of Tradition: Essays in Indian Ritual, Kingship, and Society* (Chicago: University of Chicago Press, 1985), p. 193.

48. It has also seemed extraordinary to me that so many commentators find it possible to address contemporary social, cultural, and political questions in India by primary resort to ancient history, whether textually derived or not. In the case of Europe, for example, no serious commentator would suggest that the present can be explained not only by referring to the ancient past but also by rendering the period between the late eighteenth and the mid-twentieth centuries either irrelevant, or at best of only limited importance. For another egregious example of this, see the book by the eminent Sanskritist W. Norman Brown, *The United States and India and Pakistan* (Cambridge: Harvard University Press, 1953). In one of the first books concerning independent India by an American scholar—and that too the founder of the first area studies program in South Asian Studies at the University of Pennsylvania—Brown not only wrote, "The greatest achievement of characteristic Indian civilization are in religion and philosophy" (p. 24) but suggested that this religion and philosophy had been the primary cause of the partition of India and Pakistan (p. 130). He also used his review of ancient Indian civilization as the frame for his own analysis of the depressing condition of agricultural production, the oppressive poverty both in the countryside and the cities, and the many problems confronting the establishment of democratic politics across the subcontinent.

49. Heesterman, *Inner Conflict of Tradition*, p. 8.

50. For the most recent statement of an ethnosociological approach to the study of India, see McKim Marriott, ed., *India through Hindu Categories* (New Delhi: Sage, 1990), although there are some dissenting views within. For the best reviews of recent scholarly debates on caste, see Gloria Raheja's important "India: Caste, Kingship, and Dominance Reconsidered," in *Annual Review of Anthropology* 17 (1988): 497–522, and Chris Fuller's Introduction to his edited volume, *Caste Today* (Delhi: Oxford University Press, 1996). As is clear from both works, the most significant revisions of Dumont and Marriott have come from scholars who have insisted on the importance of broad historical as well as contemporary political analyses of caste. It is worth noting that recent efforts to treat caste from a comprehensive anthropological perspective—works such as Declan Quiqley's *The Interpretation of Caste* (Oxford: Clarendon, 1993)—have continued to take Dumont's contribution as foundational to contemporary understandings, even when they are critical. Even Susan Bayly's useful historical

review of caste society from the eighteenth century to the present, published after the completion of the present manuscript, argues that "The Social Scientists who will probably have the most enduring impact on the field are therefore those who have taken Dumont's formulations seriously rather than dismissing them altogether"; S. Bayly, *Caste, Society and Politics in India from the Eighteenth Century to the Modern Age*, The New Cambridge History of India, vol. 4, no. 3 (Cambridge: Cambridge University Press, 1999).

## Chapter Four
### The Original Caste: Social Identity in the Old Regime

1. See Rosalind O'Hanlon, *Caste, Conflict and Ideology: Mahatma Jotirao Phule and Low Caste Protest in Nineteenth-Century Western India* (Cambridge: Cambridge University Press, 1985), pp. 3–49.

2. Norman Paul Ziegler, "Action, Power and Service in Rajasthani Culture: A Social History of the Rajputs of Middle Period Rajasthan," Ph.D. dissertation, Department of History, University of Chicago, August 1973.

3. See Surajit Sinha, "State Formation and Rajput Myth in Tribal Central India," *Man in India*, 42.1 (1962): 35–80.

4. I draw here from my earlier monograph, *The Hollow Crown: Ethnohistory of an Indian Kingdom* (Cambridge: Cambridge University Press, 1987; 2nd ed., Ann Arbor: University of Michigan Press, 1993).

5. André Wink has demonstrated that a similar importance was placed on inams as symbols of rule and structures of landholding in the Maratha kingdom throughout much of the seventeenth and eighteenth centuries. See his *Land and Sovereignty in India: Agrarian Society and Politics under the Eighteenth-Century Maratha Svarajya* (Cambridge: Cambridge University Press, 1986).

6. Hiroshi Fukazawa, *The Medieval Deccan: Peasants, Social Systems and States, Sixteenth to Eighteenth Centuries* (Delhi: Oxford University Press, 1991).

7. Uma Chakravarty, *Rewriting History: The Life and Times of Pandita Ramabai* (Delhi: Oxford University Press, 1998), pp. 14, 17.

8. To use M. N. Srinivas's term. See Arjun Appadurai, *Worship and Conflict under Colonial Rule: A South Indian Case* (Cambridge: Cambridge University Press, 1981); also Chandra Mudaliar, *The State and Religious Endowments in Madras* (Madras: University of Madras Press, 1976).

9. The text is called the *Maravar Cati Vilakkam*, and is included in the Mackenzie manuscript collection. The original is in the Government Oriental Manuscripts Library, Madras, D. 2743 R. 370 (restored). Quotes here are from my own translation of the text.

10. This is an example of one of the texts collected by Colin Mackenzie that was clearly scripted by one of Mackenzie's assistants on the basis of oral accounts provided by selected "informants."

11. Abbé J. A. Dubois, translated, annotated, and revised by Henry K. Beauchamp, as *Hindu Manner, Customs and Ceremonies* (Oxford: Clarendon Press, 1906), p. 25.

12. Ibid., p. 26.

13. Brenda Beck, *Peasant Society in Konku: A Study of Right and Left Subcastes in South India* (Vancouver: University of British Columbia Press, 1982).

14. The components were not, however, as open as suggested by Arjun Appadurai,

who argued that the right-left distinction was a root metaphor for factional classification in southern India. Although he showed that there was a great deal of variability in the way lists of right- and left-hand castes were organized across space, time, and account, he could not explain some regularities—he could not fully explain the extent to which some of the divisions did suggest fundamental cleavages in the social and political structure of the time. Arjun Appadurai, "Right and Left Hand Castes in South India," *Indian Economic and Social History Review* 14.1 (1976): 47–73.

15. Burton Stein, *Peasant State and Society in Medieval South India* (Delhi: Oxford University Press, 1980).

16. Burton Stein, *Thomas Munro: The Origins of the Colonial State and His Vision of Empire* (Delhi: Oxford University Press, 1989), p. 51.

17. See T. Muzushima, *Nattar and the Socio-Economic Change in South India in the 18ᵗʰ–19ᵗʰ Centuries*, Institute for the Study of Languages and Cultures of Asia and Africa, monograph 19 (Tokyo, 1986).


## Chapter Five
## The Textualization of Tradition: Biography of an Archive

1. Mountstuart Elphinstone, *The History of India: The Hindu and Mahometan Periods* (London: J. Murray, 1841).

2. T. V. Mahalingam, ed., *Mackenzie Manuscripts (Tamil and Malayalam)* (Madras: University of Madras Press, 1972), p. xviii.

3. Excerpted in William Taylor, *Catalogue Raisonné of Oriental Manuscripts in the Library of the (Late) College of Fort Saint George* (Madras: H. Smith, 1857), pp. ii, iii.

4. "Biographical Sketch of the Literary Career of the Late Colin Mackenzie, Surveyor-General of India; comprising some particulars of his collection of manuscripts, plans, coins, drawings, sculptures, etc., illustrative of the antiquities, history, geography, laws, institutions, and manners of the ancient Hindus; contained in a letter addressed by him to the Right Hon. Sir Alexander Johnston, V.P.R.A.S., etc. etc.," *Madras Journal of Science and Literature* 2 (1835): 264.

5. Ibid., p. 265.

6. W. C. Mackenzie, *Colonel Colin Mackenzie: First Surveyor-General of India* (Edinburgh and London: W. & R. Chambers, 1952), p. 53.

7. Colonel R. H. Phillimore, *The Historical Records of the Survey of India* (Dehra Dun: Survey of India, 1945), vol. 1, p. 351.

8. Vol. 68, Survey of India Records (SIR), National Archives of India (NAI), New Delhi.

9. Mackenzie, *Colonel Colin Mackenzie*, p. 269.

10. Letter from Mackenzie to Colonel Montresor, dated July 28, 1800, SIR, vol. 4.

11. Letter dated Madras July 12, 1803, SIR, vol. 42.

12. Mayaconda, for example, was chosen by the raja because when he was hunting with his dogs in its deep woods, a hare miraculously fought off the dogs and chased them back to their master. The raja then discovered that in the days of the Vijayanagara rulers a local chief had died, and his wife Mayaca had thrown "herself into the fire of her Husband's pyre according to their law." Because of the virtue accruing to this act, and the transformation of the chief and his wife into "veerooloo" ("persons remarkable for virtue"), the site had become charged with extraordinary properties and powers.

13. Mackenzie, "Memoirs of the Northern Pargannahs of Mysore, Surveyed in 1801 and 1802, under the Provincial Divisions of the Partition of 1799," Foreign Miscellaneous, NAI, vol. 92, p. 180.

14. Ibid., p. 247.

15. Second Report on the Mysore Survey, letter from Mackenzie to Close, July 12, 1803, SIR, vol. 42.

16. "Memorandum of the Means of Procuring Historical Materials Regarding the South of India," doc. 65, Box 3, Mackenzie uncatalogued miscellaneous papers, IOL.

17. Ibid.

18. Letter to P. Connor, on Survey in Coorg, January 11, 1816, SIR, vol. 42.

19. Mackenzie, *Colonel Colin Mackenzie*, pp. 274–75.

20. Mackenzie learned that his general scheme would have to be scaled down at the end of 1801, just after he had finished his initial survey of the northern and eastern frontier of Mysore. As a result, he could not continue to survey the natural history of the country, had to fire a number of his principal assistants, and had his stipend and general establishment cut in half. Despite these problems, and virtually constant problems of ill health, Mackenzie conducted an extraordinarily detailed survey. In addition to preparing general maps of each district and descriptions of salient geographical features, the survey included a census of villages, forts, houses, classes of inhabitants (that is, a breakdown of the population into its constituent castes, tribes, and occupational groups), waterworks, and so on; historical "memoirs" of each district "illustrative of the revolutions and remarkable events of the country and of the origin and succession of the several Rajahs, Polligars, and Native Rulers for the last three centuries"; and "cursory remarks and accounts of the soil, productions, manufactures, minerals, inhabitants, etc." John Malcolm wrote that the survey contained "a mass of information respecting the geography, history, commerce, revenue, police and population of Mysore which must prove of the greatest advantage to every officer connected with the conduct of administration" (Letter dated November 13, 1803, SIR, vol. 68)."

Mackenzie's survey, commissioned so soon after the fall of Srirangapattinam, was necessarily limited in nature. At the outset Mackenzie informed Colonel Barry Close, the resident of Mysore, that his survey would not "descend to the minutea of measurements of the quantity of the cultivated and uncultivated lands, with details more properly belonging to an Agricultural Survey," concentrating rather on "full information of its [Mysore's] extent, form, and capacity in a Political and Military Light" (Letter to Close dated November 9, 1799, SIR, vol. 41)." Elsewhere Mackenzie noted that "enquiries into the Revenue were altogether avoided, as tending to create an uneasiness, and possible counteraction that would have possibly retarded the progress of the other branches, without deriving sufficient advantages" (Letter to Close dated January 10, 1803, SIR, vol. 44). Some years later, when giving advice to the British surveyor of Coorg, Mackenzie advised him against making "many minute enquiries," as such would "at first alarm their minds with *friendless suspicions*" (Letter to P. Connor dated January 11, 1816, SIR, vol. 44; italics added)." In any case, the East India Company had restored the rule of the Wodiyar rajas of Mysore, overthrown forty years previously by the Mysore sultans, and had no direct reason to assemble revenue information. Although Mackenzie sought to collect information about the origins of land tenures, he specifically avoided the facts of production. Nevertheless, at one point the dewan of

Mysore expressed his concern that "all further enquiries respecting the number of Ryots and inhabitants of either sex in Mysore may be put a stop to." (Phillimore, *Historical Records*, 2, p. 367).

21. Letter to Col. Close, dated May 29, 1801, SIR, vol. 41.

22. January 11, 1816; SIR, vol. 156.

23. *History of Indian and Eastern Architecture*, 2 vols. (1876; 2nd ed. New York: Dodd, Mead, 1899), vol. 2, p. 253.

24. See the catalogues of the Prints and Drawings Room, India Office Library, London. Reference numbers are given here by reference to Mildred Archer, *British Drawings in the India Office Library*, 2 vols. (London: H. M. Stationery Office, 1969).

25. Ibid., p. 535, fol. 71.

26. Ibid., p. 537, fol. 64.

27. Ibid., p. 537, fols. 25–28.

28. Ibid., p. 536, fol. 41.

29. "No daring Chief of all the numrous band / Against his Priest shall lift an impious hand / Not even the chief by whom our Hosts are led / The King of Kings shall touch that sacred hand." The poem makes clear the importance of the purohit or priest in relation to the king rather than as a straightforward sign of Indian spirituality. Ibid., p. 536, fol. 36.

30. Ibid., p. 537, fols. 80, 67, 66.

31. Ibid., pp. 535–37, fols. 12, 15, 44, 48, 79, 35.

32. Ibid., p. 536, fol. 46.

33. Ibid., p. 536, fol. 44.

34. Ibid., p. 536, fols. 32, 33.

35. Ibid., pp. 535–37, fols. 61, 18, 8, 21.

36. Ibid., p. 497, no. 868.

37. Ibid., p. 496, nos. 857, 858.

38. Ibid., p. 537, fol. 65.

39. Ibid., p. 537, fol. 82.

40. H. H. Wilson, *Mackenzie Collection* (Madras: n.p., 1828), p. 11.

41. Public Letter, October 21, 1807, BC no. 6426, IOL.

42. Extract of Public Consultation, letter from Rennell dated March 4, 1809, in BC no. 6426, IOL.

43. Mackenzie, *Colonel Colin Mackenzie*, 366.

44. Letter to Board of Control dated March 14, 1807, in BC no. 6426, IOL.

45. Extract of a letter from Major Wilks to John Malcolm, dated February 27, 1807, in BC no. 6426, IOL.

46. Ibid.

47. Mackenzie, *Colonel Colin Mackenzie*, p. 122; C.O. Blagden, *Catalogue of Manuscripts in European Languages Belonging to the Library in the India Office* (London: Oxford University Press, 1916), p. 358.

48. "Biographical Sketch of the Literary Career of the Late Colin Mackenzie," p. 276.

49. Ibid., pp. 276–77.

50. Taylor, *Catalogue Raisonné*, pp. ix, x n.6.

51. "Biographical Sketch," pp. 265–66.

52. *Journal of the Asiatic Society of Bengal* 13.145–150 (1844): 421–63, 578–608.

53. Letter from A. Falconer to C. Mackenzie, June 25, 1813, in Report on the Mysore Survey, SIR, vol. 41, July 1803.

54. Ibid.

55. Ibid.

56. Letter from Mackenzie to Government of India dated July 29, 1808, in SIR, vol. 41.

57. "Letters and Reports from Native Agents Employed to Collect Books, Traditions, etc., in the Various Parts of the Peninsula," Mackenzie Collection, Unbound Translations (housed in the IOL), Class XII, vol. 1, no. 3. The volumes and books are idiosyncratically numbered, sometimes in contradictory ways. For the only index to this collection see the appendix to H. H. Wilson, *Catalogue of Oriental Manuscripts of Col. Mackenzie* (Calcutta: n.p., 1828).

58. "Letters and Reports," Class XII, no. 40; no. 13.

59. As all of Mackenzie's assistants corresponded with their employer in English, I use the spellings of names and places as written in the original English texts of the Mackenzie Collection.

60. "Letters and Reports," Class XII, no. 40.

61. C. V. Ram, "Letters and Reports," no. 18.

62. Narrain Row, "Letters and Reports," nos. 26, 27.

63 Walter Benjamin, *Illuminations: Essays and Reflections*, edited by Hannah Arendt (c. 1968; New York: Schocken Books, 1977), p. 60.

64. For a provocative meditation on, and illustration of, the silence of the archive, see Michel-Rolph Trouillot, *Silencing the Past: Power and the Production of History* (Boston: Beacon, 1995).

65. Phillimore, *Historical Records*, p. 483 n9.

66. "Report of the Committee of Papers on Cavelly Venkata Lachmia's Proposed Renewal of Colonel Mackenzie's Investigations," *Proceedings of the Asiatic Society of Bengal, including 3rd August 1836, 7th September 1836*, printed in the *Madras Journal of Science and Literature*, October 1836, pp. 437–42.

67. Archer, *British Drawings*, no. 586, plate 25, p. 477.

## Chapter Six
## The Imperial Archive: Colonial Knowledge and Colonial Rule

1. "Factory" is the term used for the warehouses and staging points for the collection of goods and commodities traded by the East India Company (not for their production).

2. Munro's interest in the "Poligars" of southern India was to find ways to unseat them, and make their lands available to British survey and settlement. See W. K. Firminger, ed., *The Fifth Report from the Select Committee on the Affairs of the East India Company, 1812*, 3 vols. (Calcutta: R. Cambray, 1918).

3. Mackenzie's collection was virtually allowed to disappear. After Wilson's half-hearted catalogue was completed, most of the Mackenzie manuscripts were consigned to a most uncertain fate, shipped back and forth between London and Madras, ultimately housed in Orientalist libraries rather than government archives.

4. In 1795 there was a dramatic fall in prices, making it difficult for zamindars to collect rents from peasants at the old rates. Many zamindars "had no choice but to sell out or see their right auctioned off to other bidders. It was at this time that a number of

NOTES TO CHAPTER SIX

zamindaris passed by foreclosure of mortgage, sale or auction to bankers and merchants." Irfan Habib, "Colonialization of the Indian Economy 1750–1900," In *Essays in Indian History* (New Delhi: Tulika, 1995), pp. 296–335.

5. Lawrence Stone and Jeanne C. Fawtier, *An Open Elite?: England, 1540–1800* (Oxford: Clarendon, 1984).

6. The 1793 regulations entailed no survey, records of rights, or methods of assessment; by 1820, the documentation project of the colonial regime had expanded to the point where even zamindari settlements required the recording of rights, annual assessments of cultivated land, and periodic reassessments.

7. As, for example, in southern India, first in the Baramahal district that had been absorbed from Tipu Sultan in 1792, then in Kanara after Tipu's final defeat in 1799, and finally in the Ceded Districts that had been handed over by the nizam of Hyderabad in 1800 to "defray" the cost of military support from the Company.

8. This previous paragraph summarizes for the most part the historical argument of Burton Stein, in his *Thomas Munro: The Origins of the Colonial State and His Vision of Empire* (Delhi: Oxford University Press, 1989).

9. Munro's supervisors were particularly surprised by the fact that Munro, who had so criticized the reliance of earlier regimes on inam grants—and praised Tipu Sultan for his extensive efforts to resume inams—ended up using them to reward dominant groups in village politics. What Robert Frykenberg has termed the "silent settlement" was really the recognition on the part of Munro that inam forms were fundamental to the establishment of state power—whether old regime or colonial—in the southern Indian countryside. See Frykenberg, "The Silent Settlement in South India, 1793–1853: An Analysis of the Role of *Inams* in the Rise of the Indian Imperial System," in *Land Tenure and Peasant in South Asia*, edited by Robert Frykenberg (New Delhi: Orient Longman, 1977).

10. I accept Burton Stein's argument here that the village form would have been historically more attuned to the old regime revenue system. But see my own work on the character of *mirasidar* politics in Pudukkottai, in *The Hollow Crown: Ethnohistory of an Indian Kingdom* (Cambridge: Cambridge University Press, 1987; 2nd ed., Ann Arbor: University of Michigan Press, 1993).

11. Firminger, ed., *Fifth Report*. Kingdom (Cambridge: Cambridge University Press, 1987; 2nd ed., Ann Arbor: University of Michigan Press, 1993).

12. There was some overlap between Mackenzie's survey of Mysore and the investigations of Francis Buchanan, an Edinburgh-educated surgeon who in February 1800 was commissioned to investigate the "state of agriculture, arts and commerce in the fertile and valuable dominions acquired in the recent and former war, from the late sultaun of Mysore, for the purpose of obtaining such insight in to the real state of the Country, as may be productive of future improvement and advantage." Letter dated February 24, 1800, from Governor General, extract of Bengal Public Consultation, 14 March 1800, Home Miscellaneous, IOL, vol. 256.

13. Ibid.

14. Francis Buchanan, *A Journey from Madras through the Countries of Mysore, Canara, and Malabar*, vol. 2 (Madras: Higginbotham, 1870), p. 317.

15. "The Brahmans of Tulava are allowed a plurality of wives, which must be of the same nation with themselves, but of a different Gotram or family, and which must be married before the signs of puberty appear. The widows cannot marry, but may become

Moylar. . . . It is looked upon as disreputable for a Brahman to keep a woman of this kind, and he would lose caste by having connection with a dancing girl, or with a Moylar, that did not belong to a temple; but all such women as are consecrated to the gods cohabit with some Brahman or other" (ibid., vol. 2, p. 268).

16. Lists of this kind seem to proliferate from the early nineteenth century on. As David Ludden has observed, before this local census lists or revenue accounts did not use caste at all, in the form of either jati or varna. See his "Orientalist Empiricism: Transformations of Colonial Knowledge," in Carol Breckenridge and Peter van der Veer, eds., *Orientalism and the Postcolonial Predicament* (Philadelphia: University of Pennsylvania Press, 1993), pp. 250–78.

17. Buchanan, *Journey from Madras*, vol. 2, January 15, 1801, p. 204.

18. Mackenzie's Report on the Survey of 1805, Survey General Records, SIR, vol. 42, NAI.

19. "Lectures on Hindu Law" by F. W. Ellis, Erskine Manuscripts, Eur. MSS D. 31, IOL.

20. He used the *sthala-purana* of Tondaimandalam, inscriptions as well as modern deeds of sale, and other sources in Tamil, Telugu, Kannada, Malayalam, and Sanskrit. See *Three Treatises on Mirasi Right* by the late Francis W. Ellis, Lieutenant Colonel Blackburne, and Sir Thomas Munro, edited by Charles Philip Brown (Madras: Christian Knowledge Society's Press, 1852).

21. "Caste is ignored or underplayed throughout, for in the prevalent ideology of the period a 'community' is an egalitarian group." L. Dumont, "The 'Village Community' from Munro to Maine," *Contributions to Indian Sociology* 9 (December 1966): 67–89.

22. I am grateful to David Ludden for making this census available to me and sharing his sense of its historical formation and context.

23. There seems to be one major difference between this grid and Marriott's proposals. Whereas Marriott writes about those who are willing to eat in certain houses and not in others, Mackenzie notes those who are "allowed" and those who are "exempted." In the absence of more to go on, it is difficult to know whether the difference here is just the use of particular words or whether the emphasis is more on food giving than on the Brahmanic principle of not taking food from any deemed inferior. See McKim Marriott, "Caste Ranking and Food Transactions, a Matrix Analysis," *Structure and Change in Indian Society*, edited by Milton Singer and Bernard S. Cohn (Chicago: Aldine, 1968), pp. 133–71.

24. C. V. Ramswamy, Pundit, and Son, *A Digest of the Different Castes of the Southern Division of Southern India, with descriptions of their habits, customs, etc.* (n.p.: printed at the Telegraph and Courier Press, by JeeJeebhoy Byramjee, Printer, 1847).

## Chapter Seven
## The Conversion of Caste

1. V. D. Savarkar, *The Indian War of Independence: National Rising of 1857* (London: n.p., 1910).

2. See the excellent account of the Great Rebellion in Thomas R. Metcalf, *The Aftermath of Revolt: India, 1857–1870* (Princeton: Princeton University Press, 1964).

3. Sir Sayyid Ahmad Khan, *History of the Bijnor Rebellion*, translated with notes

and introduction by Hafeez Mallik and Morris Dembo (East Lansing: Asian Studies Center, Michigan State University, 1972), pp. 122, 124, 126.

4. See David Lelyveld, *Aligarh's First Generation: Muslim Solidarity in British India* (Princeton: Princeton University Press, 1978).

5. Letter of 1869 to Sir John Kaye from Sir Syed Ahmed, dated December 14, 1869, quoted in Khan, *History*, pp. 161–62.

6. Notes by Frere and Outram of March 28, 1860 in Canning Papers Miscellaneous, No. 558, quoted in Metcalf, *Aftermath of Revolt*, p. 91.

7. See John W. Kaye, *A History of the Sepoy War in India 1857–1858*, 3 vols. 7th ed. (London: W. H. Allen, 1876); G. B. Malleson, *History of the Indian Mutiny*, 3 vols. (London: W. H. Allen, 1896).

8. C. H. Philips et al., eds. *The Evolution of India and Pakistan, 1857–1947. Select Documents* (London: Oxford University Press, 1962), pp. 10–11.

9. Thomas Metcalf, *Ideologies of the Raj* (Cambridge: Cambridge University Press, 1994), p. 48.

10. Ibid.

11. Max Müller, "Caste, 1858," in Müller, *Chips from a German Workshop* (London: Longmans, Green, 1867).

12. Duncan B. Forrester, *Caste and Christianity: Attitudes and Policies on Caste of Anglo-Saxon Protestant Missions in India* (London, Curzon, 1980), p. 57.

13. Ibid., p. 33.

14. *Minute of the Madras Missionary Conference on the Subject of Caste* (n.p.: printed for the Conference at the American Mission Press, 1850), pp. 1, 4.

15. Calcutta, 1858.

16. Forrester, *Caste and Christianity*, pp. 55–56.

17. Müller, "Caste, 1858," pp. 318–19.

18. Ibid., p. 355.

19. See Thomas Trautmann, *Aryans and British India* (Berkeley and Los Angeles: University of California Press, 1997).

20. Obituary of Robert Caldwell, *Times* (London), October 19, 1891.

21. Quoted in *Reminiscences of Bishop Caldwell*, edited by his son-in-law, Rev. J. L. Wyatt, Missionary, S.P.G., Trichinopoly (Madras: Addison, 1894), p. 190.

22. Ibid., p. 191

23. Ibid.

24. Ibid.

25. Robert Caldwell, "The Languages of India in their Relation to Missionary Work," a speech delivered at the Annual Meeting of the Society for the Propagation of the Gospel in Foreign Parts, April 28, 1875 (London: R. Clay, Sons & Taylor, 1875), p. 9.

26. Robert Caldwell, *The Tinnevelly Shanars: A Sketch of their religion, and their moral condition and characteristics, as a caste; with special reference to the facilities and hindrances to the progress of Christianity amongst them* (Madras: Christian Knowledge Society's Press, 1849).

27. Ibid., pp. 17, 13.

28. Ibid., p. 59.

29. Ibid., p. 42.

30. Ibid., pp. 42–43.

31. Ibid., p. 12.

32. Ibid., p. 25.

33. Ibid.

34. Ibid., pp. 29, 22, 37.

35. Ibid., p. 71.

36. Ibid., p. 69.

37. Robert Caldwell, *A Comparative Grammar of the Dravidian or South-Indian Family of Languages* (1856; London: Trabner, 1875), pp. 49, 51.

38. Ibid., pp. 109, 114, 117.

39. Ibid., p. 577.

40. J. M. Lechler, letter to Church Board, Salem, dated January 13, 1857; box 10, archives of the Council for World Missions, South India; housed in the Library of the School of Oriental and African Studies, London.

41. W. B. Addis, letter to Church Board, Coimbatore, dated March 31, 1854, ibid.

42. W. B. Addis, letter to Church Board, Coimbatore, dated January 6, 1852, ibid.

43. Quoted in Trautmann, *Aryans and British India*, p. 176.

44. See Joan Leopold, "The Aryan Theory of Race," *Indian Economic and Social History Review* 7. 2 (June 1970): 281.

45. See Sumathi Ramaswamy, *Passions of the Tongue: Language Devotion in Tamil India, 1891–1970* (Berkeley and Los Angeles: University of California Press, 1997).

46. Ibid.

47. See Rosalind O'Hanlon, *Caste, Conflict, and Ideology: Mahatma Jotirao Phule and Low Caste Protest in Nineteenth-Century Western India* (Cambridge: Cambridge University Press, 1985), pp. 50–132.


**Chapter Eight**
**The Policing of Tradition: Colonial Anthropology and the Invention of Custom**

1. October 23,1891. The *Madras Mail* was the largest English daily in Madras at the time.

2. Lata Mani, "Contentious Traditions: The Debate on Sati in Colonial India," in Kumkum Sangari and Sudesh Vaid, eds., *Recasting Women: Essays in Colonial History* (New Delhi: Kali for Women, 1989), pp. 88–126.

3. Individual vows, such as those that involved the piercing of the body in fulfillment of various pledges, were never subjected to administrative concern; however, when vows led to activities such as firewalking in public, collective, ritual events, some of the same concerns as we find in regard to hookswinging were also raised. For a superb anthropological account of different rites in Sri Lanka, see Gananath Obeyesekere, *Medusa's Hair: An Essay on Personal Symbols and Religious Experience* (Chicago: University of Chicago Press, 1981).

4. For an important account of the development of colonial contradictions around public space in northern India, see Sandria Freitag, *Collective Action and Community: Public Arenas in the Emergence of Communalism in North India* (Berkeley and Los Angeles: University of California Press, 1989).

5. See Arjun Appadurai, "Right and Left Hand Castes in South India," *Indian Economic and Social History Review* 14.1 (1974): 47–73.

6. For an account of missionary responses to hookswinging, see the recent book by Geoffrey Oddie, *Popular Religion, Elites and Reform: Hook-swinging and Its Prohibition in Colonial India, 1800–1894* (Delhi: Manohar, 1995).

7. Judicial Department, Madras, Government Order (G.O.) No. 83, January 14, 1892, Tamil Nadu Archives, Madras.

8. See Selections from the Records of the Madras Government, *Reports on the Swinging Festival and the Ceremony of Walking through Fire* (Madras: Fort St. George Gazette Press, 1854) IOL V/23/139.

9. Judicial Department, Madras, G.O. No. 1,257, July 7, 1892.

10. Letter from J. H. Wynne, Acting District Magistrate, to J. F. Price, Chief Secretary to Government, Judicial Department. Judicial Department, Madras, G.O. No. 856, May 5, 1892. Kallan is the singular form of Kallar. Kallars were a major landed group that tended to reside in mixed or dry agricultural zones, and had been associated in intimate ways with precolonial chiefs and their military systems. They were associated with criminality because of both their military prowess, amply displayed in early wars with or involving the British, and their forms of land control and local authority, which were based in protection systems.

11. Judicial Department, Madras, G.O. No. 856, May 5, 1892.

12. See Oddie, *Popular Religion*, pp. 47–68; also Edgar Thurston, *Ethnographic Notes in Southern India* (Madras: Superintendent, Government Press, 1906), pp. 487–501; 510–19.

13. Judicial Department, Madras, G.O. No. 856, May 5, 1892.

14. Judicial Department, Madras, G.O. No. 1,321, July 22, 1892.

15. Judicial Department, Madras, G.O. No. 2,662/3, December 21, 1893.

16. Public Consultations, Nos. 35–37, December 21, 1858, Vol. 4, pp. 385–88.

17. Letter dated September 27, 1858, ibid.

18. Quoted in Oddie, *Popular Religion*, pp. 175–84; see p. 176.

19. Extract from the Minutes of Consultation, Public Department, Madras, February 18, 1854, no. 173, quoted in *Reports on the Swinging Festival*, p. 327.

20. Judicial Department, Madras, G.O. No. 2,662/3, December 21, 1893.

21. Judicial Department, Madras, G.O. 1,418, August 27, 1890.

22. Judicial Department, Madras, G.O. 990, May 25, 1892.

23. Judicial Department, Madras, G.O. 2,662/3, December 21, 1893.

24. This is a view that is echoed in large part by Geoffrey Oddie in *Popular Religion*. After dismissing those critics of colonialism who merely focus on colonial sources rather than the truths available in them, he emerges with an analysis that could have been developed without any of the sources.

25. Judicial Department, Madras, G.O. 2,662/3, December 21, 1893.

26. Ibid.

27. Quotations in this paragraph are ibid.

28. Ibid.

29. Ibid.

30. For a helpful account of the rise of bourgeois morality in nineteenth-century Britain, see Peter Stallybrass and Allen White, *The Politics and Poetics of Transgression* (London: Methuen, 1986).

31. Judicial Department, Madras, G.O. No. 2,662/3, December 21, 1893.

32. Ibid.

33. Quoted ibid.

34. Judicial Department, Madras, G.O. No. 1,284, May 27, 1894.

35. Judicial Department, Madras, G.O. No. 2,627, November 2, 1894.

36. See my argument in "From Little King to Landlord: Colonial Discourse and Colonial Rule," in Dirks, ed., *Colonialism and Culture* (Ann Arbor: University of Michigan Press, 1992), pp. 175–208.

37. For an example of this view, see Oddie, *Popular Religion*.

38. Judicial Department, Madras, G.O. No. 2,314, September 24, 1894.

39. See M. N. Srinivas, *Social Change in Modern India* (Berkeley and Los Angeles: University of California Press, 1968).

40. The particular example comes from Pudukkottai; see Nicholas Dirks, *The Hollow Crown: Ethnohistory of an Indian Kingdom* (Ann Arbor: University of Michigan Press, 1993). For other examples, see Franklin Presler, *Religion under Bureaucracy: Policy and Administration for Hindu Temples in South India* (Cambridge: Cambridge University Press, 1987), and Arjun Appadurai, *Worship and Conflict under Colonial Rule: A South Indian Case* (Cambridge: Cambridge University Press, 1981).

41. See the argument in Eric Hobsbawm and Terence Ranger, *The Invention of Tradition* (Cambridge: Cambridge University Press,1983). See my longer critique of this position in "Is Vice Versa? Historical Anthropologies and Anthropological Histories," in T. McDonald, ed., *The Historic Turn in the Human Sciences* (Ann Arbor: University of Michigan Press, 1996), pp. 17–51.


**Chapter Nine**
**The Body of Caste: Anthropology and the Criminalization of Caste**

1. I came upon some of these reports in the first instance because they were carefully preserved and in some cases reproduced by Walter Elliot, a long-time civil servant in the Andhra region of Madras presidency who was an amateur ethnographer and prodigious collector. After his retirement from India, Elliot became one of the early promoters in England of anthropological interest in the customs and communities of India. Missionary writings constituted the primary source material for the many papers he gave in learned societies in Britain. In this, Elliot was by no means an exception; during the years leading up to and immediately following the Great Rebellion, missionary reports could scarcely be distinguished from more official (administrative) forms of ethnographic writing about caste and custom. See Robert Sewell, *Sir Walter Elliott of Wolfelee: A Sketch of His Life, and a Few extracts from His Note Books* (Edinburgh: printed for private circulation, 1896); only 100 copies were issued. See also Walter Elliott's papers in the IOL, European Manuscripts, D. 318, D. 319, D. 320.

2. IOL, European Manuscripts, D. 318; see, for example, *Church Missionary Intelligencer*, Vol. 3, No. 8 (August 1852), under the heading, "The Aboriginal Races of India."

3. One Mr. Cleveland, a British officer who labored in the Andhra highlands, was given the following epitaph in 1851: "Without bloodshed, or the terrors of authority, employing only the means of conciliation, confidence, and benevolence, attempted and accomplished the entire subjection of the lawless and savage inhabitants of the jungle territory of Rajamahal, who had long infested the neighboring lands by their predatory incursions, inspired them with a taste of the arts of civilized life, and attached them to

the British government by a conquest over their minds; the most permanent, as the most rational, mode of dominion"; ibid.

4. See "The Aboriginal Races of India."

5. Edgar Thurston, *Ethnographic Notes in Southern India* (Madras: Superintendent, Government Press, 1906), p. 511.

6. Edith Brandstadter, "Human Sacrifice and British-Kond Relations, 1759–1862," in A. Yang, ed., *Crime and Criminality in British India* (Tucson: University of Arizona Press, 1985), pp. 108–27.

7. IOL, European Manuscripts, D. 318.

8. Due to the monograph of W.H.R. Rivers, *The Todas* (London: Macmillan, 1906).

9. Paper by Walter Elliot, "On a Proposed Ethnological Congress at Calcutta," read at a meeting of the British Association of Nottingham, August 28, 1866, IOL, European Manuscripts, D. 319.

10. See Philip Mason, *A Matter of Honour: An Account of the Indian Army, Its Officers, and Men* (New York: Holt, Rinehart and Winston, 1974).

11. David Omissi, *The Sepoy and the Raj*: The Indian Army, 1860–1940 (London: Macmillan, 1994), p. 8.

12. Major G. F. MacMunn, *The Armies of India* (London: Adam and Charles Black, 1911), pp. 119, 135.

13. Bernard S. Cohn, *Colonialism and Its Forms of Knowledge: The British in India* (Princeton: Princeton University, 1996), pp. 109–11.

14. Thomas Babington Macaulay, the great-nineteenth century liberal historian, wrote in his essay on Warren Hastings: "The physical organization of the Bengalee is feeble even to effeminacy. He lives in a constant vapour bath. His pursuits are sedendary, his limbs delicate, his movements languid. During many ages he has been trampled upon by men of bolder and more hardy breeds." See T. B. Macaulay, "Warren Hastings" (originally published in October 1841), reprinted in G. M. Young, ed., *Macaulay, Poetry and Prose* (Cambridge: Harvard University Press, 1967), p. 386.

15. Omissi, *The Sepoy and the Raj*, p. 12.

16. R. C. Christie, *Handbooks for the Indian Army: Jats, Gujars and Ahirs* (Delhi: Government of India, 1937), pp. 1–6; W. B. Cunningham, *Handbooks for the Indian Army: Dogras* (Calcutta: Government of India, 1932), p. 2.

17. Ridgway, *Handbooks for the Indian Army: Pathans* (Calcutta: Government of India, 1915), pp. 14–15.

18. Cunningham, *Dogras*, pp. 89–90.

19. J. M. Wikeley, *Handbooks for the Indian Army: Punjabi Mussalmans* (Calcutta: Government of India, 1915), pp. 67, 69; R. M. Betham, *Handbooks for the Indian Army: Marathas and Dekhani Musalmans* (Calcutta: Government of India, 1908), p. 74; J. Evatt, *Handbooks for the Indian Army: Garhwalis* (Calcutta: Government of India, 1924), p. 43; A. E. Barstow, *Handbooks for the Indian Army: Sikhs* (Calcutta: Government of India, 1928), p. 151.

20. Omissi, *The Sepoy and the Raj*, pp. 26–27.

21. Ridgway, *Pathans*, pp. 48, 87–94, 167, 189.

22. C. J. Morris, *Handbooks for the Indian Army: Gurkhas* (Delhi: Mittal Government of India, 1938), p. 145.

23. Omissi, *The Sepoy and the Raj*, p. 30.

24. Betham, *Marathas and Dekhani Musalmans*, p. 96.

25. George MacMunn, *The Martial Races of India* (1933; reprinted Delhi: Mittal Publications, 1979). In addition to the books mentioned below, he wrote books such as *The Armies of India, The Indian Mutiny in Perspective, The Romance of the Indian Frontiers* and *The Religious and Hidden Cults of India*.

26. Ibid., pp. 9–10.

27. George MacMunn, *The Underworld of India* (London: Jarrolds, 1932), pp. 19, 21.

28. Omissi, *The Sepoy and the Raj*, pp. 16–19.

29. There were groups that were classified as criminal all over British India. Even MacMunn, in *The Underworld of India*, devotes a chapter to the "Criminal Castes and Tribes," pp. 149–62.

30. Public Records, Madras, G.O. No. 6/6A, January 10, 1893, Tamil Nadu Archives, Madras.

31. Frederick S. Mullaly, *Notes on Criminal Classes of the Madras Presidency* (Madras: Government Press, 1892). The preface says, "Much valuable information has been obtained from Dr. Sherring's 'Hindu Castes and Tribes,' the Abbé Dubois' 'People of India,' Mr. Nelson's 'Madura Country,' and from the various District Manuals."

32. See Yang, *Crime and Criminality*.

33. Mullaly, *Notes on Criminal Classes*, p. 82.

34. Ibid., p. 85.

35. Financial Department, Madras, G.O. No. 86, January 25, 1893.

36. Public Records, Madras, G.O. 647, June 26, 1901.

37. A. Aiyappan, "Hundred Years of the Madras Government Museum (1851–1951)," in *Madras Museum Centennial Bulletin* (Madras: Government Press, 1951), pp. 1–36.

38. *Journal of the Royal Society of Arts* 57, No. 2,942 (April 9, 1909).

39. Proceedings of the Government of India in the Home Department (Public), May 23, 1901, No. 3219/32. The Proposal for and Ethnographical Survey of India was later published in the first issue of the anthropological journal *Man* 1.1 (1901).

40. Ibid. Also see Home Department, Public Records, August 1900, Nos. 6, 8, on proposals of the British Association regarding the use of ethnography in connection with the census of 1901. The government allocated substantial funds and announced its intention to name Risley as the Director of Ethnography for India in its Public Proceeds, May 23, 1901, No. 3219/32. The Madras government followed suit by appointing Thurston as the Superintendent of Ethnography for the Madras Presidency in Public Records, Madras, G.O., No. 647, Public, June 26, 1901.

41. E. Thurston, "Syllabus of a Course of Demonstrations on Practical Anthropology Given at the Museum, October 1898," in *Madras Government Museum Building*, 2.3 (Madras: Government Press, 1899), pp. 170–80.

42. See Stephen Jay Gould, *The Mismeasure of Man* (New York: Norton, 1981), for an insightful analysis of the relation between statistics and prejudice in this kind of research.

43. Edgar Thurston, "The Madras Government Museum as an Aid to General and Technical Education," Nos. 454, 455, Educational Department, August 1, 1896, India Office Records, London (Appendix E).

44. Thurston, "Anthropology in Madras," ibid. Appendix F.

45. Judicial Department, Madras, G.O. No. 1838, September 9, 1893.

46. Ibid.

47. Judicial Department, Madras, G.O. No. 2,454, October 9, 1894.

48. Judicial Department, Madras, G.O. No. 1,472, October 9, 1897.

49. Judicial Department, Madras, G.O. No. 1,014, July 1, 1898.

50. Francis Galton, the prime mover of eugenics in Victorian England as well as the inventor of regression analysis, was the first to give prominent scientific credence to the use of fingerprinting for marking and identifying individuals. In fact, however, Sir William Herschel, chief administrator of the Hooghly district of Bengal in 1860, was one of the first to use fingerprinting, and—unaware of some experiments taking place in Europe earlier in the century—he discovered the idea in Bengal itself, where finger-prints were routinely used to "sign" documents and deeds well before the British ar-rived. Galton noted that the use of fingerprinting made particular sense in Colonial India, where officials had special difficulty identifying natives, who were both illiterate and, to the British, indistinguishable. As Carlo Ginzburg, who gives this account in his fascinating essay on the history of detection, writes, "This prodigious extension of the concept of individuality was in fact occurring by means of the State, its bureaucracy and police. Thanks to the fingerprint, even the least inhabitant of the poorest village of Asia or Europe was now identifiable and controllable." See Carlo Ginzburg, *Clues, Myths, and the Historical Method* (Baltimore: Johns Hopkins Press, 1989), p. 123.

51. Edgar Thurston, *The Castes and Tribes of Southern India* (Madras: Government Press, 1907).

52. Judicial Department, Madras, G.O. No. 792, September 5, 1903.

53. Thurston, *Castes and Tribes*, vol. 3, p. 54.

54. Ibid., p. 69.

55. Ibid., p. 64.

56. See Daniel J. Kevles, *In the Name of Eugenics* (New York: Knopf, 1985).

57. Edgar Thurston, *Ethnographic Notes in Southern India*, 2 vols. (Madras: Gov-ernment Press, 1906).

58. Thurston, *Castes and Tribes*, vol. 1, p. xi.

59. Thurston, *Ethnographic Notes*, pp. 487–501.

60. Ibid., pp. 407–432.

61. *Report of the Commissioners for the Investigation of Alleged Cases of Torture in the Madras Presidency, Submitted to the Right Honorable the Governor in Council of Fort Saint George, on the 16th April 1855* (Madras: Fort St. George Gazette Press, 1855), p. 4.

62. Ibid., p. 15.

63. Ibid., pp. 4–5.

64. See David Arnold, *Police Power and Colonial Rule in Madras* (Delhi: Oxford University Press, 1986).

65. Public Records, Madras, G.O. No. 787, November 2, 1906.

66. J. M. Kaye, *The People of India* (London: India Museum and W. H. Allen, 1872). The preface to volume 1 lists various sources for the letterpress accounts, includ-ing J. R. Melville, Meadows Taylor, J. M. Kaye, and J. Forbes Watson.

67. For a more extensive treatment of Kaye's project, and of the visual compo-nent of late colonial ethnographic representation, see Christopher Pinney, *Camera Indica: The Social Life of Indian Photographs* (Chicago: University of Chicago Press, 1997).

68. Ever since Bernard Cohn argued persuasively that the colonial sociology of India left important legacies for postcolonial social science, and Talal Asad brought together a classic group of essays that demonstrated the close links between colonial rule and anthropology, it has been widely accepted that such work sheds important light on the conceptual and political history of significant areas of anthropological practice. Until recently, however, the historical scrutiny of anthropology has been seen as largely incidental to the kind of anthropology done today, and historical investigations within anthropology have stopped far short of engaging in thorough, and wide-ranging, historical inquiry into the relations between foundational categories and historical processes. See Cohn, *Colonialism and Its Forms of Knowledge*, and Talal Asad, ed., *Anthropology and the Colonial Encounter* (London: Ithaca Press, 1973).

## Chapter Ten
## The Enumeration of Caste: Anthropology as Colonial Rule

1. Even before the rebellion, the government had been desirous of better, and more systematic, information. For example, in Madras—where the rebellion in any case caused fewer direct concerns—it was believed as early as 1855 that "defective organization" had so far "failed to yield any systematic and comprehensive results . . . for rendering . . . a faithful register of the state of the country as at present existing." However, it was only with the rebellion that this need became recognized at an all-India level. Madras Public Proceedings, No. 144–145, September 30, 1871, Tamil Nadu Archives, Madras.

2. Nelson's in 1868; Carmichael's in 1869. J. H. Nelson, *The Madura Country* (Madras: At the Government Press, 1868); David F. Carmichael, ed., *A Manual of the District of Vizagapatam in the Presidency of Madras* (Madras: Asylum Press, 1869).

3. Madras Public Proceedings, G.O. nos. 32–33, March 7, 1870.

4. Madras Public Proceedings, G.O. nos. 144–145, September 30, 1871. Richard Temple, chief commissioner of the Central Provinces, prepared a gazetteer for the Central Provinces in 1865, which was held in considerably higher repute than the works of Nelson and Carmichael. But Temple's ambitions for a separate department of statistics was thought to be too expensive a proposition.

5. W. W. Hunter, *A Statistical Account of Bengal*, Preface (London: Trubner, 1875–1877), Vol. 1, p. viii. In early 1865, W. W. Hunter had already begun his own researches in the Birbhum collectorate, and in September of 1865, the Bengal government decided to experiment with the idea of using Hunter to do this on a district-by-district basis. The outcome of this inquiry, funded by the Government of India, was Hunter's *Annals of Rural Bengal* (1868).

6. Hunter, *Statistical Account*, p. x.

7. Madras Public Proceedings, G.O. No. 197, March 25, 1892.

8. Despite the official disapproval of Nelson's manual, it is noteworthy that he provided footnotes (as we have seen in previous chapters) for many of the ethnological endeavors of the next several decades. Nelson was an interesting character whose legal writings also secured major significance in the development of Anglo-Hindu law; in southern India he is chiefly remembered for his anti-Brahman sentiments. In fact, there was a long tradition through the nineteenth century of anti-Brahman feeling among official civilians as well as missionaries. In *The Madura Country* Nelson made it clear

that he valued the literary and cultural achievements of non-Brahmans over those of
Brahmans, and believed that the term "Sudra" had been forced on non-Brahmans as a
term of denigration. He also endorsed the Abbé Dubois's account of the customs and
rituals of Brahmans—hardly the most sympathetic account, even if from the perspective of one who supported the general principle of hierarchy. Although official ethnography tended increasingly to take a Brahmanic view of caste, Indian society in general,
and Hinduism during the late nineteenth and early twentieth centuries, Nelson's comments reveal an undercurrent of critique that gave additional weight to Caldwell's exco-
riation of Brahmans and Brahmanic influence in the south. See J.D.M. Derrett, "J. H.
Nelson: A Forgotten Administrator-Historian of India," in C.H. Philips, ed., *Historians
of India, Pakistan, and Ceylon* (London: Oxford University Press, 1961), pp. 354–72.

9. See Ian Hacking, *The Emergence of Probability* (Cambridge: Cambridge University Press, 1975); *The Taming of Chance* (Cambridge: Cambridge University Press,
1990). Arjun Appadurai, "Number in the Colonial Imagination," in Carol Breckenridge
and Peter van der Veer, eds., *Orientalism and the Postcolonial Predicament* (Philadelphia: University of Pennsylvania Press, 1993), pp. 314–39.

10. See Sekhar Bandyopadhyay, *Caste, Politics and the Raj: Bengal 1872–1937*
(Calcutta: K. P. Bagchi, 1990), p. 31.

11. The imperial gazetteer was a logical extension of Hunter's first proposed statistical survey. It was designed to provide ready-to-hand information for district collectors
and magistrates, who were frequently transferred from post to post. Some old India
hands had little faith in Hunter's enterprise, however. John Beames asked, "How many
Collectors in Bengal do you think will care a sixpence for your Gazetteer? How many
of them will be bored by the whole thing and hand it over to Babu Ghose or Bose to
expiate upon? How many will have time for it or the taste and learning which fit them
to be your collaborators?" In his memoirs he was much more vicious: "About this time
we received a visit from that vivacious but not very accurate writer, Dr. W. W.
Hunter. . . . He was then a small, lean, hatchet-faced man with a newspaperman-corre-
spondent's gift of facile flashy writing, and a passion for collecting facts and figures of
which he made fearful and wonderful use afterwards. The light-headed subalterns of the
regiment at Cuttack had amused themselves by inventing for his benefit wonderful
yarns, all which he duly entered in his notebook and reproduced in his book on Orissa."
Quoted in R. Emmett, "The Gazetteers of India: Their Origins and Development during
the Nineteenth Century," M.A. thesis, University of Chicago, 1976.

12. See Bernard S. Cohn, "The Census, Social Structure and Objectification in South
Asia," in Cohn, *An Anthropologist among the Historians and Other Essays* (Delhi:
Oxford University Press, 1990), pp. 233–38; Bandyopadhyay, *Caste, Politics, and the
Raj*, pp. 28–29

13. W. R. Cornish, *Report on the Census of the Madras Presidency, 1871*, vol. 1
(London: Government Gazette Press, 1874).

14. Henry Waterfield, *Memorandum on the Census of British India of 1871–72*
(London: H. M. Stationery Office, 1875).

15. Ibid., p. 41.

16. H. Beverley, *Report of the Census of Bengal, 1872* (Calcutta: Bengal Secretariat
Press, 1872), p. 58.

17. Waterfield, *Memorandum on the Census of British India of 1871–72*, p. 41.

18. Beverley, *Report on the Census of Bengal, 1872*, p. 59.

19. Cornish, *Report of the Census of the Madras Presidency*, 1871, p. 91.

20. Waterfield, *Memorandum on the Census of British India of 1871–72*, p. 20.

21. Plowden noted elsewhere that "On the subject of caste, the results obtained . . . are by no means commensurate with the labour involved, and, unless some better arrangements are made, it would, probably be advisable to omit the column altogether. . . . In the eight reports about 200 pages are devoted to a description of the various castes, with some 1,370 pages of tables and though there is in them much interesting matter, it is very doubtful whether the information thus gained has at all repaid the trouble taken in the compilation." Proceedings of the Government of India, Home Department (Public), nos. 76–78, March 1878, NAI, p. 9.

22. See Bernard S. Cohn, "Is There a New Indian History? Society and Social Change under the Raj," in *An Anthropologist among the Historians*, pp. 172–99.

23. The total of Hindus by race is 12,530,637, broken down into 654,707 Brahmans, 142,433 Ksatriyas, 932,404 Vaisyas, and 10,801,393 Sudras.

24. J. Lumsdaine, *Report of the Census of the Bombay Presidency*, 1872 (Bombay: Government Central Press, 1872).

25. See Uma Chakravarti, *Rewriting History: The Life and Times of Pandita Ramabai* (Delhi: Kali for Women, 1998), chapter on "Caste, Gender, and the State in Eighteenth Century Maharashtra," pp. 3–42.

26. Beverley, *Report on the Census of Bengal*, 1872, p. 154.

27. Waterfield, *Memorandum on the Census of British India*, 1871–72, p. 36.

28. Cornish, *Report on the Census of the Madras Presidency*, 1871, Vol. 1, p. 116.

29. Cornish exempted two authors from his general characterization: W. W. Hunter and J. H. Nelson. He applauded Hunter for demonstrating that the Brahmans of the present day are not all of uniform origin, and Nelson for explaining that the caste system of Manu never had any vitality in southern India, ibid.

30. Ibid., p. 117.

31. Ibid.

32. Ibid., p. 118.

33. Ibid., p. 123.

34. Ibid., p. 125.

35. "The later Aryan colonists evidently saw that if they were to preserve their individuality and supremacy, they must draw a hard and fast line between themselves, the earlier and partly degenerated Aryans, and the brown and black races of the country, and hence probably we get a natural explanation of the origin of caste. It was at first essentially a distinction of race" (ibid., p. 126).

36. Ibid., pp. 125, 127.

37. Ibid., p. 129.

38. Nevertheless, it was unclear whether he had any real sense of the superiority of the original Brahman, so thorough was his racial condemnation of the population he was charged to enumerate.

39. W. C. Plowden, *Report on the Census of British India*, 1881 (London: H. M. Stationery Office, 1882), vol. 1, p. 277.

40. Lewis McIver, *Report on Census in the Presidency of Madras*, 1881 (Madras: Government Press, 1883), p. 102.

41. Ibid.

42. Ibid., p. 108.

43. Ibid., p. 104.

44. Ibid., p. 108.

45. Rashmi Pant, "The Cognitive Status of Caste in Colonial Ethnography: A Review of Some Literature on the NorthWest Provinces and Oudh," in *Indian Economic and Social History Review* 24.2 (1987): 152; see Plowden, *Report on the Census of India*, 1881, vol. 1, p. 307.

46. Cohn, "The Census," p. 245; J. A. Bourdillon to Sec. Govt. Financial Department, Bengal, G.O. No. 255I C, June 17, 1881; Proceedings of the Lt. Governor of Bengal, Financial Department, Statistics Branch, Head Census, July 1881; Circular no. 5, May 1881, IOL.

47. J. A. Baines, *General Report on the Census of India*, 1891 (London: Printed for the Indian Government, 1893), p. 183.

48. Ibid., pp. 123, 127.

49. Ibid., p. 185.

50. Ibid., p. 121.

51. In the 1891 census Baines wrote as follows: In Bengal, "it is said that there is the only opportunity to be found in the present day of judging of Brahmanism where its development has been absolutely unchecked; and something very like the code of Manu is in force in its unmitigated bigotry. It is only within comparatively recent times that the racial distribution of the population has been investigated on the line of modern science. Previous to that time philology had held the field unchecked by observations from other standpoints. A beginning has been made in Bengal by Mr. Risley, who has published anthropometrical data from about 6,000 persons. Most of them are from Bengal, but some were made in the North-West Provinces and the Panjab. Such an extensive field of survey, comprising over 146 millions of inhabitants, cannot, of course, be appreciated from the results of measuring one person in 24,000, but the results show the value of the method, and it is to be hoped that more material of the same sort may be made available."

52. Risley was obviously the most successful critic of occupation, but he was by no means alone. For example, H. A. Stuart wrote in his report on the 1891 census in Madras that "the connection between caste and function is, in my opinion, entirely a non-Dravidian idea," thus making clear his sense of the irrelevance of occupational criteria for Madras.

53. Sir Denzil Ibbetson, *Punjab Castes (reprint of the chapter on "The Races, Castes, and Tribes of the People" in the Census of the Punjab, 1881* (Lahore, Mubarak Ali, 1974); first published 1883.

54. John C. Nesfield, *Brief View of the Caste System of the North-Western Provinces and Oudh, together with an examination of the names and figures shown in the census report, 1882, being an attempt to classify on a functional basis all the main castes of the United Provinces, and to explain their gradations of rank and the process of their formation* (Allahbad: North-Western Provinces and Oudh Government Press), 1885.

55. Baines, *General Report on the Census of India*, 1891, p. 189.

56. H. H. Risley, only son of Rev. John Holford Risley, rector of Akeley, was born on January 4, 1851. He went to Winchester and Oxford, where he was selected for an appointment in the Indian Civil Service before his graduation in 1872. He stayed in India until 1910, when he was appointed permanent secretary in the India Office, a post he only held for a short time, as he died in September 1911.

57. H. H. Risley, *The Tribes and Castes of Bengal* (Calcutta: Secretariat Press, 1891), preface, p. xix.

58. Proceedings of the Government of India, Home Department (Public), no. 3219/32, May 23, 1901, NAI.

59. Baines, *General Report on the Census of India*, 1891, p. 189.

60. Risley, *Tribes and Castes of Bengal*, p. i.

61. Ibid., p. xx.

62. Ibid., p. xxii.

63. Ibid.

64. Ibid., p. vii.

65. Ibid.

66. One of the curious results of Risley's peculiar fascination with marriage customs and their racial register was his careful defense of Indian customs in matters such as child marriage. "Many hard things have been said of infant marriage, and the modern tendency is to assume that a population which countenances such a practice must be in a fair way towards great moral degradation, if not to ultimate extinction. Much of this criticism seems to me to be greatly exaggerated, and to be founded on considerable ignorance of the present conditions and future possibilities of Oriental life." Of course Risley was also convinced that the handful of "classes who have adopted more or less completely European ideas on the subject of marriage" would be the ruin of India's classical traditions. And he was hardly averse to the idea that there be some controlling authority other than the Western ideal of romantic love over the marriage decision, perhaps a coded eugenicist wish of his own to find parallels for the control of unsuitable racial mixing in Europe.

67. All of this material is found in the IOL file European Manuscript E 101, Ethnographical Papers, mostly concerning H. H. Risley.

68. Circular No. 1, July 1886, Reg. No. 4034J–300–16–7–86, European Manuscript E 101, IOL.

69. Report dated September 1, 1886. Microfilm reel, ibid.

70. This letter is included in Risley's papers but appears to have predated most other inquiries. It is dated July 12, 1881.

71. Ibid., p. 260 in file.

72. Letter from Michael Foster to the Secretary of State for India, December 1899, in Extract No. 3219–32 from the Proceedings of the Government of India in the Home Department (Public)—Simla, May 23, 1901, NAI.

73. Resolution of the Government of India, Home Department (Public) no. 3919, May 23, 1901, Simla, NAI.

74. It is noteworthy to contrast the support of the colonial administration for the collection and analysis of ethnological knowledge with the extremely limited interest of the state, a century before, in the collecting activities of men such as Mackenzie.

75. H. H. Risley, *Census of India*, 1901, Vol. 1., Part 1., *Report*, chapter 11, pp. 489–557.

76. Ibid., p. 493.

77. Ibid., p. 538.

78. Ibid.

79. Ibid., p. 543.

80. Ibid., p. 544.

81. Risley did not believe that caste was confined to India. "It occurs in a pronounced form in the southern States of the American Commonwealth, where Negroes intermarry with Negroes, and the various mixed races Mulattos, Quadroons and Octoroons each have a sharply restricted *jus connubii* of their own and are absolutely cut off from legal unions with the white races"; ibid., p. 555.

82. Ibid., p. 556.

83. Ibid., p. 539.

84. W. Francis, *Report on the Census, Madras*, 1901, Part 1 (Madras: Government Press, 1902), p. 171.

85. J. C. Maloney, *Report on the Census, Madras*, 1901, Part 1 (Madras: Government Press, 1913), p. 159.

86. L.S.S. O'Malley, *Report on the Census of India, Bengal, Bihar and Orissa and Sikkim*, Part 1 (Calcutta: Bengal Secretariat, 1913).

87. Bandyopadhyay, *Caste, Politics, and the Raj*, p. 100.

88. J. H. Hutton, *Census of India*, 1931, Vol. 1, Part 1, *Report*, p. 433. Like other census commissioners before him, Hutton went on to use his census background in his subsequent professional career. He used an appendix and one chapter from his census report in his book, *Caste in India* (Cambridge: Cambridge University Press, 1946).

89. H. H. Risley, *The People of India* (London: Thacker, 1908 [based on *Report on the Census of India*, 1901, authored by H. H. Risley and E. A. Gait [Calcutta: Office of the Superintendent of Government Printing, 1902]), p. 287.

90. Ibid., p. 293.

91. Ibid., p. 294.

92. Ibid., p. 301.

93. Ibid., p. 281.

94. See, for example, Sumit Sarkar's thorough discussion of this in his *The Swadeshi Movement in Bengal, 1903–1908* (New Delhi: People's Publishing House, 1973).

95. See Hermann Kulke and Dietmar Rothermund, *A History of India* (New York: Routledge, 1986), pp. 271–72.

96. See Ayesha Jalal, *The Sole Spokesman: Jinnah, the Muslim League and the Demand for Pakistan* (Cambridge: Cambridge University Press, 1985).

**Chapter Eleven**
**Toward a Nationalist Sociology of India: Nationalism and Brahmanism**

1. Sumit Sarkar, *Writing Social History* (Delhi: Oxford University Press, 1997), p. 365.

2. *The Hindu*, April 9, 1921.

3. M. K. Gandhi, *Collected Works* (Delhi: Government of India, 1958–1994), vol. 19, pp. 83–84.

4. Bhikhu Parekh, *Colonialism, Tradition and Reform: An Analysis of Gandhi's Political Discourse* (New Delhi: Sage, 1989), p. 226.

5. See for example ibid., p. 229.

6. Gandhi, *Collected Works*, vol. 63, p. 153, vol. 62, p. 121.

7. See Sarkar, *Writing Social History*, p. 390.

8. Nehru wrote that "If merit is the only criterion and opportunity is thrown open to everybody, then caste loses all its present-day distinguishing features and, in fact, ends.

Caste has in the past not only led to the suppression of certain groups but to a separation of theoretical and scholastic learning from craftsmanship and a divorce of philosophy from actual life and its problems. It was an aristocratic approach based on traditionalism. This outlook has to change completely, for it is wholly opposed to modern conditions and the democratic ideal." *The Discovery of India* (Delhi: Oxford University Press, 1989): p. 520. But since Nehru also sanctioned his valorization of Indian civilization through an idealized retelling of Sanskritic and Hindu genealogies, he could only appeal to a political vision in which the democratization of the masses would eviscerate the old regime. His accounts of, and relationship with, Gandhi reveal the full measure of Nehru's ambivalence and contradiction. See ibid., pp. 358–64; also see Partha Chatterjee, *Nationalist Thought and the Colonial World: A Derivative Discourse* (Minneapolis: University of Minnesota Press, 1993), pp. 131–66.

9. See, for example, Lloyd I. Rudolph and Susanne Hoeber Rudolph, *The Modernity of Tradition: Political Development in India* (Chicago: University of Chicago Press, 1967).

10. Sekhar Bandyopadhyay, *Caste, Protest, and Identity in Colonial India: The Namasudras of Bengal, 1872–1947* (Surrey: Curzon, 1997).

11. Sarkar, *Writing Social History*, p. 376.

12. Ibid., p. 390.

13. Uma Chakravarti, *Rewriting History: The Life and Times of Pandita Ramabai* (Delhi: Kali for Women, 1998), p. 64.

14. P. J. Mead and G. Laird MacGregor, *Report on the Census*, vol. 7, *Bombay*, 1911 (Bombay: Government Central Press, 1912), p. 195.

15. Chakravarti, *Rewriting History*, p. 65.

16. Rosalind O'Hanlon has demonstrated the diverse intellectual influences on Phule in her *Caste, Conflict and Ideology: Mahatma Jotirao Phule and Low Caste Protest in Nineteenth-Century Western India* (Cambridge: Cambridge University Press, 1985), p. 142.

17. Gail Omvedt, *Cultural Revolt in a Colonial Society: The Non-Brahman Movement in Western India: 1873 to 1930* (Bombay: Scientific Socialist Education Trust, 1976), p. 2.

18. O'Hanlon, *Caste, Conflict and Ideology*, pp. 220–302.

19. H. A. Stuart, *Report on the Census, Madras*, 1891 (Madras: Government Press, 1894), p. 212.

20. Ibid., p. 213.

21. W. Francis, *Report on the Census, Madras*, 1901, Part 1 (Madras: Government Press, 1902), p. 171.

22. Home Department (Public), Madras, G.O. no. 857, May 27, 1935, TNA.

23. G. T. Boag, *Report on the Census, Madras*, 1921, vol. 13 part 1 (Madras: Government Press, 1922), p. 153n.

24. These records were grouped under a special category of communal records: H.F.M. Extracts from G.O.s relating to the Communal Movement, Tamil Nadu Archives, Madras. The following citations are from this collection.

25. G.O. No. 590 (confidential), July 17, 1933; G.O. No. 622 (confidential), March 29, 1936;

26. G.O. No. 817, March 25, 1922.

27. G.O. No. 516, May 1, 1929.

28. G.O. No. 291, March 23, 1931.

29. G.O. No. 1,356, October 20, 1932.

30. G.O. No 329, February 25, 1935

31. G.O. No. 166, January 26, 1939.

32. Ibid.

33. G.O. No. 878, August 28, 1931.

34. Non-Brahman Manifesto, "printed as an appendix to Eugene Irschick, *Politics and Social Conflict in South India: The Non-Brahman Movement and Tamil Separatism, 1916–1929* (Berkeley and Los Angeles: University of California Press, 1969).

35. Quoted in Shriram Maheswari, *The Census Administration under the Raj and After* (New Delhi: Concept Publishing, 1996), p. 113.

36. S. V. Ketkar, *History of Caste in India: Evidence of the Laws of Manu on the Social Condition in India during the Third Century A.D., Interpreted and Examined, with an Appendix on Radical Defects of Ethnology* (1909; reprint Jaipur: Rawat Publishers, 1979), p. liv.

37. He also made it clear that caste in India was not only unique but also impervious to changes introduced by "foreigners" within India: "Principles antagonistic to the system were forced into society by the swords of the Mohammedans, by the bayonets of the Portuguese, and by the organized missions of Europeans and Americans of the nineteenth centuries, but they all failed to make any impression," ibid., p. 5.

38. Ibid., pp. 53–54.

39. Ibid., pp. 22–23.

40. Ibid., pp. 21–22.

41. Ibid., pp. 79–80.

42. Including M. N. Srinivas, A. R. Desai, Irawati Karve, Y. B. Damle, and M.S.A. Rao. He supervised fifty-five Ph.D. dissertations and twenty-five M.A.s.

43. G. S. Ghurye, *Caste and Race in India* (1932; 5th ed. Bombay: Popular Prakashan, 1969), p. 1.

44. Ibid., p. 27.

45. Ibid., p. 157.

46. Ibid., p. 160.

47. It is, of course, ironic that Ketkar's book anticipates the rise of American ethnosociology more than it does subsequent colonial forms of knowledge.

48. Ghurye, *Caste and Race in India*, pp. 287–90.

49. Ibid., p. 283; he went even further to suggest that "Perhaps, in the name of justice and efficiency, the time has come when the interests of the Brahmins have to be protected against the majority party" (ibid., p. 291), though ultimately he dismissed this idea as well because of his argument that special representation was unnecessary and harmful.

50. Ibid., p. 290.

51. Ibid., p. 285.

52. Ibid., pp. 283, 291.

53. For example, in his major work he never raises the question of whether Muslims have caste—a standard question, if not a major preoccupation, for most other ethnographers.

54. Ghurye, *Caste and Race in India*, p. 303.

55. A. R. Momin, ed., *The Legacy of G. S. Ghurye: A Centennial Festschrift* (Bombay: Popular Prakashan, 1996), p. vii.

56. Srinivas had a difficult relationship with Ghurye, earning the latter's displeasure

in particular when he went off to Oxford to study with Radcliffe-Brown. Srinivas complained about Ghurye's despotic proclivities as a supervisor, wryly noting that "while meeting him was a good thing for me, leaving him was better." See M. N. Srinivas, "Professor G. S. Ghurye and I: A Troubled Relationship," in Momin, ed., *The Legacy of G. S. Ghurye*, p. 12.

57. M. N. Srinivas, *Social Change in Modern India* (Berkeley and Los Angeles: University of California Press, 1966), p. 6.

58. Ibid., p. 23.

59. Ibid., p. 7.

60. Ibid., p. 23.

61. Ibid., p. 102.

62. See Chapter 13 below for a discussion of Srinivas's role in debates over reservation policy.

63. Srinivas, *Social Change in Modern India*, p. 147.

64. Ibid., p. 152.

65. E. R. Leach, review of Dumont, *British Journal of Sociology* 14.4 (December, 1963): 377–78.

66. See M. N. Srinivas, *Religion and Society among the Coorgs of Southern India* (Oxford: Clarendon Press, 1952).

67. See Partha Chatterjee's argument about the predicament of anticolonial nationalism in his *Nationalist Thought and the Colonial World* (Minneapolis: University of Minnesota Press, 1996).

68. Ketkar, *History of Caste*, p. 4.

69. When Dumont and Pocock bid farewell to their journal *Contributions in Indian Sociology* in 1966 (the year of the publication of *Homo Hierarchicus*), they bequeathed it to T. N. Madan, a prominent sociologist who soon made the New Series of *Contributions* the most influential anthropological journal published in India. Although the journal has published some of the most important contributions to anthropological research concerning India, it has also maintained an uneasy connection between Indological assertions about the primacy of Indian values, terms, and meanings and sociological commitments to develop a national social science. Madan has been one of the most influential scholars to raise questions about the cultural appropriateness of secularism in modern India, and to suggest in turn that India must acknowledge the special place that religion has had in its history and its culture. But I ask here what kind of "religion" this has been, and what implications the use of this idea of religion has for the emergence of a new nationalist sociology of India. See T. N. Madan, "Secularism in Its Place," *Journal of Asian Studies* 46.4 (November 1987): 747–60.

## Chapter Twelve
## The Reformation of Caste: Periyar, Ambedkar, and Gandhi

1. See Partha Chatterjee, "Secularism and Toleration," in *A Possible India: Essays in Political Criticism* (Delhi: Oxford University Press, 1998), pp. 228–62.

2. See Arjun Appadurai, *Worship and Conflict under Colonial Rule: A Couth Indian Case* (Cambridge: Cambridge University Press, 1981).

3. Dilip Menon, *Caste, Nationalism and Communism in South India: Malabar 1900–1948* (Cambridge: Cambridge University Press, 1994), p. 81.

4. Ibid., p. 82.

5. *Kudi Arasu* (Madras), May 2, 1925.

6. See Eugene Irschick, *Politics and Social Change in South India: The Non-Brahman Movement and Tamil Separation, 1916–1929* (Berkeley and Los Angeles: University of California Press, 1969).

7. V. Geeta and S. V. Rajadurai, *Towards a Non-Brahmin Millennium: From Iyothee Thass to Periyar* (Madras: Samya Press, 1998), pp. 298–99.

8. *The Hindu* (Madras), April 9, 1921.

9. M. K. Gandhi, *Collected Works* (Delhi: Government of India, 1958–1964), Vol. 34, pp. 510–11.

10. *Kudi Arasu*, August 7, 1927

11. *Kudi Arasu*, August 28, 1927.

12. Quoted in Geeta and Rajadurai, *Towards a Non-Brahmin Millennium*, p. 299.

13. "The Self-Respecters contended that the Vellalas' eyes were partially opened to their cultural grandeur by the English missionary Dr. Robert Caldwell, but still they remained under the spell of Smartaism, which could only be dispelled by the magic wand of the Self-Respect Movement." *Revolt*, 18 August 1929, quoted in E. Sa. Visswanathan, *The Political Career of E. V. Ramasami Naicker* (Madras: Ravi and Vasanth, 1998), p. 357.

14. See Geeta and Rajadurai, *Towards a Non-Brahmin Millennium*, pp. 210–16.

15. Ibid., p. 319.

16. Ibid., p. 320.

17. E.V.R. praised Jinnah's two-nation theory "as the sanest way of settling the baffling Hindu Muslim problem," and contended that this doctrine was the logical outcome of two years of Aryan-dominated Congress rule in the country: "Two years of Congress regime, which was so Aryan ridden, could not but create a sense of despair in the minds of all non-Aryans. . . . It is but a natural desire on the part of the Muslims to live as a separate nation." Significantly, however, there is no indication that he made any serious effort to make bridges with the Tamil Muslim community, which was hardly affected by the plan for Pakistan.

18. Geeta and Rajadurai, *Towards a Non-Brahmin Millennium*, p. 327.

19. Quoted ibid., p. 522.

20. B. R. Ambedkar, "Castes in India: Their Mechanism, Genesis and Development," in V. Moon, ed., *Dr. Babasaheb Ambedkar Writings and Speeches*, Vol. 1. (Bombay: Education Department, Government of Maharashtra, 1989), pp. 18, 15.

21. Ibid., p. 15.

22. B. R. Ambedkar, "The Annihilation of Caste," in Moon, ed., *Dr. Babasaheb Ambedkar*, vol. 1. pp. 68, 77.

23. "A Vindication of Caste by Mahatma Gandhi," Reprint of Gandhi's articles from *Harijan*, reprinted in Moon, ed., *Dr. Babasaheb Ambedkar*, vol. 1, pp. 81–85.

24. *Harijan*, July 18, 1836. Reprinted with Ambedkar's "Annihilation of Caste."

25. Ambedkar's reply to Gandhi, reprinted in Moon, ed., Dr. Babasaheb Ambedkar, Vol. 1, pp. 89, 93, 94.

26. B. R. Ambedkar, *What Congress and Gandhi Have Done to the Untouchables* (Bombay: Thacker, 1945), pp. 108, 112.

27. B. R. Ambedkar, *The Untouchables* (Bombay: Shravasti, 1948), pp. x, xi, xii.

28. Bhagwan Das, ed., *Thus Spoke Ambedkar—Selected Speeches,* 2nd ed. (Jullundur, Punjab: Bheem Patrika Publications, 1969), pp. 126–38.

29. In *The Untouchables,* he wrote about Buddhism for the first time as the only Indian religion that was genuinely committed to egalitarianism. Gauri Viswanathan has noted that Ambedkar chose conversion to Buddhism as a commitment to national regeneration; *Outside the Fold: Conversion, Modernity, and Belief* (Princeton: Princeton University Press, 1999). Although I share much of her analysis, her interest in the comparative question of religious conversion leads her to a different emphasis in her interpretation of Ambedkar's conversion. She argues that rather than being primarily reactive, Ambedkar's chief aim was the refashioning of a moral community. My argument here is that Ambedkar's conversion was made necessary by, even as it was the ultimate rejection of, the stranglehold of caste. In other words, the conversion was less about religion than it was about the extent to which religion had been implicated in the history of casteism and Brahmanism in India.

## Chapter Thirteen
## Caste Politics and the Politics of Caste

1. J. H. Hutton, *Caste in India: Its Nature, Function, and Origins* (Bombay: Oxford University Press, 1961), p. 194.

2. Marc Galanter, *Competing Equalities: Law and the Backward Classes in India* (Berkeley and Los Angeles: University of California Press, 1984), p. 134. He goes on to note that "The resulting list, then, designates all of those groups who in the view of Parliament require the special protections provided by the Constitution: it defines who may stand for reserved seats and enjoy benefits and reservations for the Scheduled Castes. But it does not necessarily include every person or group that might be considered 'untouchables' by any conceivable definition. It omits some groups which historically suffered disabilities (e.g. Ezhuvas) or which would be untouchables in terms of the 1931 census tests. And it excludes non-Hindus (other than Sikhs) who would clearly seem to be untouchables within the judicial test of 'origin in a group considered beyond the pale of the caste system'" (p. 134). Galanter also surveys the change over time in the list, finding it remarkably constant, and consistently bound to an idea the caste should play the primary role in designating the scheduled castes.

3. "Community" in recent Indian usage has come increasingly to stand for a section of the population differentiated by religion or caste or both, such as Muslim/Hindu; Brahman/non-Brahman; caste Hindu/untouchable. "Communalism," or "communalist," refers to persons or ideologies that stress community for political purposes or in the context of social/religious antagonism.

4. For full quotations and citations, see Galanter, *Competing Equalities,* pp. 73–74.

5. G. S. Ghurye, *Caste and Race in India,* 5th ed. (Bombay: Popular Prakashan, 1969), p. 292.

6. Lloyd I. Rudolph and Susanne Hoeber Rudolph, *The Modernity of Tradition: Political Development in India* (Chicago: University of Chicago Press, 1967), p. 150.

7. See Galanter, *Competing Equalities,* pp. 320–21.

8. See Rudolph and Rudolph, *The Modernity of Tradition,* p. 149 n. 49.

9. See *Report of the Commission for Scheduled Castes and Scheduled Tribes, 1982–83* (New Delhi: Controller of Publication, 1984).

10. M. J. Akbar, *Riot after Riot* (New Delhi: Penguin Books, 1988), p. 45.

11. Galanter, *Competing Equalities*, p. 166.

12. N. K. Bose, *Culture and Society in India* (Bombay: Asia Publishing House, 1967), p. 188.

13. Galanter, *Competing Equalities*, p. 166.

14. Eugene Irschick, *Politics and Social Conflict in South India: The Non-Brahman Movement and Tamil Separatism, 1916–1929* (Berkeley and Los Angeles: University of California Press, 1969), pp. 218–74, 368–72.

15. Ghurye, *Caste and Race in India*, p. 290.

16. This reckoning constituted a population of 116 million, about 32 percent of the total population of India. This figure did not include women as a separate group, although the commission recommended that all women in India made up what was in effect a backward class; Galanter, *Competing Equalities*, p. 169.

17. Ibid., p. 172.

18. Quoted in *Frontline* (Madras), September 1–14, 1990.

19. Galanter, *Competing Equalities*, p. 173.

20. Quoted in ibid., p. 175.

21. Quoed in ibid., p. 178.

22. Marc Galanter, whose splendid book provides much of the information used in the preliminary pages of this chapter, makes the point that as a result of the dropping of the report, the major story of preferential discrimination in favor of backward groups has been played out in the courts, both at the center and in the states. The bulk of his massive study concerns this legal history.

23. Galanter, *Competing Equalities*, pp. 186–87.

24. *India Today*, September 15, 1990, pp. 34, 35.

25. *Frontline*, September 15–28, 1990, p. 27.

26. *Economic and Political Weekly*, October 6, 1990, p. 2,231.

27. Ibid., p. 2,234.

28. Rajni Kothari, *Caste in Indian Politics* (New York: Gordon and Breach, 1970); Kothari, "Caste and Politics: The Great Secular Upsurge," *Times of India*, op-ed. piece, September 28, 1990.

29. This had also been argued by the political scientists Lloyd and Susanne Rudolph in *The Modernity of Tradition*.

30. M. N. Srinivas, A. M. Shah, and B. S. Bavaskar, "Kothari's Illusion of Secular Upsurge," *Times of India*, letter to editor, October 17, 1990.

31. Times of India, November 13, 1990. Mehta further argued that it was the external threat of Islam that produced modern hereditary forms of caste.

32. See interview of Veena Das in *India Today*, May 31, 1991; Dharma Kumar, "From Paternalism to Populism: The History of Affirmative Action in India," paper delivered to the Center for South and Southeast Asian Studies, University of Michigan, October 1991.

33. By this I refer to the fact that arguments made against the British, and in the context of British colonial rule, are frequently used uncritically in the post-colonial period, when despite the continued salience of national unity as a concern,

issues of social justice and redistribution must be addressed in new and less defensive ways.

34. Ashok Guha, "Reservations in Myth and Reality," *Economic and Political Weekly*, December 15, 1990.

35. Although not all arguments against Mandal can be automatically designated as unprogressive, the primary political instincts behind colonial critiques and Mandal critiques are fundamentally different, if not completely opposed.

36. Guha, "Reservations in Myth and Reality," p. 2,718.

37. Dharma Kumar, "The Affirmative Action Debate in India," *Asian Survey* 32.3 (March 1992): 290–302

38. See André Béteille, *Caste, Class, and Power: Changing Patterns of Stratification in a Tanjore Village* (Berkeley and Los Angeles: University of California Press, 1985); Béteille, *Castes: Old and New, Essays in Social Structure and Social Stratification* (Bombay: Asia Publishing House, 1969); Béteille, *Society and Politics in India: Essays in a Comparative Perspective* (New Delhi: Oxford University Press, 1992).

39. André Béteille, "Caste and Reservations: Lessons of South Indian Experience," *The Hindu*, October 20, 1990.

40. This is a point made even more strongly by Dharma Kumar, "The Affirmative Action Debate."

41. Béteille, "Caste and Reservations."

42. Op ed. article, *The Hindu*, October 27, 1990.

43. Ibid.

44. *India Today*, Special Forum, "Caste vs. Class," May 31, 1991.

45. Interview with Ashis Nandy, *Frontline*, October 13–26, 1990.

46. Interview with Upendra Baxi, *Frontline*, October 13–26, 1990.

47. P. Radhakrishnan, "OBCs and Central Commissions," *Seminar* 375 (November 1990), pp. 22–26.

48. Aditya Nigam, "Mandal Commission and the Left," *Economic and Political Weekly*, December 1–8, 1990.

49. Shiv Visvanathan, "Mandal's Mandala," *Seminar*, 375 (November 1990), pp. 31–36.

50. The concept of compartmentalization was initially that of Milton Singer, *When a Great Tradition Modernizes* (New York: Praeger, 1972).

51. Ghurye, *Caste and Race in India*, pp. 300–1.

52. *Report of the Seminar on Casteism and Removal of Untouchability*, 1955, p. 136. For Srinivas's general views, see his *Caste in Modern India and Other Essays* (London: Asia Publishing House, 1962), and *Social Change in Modern India* (Berkeley and Los Angeles: University of California Press, 1966).

53. Edmund Leach, ed., *Aspects of Caste in South India, Ceylon, and Northwest Pakistan* (Cambridge: Cambridge University Press, 1960), pp. 6–7.

54. Louis Dumont, *Homo Hierarchicus: The Caste System and Its Implications* (Chicago: University of Chicago Press, 1990), p. 222.

55. See Nicholas Dirks, "Recasting Tamil India," in C. J. Fuller, ed., *Caste in India Today* (New Delhi: Oxford University Press, 1996), pp. 263–95.

56. Partha Chatterjee, "Two Poets and Death: On Civil and Political Society in the Non-Christian World," in Timothy Mitchell, ed., *Questions of Modernity* (Minneapolis: University of Minnesota Press, 2000), pp. 35–48.

## Chapter Fourteen
## Conclusion: Caste and the Postcolonial Predicament

1. Kancha Ilaiah, *Why I am Not a Hindu: A Sudra Critique of Hindutva Philosophy, Culture, and Political Economy* (Calcutta: Samya Press, 1996), p. 7.
2. Mohandas K. Gandhi, *An Autobiography: The Story of My Experiments with Truth* (1929; Boston: Beacon, 1957), p. 504.
3. *Young India*, September 29, 1927
4. Ashis Nandy, "The Politics of Secularism," in Veena Das, *Mirrors of Violence* (Delhi: Oxford University Press, 1992), p. 90.
5. T. N. Madan, "Secularism in Its Place," *Journal of Asian Studies* 46.4 (November 1987), p. 757.
6. "Caste and the Census: Implications for Society and the Social Sciences," *Economic and Political Weekly,* August 8, 1998, p. 2,157.

## Coda
## The Burden of the Past: On Colonialism and the Writing of History

1. For a commanding summary of the outlines of the economic entailments of imperial rule in India, see Irfan Habib, *Essays in Indian History: Towards a Marxist Perception* (New Delhi: Tulika, 1995), in particular the essay, "Colonialization of the Indian Economy, 1757–1900," pp. 296–335.
2. J. R. Seeley, *The Expansion of England* (1883; reprint Chicago: University of Chicago Press, 1971), pp. 9, 12.
3. Ibid., p. 165.
4. Ibid., p. 185.
5. Ibid., p. 179; 184.
6. The "Cambridge school" was founded by Jack Gallagher, coauthor with Ronald Robinson of *Africa and the Victorians: The Climax of Imperialism in the Dark Continent* (New York: St. Martin's Press, 1961), and early on joined by Anil Seal. In its early years, the late 1960s and 1970s, the school included such figures as Gordon Johnson, Francis Robinson, Christopher Baker, B. R. Tomlinson, and David Washbrook. Christopher Bayly, who was trained at Oxford by Gallagher, among others, only joined Cambridge in 1970.
7. Anil Seal, "Imperialism and Nationalism," in John Gallagher, Gordon Johnson, and Anil Seal, eds. *Locality, Province and Nation* (Cambridge: Cambridge University Press, 1973), p. 12. The theme of collaboration had first been sounded in systematic fashion in Gallagher and Robinson's *Africa and the Victorians*.
8. C. A. Bayly, *Rulers, Townsmen, and Bazaars: North India in the Age of British Expansion, 1780–1870* (Cambridge: Cambridge University Press, 1983).
9. C. A. Bayly, *Origins of Nationality in South Asia: Patriotism and Ethical Government in the Making of Modern India* (Delhi, Oxford University Press, 1998), p. 319.
10. The words are Robinson's: Ronald Robinson, "Non-European Foundations of European Imperialism," in R. Owen and B. Sutcliffe, eds., *Studies in the Theory of Imperialism* (London: Longman, 1972), p. 120, quoted in Bayly, *Rulers*, p. 2.
11. Despite Bayly's interest in the economic character of empire, he has nowhere refuted the kinds of evidence adduced by Irfan Habib, among others, to demonstrate the

massive colonization, and impoverishment, of the Indian economy from the mid-eighteenth through the mid-twentieth centuries. Perhaps Bayly simply assumes that the *Cambridge Economic History of India* (edited by Dharma Kumar, with the assistance of Meghnad Desai, Cambridge, 1982) had put to rest to the arguments of Dutt and his successors concerning the drain of empire and the deindustrialization of India. It seems unarguable today, however, that Britain's own economic and political prosperity was integrally connected to its imperial role in India. Wealth was extracted first with the lever of new-world bullion, then through the extortionate use of land revenue to fund the management of Indian politics and the monopolization of the Indian economy; later in the nineteenth century, relying on the opium trade with China, the British used India to bankroll both its imperial and metropolitan dominance. As Habib makes clear in his essay, "Colonialization of the Indian Economy, 1757–1900," the evidence to document the extraordinary economic exploitation wrought by imperial rule is still overwhelming. For a critique of the *Cambridge Economic History of India*, see Habib, "Studying a Colonial Economy—Without Perceiving Colonialism," in his *Essays in Indian History*, pp. 336–66.

12. C. A. Bayly, *Indian Society and the Making of the British Empire* (Cambridge: Cambridge University Press, 1988), pp. 46–47. Emphasis added.

13. Bayly, *Indian Society*, pp. 48, 53, 51, 203–4.

14. David Washbrook, "Progress and Problems: South Asian Economic and Social History, c. 1720–1860," *Modern Asian Studies* 22.1 (1988): 74, 76.

15. Washbrook's Marxism seems only to concern class formation in Britain, and as a consequence has the effect of exculpating British "national" responsibility for the consequences of "world" capitalism.

16. Washbrook, "Progress and Problems," p. 84.

17. These are the very magnate classes who later entered nationalist politics, according to Washbrook. See his "Country Politics: Madras 1880–1930," in Jack Gallagher, Gordon Johnson, and Anil Seal, eds., *Locality Province and Nation: Essays on Indian Politics, 1870–1940* (Cambridge: Cambridge University Press, 1973), pp. 155–211.

18. Washbrook, "Progress and Problems," p. 85.

19. Ibid., p. 86. The main example is taken from Frykenberg, *Guntur District 1788–1848* (Oxford: Oxford University Press 1965). When Washbrook notes that "the cultural blindness, internal contradictions, and more meaningful 'corruptions' of the regime made successful 'concealment' of wealth not only possible but more the rule than the exception," he is restating Frykenberg's argument. Frykenberg called his theory of colonial Indian politics the theory of the white ant, local Indian agents being likened to white ants who, invisible to the colonial overlords, managed to consume the colonial pie from the inside out.

20. Washbrook, "Progress and Problems," p. 87.

21. C. A. Bayly, "The Second British Empire," in R. W. Winks, ed., *The Oxford History of the British Empire*, vol. 5, *Historiography* (Oxford: Oxford University Press, 1999), p. 70.

22. Robert Frykenberg has put the objection even more stridently. As he wrote in his chapter in the new *Oxford History of the British Empire*, "At least for the moment, some historians have been listening to the siren song of anti-historical literary criticism. Theory, in the names of current fashions, has become a cloak for dogma, for denial of

empirical evidence, and for scorning real events in historical understandings. By whatever name such fashions parade, whether as 'colonial discourse analysis', 'deconstruction', or whatever else such nihilist impulses might be called, fulminations of this sort cannot be accepted as genuine historical understanding." One is tempted to ask who is fulminating, but the attribution of such labels as nihilist dogma to work such as that represented in my first book would seem libelous (even if it had appeared without the authority of the editors of the new *Oxford History*) were the charges not so absurd. Robert E. Frykenberg, "India to 1858," in Winks, ed., *Historiography*, pp. 194–213.

23. C. A. Bayly, *Empire and Information: Intelligence Gathering and Social Communication in India, 1780–1870* (Cambridge: Cambridge University Press, 1996), p. 370.

24. Part of the reason for this is a profound unease with "the 'knowledge is power' theme of Francis Bacon and Michel Foucault" (ibid., p. 324)," partly because of an interest in strategic and military information rather than knowledge in the larger sense. Of course, specific information of this last kind is both at the service of larger forms of knowledge, and frequently driven by it, even as it is so literally implicated in the larger project of colonial conquest and rule. I might add that Bayly seems almost deliberately to misunderstand the thrust of new work, even as he avoids any direct comment about the work of Bernard Cohn, noting only, in a footnote, that "his seminal article attributed too great a capacity on the part of the British to 'construct' Indian society independently of the agency of its social formations and knowledge communities" (ibid., p. 287n).

25. Ibid., pp. 370, 371.

26. Ibid., pp. 47, 53, 143, 49, 313.

27. Ibid., pp. 48, 46, 167.

28. See, for example, James Clifford, "On Orientalism," reprinted in Clifford, *The Predicament of Culture* (Cambridge: Harvard University Press, 1988), pp. 255–76.

29. I have made this argument before, as for example in "From Little King to Landlord: Colonial Discourse and Colonial Rule," in Dirks, ed. *Colonialism and Culture* (Ann Arbor: University of Michigan Press, 1992), pp. 175–208.

30. Eugene Irschick's recent book, *Dialogue and History* (Berkeley and Los Angeles: University of California Press, 1996), has been held up as the model of a new kind of colonial history by Bayly (see *Empire*, p. 370, and "The Second British Empire," p. 71) and Frykenberg, "India to 1858," p. 212.

31. See David Washbrook, "Law, State and Agrarian Society in Colonial India," *Modern Asian Studies* 15.3 (1981): 649–721.

32. Bayly, *Empire*, p. 142. Emphasis added.

33. All of the authors discussed above refer to Said and his "disciples." The disciples are invariably guilty of far more than the master himself.

34. William Pinch, "Same Difference in India and Europe," *History and Theory: Studies in the Philosophy of History* 38.3 (October 1999): 389–407.

35. Pinch makes the extraordinary claim that "what underpins postmodernist-deconstructionist scholarship on colonial India generally" is the "assertion of fundamental difference between European and Indian cognition." He fails entirely to take into account that most of the colonial scholarship he considers, not to mention the work of both Said and Foucault, has precisely focused its critique on those traditions of

thought and institutional practice that have asserted fundamental (that is, essential) difference.

36. Rosalind O'Hanlon and David Washbrook, "After Orientalism: Culture, Criticism, and Politics in the Third World," *Comparative Studies in Society and History* 34 (January 1992): 141–67.

37. This, in fact, is the common charge, made by O'Hanlon and Washbrook, Aijaz Ahmed, Arif Dirlik, Neil Lazarus and H. D. Harootunian, among others. See my "Post-colonialism and Its Discontents: History, Anthropology, and Postcolonial Critique," forthcoming in Joan W. Scott and Debra Keates, eds., *Schools of Thought: Twenty-five Years of Social Science and Social Change* (Princeton: Princeton University Press).

38. See my "The Home and the World: The Invention of Modernity in Colonial India," in R. Rosenstone, ed., *Revisioning History: Film and the Construction of a New Past* (Princeton: Princeton University Press, 1993), pp. 44–63. Also see Gyan Prakash's cogent critique of Chatterjee in *Another Reason: Science and the Imagination of Modern India* (Princeton: Princeton University Press, 1999).

39. Indeed, the focus on Sanskrit texts and ideas works precisely to pose the kind of problems that Ambedkar and Periyar fought against in their own political and intellectual struggles.

40. I have used the term "hegemony" in the colonial context to specify forms of securing consent, whether in public rhetorical arenas or private law cases, that make it clear that "domination" as an analytic term is hardly sufficient to explain the nature of colonial law. Although I used "hegemony" in much of my earlier writing on colonial history, I would accept that there are differences between metropolitan and colonial hegemony. Significantly, I would argue that "hegemony" is useful precisely to counter the trope of "collaboration." Nevertheless, colonial effects were neither minor nor controlled solely by the colonized. I cannot accept, for example, Guha's argument that "The advent of Europe's reason in South Asia as part of a colonial cargo also had a transformative impact, no doubt. But thanks to the indigenous society's refusal to dignify an alien rulership with hegemony, the transformation shaped up essentially as a process of Indianizing the idioms of modernity imported by the Raj." My emphasis in this book, of course, has been on the colonialization of the idioms of tradition under the regime of colonial modernity. See Ranajit Guha, "Introduction," in his *A Subaltern Studies Reader, 1986–1995* (Minneapolis: University of Minnesota Press, 1997), p. xx. Also see Ranajit Guha, *Dominance without Hegemony: History and Power in Colonial India* (Cambridge: Harvard University Press, 1997).

41. It is in this context that I would situate the contrast between colonial and metropolitan governmentality. Whereas in my view colonial governmentality shares more with metropolitan governmentality than suggested by Partha Chatterjee, the similarities are always mediated by the complexity of relations of accountability, in short, by the limits of colonial despotism. Colonial hegemony worked precisely to lessen the sense of this contrast (through the promise that British rule would confer equivalent rights to Indians once education succeeded in creating the conditions for civil society), even as that hegemony increasingly came up against the limits of its own fundamental contradictions (from the British response to the rebellion to debates over the Ilbert Bill). The nationalist movement itself struggled for years with the problem of hegemony, ultimately overturning the conditions for limited hegemony, even as it appropriated many of the terms of colonial hegemony in the formation and implementation of nationalist

goals. Here see Partha Chatterjee, *Nationalist Thought and the Colonial World: A Derivative Discourse* (Minneapolis: University of Minnesota Press, 1993).

42. See, for example, Peter van der Veer, *Imperial Encounters: Religion and Modernity in India and Britain* (Princeton University Press, 2001).

43. See Dipesh Chakrabarty, *Provincializing Europe: Postcolonial Thought and Historical Difference* (Princeton: Princeton University Press, 2000).

# Index

Abisekapuram, 160
Abu'l Fazl, 19–20, 247
Acharjyas, 216
Addis, W. B., 141
Adi Dravidas, 240–41
administrative centralization in the East India
    Company, 86
affirmative action, 290
Afghans, 3, 63
agency and India, 151–52, 306–9, 312
agrarian revolts, 43
agricultural castes, 208
Aheers, 203
Ahmed, Aijaz, 312
*A'in-i-Akbari* (Abu'l Fazl), 19–20
Aiyar, Srinivas, 102
Aiyer, U. V. S., 262
Ajmere, 204
Akampatiyars, 66, 68
Akbar, M. J., 280
Ali, Haidar, 28, 67, 85, 86, 112, 113
All-India Congress, 257–58
All India Hindu Mahasabha, 243
All India Spinner's Association, 259
Ambedkar, B. R., 7, 16, 41, 234, 235, 263,
    277–79, 297, 299–301. *See also under* poli-
    tics of caste, caste politics, 95–99
ambivalence surrounding caste, 290–96
Amildars, 86
Ampalams, 68–69
Ampthill, Lord, 184
Ananthacharlu, P. C., 163
Andhra Pradesh, 85, 112–13
Anglican Society for the Propagation of the
    Gospel, 134
Anglicists, 33, 118, 122, 133
animal sacrifices, 175
*Annals of Rural Bengal* (Hunter), 198
annexation, 129
anthropology supplanting history as principle
    colonial modality of knowledge/rule, 43,
    150. *See also* archive, the imperial; ethnog-
    raphy; historiography, early colonial
anthropometry, 49–50, 183–87, 214, 219
antisedition laws, 262
Anukastha, 216

Appavoo, C., 101–3
*Archaeology of Knowledge* (Foucault), 303
archive, the imperial: anthropology as the his-
    tory of the colonized, 194–96; caste and,
    116–22, 306, 315; difficulties in getting ma-
    terials/information, 102–3; governmentality,
    122–23; imperial interests as the basis of the
    archives, 107–9, 306, 315; land relations and
    relations between state and society, 109–16;
    marginalization of the native scholar, 105;
    native staff used to collect local knowledge,
    100–4; origins of, 82–83; silence of, 104–6;
    voices of, 99–104. *See also* historiography,
    early colonial
Arcot, 28, 63, 66, 67, 101, 112
army recruitment and race, 177–80
Aryan theory of race, 133, 142–43, 207, 213–
    14, 220–21, 239, 245–46
Asiatic Society of Bengal, 105
Asrama, 34
atheism, 261
Augradanis, 216
Aunomacondah, 101
authenticity of Christian conversion, 137
Awadh, 15, 63, 111, 201
Ayyar, P. S., 160

Babhans, 203, 210
backward castes, 243, 280–83. *See also*
    Naicker, E. V. R and Ambedkar, B. R. under
    politics of caste, caste politics and the; reser-
    vations, caste
Backward Classes Commission of 1953, 281,
    283
Badhwar, Inderjit, 286
Bahadur, 20
Bahadur Shah, 128
Bahudundas, 116
Baidya, 216
Baines, A., 210–13
Balagopal, K., 286
Banerjee, B. S., 216
Baramahal, 113
barbarism, 173–76, 189, 190–91, 194, 196,
    232
Barbers, 240

Meriahs, 173

Metcalf, Thomas, 130

Metcalfe, Charles, 15, 28, 29, 37

metropolitan experimentation, imperial societies as useful laboratories for, 314

Mhairwara, 204

Middleton, Mr., 248

Mill, James, 31–38, 54, 118, 304, 306

Miller, L. C., 164, 168

minority and majority communities created by the census, 255–57. *See also* Naicker, E. V. R *and* Ambedkar, B. R. *under* politics of caste, caste politics and the

missionaries, 41; barbarism focused on and reported by, 173–74; Carey, William, 26–27; caste and, 27–28, 130–34, 147–48; *Description of the Character, Manners and Customs of the People of India, and of Their Institutions, Religious and Civil*, 21–26; Enfield rifle and cartridges packed with beef/pork, 127; Great Rebellion of 1857, 127, 128; hookswinging, 171; noninterference/nonintervention policy, 41, 130. *See also* conversion, Caldwell (Robert) and religious

Mitra, Rajendra Lal, 210, 216

mixed castes, 216–17, 236–37, 247

modernization theories, 53–54

Mohamedans, 120

Momin, A. R., 250

Moodeliar, A. S., 161–62

Morley, John, 226

Morley-Minto reforms of 1909, 227, 233

Morris, G. E., 158

Mudaliar, P. R., 162, 163

Mudaliyars, 120, 164

Mughal rule, 3, 19–20, 63, 64, 67, 111, 112, 305

Muhammedan Anglo-Oriental College, 128

Muhammedans, 222. *See* Muslims

Mullaly, Frederick S., 181–83, 188, 191

Müller, Max, 23, 38–40, 47, 131–33, 142, 146, 217, 298

Munro, Thomas, 28–29, 37, 102, 109, 110, 112, 113–16, 119

Murr, Sylvia, 21

Muslim League, 227

Muslims: archives (imperial), 117; army recruitment, 177, 178; Ghurye, G. S., 249; minority and majority communities created by the census, 255–56; Partition, 16, 59, 227; politics, 227, 272–73; Risley, H. H., 218, 227

Mysore: archives (imperial), 115, 117; backward castes, 282; census, 204, 205; conquest, colonial, 28, 63, 64; decentralization of political forms, 67; Hastings, Warren, 111; historiography (early colonial), 85–87, 95; non-/anti-Brahman movement, 11; revenue settlement/collection with peasants/village communities, 30

Nadars, 134–35, 147, 239, 240

Naicker, E. V. R., 41, 144, 243, 260–61, 264, 299–301. *See also under* politics of caste, caste politics and the

Naina, Nitala, 101

Nair, T. M., 242

Nandy, Ashis, 290, 299

Narayan, Jayaprakash, 284

Nasik, 266

nationalism: Ambedkar, B. R., 271; Brahmans linked to, 237, 243–54; caste question missing from the nationalist discussion, 231, 232; Chatterjee, Partha, 313; collaboration of Indians crucial to British rule, 306–7; complicity in caste privilege and power, 243; Gandhi, Mohandas K., 232–33; Ghurye, G. S., 249; Guha, Ranajit, 313; Hindu, 255–57; Naicker, E. V. R., 263, 265–66; Nehruvian secular vision of society, 16; religious community replacing caste, 7; Risley, H. H., 227; Seeley, J. R., 305; temple entry for the untouchable caste, 258; women's question missing from nationalist discussion, 232, 294

native scholar, marginalization of the, 105

native staff used to collect local knowledge, 90–91, 100–5

Nattars, 78, 241

Nayaka, 67

Nayakar, T. A., 223

Negroes, 185

Nehru, Jawaharlal, 3–5, 16, 234, 281

Nelson, J. H., 187, 198

neotraditional view of caste, 295

Nesfield, John C., 211, 214, 220

Nigam, Aditya, 290

Nobili, Roberto de, 25

noncooperation campaign of 1919–1922, 237, 242, 257

noninterference/nonintervention policy, 41, 130, 133, 147–51, 157

North American/European political domination, 303–4